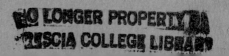

THE WORD WAR

THE WORD WAR

The Story of American Propaganda

By THOMAS C. SORENSEN

HARPER & ROW, PUBLISHERS

NEW YORK, EVANSTON, AND LONDON

1817

For Ann, Alan and Chris

Contents

Contents

Foreword

American foreign policy two-thirds of the way through the twentieth century is founded upon the fundamental fact that we cannot afford to be alone in the world—militarily, economically, politically, or even psychologically. While popularity overseas can never be the test of our actions, we cannot ignore the reactions of others. If we cannot always be loved, it is important that we at least be understood and respected.

In the course of my own travels abroad, I have repeatedly noticed the high degree of interest which the people of every other country take in our own, the intensity of their feelings about us—good and bad—and the sweep of their information and misinformation. When foreign governments react adversely to American interests because of the misconceptions or misunderstandings of their citizens, we tend to put both the blame and the burden of remedying the situation upon the USIA—the United States Information Agency.

In fact, this task cannot be performed by the USIA alone. All agencies of the government, domestic as well as foreign, and the President most of all—indeed, all of us as private citizens, as tourists, as traders and hosts and creators of images and trends—have an effect on what others think of our country. All of us must be mindful of the impact around the world of what we say and do. Our actions and attitudes on civil rights, as well as our actions and attitudes on Vietnam and virtually every other domestic and foreign controversy, affect the respect with which we are held.

The USIA, however, has the primary and difficult responsibility of putting all our actions and attitudes into proper focus overseas. It cannot make poor policies look good, it cannot make shameful acts appear virtuous; but it can provide essential perspective to the rest of the world by conveying in every way possible an honest but balanced and persuasive message about our policies and our people, our motives, our goals, our ideals, our history, and our culture.

President Kennedy recognized the importance of USIA in this context. He was fortunate to have had as his Director an extraordinary man, Edward R. Murrow, who was in turn assisted by two extremely able and imaginative deputies, Don Wilson and the author of this book, Tom Sorensen.

Mr. Sorensen's analysis and history of our foreign information program, to which his own service was a valuable contribution, should be read by every official, scholar, and citizen concerned with the course and conduct of our foreign policy. He relates where it has performed well, where it has performed poorly, and how it can be improved. His book reinforces my conviction that USIA, if not given proper leadership, funds, and backing, can do far more harm than good to our posture overseas. With prods such as those provided by Tom Sorensen, those of us in official positions as well as concerned members of the public must act to improve our overseas information program if America is to loom as large in the hopes of men as it currently does in their fears.

ROBERT F. KENNEDY

United States Senate
November, 1967

Author's Note

Annoyed with the "reverence" in which public opinion is held in this country, Mark Twain once snorted: "Some think it is the voice of God." That it is not, but it *is* the voice of the people, and there are few nations—even among the least democratic—where it does not largely determine the course of history. This book is about our government's efforts to influence foreign public opinion.

The story begins with World War I. Before that cataclysmic event, it mattered little what others thought of us; they were too remote to affect our destiny. In the last half-century, however, we have learned—often unhappily—that there are few spots on earth so remote that what happens there cannot have an impact here. The attitudes of Vietnamese villagers, for example, have been more important to us in recent years than the opinions of all the crowned heads of Europe and Asia.

Still, there are those who believe, as a *Wall Street Journal* writer recently put it, that "world opinion comprises chiefly the editorials of Europe's left-wing political press and the posturing of the United Nations' fuzzy-minded neutralists." And others share the view of former Secretaries of State Dean Acheson and the late John Foster Dulles that there is no such thing as world public opinion, and if there were it would be of no concern to us.

These estimable statesmen were demolishing a straw man. There indeed is no easily identifiable "world public opinion" as such, but there are in each country—as there are here—the articulated opinions of important individuals and groups that always influence and usually determine what their governments do. If we are to have the kind of world we want, we must go beyond traditional diplomacy to influence the opinions and attitudes of these men and women.

This means engaging in propaganda, a label most people might apply to the utterances of their opponents but never to their own. When I joined the U.S. Government's foreign information program in 1951, I had the typical liberal's suspicion of the word. I did not consider my colleagues and myself to be "propagandists." We were disseminating only "information" designed to "tell America's story to the world," and our hope was that if others could come to know us better they would learn to appreciate, respect, and sometimes even love us.

I was wrong; it is not that simple. I spent most of the 1950s as a government Information Officer abroad, and I found that merely "informing" people was not enough. We had to make a case for our views, as others were doing for theirs. We had to be advocates, persuaders—propagandists. We did not lie, or distort the news, or subvert the media, but neither were we disinterested. We accomplished no miracles, but had we not been propagandists we would have accomplished nothing.

There was, I found, much concern in the world about America, and much misunderstanding—some of it innocently acquired, some of it maliciously engendered. The concern should not surprise us. America is viewed as the "new trial place for the human race," as Robert Frost called it. If this trial goes badly, it goes badly for everyone.

Some need to be reassured, and others persuaded, that modern America still believes in the revolutionary goals of the Declaration of Independence, in the humanity of Abraham Lincoln, and in the Four Freedoms of Franklin Roosevelt. The private American news media cannot do the job; they cannot, in James Reston's words, serve "as cheerleaders for our side." Nor can the job be done alone by the thousands of private American citizens living and working abroad, nor by Hollywood's version of the American dream. What is needed is an organized, deliberate effort of persuasion.

If I had any remaining doubts on this score, they were resolved in 1961 when Edward R. Murrow was appointed head of the U.S. Information Agency. Here was a man of unimpeachable integrity, renowned the world around for his relentless pursuit of truth on radio and television. He had no illusions about America's deficiencies, and he recognized, as he often said, that this country "has no patent on the truth." But he knew the nation's strengths and virtues better than most, and neither truth nor America ever had a better advocate in high office.

In his three years in office, Murrow won the confidence of his President and the respect of Congress, educated the public on the realities of propaganda, obtained a more reasonable budget for USIA, improved its staff, and—most important for the long run—redefined and clarified the role and purposes of American propaganda. There are those today who question the efficacy of our foreign propaganda; few, since Murrow, question its necessity—even though they may shy away from the word itself.

Murrow is dead now, and some of the vision and excitement have gone with him, but the standards he set and the goals he articulated will not soon be forgotten. He liked to say that American propagandists were in a war not to capture men's minds but to free them. This is the story of that war, the word war, and of the men and women who have fought it—before, during, and since the days of Ed Murrow.

THE WORD WAR

THE WORD WAR

1 *We Become Propagandists*

"The public be damned!" exclaimed William H. Vanderbilt nearly a century ago, but the public would not be damned. Today its voice is heard and heeded around the world. In America, public opinion is king: the man in the White House nervously awaits its next reading by Gallup or Harris, and so do a great many other people.

There are those who scorn public opinion, who agree with Thoreau that it is "a weak tyrant compared with our own private opinion." They may be right, but public opinion nonetheless must be reckoned with—and not only in our own country. It can elevate men and ideas to great power, and break them overnight. It can sometimes start wars, and sometimes stop them. A nation sensitive about its relations with other nations had better also be sensitive about the attitudes and enthusiasms of other peoples.

Before World War I most Americans were curious but not overly concerned about foreign opinion. Protected by two oceans, weary of the internecine quarrels of the Old World and absorbed in the task of building a new civilization, this country went its own way. When others criticized them, Americans were either angry or unconcerned. Theirs was "God's country"; what did it matter what others thought?

In time of war the situation was a little different. God and right were on America's side, of course, but it was fervently hoped that others also recognized it. At the very beginning of the nation, the merits of the colonialists' cause were proclaimed abroad by a talented collection of indefatigable propagandists headed by wily old

Benjamin Franklin. At the battlefront, crude leaflets promised amnesty and free land to Hessian mercenaries and British soldiers if they would desert, and five thousand Hessians—one-sixth of the total force—did defect.

During the Civil War the Union sought support from antislavery elements in Europe. In 1863 a group of laborers in Manchester sent President Lincoln a resolution supporting his Emancipation Proclamation, expressing a view contrary to much influential opinion in England. Lincoln replied in an open letter that created some excitement, for in disregard of diplomatic precedent he spoke directly to the people of another country:

I have understood well that the duty of self-preservation rests solely with the American people, but I have at the same time been aware that the favor or disfavor of foreign nations might have a material influence in enlarging or prolonging the struggle.

"The favor of nations." The United States has needed it in every crisis and conflict, but it has never come easy. For it is based, after all, on the much-discussed "image" of America abroad, and that image is a highly elusive picture: part fact and part mirage, part expectation and part disillusionment. It is a picture magnified by the modern mass media, blurred by the fantasies of Hollywood, distorted by the falsifications of our adversaries, and complicated by the sheer size of America's population, wealth, power, and problems.

The image is actually many and often contradictory images: great wealth and grinding poverty, unparalleled freedom and racial discrimination, awesome power and frustrating impotence, responsible leadership and irresponsible policies, sophisticated technology and unsophisticated politicians. Some of the flickering foreign images of America are true, some half true, and others simply false.

"It is fashionable in certain circles," Walter Lippmann has written in the Washington *Post,*

to dismiss scornfully a serious concern about what foreign nations think of us. This is a reaction to the naïve and often silly American wish to be loved by everybody. But the reaction has gone much too far. For it is not true that in the real world of affairs a great power, even the strongest, can afford to ignore the opinions of others. It cannot overawe them all. It must have friends who trust it and believe in it and have confidence that its power will be used wisely.[1]

If this nation is to have such friends, especially when it needs them most, then it must actively seek the friendship of others. Our example alone is not sufficient, so we must persuade others of its validity. We call this our "information program"; others call it propaganda.

That label, in this century, has become widely distasteful. Most Americans identify it with Hitler's "big lie," Soviet speeches in the United Nations, and—for an older generation—"perfidious Albion" enticing this country into World War I. To propagandize means in many minds to lie, to exaggerate, to manipulate, to subvert. So the U.S. Government employs a euphemism, but in this book we will not.

The word *propaganda* first appeared in the seventeenth century, when Popes Gregory XV and Urban VIII established a College of Propaganda to educate priests for missionary work; the Catholic Church still maintains a committee of cardinals, the *Congregatio de Propaganda Fide,* to supervise its world-wide missions. In modern times the word has become associated with the efforts of secular organizations or nations to influence the thinking and actions of others.

There are several categories of propaganda used by nations to influence one another. Each involves different but overlapping methods: battlefield psychological warfare, to undermine the enemy's will to fight; tactical political propaganda, seeking to win support on immediate issues of the day; the long-range influencing of motivations and attitudes in support of long-term national objectives; and indirect propaganda through the influencing of the educational processes of other nations.

The American Government today is engaged in all these types of propaganda. Yet, despite a firm American belief in the importance of public opinion, no one prior to the mid-1940s ever seriously considered an organized, government-sponsored effort to influence foreign peoples in peacetime. It seemed to many an unclean and improper function of a democratic government, particularly after international persuasion was debased by the false propaganda of the Nazis, Fascists, and Communists. It took Cold War with the Soviet Union to make foreign propaganda a permanent feature of American government.

There would, perhaps, be fewer qualms about American propaganda if it were better understood that there is not necessarily a conflict between veracity and advocacy, that it is possible to be both truthful and persuasive. American propaganda has not always been persuasive, but it has always tried to be truthful.

In this day of rapid and multiple communications, few lies will stand undetected for long. Everyone is watching everyone else, and the spotlight is brightest on the most powerful and the most righteous. Once a politician or a nation is caught in a lie, an increasingly sophisticated public will view subsequent utterances with skepticism if not outright disbelief. And the greater the number of lies, the greater the skepticism.

When he was head of America's propaganda program, Edward R. Murrow put it this way: "To be persuasive we must be believable; to be believable we must be credible; to be credible we must be truthful. It is as simple as that."[2]

Of course, closed societies, Communist or otherwise, do have a certain advantage, especially over the short run. They can suppress or lie about what goes on in their own countries, while preventing others from checking the facts. But the truth will out, even in tyrannies (as the truth about Stalin did in the Soviet Union, once his successors started admitting it), and in any case dictators cannot prevent outsiders from telling the truth once it becomes known.

American propagandists do have a problem, however, for which the truth is no solution: the double standard applied to the conduct of nations. More is expected and demanded of the United States than of other nations. The ink-throwers and window-breakers went after U.S. libraries and embassies when the United States supported the Bay of Pigs invasion of Cuba in 1961, but they were silent when the Soviet Union nearly precipitated World War III by smuggling missiles into Cuba in 1962. The pickets and paint-splashers harassed President Johnson and Vice President Humphrey about Vietnam during their travels abroad in 1966 and 1967, but they made no complaint when Hanoi and the Vietcong launched their campaign of terror and subversion in South Vietnam.

For U.S. propagandists this double standard is often frustrating and always exasperating, but perhaps in the long run it works to America's advantage. For it exists in part because many foreigners know and cherish the principles of Jefferson, Lincoln, Wilson, and Franklin Roosevelt, and they expect Americans to live up to them —even if the rest of the world does not.

The truth, then, is no cure-all. Nevertheless, Murrow was basically correct: credibility, in the long run, cannot be achieved without truthfulness. "There was never a country in the world that aired its dirty laundry the way the U.S.A. does," commented an influential Cologne publisher to an American friend, but he spoke with great admiration and sympathy, not disapproval.

While good propaganda is truthful, the truth—out of context and unexplained—is not always good propaganda. It is not good propaganda to tell the world of racial disturbances without, at the same time, reciting the steady if unspectacular progress toward an integrated society. It is not good propaganda to tell the world of an increased commitment of American military power in some far corner of the world without making it clear why that power is there.

Moreover, the sheer volume of events forces any medium, government or private, to be selective, not inclusive, and to pay attention to one development at the expense of another. No disseminator of information can tell all the truth all the time, even if it does not tell any falsehoods. It must select bits and pieces of the truth, although to remain credible it must not omit any of major significance.

Effective U.S. Government propaganda is the selective but credible dissemination of truthful ideas and information for the purpose of persuading other people to think and act in ways that will further American purposes. It is a definition that has stood the tests of time and trial.

The Creel Committee

The first major test came in 1917, when the American Government for the first time since the Revolution launched a serious campaign of foreign propaganda. A week after Congress declared war, President Wilson by Executive Order created a Committee on Public Information composed of the Secretaries of State, War, and Navy, and headed by a journalist friend, George Creel. Creel did not call his operation propaganda, "for that word, in German hands, had come to be associated with deceit and corruption,"[3] but propaganda was what it was, nonetheless.

The committee's representatives, working with the Military Intelligence Bureau, arranged for leaflets to be sent by gun, balloon, and airplane over the German lines. Enemy soldiers were encouraged to surrender by promises of food and fair treatment. Stories were fed to newspapers in neutral countries, and then often unwittingly transmitted to German papers by neutral and even German correspondents. Books, exhibits, pamphlets, and movies were produced for foreign consumption. Copies of Wilson's speeches and his photograph were distributed in great numbers.

Creel and his associates sought to educate their colleagues in the government, and in Allied governments, on the significance of public opinion to the war effort. Publicist Edward L. Bernays, a youthful member of the committee's Foreign Press Bureau in New York, talked Tomáš Masaryk into proclaiming Czechoslovakia's independence on a Sunday rather than a Friday, in order to assure better press coverage. ("That, sir, is making history in the cables," Masaryk protested at first. "Sir, cables make history," Bernays replied. Masaryk went along.)

The fledgling propagandists had to learn while doing, and they made many mistakes. "When we started out," Creel recalled later, "it was as if the Babylonians were asked to invent the threshing machine." But they learned fast. Though often flamboyant and amateurish, the Creel Committee played a major part in making Wilson and U.S. war aims widely known and appreciated throughout the world. And it did so in the face of severe handicaps. In neutral nations its representatives frequently found themselves undercut by chauvinistic British and French propagandists, as well as by Germans. In this country Creel and his associates, like their successors of later years, were viewed with suspicion by the Secretary of State, most U.S. diplomats, and important elements of the press, public, and Congress.

Annoyed by Congressional sniping, Creel nearly sank the whole effort with an imprudent remark to reporters in May, 1918. Asked if he thought all Congressmen were loyal, Creel shot back: "I do not like slumming, so I won't explore into the hearts of Congress for you."

He later apologized publicly, but Congress never forgave him, even though Wilson told a group of angry Senators, "Gentlemen, when I think of the manner in which Mr. Creel has been maligned and persecuted I think it a very human thing for him to have said."[4]

Creel had been an early supporter of Wilson; during the 1916 campaign he had written a partisan book, *Wilson and the Issues,* and his actress wife was a long-time friend of Wilson's daughter Margaret. Consequently, there were some, especially Republicans, who saw Creel more as a propagandist for the Wilson Administration than for the American nation. Although the House Appropriations Committee gave his operation a clean bill of health after a thorough investigation at the height of the war (even as Congress cut his budget request in half), the lawmakers interrupted an orderly termination of the Creel Committee by abolishing it in mid-1919, leaving it without "power to rent a building, employ a clerk, transfer a bank balance, or to collect a dollar."

Creel's difficulties may have made him overly sensitive to criticism. According to Bernays, Creel's failure to work closely with the press at the Paris Peace Conference "helped to lose the peace for us."[5] After the Armistice, eleven employees of Creel's New York office were assigned to attend the Peace Conference, although Creel had earlier announced that propaganda operations were being terminated with the end of hostilites. On November 21, 1918, the press quoted Bernays as saying that the purpose of the "press mission" was "to interpret the work of the Peace Conference by keeping up a worldwide propaganda to disseminate American accomplishments and ideals."

Congressional Republicans immediately accused Creel of planning to control American press coverage of the conference. He promptly denied it: "The one proper effort of the Committee . . . will be to open every means of communication to the press of America without dictation, without supervision, and with no other desire than to facilitate in every manner the fullest and freest flow of news."[6] Then he cabled his Paris office: "Contrary to the press, the people I sent abroad . . . will have nothing to do but purely mechanical work in connection with distribution."[7]

Creel followed this with another public statement: "The representatives of the Committee [do] not in any manner constitute an official Peace Conference press mission. . . . Their sole duties will be the completion of the Committee's foreign work and settlement of contracts and business details." He told Wilson he would insist upon "the government's immediate and complete surrender of every supervisory function as far as news was concerned."[8] But freedom of the press was not the issue; everyone favored that. The need was to make America's position at Paris clear to the world and rally support for it. This was not realized, and not done.

Creel himself did little in Paris, and prevented the New York group from working with the press. Wilson put Ray Stannard Baker in charge of press relations, but Baker was inexperienced and inept. Had Wilson been able to deal with the press himself, with the flair of a Roosevelt or a Kennedy, little damage would have been done. But he was not, and the government failed to make its case effectively with the news media. Bernays believes that if Creel "had insisted on following the original plan, [Wilson's] communication with the media in the U.S." would have been assured and "the course of history possibly altered."[9]

But Creel did not insist, Wilson was defeated on the treaty issue, and America again turned its back on the world. The "normalcy" of Warren G. Harding succeeded Wilson's "New Freedom," and there was no place for foreign propaganda in the frenzied twenties or the depression years that followed.

Then Adolf Hitler came to power in Germany. Relying heavily on the propaganda of fear, he occupied the Rhineland in 1936, seized Austria in early 1938, blackmailed Britain and France at Munich into letting him take the Czech Sudetenland that autumn, and swallowed the rest of that hapless democracy the next spring. The Bolsheviks, after their takeover in Russia, also made propaganda an important instrument of foreign policy. So did the short-lived Communist regime in Hungary. Holland began international broadcasting in 1927, France in 1931, and Britain in 1932 with the British Broadcasting Corporation (BBC) Empire Service. Fascist Italy had a Ministry of Propaganda, similar to Hitler's.

The Propaganda of War

The most active early practitioners of modern political propaganda were the European dictators, and they gave it the bad name which has lasted to this day. As Hitler's mouthpiece, Dr. Josef Goebbels, saw it, "Propaganda has only one object—to conquer the masses." The Nazis believed in total propaganda: total control over the minds of the German people and as much control as could be obtained over the minds of others. Vast sums were spent. Propagandists were assigned to German embassies abroad, and "front" groups established. Hitler and the Third Reich were exalted, and every weakness—real or invented—of the democracies was proclaimed and reiterated.

Too little and too late, in propaganda as in military prowess, the United States sought in the late 1930s to develop a capability of its own. The initial concern was with Nazi and Fascist propaganda in Latin America. President Roosevelt in 1938 established an Inter-departmental Committee for Scientific and Cultural Cooperation and, within the State Department, a Division of Cultural Cooperation. In August, 1940, after the fall of France, Roosevelt appointed young Nelson Rockefeller to be Coordinator of Commercial and Cultural Affairs between the American Republics (later retitled Coordinator of Inter-American Affairs). Rockefeller launched an exchange-of-persons program with Latin-American countries, and opened offices in them to cultivate opinion leaders and sponsor libraries and jointly operated binational cultural centers.

In 1941 the war drew nearer. Britain was given desperately needed Lend-Lease assistance and U.S. war production greatly increased, but the country was sharply divided between "interventionists" who favored all-out help to the Allies and "isolationists" who believed the war was none of our business or too far gone to win. In this climate Roosevelt created a government bureau to provide Americans with information on the defense effort. Delighting in alliteration and chary of anything smacking of the propaganda machines of the enemy, he named the new organization the Office of Facts and Figures, and appointed not a huckster or a journalist but a poet—Archibald MacLeish—to head it.

Also in 1941 Roosevelt established yet another agency, this one for foreign intelligence and clandestine political action and sabotage. Heading it was a lawyer and former military officer, William J. (Wild Bill) Donovan, who was given the deliberately innocuous and misleading title of Coordinator of Information. Playwright Robert E. Sherwood, a Roosevelt speech writer during the 1940 campaign, persuaded Donovan to set up what in effect was a division of the new agency called the Foreign Information Service. Sherwood recruited a few friends to help him and began beaming broadcasts and news material abroad. Congress and the public knew little about this foreign propaganda effort, and it was probably just as well, for its legal basis was questionable.

On December 7 the Japanese attack on Pearl Harbor put America in the war all the way. It now was both necessary and politically possible to step up propaganda abroad. In February, 1942, bringing together the facilities of eleven private shortwave stations, Sherwood launched a government-sponsored shortwave broadcasting station and named it the Voice of America.

Four months later, on June 13, Roosevelt consolidated the bits and pieces of the foreign and domestic propaganda effort into an Office of War Information (OWI). He instructed OWI to supervise or coordinate all government information activities except Rockefeller's Latin-American operation. Elmer Davis, a renowned and scholarly Indiana-born journalist who had gone from the *New York Times* to become a celebrated radio news reporter, was installed as OWI's Director. Sherwood remained head of what then became the Overseas Branch of OWI. Offices abroad were named the United States Information Service (USIS).

From its birth the Office of War Information was embroiled in controversy. Davis had few peers as a thinker, writer, and broadcaster, but he was never comfortable in the bureaucratic jungle of wartime Washington. A part of Congress and the public considered propaganda to be unclean and un-American, and—as in Creel's time a generation earlier—some suspected that OWI was chiefly interested in propagandizing on behalf of the Democratic Administration.*

OWI's staff was also a problem. Davis and his colleagues naturally recruited personnel from two sources: the communications media and the foreign-born community, especially those of the latter who had a good grasp of the language, culture, and mentality of the Old World. OWI's employees were well educated and unusually articulate. But some were more concerned with the politics of their native lands than with American policy; a high percentage were political liberals or even farther to the left, and most had been exempted from military service. All this aroused doubts about OWI among those elements

---

* Creel wanted an important position in OWI, but was turned down by the Roosevelt Administration.

of Congress and the public that viewed intellectuals, the political left, and "foreigners" with suspicion.

With some justification, it was the domestic activities of OWI that at first were most criticized, just as Creel's home-front operations had been during World War I. A domestic "ministry of propaganda" was anathema to most Americans who gave the matter much thought. As a result, the domestic operation never really got under way; pleased, the critics then turned their fire on OWI's overseas effort. Davis himself was the target of repeated personal attacks, and his impatience with critics and criticism only further antagonized his opponents.

Moreover, OWI was plagued with internal problems. Davis' hastily recruited staff had a high proportion of prima donnas, all competing with one another. Sherwood's Overseas Branch in New York, which had been in action before OWI was formed, resented and sometimes ignored Davis and his senior staff in Washington. After Roosevelt finally gave Davis his full support, three of Sherwood's principal assistants quit in a huff in early 1944. Later in the year, Sherwood himself resigned to work in the Roosevelt re-election campaign and was succeeded by Edward W. Barrett, a former associate editor of *Newsweek*. Under his skillful direction, harmony was restored.

Not all the trouble was internal. Other elements of the government, from the White House on down, were neither as understanding nor as helpful as they should have been. The State Department, the War and Navy departments, and especially the Office of Strategic Services (OSS)*—the new subversion-espionage-intelligence agency—were jealous of their prerogatives and not fully cognizant of the uses of propaganda and psychological warfare. Consequently, they often

---

* This forerunner of the present-day Central Intelligence Agency was headed by the same Colonel Donovan who had briefly served as Coordinator of Information and in that capacity supervised Sherwood's pre-OWI Foreign Information Service. It took nine months after OWI's creation to define and divide foreign propaganda responsibilities betwen OWI and OSS, and during that period they spent almost as much time fighting each other as fighting the enemy. Donovan's organization wanted as much control as possible over American propaganda, and believed the emphasis should be put on unattributable "black" propaganda. OWI, on the other hand, felt that truthful information disseminated under the American label would be the most effective propaganda in wartime. In the end OWI prevailed, the feud was brought to a halt, and good working relations developed.

sought to keep OWI—at worst—impotent and—at best—out of their hair.

OWI was told too little and too late about what was going on. The State Department and the military were given the responsibility of providing it with policy guidance, but the guidance was often neither prompt nor specific. OWI did not participate in policy-making, and Davis was not a member of Roosevelt's "war cabinet." In fact, Davis rarely saw the President and almost never alone, in sharp contrast to Creel's close relationship with Wilson. Roosevelt, the consummate politician who should have had a good understanding of the potential of propaganda, seemed to view OWI as a censorship agency, which, unlike the Creel Committee, it was not.

Many military officers thought of war exclusively in terms of men and weapons, not of words, although General Eisenhower in Africa and Europe, General MacArthur in the Pacific, and General Stilwell in Burma did encourage psychological warfare operations in their theaters. One sarcastic Allied officer wrote Eisenhower's psycho-logical warfare chief: "The army insists on the killing of our enemies, not persuading or arguing them out of the war. . . . Paper will not kill Germans."[10] No one, of course, claimed that it would. Davis under-stood "that the war is going to be won primarily by fighting, but we can point to plenty of proof in history . . . that victory of the fighting forces can be made easier" by psychological warfare and propaganda.

Davis won some converts, but not enough. Psychological factors were not adequately considered in making and enunciating policy, and OWI had only partial success as an advocate and clarifier of Ameri-can war aims. Wallace Carroll, an OWI senior official, wrote later that "while Americans attained considerable skill in the use of propaganda as an instrument of war, they failed completely to de-velop the arts of persuasion as an instrument of foreign policy."[11] And the Army General Board, in its final report on the war, con-cluded that propaganda had been "a neglected and ineptly used political and diplomatic weapon."

Two Big Problems: Vichy and "Unconditional Surrender"

OWI had little success in dealing with the two biggest propaganda problems of the war. Both were prime examples of the neglect and ineptness of which the Army General Board spoke.

The first grew out of the Allied invasion of French North Africa in November, 1942. At the beginning, all was rosy. Eisenhower told OWI's Deputy Director: "I don't know much about psychological warfare but I want to give it every chance."[12] Percy Winner, a former foreign correspondent, went on Eisenhower's staff as his propaganda adviser. He obtained the cooperation of the British counterpart to OWI and organized an Anglo-American team that planned broadcasts, drafted statements for issuance by Allied leaders, and produced thirty million leaflets for distribution in Africa and metropolitan France. "From that time on," Sherwood recalled later, "there was no major Allied landing from Normandy to the Philippines that did not have a Psychological Warfare Division as part of the force."[13]

But unforeseen political difficulties limited the impact of OWI's propaganda. The main objective, of course, was to minimize or eliminate French military resistance in North Africa. A secondary goal was to keep alive French hopes for liberation. Achievement of the first objective required gaining the support of—or at least neutralizing —Marshal Pétain's Vichy-based government of unoccupied France which still exercised sovereignty over North Africa. This meant excluding General Charles de Gaulle and his Fighting French movement, whom Vichy viewed as traitors.

The hoped-for soft response from Vichy was not forthcoming, however. The embittered Pétain cried, "We shall defend ourselves," and there was scattered opposition by French forces. Vichy's top military man, Admiral Jean Darlan, happened to be in Algiers when the invasion took place. After brief resistance, he surrendered French forces there. But fighting continued in Oran and Morocco, whereupon Darlan—with the approval of Pétain—offered to cooperate, at a price.

Eisenhower had the choice of dealing with the Fascist-minded Darlan or continuing to fight. Ike chose the former, and French resistance was ended by Darlan in the name of Pétain. The Darlan accord prompted a wave of surprise and anger in America and Britain. The conquered peoples of Western Europe wondered if a precedent had been set for dealing with Hitler's stooges after liberation. Enemy propagandists were quick to exploit the situation.

Partly at the prompting of OWI, President Roosevelt sought a week later to reassure the world. Describing the Darlan deal as "only a temporary expedient justified solely by the stress of battle," he agreed that "no permanent arrangement should be made with Admiral Darlan. . . . We are opposed to Frenchmen who support Hitler and the Axis. The future French government will be established . . . by the French people themselves after they have been set free." He said he had "asked for the abrogation of all laws and decrees inspired by Nazi governments or Nazi ideologies."

Despite Roosevelt's words, the deeds OWI needed to reassure world opinion were not quickly forthcoming. Under the Eisenhower-Darlan agreement, the communications media of North Africa remained largely in the hands of Vichyites. And, to avoid offending them and anti-Zionist Arab leaders, Eisenhower's headquarters imposed a ban on OWI references in North Africa to the reforms Roosevelt had promised.

Anxiously trying to appraise the situation, Elmer Davis sent one of his deputies—Milton Eisenhower, the General's brother—to North Africa for a firsthand report. Eisenhower concluded that reforms were going forward but could not be publicized without unnecessarily antagonizing local French and Arab authorities, that the military advantages of the deal outweighed its political liabilities, and that OWI should therefore suffer in silence.

Understandably, De Gaulle was enraged by the American recognition of Darlan, which undermined his whole position. His radio in Brazzaville and his representatives in the United States and Britain attacked the Darlan accord and pressed De Gaulle's claim to be the exclusive legitimate spokesman of France. In one of the more curious if temporary alliances of the war, the Russians—and Communists everywhere—joined in the attacks, and Dr. Goebbels exploited the controversy to suit Nazi ends.

Time and the Casablanca Conference of Roosevelt and Churchill eventually reduced the controversy to controllable proportions. Darlan was assassinated, Gaullists were included in the North African administration, and the worst of the Vichy laws repealed. German and Italian resistance in North Africa ended in the spring of 1943. A French Committee of National Liberation, dominated by De Gaulle, was established, and in August won full U.S. and British diplomatic recognition.

Eisenhower probably made the right decision in quickly ending French resistance by dealing with the Vichyites. Lives were saved, and the campaign was brought to a successful conclusion sooner than if the French had fought us. But politically it was a defeat: it cast doubt on the Roosevelt-Churchill proclamation of the Atlantic Charter, aroused suspicions of American motives among the captive peoples of Europe, handed both the Nazis and the Communists a useful club with which to beat us, and generated animosities in the heart of Charles de Gaulle which still trouble Britain and America.

Although the Casablanca Conference helped smooth over one major psychological problem, it also added another: "unconditional surrender." The official communiqué of the January, 1943, conference made no mention of the doctrine. However Roosevelt, at a press conference, had remarked that the Allies would settle for no less than "unconditional surrender" by the Axis Powers. Churchill apparently had opposed the concept when FDR first mentioned it to him, but he told the House of Commons three weeks later that Roosevelt, "with my full concurrence . . . decided that the note of the Casablanca Conference should be the unconditional surrender of our foes."

Both men had been concerned about persistent rumors of a negotiated peace. They also wanted to avoid a repetition of what happened after World War I: the rise of the myth in Germany that German armies had not been beaten but were betrayed on the home front. Roosevelt wanted to make it clear that this war would end only when the Axis Powers were unquestionably defeated, and acknowledged and accepted that defeat unconditionally. He explained that unconditional surrender did not mean oppression of the defeated populations but punishment of their leaders and elimination of their ideology.

Dr. Goebbels' propagandists, however, told the German people that unconditional surrender would mean total destruction of their nation. The Nazi line was unwittingly given a boost in September, 1944, by public disclosure of the Morgenthau Plan to turn industrial Germany into an agricultural nation. OWI played down this draconian scheme, but it caused an international uproar, nonetheless.*

* The plan was named after its principal author, Secretary of the Treasury Henry Morgenthau, Jr., who was one of the few officials doing much thinking about postwar Germany. Roosevelt, like many Americans haunted by visions of another aggression-bent Germany rising from the ashes, approved Morgenthau's scheme and obtained Churchill's endorsement. The plan was, of course, never carried out.

Even Stalin at his 1943 Teheran meeting with Roosevelt and Churchill warned that the demand for unconditional surrender would only stiffen German resistance. OWI joined Secretary of State Hull, General Eisenhower, and others in recommending that the Allies soften the phrase or at least define more precisely what it meant. But Roosevelt refused to water down or back away from the words. "Germany understands only one kind of language," he wrote Hull. And he pointed to Lee's capitulation to Grant at Appomattox as both unconditional and generous—a comparison questionable on both counts.

After the war, Allen W. Dulles—who had dealt with the German underground for OSS and later became head of CIA—argued that Goebbels twisted the formula of unconditional surrender "into the formula 'total slavery' and very largely succeeded in making the German people believe that was what unconditional surrender meant."[14] Eisenhower, in 1964, agreed. Nonetheless, it appears today that the quarrel over the doctrine was largely meaningless. There is little proof that the outcome of the war, or postwar developments, were substantially affected one way or another. Polls taken after the war showed a majority of Germans had been prepared to accept unconditional surrender, if not the Morgenthau Plan. And the doctrine did enhance the confidence of the conquered peoples of Europe in our ultimate war aims and quiet fears raised by the Darlan deal.

OWI's Contributions to Victory

OWI made its mark not so much in the Darlan and "unconditional surrender" controversies as in day-to-day, mostly unsung efforts to maintain Allied morale, undermine the morale of the enemy, and weaken his will to resist. OWI started from scratch, learned while doing—and often failed while learning. Its propagandists were inexperienced and untrained, and what was remembered of the Creel Committee offered few helpful precedents. But OWI did learn, and its successes were not inconsiderable.

Then as now, some of the most effective propaganda projects were the simplest. One was the brain child of author Leo Rosten, who was serving a stint with OWI in Washington. He was asked to come up with a propaganda scheme for January 30, 1943, which was both the tenth anniversary of Hitler's accession to power and Roosevelt's birthday. The war was still running in Germany's favor, and Hitler and Goebbels were certain to make the most of the anniversary.

When it appeared likely that Hitler would broadcast to the world at 11 A.M., the hour he became Chancellor, Rosten proposed that the RAF bomb Berlin at that precise moment and knock the Nazi radio off the air while the world listened. The project went off without a hitch. With perfect timing, RAF Mosquito bombers hit Berlin a few seconds after 11 o'clock. Hitler had a sore throat, but Hermann Goering spoke in his place. A few seconds after the fat *Reichsmarschall* began speaking, explosions were heard in the background. Shouts and sounds of confusion followed, then Radio Berlin went off the air. Germany was not invincible, after all.[15]

That first daylight raid on Berlin did not win the war; it probably did not even shorten it by one day. But it gave new hope and courage to the conquered peoples of Europe in a striking example of successful propaganda of the deed. And it was probably the only time the enemy's radio broadcast our own propaganda message!

Allied radios had their effect, too. Despite Nazi jamming, nearly two-thirds of the German population listened to broadcasts from the West. While the BBC had a head start, and its programs were superior to those of the Voice of America, VOA had its share of the audience, and that share grew as the war progressed.

In 1942 OWI began producing a four-page tabloid newspaper, *L'Amérique en Guerre*, for distribution in France. At first, only a few copies were circulated in unoccupied France through our embassy at Vichy. Then the British Royal Air Force, and later the U.S. Army Air Corps, began dropping the little newspaper over the cities of occupied France. Circulation rose to seven million per week before D-day in 1944, compared to the grand total of three million American leaflets distributed throughout all of World War I. *L'Amérique* was factual, nonargumentative, and attractive in design. It emphasized Allied victories and held out hope of liberation. Similar newspapers were produced for conquered Norway and neutral Spain and Ireland.

Various other specialized publications, designed for specific audiences or specific purposes, were distributed. In North Africa leaflets were scattered over enemy lines by artillery and air drops, encouraging "honorable" surrender in the face of "overwhelming odds."

Labeled safe-conduct passes, the leaflets were so successful that they were used with increasing effectiveness throughout the war (and later in Korea and Vietnam). OWI produced posters for pasting on walls in the wake of advancing Allied armies.

In mid-1943 the U.S. Eighth Air Force began dropping OWI leaflets in its daylight bombing raids over Germany. The first leaflet, a million of which were scattered over two cities, had an American flag on one side and on the other the simple but ominous statement, "Adolf Hitler declared war on the United States on December 11, 1941." Later, a little weekly newspaper, *Sternebanner* (*Star-Spangled Banner*) was produced and dropped in great numbers. The newspaper was good propaganda: straightforward, low-key, and factual—so factual that it occasionally carried news unfavorable to the Allies. There were some objections to inclusion of this kind of material, but the purpose was to make *Sternebanner* believable to its German readers, and credibility could not be achieved without objectivity.*

Partly as a result of a massive propaganda campaign, more than a million Italian troops still behind Axis lines when Marshal Badoglio surrendered refused to stick with Mussolini and had to be interned by the Germans. The Italian Navy, after being urged by U.S. radio broadcasts every quarter-hour to deliver itself to the Allies, did just that—prompting a British admiral to comment that American propagandists had "accomplished in one day" what he had not been able to do in three years.

The admiral's remarks were timely if exaggerated because OWI had gotten into trouble at the time of Mussolini's overthrow by Badoglio. The Duce was ousted without warning on a Sunday night, and in the absence of guidance OWI had to devise its own line for VOA broadcasts. It decided to say that the Allies should not celebrate prematurely because the King and Badoglio were Fascists who were continuing the war. The BBC took a more optimistic note, which turned out to be the official line. Newspapers scolded OWI for working at cross-purposes with Allied policy, and President Roosevelt publicly reprimanded it. As a result, a binational committee

---

* Some military men had their doubts about the leaflets. One of Bill Mauldin's famous "Up Front" cartoons showed "Joe" loading and firing a cannon while "Willie" instructed the telephone operator: "Tell them leaflet people the Krauts ain't got time fer readin' today."

to coordinate propaganda in Europe and avoid contradictory lines was established.

Except for fast-breaking or unexpected developments, OWI had a reasonably efficient system for providing policy guidance to its staff. Each week a Central Directive was drafted, approved by an Overseas Planning Board (which included representatives of OWI, the Office of Inter-American Affairs, the State Department, OSS, the Joint Chiefs of Staff, and Britain's Political Warfare Executive), and flashed to all OWI offices.

Most major projects were jointly planned by overseas posts and Washington headquarters. Among these were psychological pressures on the Germans to make Rome an "open city," clever baiting of Goering's *Luftwaffe* in 1944 to get German planes up in the air where they could be destroyed, efforts to make it appear the Germans were committed to holding the Atlantic Wall against the Allied invasion so that our successful landings would look all the more impressive, and (after D-day) pressing the theme of "overwhelming force" to give German soldiers an honorable rationale for surrendering.

With the end of the European war, OWI turned its full attention to telling the Japanese that their cause was hopeless. In July, 1945, the Japanese Government advised Washington through neutral diplomats that it was prepared to discuss surrender. But the Japanese armies and people were not told, and they fought on—until OWI told them through radio and a massive leaflet drop. The surrender would have come in any event, but Japanese officials later admitted that, once their people knew peace was in the offing, they had no choice but to surrender on our terms. Foreign affairs expert Paul Linebarger subsequently wrote that this "one operation alone probably repaid the entire cost of OWI through the war."[16] *

Assessing the effectiveness of propaganda is difficult in war or peace, because it is only one factor leading to a given result. And propaganda's failures are more visible than its successes. During World War II Allied propaganda could not break the morale of the German home front, but neither could strategic bombing, which cost

* From start to finish, OWI's Overseas Branch spent $110,800,000, a tiny fraction of the hundreds of billions spent on the war and only 60 percent of one year's budget of the peacetime U.S. Information Agency in the late 1960s.

thousands of lives and billions of dollars. It was crushing military defeat—not propaganda—that finally undermined the faith of the German people in Hitler, and the atomic bomb—not propaganda—that finally ended Japan's will to resist. Yet U.S. propaganda did have considerable impact.

After the war Secretary of War Stimson and General Eisenhower paid tribute to OWI. Stimson said that "the political and social stresses created within Germany and Japan [by propaganda] were cogent forces which undermined the enemies' strength and sapped their resolution." Agreeing, Eisenhower wrote that "the spoken and written word was an important contributing factor in undermining the enemy's will to resist. . . . Psychological warfare has proved its right to a place of dignity in our military arsenal." And one of the sharpest Congressional critics of OWI, Representative Everett Dirksen of Illinois, reversed his position after a tour abroad and went out of his way to praise the agency.

James P. Warburg, Deputy Director of OWI, concluded after the war that, in the year following the North African invasion, "Allied strategic propaganda contributed greatly toward driving Italy out of the war; Allied front-line propaganda brought about the surrender of large numbers of German and Italian troops, prevented the French fleet from falling into the hands of the Germans, and delivered the Italian fleet into Allied hands"—a much too generous appraisal. After the Italian surrender in 1943, however, says Warburg, "strategic propaganda accomplished but little, due to the absence of a clear pro-democratic foreign policy," although "front-line propaganda continued to be effective."[17]

Wallace Carroll, who held important OWI positions in London and Washington, believes World War II "showed that propaganda is a weapon of a definite but limited utility. Used wisely against suitable targets and *in conjunction with military or political action,* it can achieve notable results. Used unwisely *without regard for its limitations,* it can prove as futile as a badly calculated air or artillery bombardment."[18]

The italics are mine, and this rule applies equally in war or peace. Propaganda unrelated to policy is almost certain to be ineffective and can be harmful. Used as one of several instruments in a co-ordinated campaign with specific and realistic objectives, it can do much. That, perhaps, is the most important lesson of propaganda taught by World War II; it is a lesson repeatedly retaught in the peacetime propaganda operations that followed.

It would be comforting to think the lesson was so obvious and so well learned that we could take it for granted, but the record of the two decades since the war indicates otherwise. U.S. propagandists now as then must continually fight for a place at the policy-makers' table. Sometimes they succeed and sometimes they do not. In OWI's time and today, American propaganda is vastly more pertinent and more effective when they do.

The Propaganda of Peace

The experience gained in the early 1940s provided the framework and the trained cadres for peacetime propaganda. But the transition was not easy. Americans were tired of war agencies, war controls, and war spending. Even before the Japanese had signed the surrender documents, President Truman by Executive Order transferred OWI and the propaganda functions of the Office of Inter-American Affairs to a newly created bureau in the State Department, the Interim International Information Service. He asked Secretary of State James Byrnes to make recommendations on the future of American propaganda.

Truman did recognize that "the nature of present day foreign relations makes it essential for the United States to maintain information activities abroad as an integral part of the conduct of our foreign affairs."[19] But most of the old hands in the State Department, traditionalists in the conduct of diplomacy, took a contrary view, and they set out to put propaganda in its place—as they saw it. They had support from many members of Congress who had disapproved of OWI and saw little need for a similar program in peacetime. And their boss Secretary Byrnes, himself a former Senator, shared many of their views.

Elmer Davis and hundreds of his wartime OWI colleagues, among them many of his most talented people, returned to private life. William Benton, who had made money and a name for himself in advertising (Benton & Bowles), education (University of Chicago), and publishing (*Encyclopaedia Britannica*), was appointed to the newly created position of Assistant Secretary of State for Public Affairs and given the task of reducing and reorganizing the propaganda machine.

Benton set out to cut the staff (thirteen thousand at war's end) and programs to acceptable size. He consolidated broadcasting operations in New York City, eliminated all OWI magazines except the Russian-language *Amerika*, reduced the news service by four-fifths, and dropped OWI's radio-photo transmission system. In the wake of large-scale resignations, he cut the staff back even further.

Where Benton used a scalpel, however, the Bureau of the Budget used a cleaver and Congress an ax. Despite the fact that the United States was already having trouble with Russia and diplomats were warning of more to come, despite the fact that much of the war-weary world was confused and hostile, Benton had to fight the Bureau of the Budget, and then Congress, for every penny needed to maintain even a skeleton propaganda service.

Although he assiduously wooed Congress, Benton's abrasive personality did not always help. The Voice of America was cut back from 3,200 live programs in some forty languages to slightly more than half that. Many other operations were eliminated entirely. Benton finally got an appropriation of $19 million and acceptance of a "permanent" Office of International Information and Cultural Affairs in the State Department, comprised of what was left of OWI and State's limited cultural program.

Yet, despite the drastic budget cuts and the hostility within the State Department and in Congress, the program remained alive. Benton made dozens of speeches across the country to promote his cause. He persuaded the skeptical American Society of Newspaper Editors to appoint a committee to study the program and tour overseas posts; it concluded that a real need existed and that Benton's people were doing a good job.

One man, however, more than any other, contributed to the growing sentiment in America that a strong, permanent information program was a necessity. That man was Josef Stalin. In conference after conference, Soviet intransigence blocked efforts to settle the issues of the postwar world. Allies in battle became adversaries in peace, and the newly created United Nations was more disunited than anything else. In Churchill's memorable words, Stalin had rung down an "iron curtain" from "Stettin in the Baltic to Trieste in the Adriatic." Communist governments, backed by the occupying Red Army, were installed in the capitals of Eastern Europe. Although the Soviets did reluctantly withdraw from the Iranian province of Azerbaijan, Communist guerrillas threatened to take over Greece and Moscow applied increasing pressure on Turkey.

Americans grudgingly faced up to a world that was unpleasantly different from their wartime anticipations. In a striking analogy with 1918, the people in 1946 repudiated the Administration that had led them to victory and elected a Republican Congress. But there the analogy ended; where the mood after World War I had been strictly isolationist, this time it was internationalist, at least among the leadership. Henry Cabot Lodge, Sr. had been a bitter foe of Wilson's blueprint for peace, but the chairman of the Senate Foreign Relations Committee in the Eightieth Congress—Arthur Vandenberg of Michigan—was a stout collaborator in constructing a bipartisan foreign policy. In the spring of 1947 Congress approved the Truman Doctrine for unprecedented U.S. assistance to Greece and Turkey. Two months later, Secretary of State George C. Marshall proposed, and Congress subsequently approved, a program of massive economic aid to the shattered nations of Europe.

For the foreign information program, the change in Congressional sentiment came none too soon. The second time Benton went to the Hill for an appropriation, he was cut back $5 million, and it would have been more had not Truman and Marshall intervened. The information program all but disappeared in another State Department reorganization. But Stalin's ambitions, Benton's educational campaign, and the new bipartisanship in Congress resulted in the passage in early 1948 of Public Law 402, the Smith-Mundt Act.

Senator H. Alexander Smith of New Jersey and Representative (later Senator) Karl Mundt of North Dakota, both Republicans, became convinced that the country needed an effective foreign information program. They believed such a program required specific authorization by Congress so that it would not—in the words of one observer—continue to be viewed in the State Department as an "illegitimate child at a family reunion."[20] A few Senators were opposed, and there was even more resistance in the House, but Smith and Mundt, greatly aided by Vandenberg, stuck to their guns.

As finally passed, the legislation was neither very sophisticated nor very explicit. But it did provide a statutory basis for a permanent foreign information program, the basic legislation which to this day underlies the operations of the U.S. Information Agency. (USIA was not created by P.L. 402, however; that came more than five years later.)

The objectives of the Smith-Mundt Act were "to promote a better understanding of the United States in other countries, and to increase mutual understanding" between Americans and foreigners. The Act provided for "an information service to disseminate abroad information about the United States, its people and policies," and "an educational exchange service to cooperate with other nations in (a) the interchange of persons, knowledge, and skills; (b) the rendering of technical and other services; (c) the interchange of developments in . . . education, the arts and sciences."

Carrying out the new law, the State Department created two new offices, the Office of International Information (OII) and the Office of Educational Exchange (OEX), under the Assistant Secretary of State for Public Affairs. A year later, following a recommendation by the Hoover Commission on Government Reorganization that the Assistant Secretary be relieved of daily operational burdens, a general manager was appointed under the Assistant Secretary to direct the International Information and Educational Exchange Program (USIE), which included both OII and OEX.

The Smith-Mundt Act provided the authority for the foreign information program, but of course it did not provide the appropriations. Members of the Appropriations Committees were less international-minded than their brethren who specialized in foreign affairs. Radio scripts, art exhibits, nearly everything that was produced, were carefully scrutinized on Capitol Hill, and there was hardly a product that was not found wanting by some legislators. One Congressman even proposed that all VOA scripts be edited by a committee of the Daughters of the American Revolution.

In early 1948, his welcome with Congress well worn, Benton returned to his encyclopedic interests and was succeeded by a career Foreign Service Officer, George V. Allen. Only forty-four, the North Carolina-born Allen had risen rapidly in government service to become Ambassador to Iran two years earlier. A former newspaperman, he had some appreciation of the communications media. More importantly, he could impress his skeptical fellow Foreign Service Officers on the importance of the program. More effective than Benton with Congress, Allen talked the Hill into appropriating $11,320,-000 for foreign relay stations to make the Voice of America more audible in many corners of the world, including the Soviet Union.

There was much for the Information Service and its Voice to say. A "full and fair picture" concept resulted in too many stories about the wealth of America, with its countless automobiles and refrigerators, and such stories alienated as many foreigners as they attracted. But stories of greater urgency were also communicated. Although the Marshall Plan program had its own information service in Europe, State Department propagandists elsewhere told the exciting story of European recovery under freedom, contrasting it with the declining living standards in Soviet-held Eastern Europe. When the Communists blockaded Berlin, USIS posts went all out in publicizing the Western airlift which kept the former German capital supplied—and free—in the winter of 1948-49. Similar treatment was given President Truman's "Point Four" proposal, in his 1949 Inaugural Address, for extending technical assistance to underdeveloped countries.

The "Campaign of Truth"

But it was Stalin who again gave the information program a big boost. In late 1949 the Soviet Union exploded its first atomic bomb, and the shock waves were felt more in Washington than anywhere else. The National Security Council, in a detailed study of Soviet capabilities and intentions, came to the conclusion that a major propaganda effort should be undertaken in addition to massive U.S. rearmament. Edward W. Barrett, summoned back from *Newsweek* to be Assistant Secretary of State, agreed after making his own quick study.

Barrett was a good choice to succeed Allen, who had been named Ambassador to Yugoslavia. Among the ablest of the wartime propagandists, Barrett also was well regarded by his fellow American journalists. Secretary of State Acheson summoned him to Washington shortly after Christmas, 1949, to urge him to take the job, then took him to see the President. Barrett was deeply impressed by Truman, but in a different way than he had been when he met Roosevelt during the war. Truman had "the simplicity and friendliness of, say, the corner merchant," he wrote later. "Yet here was a man who clearly understood the problem of international information work far better than Roosevelt ever had."[21]

Once in office, however, Barrett had no more access to Truman than Allen. But he was helped by the presence in the White House of George Elsey, a young aide who became interested in propaganda, passed Barrett's suggestions to Truman, and served as a friend at court.

Influenced by recommendations from all sides, Truman decided to propose a major propaganda offensive in a Washington speech to the American Society of Newspaper Editors in April, 1950. Barrett suggested that he call his proposal a "campaign of truth" to avoid the "propaganda" label, and Truman agreed. The President's words were widely publicized:

> We must make ourselves heard round the world in a great campaign of truth. This task is not separate and distinct from other elements of our foreign policy. It is a necessary part of all we are doing . . . as important as armed strength or economic aid.

Barrett set four goals for the new campaign: (1) Creating a "healthy international community" with confidence in American leadership; (2) presenting America fairly and countering misrepresentations and misconceptions about it; (3) discouraging aggression by showing that America wants peace but is prepared for war; (4) reducing Soviet influence by weakening the will of its officials at home while encouraging non-Communist forces elsewhere.

In retrospect the Barrett program appears overambitious if not naïve. But our propagandists did not know what they could accomplish until they tried—and once again skepticism in Congress was a major obstacle. Like his predecessors and successors, Barrett spent a disproportionate amount of time cajoling on Capitol Hill, with only partial success. Senator Pat McCarran of Nevada almost succeeded in getting the program abolished in early 1950. Then Stalin, once again, came to the rescue. On June 25, 1950, the Soviet-backed government of North Korea invaded South Korea, American forces rushed to the rescue, and Moscow began a propaganda offensive to persuade the world it was the United States that was at fault. That year, at least, Congress was generous in its appropriation, nearly tripling the program's funds.*

In the wake of the Korean outbreak, the world-wide propaganda operation grew rapidly. It was not without growing pains: some decisions were made hastily and carelessly; not all of the thousands of persons hurriedly employed were of top caliber; and some USIS posts were assigned more people than they needed. But the program had its effect, as the Soviets demonstrated indirectly through their increased attacks upon it. Although jamming limited the audibility of the Voice of America in Soviet cities, *Pravda* and Tass revealed the Kremlin's sensitivity by replying to VOA "lies." One by one USIS offices were forced to close in the satellite countries of Eastern Europe. The Soviets made distribution of the USIS magazine *Amerika* so difficult that it was discontinued in 1952 (though resurrected four years later).

On this side of the Iron Curtain, staffs and budgets were enlarged, and the beginnings of a genuine professionalism began to appear. Washington permitted more decisions to be made in the field on what to say and how to say it. A management consultant firm, called in to make an independent study, concluded in 1951 that "the program today is in a sounder position, conceptually and management-wise, than at any time since the Department of State took over" in 1945.

By mid-1951 Barrett could boast of a number of accomplishments, although on examination they proved to be more accomplishments of growth than of persuasion. He told members of his staff, whose morale was slipping under a mounting barrage of Congressional criticism, that they could "look with pride" on having: improved and expanded VOA broadcasts to make them the "most effective single weapon the free world has behind the Iron Curtain"; recruited "two of the nation's ablest advertising men, a dozen well-known newspaper correspondents, [and] an outstanding radio executive"; opened six and laid plans for another twenty-nine new USIS posts abroad, for

---

* A year later, though, tired of the Korean War, Congress was its old stubborn self. In 1950 the chairman of the Senate Appropriations Committee, Kenneth McKellar of Tennessee, had lavishly praised the Alabama-born Barrett as a true Southern gentleman. In 1951, however, he opened a hearing by asking him, "Are you a Communist?" McKellar's colleagues were equally difficult if more rational.

a total of 133; issued two million copies of 277 American books and documents in foreign languages; tripled the audience for USIS films "to a rate of 400,000,000 persons a year"; and won participation "in top policy-making."

It was a record of impressive growth under difficult circumstances. "However unfair the current sniping may seem," Barrett told his staff, "keep up the good work—well aware that your efforts, added to those of loyal public servants in other fields, may well mean the difference between peace and war."[22]

Reorganization Again

Shaken by the mixed foreign reaction to events in Korea, the Pentagon pressed for a still stronger information service, one in which it would have a hand. The State Department objected to too much military control of the program, and President Truman compromised by creating an interdepartmental strategy committee with representatives of the Secretary of Defense and the Joint Chiefs of Staff. Barrett served as chairman. Later in 1951 the President established a higher-level group called the Psychological Strategy Board, comprised of the Under Secretary of State, the Deputy Secretary of Defense, and the Director of Central Intelligence. The original group then became the Psychological Operations Coordinating Committee.

The two bodies had little impact, however. Both were long on ideas but short on power to carry them out. Though members of PSB were high-ranking, they were not the heads of their departments, and the departments resisted what they considered encroachments on their preserves. Philosophical abstractions and recommendations on operational tactics were handed down; both were largely ignored.

Barrett, meanwhile, was never fully satisfied with the administration of the program within the State Department. Rigid departmental regulations, written more for negotiators and diplomatic observers than for propagandists, limited the program's flexibility. The Assistant Secretary for Public Affairs, one of several Assistant Secretaries, had to compete with his colleagues for the Secretary's attention— and he had almost no contact with the President. Immersed in daily operations (despite the help of a general manager), he had little time to work with the department's top officers on basic policies.

Barrett and others recommended consolidation of USIE's two offices into an International Information Administration (IIA), still within the State Department but semiautonomous in administration. Its administrator would receive policy guidance from the Assistant Secretary but would report directly to the Secretary, and would have a relatively free hand in operations. The reorganization plan was accepted and Barrett resigned in early 1952. At Secretary Acheson's recommendation, President Truman appointed Howland Sargeant, who had been Deputy Assistant Secretary from 1947 to 1951, to succeed him.* Dr. Wilson Compton, president of Washington State University, was appointed the first administrator of IIA.

Sargeant's appointment was logical; he had considerable experience in the field, and it probably would have been difficult to find anyone as competent outside the government in the last year of the long Roosevelt-Truman Administration. But Compton, sixty-one, was an unlikely choice, best known as the least famous of the famous Compton brothers. A former college teacher (of economics) and administrator, he had little government experience and none in communications. But he was a Republican and knew Congress from his twenty-six years as a lobbyist for the National Lumber Manufacturers Association, and those apparently were the qualifications that Acheson, under heavy fire from Republicans on Capitol Hill, prized most highly.

Compton never had a chance. Congressional criticism increased instead of slackening, and the experienced bureaucratic infighters in the State Department ran rings around him. After a few months in office, Compton complained to Acheson that the promised "semi-autonomy" in personnel and budget had not been forthcoming. "To achieve such semi-autonomy implies a high degree of consolidation of authorities and responsibilities which heretofore have been widely dispersed. There is within the Department a reluctance to accept these changes, and if not a resistance at least a formidable inertia."

Some of that "formidable inertia" stemmed from the Secretary of State himself. Acheson believed the information program had only marginal value because, as he wrote later, "world opinion simply does

---

* Barrett later became dean of the Columbia University School of Journalism in New York; Sargeant now heads Radio Liberty, which broadcasts to the Soviet Union.

not exist on matters that concern us." And he complained of the tendency of the American "to stare like Narcissus at his image in the pool of what he believes to be world opinion."[23]

Inertia and indifference in Washington handicapped overworked field officers, but many nonetheless improved their operations and came up with imaginative projects. One of the most imaginative—and most successful—flowered in the Middle East. Annually, many thousands of Muslims travel long distances to make the required pilgrimage or *haj* to Mecca. In the hot summer of 1952, several thousand pilgrims were stranded in Beirut when airlines oversold their space. At the suggestion of the American Legation and USIS in Beirut, U.S. Air Force transports carried 3,318 *hajis* to Saudi Arabia. Although the United States was not in good favor in the area because of its support for Israel, Muslims of every nationality praised the gesture. Local newspapers published thousands of USIS-supplied pictures and words on the airlift, and pamphlets, radio programs, and posters were produced to keep the story alive for months.

At home, however, there were only setbacks for the propaganda program during 1952. It was an election year, and partisanship intensified the bitterness of the attacks on the State Department, on Secretary Acheson, and on the Information Administration. General Eisenhower, the Republican candidate for President, made the information program a campaign issue. Senator Joseph R. McCarthy of Wisconsin, riding the crest of an irresponsible campaign against "Communists" in the State Department, let his charges far outrun the facts, and fear and uncertainty lay heavily on the land.

The real danger to America continued to be foreign, totalitarian, Communist. But many Americans, seeking scapegoats for their frustrations, looked for devils at home, not abroad. In the year ahead, the greatest opposition to an effective U.S. foreign information program would come not from Stalin or Mao Tse-tung but from the junior Senator from Wisconsin.

2 *Villains and Heroes*

During World War II Dwight D. Eisenhower had learned much about the uses of propaganda. In the years that followed he spoke often of the need for an effective peacetime information program, in 1950 calling for a "Marshall Plan of ideas." As the Republican candidate for President in 1952 he proclaimed that America cannot "win the struggle for men's minds merely by tripling Congressional appropriations" for foreign information. "Rather," he said, "it will be the message which we give the Voice [of America] to speak" and "the spiritual strength, the understanding and the compassion which we . . . put into that message." In his first State of the Union Message, Eisenhower promised to "make more effective all activities related to international information" because they were "essential to the security of the United States."

Eisenhower's election should have signaled an end to the doubts and confusions that had characterized the program since the end of the war. But it did not, at least not for many months, chiefly because the President failed to stand up to a Senator from his own party, Joseph R. McCarthy, who viciously attacked the operation, shattered (at least temporarily) the reputations of some of its most dedicated public servants, and reduced morale in the International Information Administration to zero. McCarthy's first victim was the holdover head of IIA, Dr. Wilson Compton.

McCarthy, a small-town Wisconsin lawyer, had been elected in 1946 to the Senate, where he drew little public attention until he proclaimed in a 1950 speech that there were "205 Communists" in

31

the State Department. Overnight, McCarthy became a national figure and the darling of the radical right. Accusation followed accusation, although he was careful not to engage in specifics off the Senate floor where he could be sued for libel.

The country watched with mixed emotions. Many Americans, deeply concerned by the postwar revelations that career State Department man Alger Hiss and a few other government officials had been Communists and even Soviet agents, were persuaded that McCarthy had something. Most of his colleagues in the Senate, with a few courageous exceptions, avoided crossing him publicly, though privately many had no use for him. Some of his fellow Republicans, including the redoubtable Robert A. Taft, held no brief for his character or methods but were delighted to see the Democratic Administration squirm under his assaults.

In 1952 McCarthy was re-elected, and the Republicans won control of the Eighty-third Congress in the Eisenhower landslide. When McCarthy returned to Washington in early 1953, he was riding high. The change in party control made him chairman of the Permanent Committee on Investigations of the Senate Committee on Government Operations, but did not increase his superficial party loyalty. McCarthy put two young firebrands, lawyer Roy Cohn and hotel heir G. David Schine, on his committee staff and looked around for a target. None appeared more inviting than the much-criticized International Information Administration.

Although Dr. Compton was a lifelong Republican, he received no support from the White House. The new Administration was only days old when IIA found itself in deep trouble. There had been some discussion the previous year over whether IIA should ever use for any purpose the writings of Communists, fellow travelers, and those accused of pro-Communist tendencies. A distinguished advisory committee, headed by a Catholic educator, had recommended that content and purpose be the sole guiding criteria, not the political views of an author. But two weeks after Eisenhower took office, IIA Policy Order 5 advised caution in the use of works by "controversial" writers, a concession to the political climate current in the country. However, the Policy Order did concede there could be exceptions to this rule when writers had a "special credibility" with certain audiences, and it was this clause that caused trouble.

A McCarthy spy in IIA provided him with a copy of the directive, and he hit the ceiling.* The White House, eager at this point to appease Congress in general and the McCarthy element in particular, was thoroughly annoyed. The Policy Order was canceled. Less than two weeks later, Dr. Compton was informed by telephone while at lunch that he was finished. John Foster Dulles, the new Secretary of State who announced Compton's "resignation," said it had been accepted as part of the Administration's· policy of bringing new faces into government.

A new IIA directive on February 19 ordered that "no material by any controversial persons, Communists, fellow travellers, etc., will be used under any circumstances." Although the directive said it sought "to avoid all misunderstanding," it had just the opposite effect, for who could define what "controversial" and "etc." meant?

Alfred H. Morton, an experienced radio executive who had been head of IIA's radio arm, the Voice of America, since the previous October, advised his writers that they should not take the policy literally until it had been clarified. The State Department promptly suspended Morton, and, although he was reinstated with a reprimand a day later, he left his job shortly thereafter. Meanwhile two Dulles deputies promised McCarthy that no reprisals would be allowed against employees who gave him information.

On February 16 McCarthy's committee opened public, televised hearings on the Voice of America. He badgered and browbeat witnesses, particularly the quietly able Reed Harris, the Deputy Administrator of IIA who was in charge of the agency briefly after Compton's departure. Charging "gross mismanagement" of VOA, McCarthy proclaimed it "could not be merely the result of incompetence or stupidity," but must be deliberate and therefore Communist-inspired.

As a student two decades earlier, Harris had written a sophomoric book entitled *King Football,* swinging wildly at college athletics in particular and society in general. Harris had quickly outgrown the book's views, regretted having written it, and had served his country with distinction as a public servant for many years. But McCarthy

---

* McCarthy had a number of informers in IIA. They dubbed themselves the "loyal American underground." Some were refugees from Communist countries or ex-Communists; others were right-wing or disgruntled employees who saw a chance to punish their foes or reverse their superiors.

cared nothing about that. He put Harris on the stand in early March for several grueling days, screaming at him, interrupting his testimony, and constantly harking back to the "pro-Communist" book. Harris lost neither his dignity nor his courage. "You are casting innuendoes and aspersions here without any support," he quietly told McCarthy at one point. "I think you should let me tell what I have to say."

Harris noted that "if this particular proceeding were held in a court of law, where it were possible to question the questions, as it were, where the legal counsel could be on both sides of the table and not merely on the prosecution side, I could satisfy anybody in the United States that I am a loyal American citizen." But McCarthy, uninterested in due process and even less in arriving at the truth, continued his harangue, while other members of the committee sat mostly silent.

"I resent the tone of this inquiry very much," Harris said bravely. "Not only because it is my neck, my public neck, that you are . . . trying to wring, but because there are thousands of able and loyal employees in the Federal Government who have been properly cleared according to the laws and the security practices of their agencies, as I was. . . . I have had two full field investigations. Can Mr. Cohn say that? Has he . . . been examined all the way back to his birth? I have." McCarthy's only response was to repeat that the situation at VOA was "fantastic beyond words."

One of McCarthy's allegations was that "Communist influence" had led the Voice to eliminate its Hebrew-language broadcasts to Israel. In fact, VOA had terminated the broadcasts because budgetary pressures required cuts somewhere, the VOA audience in Israel was minuscule, and—due to a wave of official anti-Semitism in the U.S.S.R. and Eastern Europe—the new Jewish state was safely anti-Communist anyway. McCarthy had the support of a few Voice employees whose jobs were affected by the elimination of the Hebrew service; one of them, Gerald Dooher, called the cancellation "a well struck blow for the Communist cause . . . part of a deliberate pattern to destroy or nullify the Voice broadcasts to the non-free world." Dooher, who was treated with great courtesy by McCarthy, said he did "not believe it could be stupidity, because stupidity does not fall into a design."[1]

Beyond our shores the McCarthy spectacle was greeted with incredulity by America's friends and cynical pleasure by its adversaries.

The hearings were covered in detail by foreign news media, and it was clear to most of them that McCarthy was not interested in finding the truth. They knew what some of the program's weaknesses were, and they saw that McCarthy by-passed them (if he knew of them) in favor of meaningless but more sensational tidbits. Above all, foreigners could not understand how one Senator of the President's own party could so frighten the government of the powerful United States. Confidence in America was perceptibly damaged.

Particularly damaging was the highly publicized European expedition of McCarthy's two young aides, Cohn and Schine. Arrogant carbon copies of their boss, they insulted both foreigner and American as they toured USIS offices and libraries in Europe during early April, looking for evidences of Communism, subversion, and sexual deviation. Astonished Europeans watched, laughed—and wept for America. The two inquisitors spent a grand total of forty hours in Paris, sixteen in Bonn, nineteen in Frankfurt, sixty in Munich, forty-one in Vienna, twenty-three in Belgrade, twenty-four in Athens, twenty in Rome, and six in London, then returned to Washington as "experts." Some USIS people fawned over them; others—to their lasting credit —did not, and some of these (notably Theodore Kaghan in Bonn) paid for their lack of obsequiousness when McCarthy dragged their names into the hearings.

Everywhere abroad, USIS public affairs officers and librarians waited fearfully for the ax to fall. The Cultural Affairs Officer at one post rushed back to the office in a panic one afternoon; she thought she had seen McCarthy lunching at a local hotel. On another occasion an American tourist, idly looking over books in a USIS library, sent the staff into an uproar; they thought he was a McCarthy agent.

Robert Johnson Tries—and Fails

Meanwhile, on the same day that Compton was sent packing, Eisenhower and Dulles appointed Robert L. Johnson, a Philadelphia millionaire with impeccable conservative credentials, to be the new head of IIA. A co-founder of *Time* magazine, he had been president of Temple University since 1941. He was at various times a director of several corporations, president of Americans for the Competitive Enterprise System, a director of the Freedoms Foundation, and—in later years—a member of the Republican National Committee. Prior to Eisenhower's election he had been chairman of a Citizens Committee for Reorganization of the Government, a group that had aroused public support for the Hoover Commission report. He was also a very decent man.

Johnson knew little about the government information program, and even less about the ways of Washington politics. He soon was to learn a good deal about both. Reporters asked Johnson what he thought of McCarthy. "I think he is trying to be helpful," he responded hopefully. "Maybe he'll dig up stuff that will help us. I think he is a good American who wants to see that the Voice works properly."[2]

But Johnson ignored the suggestion of Scott McLeod, the McCarthy ally and former aide to Senator Styles Bridges who now was chief security officer in the State Department, that he hire Frances Knight, a McCarthy friend in IIA, as his assistant. (McLeod subsequently transferred her to his staff and she later became the powerful head of the Passport Division.) Johnson also resisted Dulles' suggestion that he hire O. K. Armstrong, a lame-duck Missouri Congressman of questionable qualifications, as his chief deputy.

McCarthy, at this point, was not publicly critical of Eisenhower or Johnson. But he continued his relentless attacks on Johnson's underlings. Gravely disturbed, the new information chief carefully checked the histories of his senior staff and found them to be loyal and competent without exception. Worried about both McCarthy and upcoming budget hearings on Capitol Hill, Johnson asked Herbert Hoover to intercede with his friends in Congress. But the former President turned him down, asserting that IIA was "full of OWI hangers-on, Communists, left-wingers and incompetents." It "ought to be liquidated," Hoover said coldly.[3]

Hoover's reaction was not much worse than that of top Administration officials. Although Johnson had been urged to take the job and was promised full cooperation and support, he received little from the President, the Secretary of State, or the Vice President. When Johnson went to Richard Nixon for help, the new Vice President showed an appreciation for the program and was enthusiastic in his support. As for McCarthy, however, Nixon blandly reassured Johnson: Joe wasn't a bad guy; you simply had to understand him. Nixon arranged for Johnson to meet McCarthy in the Vice President's office, but the Senator at the last minute refused to come.[4] The two finally did get together, with the help of columnist George Sokolsky, but nothing came of it.

Whatever Eisenhower's personal opinion of McCarthy may have been (and it apparently hit a new low during this period), the new President was not prepared at the time to support those in the Executive Branch who fell into the Senator's clutches. Eisenhower had a "passion" against "offending" anyone in Congress, a White House assistant told Johnson. Besides, Eisenhower repeatedly told his aides, "I refuse to get into the gutter with that guy!" A less charitable observer said that the White House was as "terrified" by McCarthy "as the most vulnerable senator."[5]

Despite McCarthy's and McLeod's efforts, no Communists were found in the program although six employees were discharged on "suitability" grounds dealing with their personal habits. More than six hundred other employees were dismissed through normal "reduction-in-force" procedures, not because Johnson wanted to fire them but because the Bureau of the Budget and the House Appropriations Committee insisted. Johnson canceled contracts for two controversial radio transmitters, although not because he agreed with McCarthy's claim that they had been deliberately mislocated through Communist influence.

Johnson found the famous February 19 directive on books no easier to interpret than Morton had. He pressed for a clarification, and on March 18 received one from Carl McCardle, a Philadelphia newspaperman who had succeeded Sargeant as Assistant Secretary of State for Public Affairs. Unfortunately, the clarification was not too clear, and like the earlier directive was greeted with horror by civil libertarians in this country and with ridicule abroad.

While the new directive did say that material "produced by Communists or their agents or sympathizers" could be used "to confound international Communism with its own words," it banned from USIS libraries all works by Communist authors and periodicals containing articles "detrimental to United States objectives," whatever that meant. McCardle also instructed IIA "not to identify by name any international Communist unless absolutely necessary" so as "not to build up our living opponents by naming them," making the preparation of news stories and features difficult if not impossible.

IIA sent a new policy directive to the field, based on McCardle's memorandum, and the State Department's Security Office prepared "blacklists" to guide IIA librarians, broadcasters, and writers. The lists proved to be unfair and undiscriminating, containing the names of many prominent liberals who were no more Communist than Eisenhower or Dulles. One banned author was a cousin of the Secretary of State.

Some USIS librarians abroad, frightened at the prospect of attack by McCarthy or criticism from the State Department, went beyond the blacklists and stripped their shelves of any and all works they thought might get them into trouble. Books by Eleanor Roosevelt, Elmer Davis, Upton Sinclair, and Marshall Field joined Lenin, Stalin, and mystery writer Dashiell Hammett on the scrap heap. Some overzealous librarians burned forbidden books because they lacked storage space for them. This prompted a new wave of criticism, here and abroad.

Even Eisenhower objected. "Don't join the book burners," he admonished students at a Dartmouth College convocation in mid-June. "Don't be afraid to go into your library and read every book." Morale rose at USIS posts around the world, but it was short-lived. Dulles, at a press conference, "explained" that Eisenhower was talking not about USIS libraries but about books in this country. Dulles ducked questions about the directive on authors; that, he said, was Johnson's responsibility. Two days later, asked by reporters if his Dartmouth speech was a slap at McCarthy, Eisenhower responded that he would not engage in "personalities" and confirmed that his address had referred only to libraries in this country.

Unsatisfied, Johnson told a press conference later that month that "in keeping with the American principle that the individual is innocent until proven guilty, it has been virtually impossible to define who is and who is not a Communist. . . . We have only been able to specify certain authors who either are avowed Communists or have publicly refused to answer questions regarding possible Communist affiliations. . . . Beyond this limited list, our people in the field have had to use their own judgment as to what works should be excluded. . . . We are preparing clarifying instructions which will base the decision . . . upon the effect reasonably to be expected from [a book's] presence in a Government-sponsored library abroad."

That same day, the American Library Association adopted a resolution saying that "though no one could justify . . . the use of the overseas libraries to disseminate material harmful to the United States, it is simply unworkable to abandon the simple criterion of whether a book is useful to the purpose of the libraries and to substitute elaborate, irrelevant and offensive schemes of 'clearance' of authors."

Buoyed by the librarians' manifesto, IIA on July 8 issued a new directive. It was largely the work of Johnson's aide Martin Merson, assisted by the IIA staff and several outsiders including Norman Cousins of *Saturday Review* magazine and George Brett, president of Macmillan. In effect it returned to pre-Eisenhower, pre-McCarthy policy. Librarians were instructed to exercise their judgment on the basis of a book's contents, not its author. The occasional use of books by Communists was allowed "if such authors may have written something which affirmatively served the ends of democracy." As for "controversial" books, they "are of course acceptable and indeed essential if by 'controversy' we mean honest differences of opinion honestly expressed. . . . We must not confuse honest controversy with conspiracy."

That ended the book debate within IIA, and closed one of the propaganda program's sorrier chapters. But there was still McCarthy to deal with, and if anything he had become more of a problem. In April, Reed Harris resigned. Eisenhower and Dulles had refused to stand up for him in the face of McCarthy's personal attacks, and Johnson had been unable to do so effectively. Johnson had not asked for Harris' resignation, and wrote him: "Frankly, I hate to see you go. I have learned to depend upon you and respect you for the fine contribution you have made."[6] Harris was understandably bitter when he departed, but he spoke not one public word of criticism of the Administration that had failed to support him.*

But it was not Harris alone who lacked support from the Administration. As the weeks went by, Johnson got less and less backing from his superiors. They remained silent when McCarthy hounded several other officials out of the program; Johnson wept when he heard of one case. To add to his troubles, Johnson, having appointed advertising executive Leonard F. Erikson to succeed Morton as head of VOA,

---

* Eight years later Harris returned to the program as Executive Assistant to USIA Director Edward R. Murrow. As of this writing, Harris is a senior official of USIA's Office of Policy.

was scolded privately by Eisenhower Assistant Sherman Adams and Republican National Chairman Leonard Hall because Erikson was a Democrat who had supported Adlai Stevenson for President. Finally, Johnson heard from a mutual friend that Eisenhower believed Johnson himself was doing "a lousy job."[7] Under all this pressure Johnson's health, never very good, worsened. Discredited and discouraged, he resigned, effective at the end of July, to return to Temple University.

Now that he was leaving, Johnson saw no need to appease McCarthy further. When the liberalized book directive was issued in early July, McCarthy was outraged. He counterattacked with the charge (through an aide) that USIS libraries contained no anti-Soviet publications. Johnson publicly denied it. In a cold letter to McCarthy he called the statement "patently false and clearly damaging to the vital interest of the American people abroad." The reputation of America, said Johnson, "has suffered enough as the result of irresponsible charges and actions in connection with our program."

McCarthy, who was a member of the Senate Appropriations Committee, threatened to retaliate by further cutting the already battered IIA budget. "If you had deliberately set out to sabotage any possibility of getting adequate funds to run a good information program, you could not have done a better job," the Senator wrote Johnson. The Washington *Post* called it an effort "to cut off the Voice of America's tongue to spite Dr. Johnson's face" and warned that "a crippled IIA can tell the world only that Senator McCarthy dominates America's foreign information activities."[8]

Martin Merson, Johnson's assistant, later disclosed that Senator Mundt, a member of McCarthy's committee, had called the White House to "raise hell" about Johnson's criticism of McCarthy. Mundt, co-author of the law authorizing an information program but a supporter of McCarthy, promised that if Johnson were gagged the budget would not be slashed. Sherman Adams promptly ordered Johnson to keep quiet and stay away from the Senate budget hearings.[9]

It did not help much. In the end, the propaganda program was voted only $75 million, compared to $96 million the previous year (when Eisenhower campaigners had complained of an inadequate effort). Of the final figure, $15 million was for the exchange program, $5 million for "termination costs" in connection with the discharge of excess employees, and $4 million was earmarked for moving Voice of America offices and studios from New York to Washington, a move which Congress (wisely) had insisted upon.

Dispirited but not apologetic, Johnson paid his farewell call on Eisenhower. He presented the President a report on his accomplishments, which were understandably thin. And he pointedly told Eisenhower that "in no single case which has been brought to my attention has there been any allegation—or suspicion—that the person under fire [by McCarthy] was or had been disloyal to the United States." The President thanked him, and Johnson left the White House, Washington, and government service. Months later, Eisenhower, Congress, and the nation would lose their patience with McCarthy and cut him down—but too late to undo the damage done to the foreign information program.

The Jackson Committee: A Voice of Reason

While McCarthy was persecuting the propagandists in televised hearings, there were three other inquiries in the mill—if less in the news— to strengthen the faltering program. A special subcommittee of the Senate Foreign Relations Committee had begun an evaluation of the operation in the previous session of Congress, and it was continued in 1953. The Advisory Commission on Information, established by the Smith-Mundt Act and now headed by Dr. Mark A. May of Yale, was conducting its own inquiry. And, six days after he took office, Eisenhower created a President's Committee on International Information Activities. He ordered all executive departments to cooperate fully with the group, which soon became known as the Jackson Committee after its chairman, William H. Jackson, a New York investment banker and former Deputy Director of Central Intelligence.*

The committee was told to report to the President no later than

* Other members of the committee, some of whom were highly knowledgeable, were C. D. Jackson, a wartime propagandist on leave as publisher of *Fortune* magazine to head Radio Free Europe; Robert Cutler, the President's foreign affairs assistant who had been deputy head of the Psychological Strategy Board; Gordon Gray, president of the University of North Carolina, former Secretary of the Army, former head of the PSB (and later Eisenhower's Assistant for National Security Affairs); Roger M. Kyes, the new Deputy Secretary of Defense; Sigurd Larmon, advertising agency president; and two businessmen, Barklie Henry and John C. Hughes.

June 30, and it began work immediately. Abbott M. Washburn, a Minneapolis public relations man who had been an official of Radio Free Europe and then worked for Eisenhower during the campaign, was named executive secretary. A staff was drawn from the foreign affairs agencies of the government, and more than 250 witnesses were interviewed. Of the three concurrent studies, the Jackson Committee's was the most thorough and the most perceptive, although admittedly it was influenced by the findings of the other two groups.

On its June 30 deadline, the committee submitted its report to Eisenhower. While much of it was highly classified, particularly portions recommending specific themes and operations, a "sanitized" version was made public by the White House eight days later. The report:

• Recommended that the program's primary purpose should be "to submit evidence to the peoples of other nations that their own aspirations for freedom, progress and peace are supported and advanced by the objectives and policies of the United States."

• Flatly stated that "any program supported by government funds can only be justified to the extent that it assists in the achievement of national objectives."

• Rejected such simple slogans as disseminating truth, winning friendship, and fighting Communism as adequate expressions of the information and propaganda mission.

• Criticized the "haphazard projection of too many and too diffuse propaganda themes."

• Recommended a steady level of appropriations and greater flexibility in budgeting and personnel, in part to permit "rapid concentration on targets of opportunity."

• Stressed the importance of first-rate personnel in the overseas installations, strongly supported in Washington to assure high morale.

• Urged that broadcasts and printed materials "concentrate on objective, factual news reporting," avoiding a "propagandist note" but "making forceful and factual refutations of false Soviet accusations" when required.

• Recommended the use of more unattributed material, less direction in Washington, and more tactical control in the field.

Taking indirect note of the McCarthy attacks, the report said government propagandists "should not hesitate to distribute books and publications just because they contain criticism" of America, although they "certainly must not aid in the distribution of subversive books or communist propaganda." Recognizing that much of the national uncertainty about the foreign information program was rooted in a lack of knowledge, the report urged that IIA be authorized to tell the American people more about its activities.

The committee took a dim view of the Voice of America. It recommended that another name be considered for the radio operation because VOA programs "have been widely criticized and discredited." It questioned the wisdom of spending a third of the budget on broadcasts to the Soviet Union since little was known about the audience, its reactions to VOA, or the effectiveness of Soviet jamming. As for the rest of the world, the committee recommended that shortwave broadcasts be continued only where, after consultation with U.S. ambassadors, "there is some expectation of accomplishing propaganda objectives" through radio.

VOA objected strongly to a change in name, and there was none. Broadcasts to the Soviet Union were continued, but transmissions in three minority languages—Tatar, Turkestani, and Azerbaijani—were eliminated. While ambassadors had mixed views about the effectiveness of VOA, the over-all program was not reduced although there were changes in emphasis.

Many in the Administration in 1953 believed that the populations of the Soviet-controlled countries were vigorously anti-Kremlin. This was probably true, at least to a considerable extent, in most of Eastern Europe, where Kremlin-installed regimes held power with the help of the occupying Red Army. It may not have been true in the Soviet Union itself. VOA Chief Erikson was a believer in the "hard sell." Commenting on the Jackson recommendation that the Voice "avoid a propagandist note," he argued for a distinction "between broadcasts to Iron Curtain listeners, who have a strong emotional need for a hard-hitting anti-Communist message, and broadcasts to Free World listeners who tend to be hypersensitive to a propagandistic approach. In Iron Curtain broadcasts the primary emphasis should be on force and directness," not on "a dispassionate presentation."

It was this insistence on a "hard-hitting anti-Communist message," rather than on subtle persuasion, that damaged the credibility of VOA broadcasts for years. The broadcasters had forgotten—or never heard

—the old African proverb: "The lion that roars is not the lion that kills."

To an Administration whose leaders had been talking boldly of "rolling back the Iron Curtain," the Jackson Committee had some wise if not always heeded words:

The United States will be judged not only by the things it is able to do and does, but also by the gap between these and its announced policies. A clear distinction must be made between policies and aspirations. Objectives with respect to which the United States commits itself to act must be clearly identified as distinct from those ends to which we, as a nation, aspire but regarding which the Government is not committed to take action.

Had that distinction been clearer three years later, the United States might have avoided acute embarrassment at the time of the Hungarian revolt.

The Jackson Committee recommended abolition of the Psychological Strategy Board on the grounds that it had been

founded upon the misconception that "psychological activities" and "psychological strategy" somehow exist apart from official policies and actions and can be dealt with independently. . . . In reality there is a "psychological" aspect or implication to every diplomatic, economic or military policy and action. . . . The important task is to build awareness throughout the entire Government of the impact of day-to-day governmental actions and to coordinate and time such actions so as to derive from them the maximum advantages.

To that end the committee recommended an Operations Coordinating Board, which under the National Security Council would "coordinate the development by departments and agencies of detailed operational plans to carry out national security policies." Eisenhower established the OCB on September 2, but it did little to infuse psychological considerations into policy-making or execution.

While the Jackson Committee was engaged in its study, the Eisenhower Administration considered how to organize the propaganda program. Nearly everyone, including the Jackson group, believed that all government foreign information operations—IIA, the Marshall Plan publicists, and the "Point Four" Technical Cooperation Administration's information staff—should be consolidated into one service.

But where? Some thought all should be put into the State Department with IIA, so the Secretary of State could exercise policy and operational control. IIA executives, weary of trying to operate efficiently within State Department machinery which seemed to them needlessly cumbersome, believed there should be a separate, autonomous agency over which the department would exercise only policy control.

The U.S. Advisory Commission on Information went a step further and recommended that the program be "placed in a new agency of Cabinet level" with "authority to formulate psychological strategy and to coordinate information policies of all Government agencies and consolidate all overseas information programs." The Commission complained bitterly about the State Department's "internal resistance" and "singular lack of enthusiasm" for foreign information activities.[10]

The special subcommittee of the Senate Foreign Relations Committee recommended that the program stay in the State Department with greater autonomy but that, should it be moved out, "the exchange of persons program should remain in the Department." Secretary Dulles, opposed to his department being saddled with large operations and uninterested in the propaganda function, favored an independent agency under State policy control—and it was Dulles' voice that was heard most often and most clearly at the White House. In fact, Dulles had promised Johnson, when he offered him the IIA job, that the program would be taken out of the State Department.

A Fresh Start: The U.S. Information Agency

Back in 1949, on recommendation of the Hoover Commission, Congress had voted the President broad powers to reorganize the Executive Branch. Congress retained for itself only the right to reject (by two-thirds vote) the President's proposals within sixty days. On June 1, 1953, President Eisenhower submitted to Congress Reorganization Plans 7 and 8. The first created a Foreign Operations Administration (FOA), consolidating in a single organization the foreign aid programs then dispersed among several agencies, chiefly the Mutual Security Administration (MSA) and the Technical Cooperation Administration (TCA). The second plan established a United States Information Agency (USIA), consolidating in it the foreign information programs which had been administered by IIA, MSA, TCA, and the U.S. occupation authorities in Germany and Austria.* The exchange-of-persons program was retained in the State Department.

The Reorganization Act provided for a Director and a Deputy Director of USIA to be appointed by the President and confirmed by the Senate. While the Director would report to the President through the National Security Council, the Secretary of State would "direct the policy and control of the content" of the information program and provide "full guidance concerning the foreign policy of the United States."

In a letter to department heads, Eisenhower made it clear that he did not want the new arrangement to reduce Dulles' authority; to the contrary, he said, the reorganization "is designed to emphasize the primary position of the Secretary of State within the Executive Branch in matters of foreign policy. . . . It will be my practice to employ the Secretary of State as my channel of authority within the Executive Branch on matters of foreign policy." The directors of USIA and FOA "will assure the concurrence or participation of the appropriate Secretary before taking up with me any policy matters of concern to that Secretary."

Eisenhower did not specify whether he wanted advice on the psychological factors of foreign affairs from USIA's Director, the Secretary of State, or the Assistant Secretary for Public Affairs. Perhaps the answer was none of these, for Eisenhower had his own "psychological adviser" on the White House staff—first C. D. Jackson and later Nelson Rockefeller. Seven years later, the first Director of USIA told me he believed "USIA should have every opportunity in advising the White House as to the public relations or psychological aspects of all actions and policies involving foreign relations. . . . It should have the opportunity to participate in foreign policy-making."

---

* Then and since there has been some confusion in the public mind regarding the kind of information dispensed by an information agency. For example, one young man wrote: "I would like to find out some information about a Girl. Her name is Susie Smith. She lives in Lancaster, Pa. I would like to know how old she is now, how tall she is, the color of her hair, what school she goes to." A student wrote for "pamphlets, interviews, charts, accounts, book lists, articles or statistics" on "the nationwide problem of prostitution." A mayor's wife asked for "any information you have concerning testing to determine compatibility before marriage. . . . I have enclosed $1 for samples." When I was USIS Information Officer in Beirut, an irate tourist berated me when I could not tell her where to get the best price on brocade.

In early March, 1953, Theodore C. Streibert, former chairman of the board of the Mutual Broadcasting System radio network and president of Station WOR in New York, had been hired as a consultant to VOA. He had also gone to Germany to assist in the reorganization of the large U.S. information program there. On July 30 Eisenhower appointed him first Director of USIA and emphasized the importance of the job. "Our overseas information service never carried a heavier responsibility than it does now," said the President. "It is not enough for us to have sound policies. . . . These policies must be made known to and understood by all peoples throughout the world."

The fifty-four-year-old Streibert, a gruff, no-nonsense sort of man, had—unlike his immediate predecessors—long experience in communications. A graduate of Harvard Business School, he had worked with Cinema Credits Corporation, FBO Pictures, and Pathé before joining WOR and Mutual in 1935. Equally important, he also was—again unlike Compton and Johnson—a tough, aggressive administrator. He was not accustomed to being pushed around, and few tried to do so while he was Director of USIA.

Eisenhower selected Abbott Washburn, the executive secretary to the Jackson Committee, as the first Deputy Director of the new Agency. In contrast to Streibert, the thirty-eight-year-old Washburn was the most amiable of men, and he, too, had an excellent background in communications. He handled public relations for General Mills in Minneapolis for thirteen years before becoming executive vice chairman of Crusade for Freedom, Inc., the parent organization of Radio Free Europe. During the campaign he helped organize national headquarters for the Citizens for Eisenhower Committee, and served briefly as the General's correspondence secretary.

USIA came into being on August 1, 1953. Although Johnson, in his final report to Eisenhower, had said he was "amazed at the high level of morale" considering "what the organization has gone through," in fact morale was at rock bottom. Streibert had to raise it if USIA was to perform effectively, and he had to do it while continuing to fire employees for economy reasons. That was no easy matter.

(It helped, however, when McCarthy, after Johnson's departure, turned his attention away from USIA, apparently believing he had milked it for all it was worth. His new target was the Army, which had the gall to draft Schine and put him into basic training as if he were no different from any other young man. This led to televised hearings at which McCarthy, at long last, outraged the sensibilities of millions of American viewers. Edward R. Murrow of CBS produced a devastating television documentary on McCarthy which contributed to the Senator's downfall. Eisenhower finally turned on McCarthy; the Senate voted to censure him, and he faded from prominence. McCarthy died in 1957.)

Streibert began by reorganizing the sprawling operation once again. He consolidated two largely advisory divisions into a powerful Office of Policy and Programs to define objectives, set information policy, and generally supervise the content of programs. The new office was headed by an Assistant Director (later upgraded to Deputy Director), Andrew H. Berding, a veteran foreign correspondent who had held key positions in the Marshall Plan information program and in the Defense Department.

Next, Streibert established a long-needed direct line of command over the 217 USIS posts in seventy-six countries (which he had reduced from 225 in eighty-five nations), appointing assistant directors for the American republics, Europe, the Far East, and the Near East–South Asia–Africa region. He asked them to serve as his "eyes and ears" in their areas, ordered them to spend at least half their time in the field, and gave them authority to act for him overseas. The area assistant directors, whom Streibert described as his "traveling vice presidents for sales and supervision," carried the new gospel of hope in their travels abroad, and morale began to improve.

Some of Streibert's appointments to top positions were first-rate, and this, too, helped morale. G. Huntington Damon, a professional with much overseas experience, was put in charge of the largest area, the Near East, South Asia, and Africa. Saxton Bradford, a former newspaperman who had skillfully directed the information program in Japan, became Assistant Director for the Far East. Henry Loomis, a young scientist who had been on the staff of the Psychological Strategy Board, contributed much as Streibert's special assistant. A large proportion of the new Agency's top staff were graduates of Harvard; three were graduates of Oxford.

One of the less distinguished appointments was that of J. R. Poppele to head the Voice of America. A former associate of Streibert at Mutual and WOR, Poppele was a radio engineer, not a broadcaster or foreign affairs expert, and he was greatly handicapped by these gaps in his training and experience. Wags referred to VOA during this period as "Vox Poppele."

Streibert was not always easy to work for, sometimes humiliating his executives in public. On one occasion he so tongue-lashed the head of the Public Information staff that the incident was still being talked about a decade later. Another time he interrupted his senior staff meeting to order Poppele to climb on a chair and adjust the wall clock which was two minutes off. One executive resigned—twice—when subjected to this treatment, but each time Streibert talked him out of it, for the Director also possessed great charm and per-suasiveness. He was respected by all, feared by some, and loved by very few—and that, apparently, was just the way he wanted it. Neither fear nor love could raise morale; respect could and did.

Eisenhower's Statement of Mission

On October 22 the National Security Council approved, and the President promulgated, a Statement of Mission for USIA. It drew heavily on the language and emphasis of the Jackson Committee report:

The purpose of the United States Information Agency shall be to submit evidence to peoples of other nations by means of communication techniques that the objectives and policies of the United States are in harmony with and will advance their legitimate aspirations for freedom, progress and peace.*

This was to be done, the directive continued, primarily by:

• "Explaining and interpreting to foreign peoples the objectives and policies of the United States Government."

• "Depicting imaginatively the correlation between United States policies and the legitimate aspirations of other peoples of the world."

• "Unmasking and countering hostile attempts to distort or to frustrate the objectives and policies of the United States."

• "Delineating those important aspects of the life and culture of the people of the United States which facilitate understanding of the policies and objectives" of the U.S. Government.[11]

In a letter to Eisenhower, Streibert called the directive "a great

---

* Unfortunately, the implied—and inferred—meaning of "legitimate" as used here was "wholesome little aspirations that the United States approves of."

stride forward." Under the new mission, he said, "avoiding a propagandistic tone," the Agency would "concentrate on objective, factual news reporting and appropriate commentaries. . . . The new approach . . . is *based on the idea of getting across a message that will be convincing. . . . From here on the Agency will pinpoint its activities on fewer but more vital programs*." Streibert characterized the common beliefs shared by Americans with "millions of other men and women we are attempting to win to our side" as "belief in a Deity, in individual and national freedom, in the right to ownership of property and a decent standard of living, and in the vision of a peaceful world with nations compromising their differences."[12]

Reaction to the two documents was mixed. One cynic complained that the Administration was "trying to turn all foreigners into Republican Episcopalian Americans. They'll only hate us for it." The complaint had some merit, particularly as it applied to Streibert's letter.* The Statement of Mission was somewhat vague and subject to many interpretations (and it had many in the nine years it remained in force). But at least there was an implied intention to *persuade* foreign audiences while concentrating on limited, specific themes and objectives, rather than merely to engage in the general dissemination of information about America with the hope it would win friends. Unfortunately, however, not everyone in the Agency interpreted it that way.

Whatever the merits of the Statement of Mission, it was important in lifting the morale of USIA officers in Washington and overseas. At last they had reasonably specific marching orders, and they had come from the President himself with a reaffirmation of the importance of their work. Framed copies of the statement were proudly hung on Agency office walls around the world, alongside a new "Seal of the United States Information Agency."

Redirection and Renewal

Libraries suffered the least as Streibert cut the program to fit the new austerity budget. Their numbers were reduced from 184 in sixty-

---

* The Agency was ridiculed when the new Chief of Religious Information remarked publicly that USIA hoped to win millions of "card carrying Christians" abroad. In fairness to Streibert, this was not at all what he had in mind.

five countries to 158 in sixty-three. The July 8 policy directive on books was reaffirmed.

Nonetheless, restoration of complete confidence in the library program was delayed by the appointment of Dr. Franklin Burdette, a University of Maryland professor with pronounced right-wing views, to head the Center Service which administered all USIA book operations. Burdette reportedly questioned the use of books by Thoreau, not because the sage of Walden Pond was a "Communist" but because his writings had influenced foreigners who became Communists. And Burdette prepared a "gray list" of some four hundred authors, including Ernest Hemingway and Dorothy Parker, whose books were not to be sent abroad without special justification and his personal approval. Abbott Washburn learned of the "gray list" and abolished it in time to deny its existence when the matter leaked to the press.

In other economy moves, motion picture production was curtailed, with "Americana" films dropped in favor of those with anti-Communist themes or that directly supported U.S. foreign policy. Seven languages were eliminated from the VOA schedule, reducing to thirty-four the number of languages in which programs were transmitted. (The Hebrew service, despite McCarthy, was not restored.)

The only activity to receive an increase was the Office of Private Cooperation, whose budget was doubled. Streibert believed that using American business, labor, and other nongovernmental services was "one of the most effective ways to strengthen the entire program," but the "private cooperation" effort had little impact abroad. It did sponsor some useful activities, however; for example, 300,000 copies of the highlights of an Eisenhower speech on peaceful uses of atomic energy were distributed in ten languages by 263 American business firms in their regular correspondence going overseas.

The program reductions left USIA with adequate resources to work with, but the personnel cuts went too far. Congress gave Streibert the authority to discharge without cause any nonveteran above the clerical level before January 1, 1954, Civil Service regulations notwithstanding. By the end of October, employment had dropped from 13,500 to 9,281, and many field posts were hard pressed to do their jobs.

To reassure USIA employees, Streibert persuaded Eisenhower to make an unprecedented appearance at a Washington staff meeting on November 10, at which he expressed his "deep conviction" of the importance of the information program and promised his personal support (which had not been forthcoming eight months earlier) to the men and women of the Agency. Streibert announced that a freeze on promotions had been removed and pledged that "anyone who is doing a good job in this Agency can feel perfectly secure in his job from here on." He was as good as his word; in fact, because the reductions had been too severe, USIA launched a great recruitment campaign in 1954. Ironically, among those hired were some who had been let out a few months before.

One of the more desirable by-products of becoming an independent agency was independence from Scott McLeod's State Department security operation. Not surprisingly, in view of recent history, careful attention was given to setting up the Agency's own Office of Security. Like McLeod, its chief, Charles M. Noone, was a former FBI agent; unlike McLeod, he was a cool professional without partisan political motivation. At the end of 1953 Streibert proudly reported that "there were no Communists discovered." The Security Office's philosophy, he said, "is to be fair to the rights of the individual, while at the same time taking all measures necessary to protect the safety of our country."

All this, of course, was secondary to the job itself: informing and persuading foreign audiences. Distracted for many months by the turmoil in Washington, USIA employees once again were free to concentrate on what they had been hired to do. The problems were plentiful.

Stalin had died in early March, 1953, and VOA was used to send the Russian people a personal message from Eisenhower: ". . . the prayer of us Americans continues to be that the Almighty will watch over the people of that vast country and bring them, in His wisdom, opportunity to live . . . in peace and comradeship." The new Soviet leaders immediately launched a "peace offensive" that raised questions about American policies. Eisenhower countered with a dramatic peace speech in mid-April, proposing steps toward disarmament with "a substantial percentage of the savings" to go to "a fund for world aid and reconstruction" in a "new kind of war" on world poverty. For months American propagandists publicized the speech through all media.

The June 17, 1953, workers' uprisings in East Berlin and several hundred other cities and towns in East Germany greatly embarrassed the Communists, particularly because the events in Berlin took place in full view of Western news media. USIA distributed thousands of photographs showing angry, frustrated young Germans throwing rocks at Soviet tanks. The pictures, and the story that accompanied them, made a deep impression everywhere.

On July 27 a truce ended the three-year-old war in Korea and strengthened America's posture as a peace-seeking nation. The refusal of many thousands of Chinese and North Korean prisoners of war to return home provided the Agency with another choice propaganda plum. A motion picture, broadcast interviews with prisoners, and innumerable pamphlets, press features, and photographs carried the story to all parts of the globe.

While the Geneva Conference was determining—or so it thought—the future of Indochina, USIA opened new posts in Cambodia and Laos and strengthened its operation in South Vietnam, the three countries that (with North Vietnam) comprised the former French colonial area. In what turned out to be the understatement of the decade, the Agency noted that "these areas are expected to be ideological battlegrounds with Communist infiltration and subversion literally at the paddy level." At the request of the Thai Government, three USIS centers were opened in northeast Thailand adjacent to Vietnam.

In Latin America and elsewhere, USIS posts made much of the downfall in Guatemala of the pro-Communist Arbenz regime and widely publicized the anti-Communist resolution adopted by the American republics at their Tenth Inter-American Conference at Caracas. (The behind-the-scenes role of the CIA in the Guatemalan victory was, of course, not mentioned.) At Milton Eisenhower's suggestion, USIA increased its output to Latin America on the merits of private U.S. investment in the area, though with little result.

In the Middle East and South Asia, Dulles began to promote various plans for collective security. He and Harold Stassen, the quadrennial Presidential candidate who then headed the foreign aid program, toured twelve countries in the area, seeking support for the concept, which never before had been applied to such unequals in power. Their efforts culminated in the "northern tier" alliances—the Baghdad Pact and the South East Asia Treaty Organization (SEATO)—which brought a mixed reaction in the Asian countries that joined them and a very hostile reaction from some of their neighbors, notably India and Egypt, which prized their neutrality. USIA encouraged Western alliances for those two countries as well (Dulles believed neutrality was "immoral"), but the more it argued, the less convinced were its audiences.

From his predecessor, Eisenhower inherited the sticky case of Julius and Ethel Rosenberg, who had been sentenced to death for passing atomic secrets to the Soviet Union in the final months of World War II. In February, 1953, Eisenhower announced he would not grant Presidential clemency, and the Communist press around the world raised a storm of protest, supported by pickets and an intensive letter-writing campaign. USIS posts pointed out that the Rosenbergs had received all the protection due process could offer, including appeals to the Supreme Court, and defended the President's decision. The pair was executed on June 19, but for months hostile foreigners used the Rosenberg case as a club with which to beat the United States.

In the spring of 1954 came the landmark decision of the Supreme Court outlawing segregation in public schools. Long hurting from years of Communist propaganda about racism in America, the Agency went all out in telling the story. Understandably but unfortunately, little note was taken of the follow-up order to the Court's decision by which desegregation was to be effected "with all deliberate speed," not, as some USIA output implied, immediately. As a consequence, many of the propaganda gains made in 1954 were lost three years later at Little Rock.

USIA launched what it called "a worldwide offensive to expose the spurious intellectual and ideological appeal of Communism." As part of this campaign a special collection of fifty-four books was sent to all USIS posts for use in the libraries and distribution. Among the titles were: Dallin and Nicolaevsky, *Forced Labor in Soviet Russia;* MacEoin, *The Communist War on Religion;* Haines, *The Threat of Soviet Imperialism;* and Zirkle, *Death of Science in Russia.* Whether these books influenced any beyond the already persuaded is difficult to determine; Streibert believed the effort was "one of our most effective book distributions."

The Voice of America began the vast job of moving its studios and offices from New York to Washington, and the even vaster job of restoring shattered morale. Although the Agency prudently did not punish McCarthy's spies in the Voice, neither did it reward them. Some were transferred to other divisions of USIA; others resigned. Straight news broadcasts were increased, as were interviews with defectors from Communism. VOA was pleased when one of them, an ex-colonel in the Soviet secret police, reported that "practically every Soviet officer has a radio and almost all of them listen" to the Voice.

The Agency began to do a little more with television. Weekly news and feature films were sent to twenty-four stations in nineteen countries, as were several program series acquired from outside sources, among them the National Association of Manufacturers' *Industry on Parade* and the *Voice of Firestone*.

Cecil B. De Mille, that flamboyant producer of Hollywood spectaculars, was appointed the Agency's chief consultant on motion pictures. A USIA film on Nixon's trip to the Near and Far East was distributed abroad by Paramount Pictures. Two others, *Atomic Power for Peace* and *The Korea Story*, were also widely shown.

As promised in Streibert's letter to Eisenhower, the Agency concentrated on fewer themes, the most important being the "unity of the free world" and the "peaceful use of atomic energy." USIS posts were instructed to redefine their country objectives and reduce their number. The criterion for everything USIA was now doing, Streibert said, was: "Does it help support and explain our foreign policy in terms of others' legitimate aspirations?"

In Washington and in the field, under Streibert's forceful direction, USIA's wounds began to heal. True, there were timid civil servants who, after the McCarthy ordeal, would be forever afraid to speak up. Men of ability and dedication had been lost who would be hard to replace. And Streibert's operation was not viewed with enthusiasm by Secretary of State Dulles.

But there was a new Agency, with new leadership and new hope. A fickle public turned its eyes elsewhere, and in their new and welcome anonymity American propagandists turned gratefully to the challenging tasks at hand.

3 *Talking and Listening: The Propaganda "Dialogue"*

Streibert established organizational patterns in the mid-1950s that have prevailed to this day with little change. USIA's Washington headquarters provides policy direction, money, administrative support, equipment, and supplies—the tools of the job—but the job itself is done in the field, and it is there that the effectiveness of the Agency is principally tested.

USIA employees abroad are members of the U.S. Embassy or Consulate staffs, not primarily for the protection diplomatic immunity affords but because propaganda is an integral part of modern diplomacy. Of what lasting value is an agreement negotiated between the American Embassy and the host government if public opinion in the country does not support its government's position? Even in the harshest of tyrannies, governments will not continuously go far beyond the limits set by their people—and if they do, it is at their own risk.

Modern diplomacy is no longer conducted exclusively in hushed, high-ceilinged chanceries. It also takes place in the press, in the marketplace, and in the street, in a daily, unremitting war of words. This makes the overseas propagandist as much a diplomat, and sometimes as important a diplomat, as the embassy's Political or Economic Officer.

This view is not accepted by all American diplomats, particularly the older generation which learned its profession before World War II. There are still some ambassadors who underestimate the talents of USIA's "upstarts," although these talents are often considerable.

The first-rate American propagandist usually speaks the language of those he is seeking to persuade, and has a reasonable grasp of their history, aspirations, prejudices, motivations, and thought processes. He also is knowledgeable about the United States and its people, history, culture, and policies. He understands the media of communication which are the tools of his trade, and can skillfully engage in one or more of the following: writing a news story, laying out a pamphlet, administering an exchange-of-persons program, making a speech, preparing a radio or film script, operating a public library, or designing an exhibit. He is willing to put up with monsoons, insects, and inadequate schooling for his children. He is willing to live on a government salary and away from the familiarity and security of his own country, amidst a different people of a different culture—and sometimes amidst hostility.

Each USIS field post is headed by a Public Affairs Officer (PAO).* A Country Public Affairs Officer is based in the American Embassy in the capital city and directs the work of all USIA employees in the country. The PAO is assigned and directed by the Agency in Washington, but he and his colleagues are responsible on a day-to-day basis to the American ambassador in the country. The USIS staffs range in size from 160 Americans and 500 local employees in Vietnam to one American and three locals in Burundi (and no locals in the U.S.S.R.). A typical post has five to fifteen Americans and twenty to fifty locals, the latter serving as translators, writers, librarians, projectionists, drivers, artists, secretaries, printers, and the like.

Senior members of the PAO's staff are the Information Officer, who handles relations with the news media and other functions relating to the direct dissemination of information, and the Cultural Affairs Officer, who is responsible for libraries, book translations, English-teaching, exhibits, and other activities the Agency labels "cultural," including the large exchange and artistic presentation programs directed in Washington by the State Department but administered in the field by USIS.

---

* Although the organization as a whole was renamed U.S. Information Agency (USIA) in 1953, its field posts continued to call themselves U.S. Information Service (USIS), the designation they had used since OWI days. When we speak of USIA, we mean the Agency as a whole or its Washington headquarters; when we speak of USIS, we mean an overseas office or "post" of the Agency. There are now 301 USIS field posts in 111 countries, employing 1,200 Americans and 5,300 foreigners or "local employees."

The successful PAO is equally effective as an administrator, counselor, and communicator. He must plan a program, persuade his ambassador and Washington of its validity, and then direct his staff in carrying it out. He must counsel the senior embassy staff on the propaganda implications of what they are doing. He must be able to entertain gracefully and purposefully, for persuasion is as often effected over a drink as over a desk. The average salary (in 1968) of this paragon is in the neighborhood of $23,000; most PAOs could command more in private life.

Let us take a look at a typical day in the life of a typical PAO. Beirut, Lebanon, is not the most important capital in the world, but neither is it the least important. Although a tiny country, Lebanon is the commercial and in many ways the intellectual center of the Arab Middle East.

Like most of his counterparts in other capitals, the Beirut PAO is on call around the clock. His workday begins at breakfast in his pleasant, airy apartment, which probably affords a view of the blue Mediterranean or the snowcapped Lebanon Mountains. But at this point the PAO is concentrating not on postcard horizons but on those of Beirut's plethora of morning newspapers that he is able to read himself, the several dailies in English and French. (USIS translators are reading the Arabic-language papers, and the PAO will receive summaries of their contents—particularly articles and editorials related to U.S. interests—when he reaches his office.)

Having scanned the press, the PAO carefully reads the ten-thousand-word Wireless File which the Agency's Press Service in Washington has radio-teletyped to all USIS posts in the Middle East and South Asia during the night. (Similar files geared to the interests of other areas have been sent to Western Europe, Africa, Latin America, and East Asia.) The Wireless File contains texts of major policy pronouncements plus news, features, and editorials supporting U.S. objectives. The most useful of the material will be adapted for local use by USIS's Press Officer and staff, translated into Arabic, French, and Armenian, and distributed to local newspapers and government officials. The PAO and his embassy colleagues rely on it as an immediate source of policy guidance, to be supplemented later by secret cables from the State Department and USIA.

When the PAO arrives at his office in Beirut's seven-story embassy building, his American secretary (who handles all classified correspondence and files) will have the incoming cables ready for him. He must prepare quickly for the Ambassador's daily meeting of the Country Team, only an hour away.

The meeting's participants—the Deputy Chief of Mission, the Political and Economic Counselors, the PAO, the head of the AID (Agency for International Development) mission, the CIA (Central Intelligence Agency) Chief of Station, and the military attachés— rise as the Ambassador enters. The Ambassador reports on his previous day's activities, including a long negotiating session with the Foreign Minister and a revealing conversation with the Prime Minister at dinner. Then each of the others reports. All take careful notes, not only to guide them but so they may brief their own staffs.

The PAO summarizes what was in the morning newspapers, and briefly reviews the Wireless File (which the Ambassador has already read, and on which he has some suggestions for use). The PAO says he has received from the Agency a kinescope of a recent *Meet the Press* television program in which the Secretary of State explains the U.S. position on Vietnam. An effort will be made to place the program on a local TV station; the Ambassador says he wants to have a screening for himself and his senior staff.

Also reported to the meeting is the receipt of a new USIA color documentary film on the President. The PAO says he will have a special dinner showing for editors and other opinion leaders before attempting placement in local theaters. "If it's any good, I'd like to show it to the President of Lebanon when next he comes to dinner," says the Ambassador. "And by the way," he adds, "have you received that new book by Stalin's daughter? In addition to using it in the library, we ought to distribute a few copies to the right people." The PAO agrees, and tells of plans to have it translated into Arabic.

The PAO tells of the arrival of a distinguished American sociologist who will lecture at the American University of Beirut and the Lebanese National University under the auspices of the USIS- administered State Department exchange-of-persons program. He describes progress in planning an exhibit on American space science which will be jointly sponsored by USIS and Lebanon's Ministry of Culture. He reports a conversation he had with the editor of *An Nahar,* a leading Arabic-language newspaper.

The Ambassador closes the meeting with a report on the current status of various U.S. policies and programs and instructions for the day. He asks the PAO to stay for a moment and when they are alone inquires about the new Cultural Officer. "I want him to spend more time with those people at the French University [St. Joseph's]," he exclaims. "Some of them are unconsciously spreading De Gaulle's poison about the U.S. Let's see if we can't broaden their horizons a bit."

Back in his office, the PAO holds quick conferences with his Information and Cultural Officers on the day's activities and then tackles his paperwork. Queries from the Agency must be answered, performance evaluations on his staff are due, and the budget needs to be reviewed. The telephone intrudes: the Ambassador's secretary wants a list of editors to be invited to the next embassy reception; the Press Officer reports on an unpleasant conversation with a left-wing editor; the Ministry of Information calls to confirm the PAO's luncheon date with the Minister; and the PAO's wife calls to ask him not to forget to pick up supplies at the commissary for Friday's reception honoring visiting Congressmen. His secretary rushes in with a cable: USIA's Deputy Director will arrive for a three-day visit two weeks hence ("Oh, God, another visitor from Washington just when we're busiest").

Despite the interruptions, there is still time for a few quick conferences before lunch. The Motion Picture Officer is summoned to report on the status of a film being produced locally on an AID project. The Information Officer brings in the draft of a new pamphlet tracing the history of American friendship with the Arabs. The Cultural Officer advises that the demand for English classes has grown to the point where a half-dozen embassy wives or other native-born Americans will have to be recruited to supplement the three professional USIA teachers.

Then the PAO goes down the elevator and out to his plain, government-issued Chevrolet for a nerve-racking chauffeur-driven ride to the Hotel St. Georges for lunch. Luckily, for the Minister of Information is a stickler for protocol, the PAO arrives a minute or two before His Excellency. Actually, the Lebanese official is an amiable man of considerable intelligence, although he is a lawyer-politician, not a journalist, and knows little about communications. No business as such is discussed; the PAO's purpose is to strengthen his personal relationship with the Minister, and the purpose is achieved with a little help from two martinis.

After a leisurely lunch, the Minister goes home for his daily siesta, but the PAO returns to his office, wishing he had skipped that second martini. He relaxes by reading the Paris edition of the New York *Times-Herald-Post*. At home, he finds, attention is focused on a tight National League pennant race. America seems very far away.

The abbreviated afternoon passes quickly. The space exhibit is checked and found wanting; the PAO orders revisions. A young junior officer trainee, in Beirut on his first assignment, comes in hesitantly for a chat. His wife does not like living abroad and his job seems aimless. Should he quit and go home? The young man has talent, and the PAO pushes his papers aside for a long, fatherly chat about current work and future prospects. After the trainee departs, greatly cheered, the PAO telephones his wife and asks her to see what she can do to help the young man's wife.

The Information Officer dashes in with an urgent problem. There has been another race riot in a major U.S. Midwestern city; several are dead, many more injured, property damage is widespread, and the National Guard has been summoned. What can be done to ease the impact of the inevitable nasty headlines and editorials in tomorrow's newspapers? They review their resources.

"Get Joe [the Assistant Cultural Officer and a Negro] on tonight's TV panel show," suggests the PAO. "He can help put the matter in perspective, and as a Negro he's believable. Let's get that long feature story on Negro progress out to the press tonight. And why don't you and Sam [the Press Officer] divide the principal newspapers among you and go talk to the editors. You ought to be able to have some influence on their handling of the story." Tomorrow, he decides, a staff meeting will explore other, longer-term measures to meet the problem.

The PAO is weary as he is driven home, but a spectacular sunset over the Mediterranean reminds him it isn't such a bad spot after all. The day is not over, however. A quick shower, a quicker shave, a fresh shirt, and he is ready for the evening's labors. This night he and his wife are invited to three cocktail parties and a dinner— social events, but also business, for it is at these affairs that the

PAO has an opportunity to make contacts with and explain American policy to some of Lebanon's top citizens.

The cocktail parties are being given by a Lebanese journalist, a French diplomat, and an American Embassy colleague. His best friends will be at the last party, but there is time to look in at only two of the affairs, and his job dictates that he attend the first two. Afterward, he is not sorry, for both parties prove to be rewarding.

Dinner at the home of a wealthy Lebanese merchant is less satisfactory. Often dinners provide occasions for sustained conversation with prominent Lebanese, but this time he is stuck with the wife of the Minister of Interior, who seemingly can discuss only children, the servant problem, and the weather. But the PAO smiles his way through, rewarding himself with a cigar at evening's end.

Falling into bed at midnight, he knows he should waste no time going to sleep; six-thirty will come all too soon. But he tosses and turns a bit, reviewing the day's events and planning the morrow's. Before long, sleep does come, and when in the dark hours just before dawn the *muzzein* calls out his amplified morning prayers from the top of a nearby minaret, the PAO stirs but does not awaken.

Blueprint: The Country Plan

At first glance, the PAO's day may appear to be disorganized, without specific plan or purpose. But this is not true, at least not any more. When Streibert decentralized USIA operations and gave PAOs broad leeway in deciding what to do and how to do it, some USIS posts—responding to local pressures or following the whims of local officers—drifted into unpurposeful, nontargeted activities.

To deal with this problem, Agency headquarters in the late 1950s strengthened its control over USIS Country Plans, the blueprints that guide each country program. Later, the precepts for the Country Plan were revised to require post activities to be mission-oriented—that is, directly related to specific, official U.S. country objectives. This rational approach to program planning was further refined and strengthened in the mid-1960s when President Johnson instructed USIA and other Federal agencies to introduce PPBS—Planning, Programming, Budgeting System—which Secretary of Defense Robert McNamara and Assistant Secretary Charles J. Hitch had developed and applied so effectively in their sprawling department.

Although some propagandists grumbled that PPBS required quantitative measurements of an activity whose quality and effectiveness could not be measured by numbers or dollars and cents, the system forced PAOs to set priorities and find the least costly ways of working toward established objectives. And it permitted the Agency to organize and budget its Washington activities in such a way as to provide maximum support for overseas operations at minimum cost.

The PAO writes his Country Plan Program Memorandum (plans his country program) in this fashion: First he examines the situation in "his" country and USIS's capability for contributing to the achievement of each official U.S. objective there. Next he formulates the USIS or Psychological Objectives, defining what people in the country need to be persuaded of if the U.S. is to attain its country objectives. Then the PAO identifies his Target Audiences, those who must be reached and persuaded if the Psychological Objectives are to be achieved.

Who makes up these audiences? For years, USIA officials have debated the matter. A few have argued that USIA cannot succeed unless it reaches a "mass" audience, not just "opinion leaders." Most believe that, given its limited resources of men and money, the Agency is likely to accomplish more if it concentrates its attentions on the relatively few leaders of opinion who influence others.

In most countries the Target Audiences include persons in the political and economic power structure—not only policy-makers, but also those who influence the policy-makers and those who are not now in power but are likely to be. In many underdeveloped countries elements of the military with a potential to stage *coups d'état* are included. Usually the owners, editors, and writers of the mass media are among the Target Audiences, as are college and high school professors and teachers, and the leaders of major political movements and parties. In many places the Target Audiences include the leaders of trade unions and confederations, in some the spokesmen for rural and village thinking, in most of the new nations student leaders. In some countries the leaders of women's groups are a Target Audience; in others, the leaders of ethnic or cultural minorities. And in nearly all countries USIA is attempting to influence those who have the desire and the capability to block their governments' collaboration with the United States through demagoguery or violence.

Having selected his audiences, the PAO—with the advice and consent of his ambassador—devises informational and cultural projects and activities that will further the attainment of each Psychological Objective. The mere act of communication is not, of course, enough. Any message can be garbled—by the sender, by the transmitter, or by the receiver—and a garbled message will confuse or irritate the intended audience, if it pays any attention to it at all. Moreover, we are familiar in this advertising-oriented country with the difference between being reached and being persuaded. From all sides Americans are urged to believe this and cajoled to buy that, but most of us have developed some immunity to advertising and other special pleading. We are reached, all right, but not always influenced.

The problems of the Public Affairs Officer and his staff are different from those of the soap merchandiser. Foreigners, too, have developed defense mechanisms against propaganda. Moreover, the American advertiser is appealing to an audience which shares a common language, common traditions, common prejudices, and mostly common aspirations, whereas the American propagandist is speaking to peoples of many tongues, different traditions, contradictory prejudices, and varying aspirations. He is talking to peoples whose very assumptions, definitions, and mental processes are often far different from his own. Another difference, to the propagandist's advantage, is that while most advertising is clearly attributed, not all propaganda is.

It is important to distinguish between *attributed* activities and what is unlabeled but *attributable*. Not all Agency materials carry the USIA label—that is, are attributed to USIA, when they reach their audience—and it is not desirable that they should. Such a label is bound to be a notice to the reader to "watch out, this is something the Americans want me to believe." Sometimes such notice is desirable; for example, in the dissemination of official U.S. policy statements. But more often it is not. In nearly all circumstances, however, USIS press stories and other media products are attributable even when not attributed; that is, USIS is always prepared to acknowledge its authorship if necessary. (One important exception is a weekly newsreel produced for USIA under Agency direction by Associated

Films, a combine of U.S. newsreel makers formed exclusively for the purpose of turning out the USIA newsreel for audiences in Africa and Asia. The Agency labels the project "Kingfish" and treats it in a very hush-hush manner.)

Unattributable material, on the other hand, is that which is prepared and disseminated in such a way as to obscure or mislead the audience as to its origins. USIA does not engage in this kind of propaganda, leaving it to the Central Intelligence Agency, which specializes in covert operations. In 1967 controversy flared when the press revealed some of the theretofore unattributable propaganda operations of CIA involving the National Students Association, the AFL-CIO, various foundations, and such ostensibly private groups as the Asia Foundation and the American Friends of the Middle East.

The disclosures of covert CIA propaganda activities raised the question in many minds, American and foreign, as to the connection if any between USIA and CIA. Although the two agencies often consult, USIA operates at arm's length from CIA. Periodic Communist accusations notwithstanding, there are no CIA agents operating under USIA "cover."

USIS posts operate wholly in the open, disseminating "white" attributed propaganda and "gray" unattributed but attributable propaganda, but seldom "black" or unattributable propaganda. Foreign governments do not necessarily approve of everything USIS tells their people, but they must be willing to tolerate it or out USIS goes.

Governmental tolerance is not, of course, enough. If USIA media materials are to be used, they must be welcomed by the local media on their merits. The Agency has a long-standing rule against buying space in news columns or on the radio, or paying journalists to do its bidding (though it may sometimes pay their travel expenses without attaching conditions*). There is an axiom among U.S. propagandists that journalists cannot be bought, only rented. In any case,

---

* Even this was too much for Senator J. William Fulbright, chairman of the Foreign Relations Committee. When he learned in the summer of 1966 that USIA had paid the air fare to South Vietnam of thirty Canadian, European, and Asian journalists, he asked USIA Director Leonard Marks, "Doesn't this point to a possible conflict of interest that might compromise the objectivity newspapers owe their readers?" Marks explained that the Agency openly paid the bills because the reporters' papers could not otherwise have afforded to send them, and that in any case the foreign newsmen were not obliged to write anything other than what they saw and believed. Fulbright was not convinced.

influential newsmen rarely will rent or sell their integrity for any price.

To reach its Target Audiences, a USIS post must produce superior products that the local media find useful, or it must depend on its own publications and facilities, which are more limited and less credible than indigenous media. Just as a story on the Berlin Wall in the *New York Times* will carry more weight with an American reader than would the same item if he read it in a handout from the German Embassy in Washington, so an unattributed USIS story in the London *Times* defending the U.S. position in Vietnam will be more persuasive to British readers than if they see it in a bulletin issued by USIS-London.

Once the Country Plan has been approved by his ambassador and by the Agency in Washington, the PAO and his staff go to work. They put a premium on personal contact, spending as much time as possible talking to editors, columnists, educators, labor and student leaders, government officials, and other members of their Target Audiences who influence the opinions of many more.

Libraries and Book Programs

The libraries, 223 of them in eighty-four countries, are USIA's best-known foreign operation. They are the center of each post's cultural activities, offering lectures, musicales, and exhibits as well as the customary books and periodicals. By U.S. standards, most of the collections are not very large (ranging from five hundred in a reading room in Bolivia to thirty thousand volumes in West Berlin), but the USIS Cultural Center—as it is frequently named—is often the only free public library in the city.

In an average year, USIA's Information Center Service, which backstops the libraries, examines some eight thousand books. About fifteeen hundred are finally recommended for the libraries, translation, and presentation to important foreigners. PAOs and librarians may order books not on the recommended list if they have a need for them.

USIS library shelves carry books in English, in the local language of the country, and in such other languages as might be useful. They run the gamut from escape fiction to standard reference works and highly technical textbooks, and include at least a smattering (and often more) of biography, the social and physical sciences, and the arts. Books are selected primarily for their significance and interest. Books promoting Communism are absent, but there are works critical of U.S. policies and personalities.

There are biographies of Lyndon Johnson and Dwight Eisenhower, of Robert E. Lee and Martin Luther King. Although "controversial" authors were banned for a time during the McCarthy era, the Agency's standards today are liberal. Occasionally, however, Agency officials become censors. The publishers of *Lyndon Johnson: The Exercise of Power,* a thoughtful but often critical study of the President by the syndicated columnists Rowland Evans and Robert Novak, were annoyed when USIA declined to buy the book for its libraries. '

Wherever possible, the Agency resists foreign censorship of its books. They are sent to USIS libraries through the diplomatic pouch in order to avoid examination by politically minded foreign customs officials. Nonetheless, USIA will not deliberately insult its host governments. USIS libraries in Yugoslavia do not carry books critical of Marshal Tito; even in democratic England there are no volumes on the shelves attacking the Queen.

(In 1967 Senator Hugh Scott of Pennsylvania revealed that the Syrian Government was imposing censorship over periodicals in the USIS-Damascus library. The Agency admitted that it submitted some magazine articles to Syrian censors for review and kept off its shelves books which it believed would be objectionable to Syrian authorities, i.e., those sympathetic to Zionism or Judaism. Scott was outraged, calling the Agency's acquiescence "an affront to our friends and allies in neighboring countries," meaning Israel. USIA replied: "While this is not an ideal situation, we strongly feel that the return from this operation is worth the resources invested. The Information Center, which includes an auditorium, is open every day of the week and is normally used to near capacity for English teaching classes, film showings, discussion groups and exhibits." In other words, by remaining in Damascus USIS offers the Syrian people hope and horizons they otherwise would be deprived of.)

The periodicals found in USIS libraries are mostly the ones available in small libraries in the United States, covering the political spectrum from left (*Nation* and *New Republic*) to right (*Reader's*

Digest and *National Review*) and including a number of scholarly and specialized journals—though not *Playboy*. Within hours after they are put out, the most popular magazines (*Life, Look, Time,* and *Newsweek*) are smudged and tattered from use. Some magazines and books are stolen, but most USIS posts benignly accept this as welcome evidence of interest.

The Agency has also become accustomed to occasional—and well-publicized—attacks on its libraries; there have been about one hundred such incidents since 1947. Communist and other anti-American elements strike at the libraries because they are the most visible evidence of the U.S. presence, often located on busy downtown street corners. "They wouldn't attack the libraries if they weren't doing some good," USIA reasons, and rallies local citizens to repair damages and restore books, thus turning apparent defeats into propaganda victories.

In addition to the library, USIA has several other book programs, managed at some posts by the Cultural Affairs Officer and at larger installations by a full-time Publications Officer. A translation program encourages the publication in foreign languages of American books, mostly nonfiction, pertinent to USIA objectives. A few important technical works are translated, and in several countries—notably India and Egypt—USIA cooperates with government bodies or private publishers in the translation and publication of great numbers of American textbooks. The Agency obtains translation rights to a book published in the United States, then offers the rights to (and sometimes pays the cost of translation to) foreign publishers. Usually, USIS buys a guaranteed number of copies—ranging from a few hundred to several thousand—for libraries and presentation, so that the publisher may minimize his business risk. For his part, the latter produces an agreed-upon number of copies and sells them at a price which is often below the going rate. With few exceptions, the books are paperbacks.

In its "low-priced book program," the Agency contracts with American paperback publishers to add to their press runs on certain titles and sell the books through commercial channels abroad at a price lower than that charged in the United States. Up to eight million copies of English-language American books are sold annually through this program, mostly in Latin America and the Near and Far East.

Other USIA-supported book operations include a limited-vocabulary "Ladder Series" for those whose English is weak, an international nonprofit publishing house which sells several hundred thousand American books annually in foreign languages, and various book-donation programs that produce more than a million books annually from U.S. publishers, libraries, private citizens, and the dead-letter office of the Post Office.

A few of these books carry a USIS attribution, but most do not. Criticism arose in this country when it was disclosed that some USIA-sponsored books were appearing on the American market without any attribution to the Agency. The problem stemmed from USIA's so-called "book development" program.

The Agency started the program in 1955 because it felt that certain needed books either did not exist or were not available for translation and reprinting abroad. So the Agency began occasionally to commission authors to produce books on specific subjects. When U.S. publishers felt the manuscripts were salable, USIA would revert to its customary role of buying copies of the American edition and negotiating for foreign rights. When publishers felt a book did not meet commercial standards, USIA would subsidize them by agreeing in advance to buy sufficient copies to eliminate the publisher's risk.

The program cost $100,000 annually, and Congress regularly approved money for it, usually without comment. Then, in 1966, it occurred to some members of USIA's Appropriations Subcommittees that the books were being sold by American publishers to American readers without the latter knowing that they were government-subsidized. Among those on the list that year were *The Truth About the Dominican Republic* and *President Kennedy and Africa.*

"Why is it wrong," asked California Congressman Glenard Lipscomb, "to let the American people know when they buy and read the book that it was developed under government sponsorship?" The trouble, replied USIA Director Leonard Marks, is that foreign readers would then also know, and this would "minimize" the book's value to USIA. Lipscomb asked the U.S. Comptroller General to rule on the legality of the program; he replied that it was not "improper." However, the Agency announced shortly thereafter that it was "relaxing its editorial supervision with regard to books it will subsidize in the future."

In March of 1967, however, the controversy broke out anew when

Senator Fulbright attacked USIA's book development program as "doubly subversive of our system." Fulbright, a critic of Johnson Administration policies in Vietnam, was especially angered by the sale in the United States of subsidized books supporting those policies, among them *Terror in Vietnam* by Jay Mallin and *Why Vietnam?* by Frank Trager.* Marks responded by disclosing that he had ordered the practice of secret subsidies stopped. "I do not intend to carry out any further book development program," he said.

In fact, the Agency did not abolish its book development program, authorizing books to be commissioned "under exceptional circumstances," but it did require subsidized authors to assign all rights to USIA to assure there would be no domestic distribution, meeting the key objection raised by Lipscomb and Fulbright. Why USIA insisted on retaining the program is not clear. It was useful in getting friendly foreign authors into print who otherwise could not find publishers. But many of the manuscripts obtained from American authors were dull and unpersuasive, and often so long in preparation that they were published too late to meet the Agency's needs. It is hard to believe that, out of the thousands of books published in the United States every year, USIA cannot find enough for its purposes.

USIA is forbidden to propagandize the American people, and for good reason. Most Americans probably would agree that it is desirable for our government to propagandize abroad, but not for the Administration in power to do so in this country at the taxpayers' expense. Domestic distribution under the Agency's book development program was unthinkingly and unintentionally doing just that with titles on Vietnam and the like; it was right to stop it. Probably the only reason it was not stopped earlier was that previous directors of USIA had paid little or no attention to this small part of their book operations.

Is "Culture" Propaganda?

Nearly everyone agrees that educational and cultural exchanges are worthwhile. There is a widespread belief that "mutual understanding"

* There was some irony in all this. The principal defender of the subsidized anti-Communist program was the then head of the Agency's Information Center Service, Reed Harris, who fifteen years earlier had been driven from government service by Senator McCarthy on the grounds that Harris, in his youth, had written a "pro-Communist" book.

is a good thing: if only other people could get to know us better, they would like us better. Although this is not always the case in personal relations, as witnessed by the volume of business in the divorce courts, it is generally believed to be a truism in international relations. It doesn't always turn out to be so.

A USIA-sponsored poll of African students in the United States revealed that their views of this country had become less rather than more favorable as a result of their experiences here. It was graduates of London and Paris universities who led the struggles for independence from Britain and France in two score African and Asian nations.

Nonetheless, few question the desirability of cultural and educational activities abroad, but many question whether they should be a part of, or have the same objectives as, the information program. Some believe that government-sponsored cultural activities, while different in method, are identical in purpose to information activities: the influencing of foreign attitudes to further U.S. policy goals. Others believe that cultural activities serve long-range U.S. interests in a broad sense, but should not be employed for tactical propaganda advantage, that they should be separated from propaganda operations so as not to be tarnished by them.

Part of the confusion is over the proper missions of USIA and the State Department. The Agency's current mandate is a 1963 Presidential directive to help "achieve United States foreign policy objectives by influencing public attitudes" abroad and to emphasize, in its cultural programs, "those aspects of American life and culture which facilitate sympathetic understanding of American policies"—in other words, to work toward political goals. The State Department's cultural activities, however, are guided by the Fulbright-Hays Act of 1961, whose preamble defines its purposes in apolitical terms: "to increase mutual understanding between the people of the United States and the people of other countries . . . by demonstrating the educational and cultural interests . . . of the people of the United States and other nations."

These directives are not necessarily contradictory, but they are often interpreted that way by partisans of one view or the other in State and USIA.

Since USIA was created in 1953 it has been responsible for a portion of the government's foreign cultural activities: libraries, art and other exhibits, English teaching, and book translation and publishing. The State Department has been responsible for exchanges of people, including students, professors, "leaders," performing artists, and athletes. The two operations are intertwined under a curious bureaucratic arrangement whereby the State Department cultural programs are administered abroad by the same USIA employees who administer the Information Agency's cultural programs.

This arrangement works, but not without friction. In general the people in the State Department's Bureau of Educational and Cultural Affairs are more likely to feel that specific policy purposes degrade cultural activities. USIA officials—particularly those with a media or public relations background—tend to believe that the more purposeful a cultural activity is, the more worthwhile it is likely to be; therefore informational and cultural activities should be planned and used together to further specific U.S. objectives.

Philip H. Coombs, the first head of State's cultural program to have the title of Assistant Secretary of State, believed his mission was to dispense "policy guidance and even-handed justice to all agencies in this field, including USIA," though there was never any Presidential sanction for his authority over USIA. Coombs believed "informational and cultural activities are in practice very different things—or at least should be." The "cultural approach," he argued, "is not concerned . . . with explaining and justifying specific U.S. policies and actions."[1]

Coombs, a Kennedy appointee, was replaced in 1962, not because of a difference in philosophy (to which the President probably had not given much thought) but because Kennedy believed Coombs had failed to develop effective programs, especially for the Alliance for Progress in Latin America. Coombs's successor was an energetic Foreign Service Officer, Lucius D. Battle, who took a practical approach to his job. Battle sought to avoid the propaganda label or tone for State Department cultural activities, but he appreciated the importance of their being purposeful.

When Battle became Ambassador to Egypt in 1964, he was succeeded by Harry McPherson, a talented protégé of President Johnson who combined an appreciation of the arts with the pragmatism of a Texas lawyer. Even more than Battle, he sought to relate the cultural programs to the national interest. But Johnson soon summoned McPherson to the White House staff, and he was succeeded by a

Columbia University professor of philosophy, Charles Frankel.

After less than two years, Frankel resigned at the end of 1967 in something of a huff. In part he blamed the government's neglect of his programs because of its preoccupation with Vietnam; in part he blamed the refusal of Congress to fund the International Education Act of 1966, which had been passed largely because of his efforts. But he also felt that his superiors had ignored his view that foreign educational and cultural programs "should not be viewed primarily as a means for the achievement of passing objectives. . . . Their main purpose, properly, is to release and stimulate the energies of the non-Federal and private sectors of our country."[2] He complained to newsmen that "the government's international education actions are too precisely targeted."

To many in USIA, it seemed that the contrary was true. (What, for example, was the State Department's "target" in sending vaudeville comedian Joey Adams abroad?) They quarreled not with Frankel's concept but with its execution, believing that when cultural activities are designed for overseas audiences with no other criterion than culture for culture's sake (or entertainment for entertainment's sake), the results are bound to be pure chance. But, they reasoned, when cultural activities are planned with broad U.S. policy objectives in mind, and carried out with skill and subtlety, the taxpayers' money is well spent. Such activities, they argued, are more purposeful without being less cultural.

When an American Nobel laureate in physics addresses an assembly of Latin-American physicists, his speech may be pure science. But his appearance also tells something about education in the United States and about American cultural values, and that is good propaganda. It is also good propaganda for the U.S. Government to subsidize the education of African and Asian political scientists and economists, for if the new nations are to have constructive relations with America and their neighbors they need men and women who can build viable political systems and economies.

Applying policy considerations to foreign educational and cultural programs does not mean, as one observer put it, that U.S. officials should be "chauvinistic vigilantes lurking behind the syllabus." It does not mean that the government should impose or even suggest limits on academic, artistic, or literary expression. Nor does it mean that the

State Department should shy away from sending abroad, let us say, a troupe to perform plays by Tennessee Williams simply because the plays reflect a less savory side of American life.

But it does mean that the government should apply some rational criteria in administering these programs. It made little sense in 1966-67 for the State Department to send abroad lecturers who denounced U.S. policy in Vietnam at a time when the department and USIA were urgently seeking to build foreign support for the policy. If Kenya has a surplus of lawyers and a shortage of engineers, the U.S. Government should not subsidize the education of still more Kenyan lawyers. If Tennessee Williams' plays or Martha Graham's modern dance troupe are understood and appreciated as art in one country but not in another, they should go to the first but not to the second.

Those who favor the "culture for culture's sake" approach sharply criticize USIA for its handling of both Agency and State Department cultural programs. Many of them want to transfer the Agency's cultural activities, and its Cultural Affairs Officers, into the State Department. After Coombs left the government, he recommended creation of a semiautonomous agency within the State Department "which would amalgamate the principal educational and cultural activities now in the hands of [State], USIA and AID. . . . USIA would continue to function, but now as a specialized information agency unencumbered by educational and cultural activities."[3] In recent years the proposal has won much high-level support in the government, Frankel's resignation notwithstanding.

Many in USIA, on the other hand, weary of devoting time and resources to what they consider marginal cultural activities, believe the State Department's cultural and educational programs should be transferred to the Information Agency, where they could be given a greater sense of purpose.

Dr. Cleanth Brooks, professor of rhetoric at Yale, wrote after two years with USIS in London that "the problem of the Cultural Attaché is constantly to fill in the picture, to round it out, to point to the 'other' side, and most of all not so much to argue a case as to present the American world as it is in something like its proper proportion."

Brooks cited a lecture by anthropologist Margaret Mead at the University of London. "What she accomplished through her talk and through her handling of questions—some of them vaguely hostile—

was impressive. Without in the least trying to, she conveyed to a rather suspicious audience of young intellectuals volumes about American common sense, moderation and maturity." Mentioning another example, Brooks said a "story by Katherine Anne Porter or by William Faulkner . . . can put into perspective all sorts of troubled relations of American life."[4]

As long as there are intelligent and effective Cultural Affairs Officers such as Professor Brooks representing the United States abroad, it probably matters little whether they receive their paychecks from USIA or the State Department. What does matter is the character of the cultural program. It must be purposeful without being propagandistic, artistic without being arty. This has been, and will be, no easy task.

Making Propaganda a Dialogue

In Streibert's time and since, USIA has measured the impact of its cultural and informational activities in a variety of ways, none of them entirely satisfactory. The way foreign governments behave is one clue; the way foreign peoples vote is another. In free countries the press reflects public opinion in varying degrees. Where it is permitted, public opinion polling provides useful insights.

When the Agency is able to determine how well it is doing, the information is for internal use only. While USIS posts operate in the open, they are reluctant to be explicit about their victories. This is understandable; detailed public trumpeting of successes would have the same results as a young man boasting to his pals, within hearing of his girl friend, that he had just seduced her. USIA cannot proclaim publicly that it won over this Indonesian labor union or that Argentine editor, even if it could prove it. The minute the Agency did so, both the credibility and the usefulness to USIA of the union and the editor would be destroyed, and so would USIA's position with them.

Thus when the Agency goes to Congress each year for money, it cannot in open hearings claim many specific accomplishments. It can only describe its products and policies, claim prudent use of manpower and such items as air conditioners and newsprint, and generalize about its successes. USIA's budget hearings go into dreary detail about things, but they rarely touch on people and almost never on ideas and strategy. Consequently, members of the Appropriations Subcommittees that consider USIA's budget requests often master an impressive amount of detail about the Agency's operations, yet sometimes are unable to see the forest for the trees.

This leads to frequent misunderstandings or simply an absence of understanding. Worse yet, it tends to keep some Agency executives overly preoccupied with mechanics. They talk, but they do not listen enough. Yet the first requisite of a good propagandist is the ability to listen to what his audiences are saying so he may understand them better. It is true that while traditional diplomacy is a dialogue, propaganda is a monologue. But the most effective propagandists construct a simulated response through opinion research—and by just listening.

The ablest USIA officers devote much time to considering what other people think and the consequences of that thought. There are three good reasons for doing so, the third and least of which is to measure effectiveness. First, USIA must be able to advise the President, the State Department, and the nation's diplomats on how people are reacting or are likely to react to U.S. policies and programs. Second, USIA needs to know about foreign criticisms and misconceptions of America so it may organize its program to counter them.

USIA goes about this task in a variety of ways. USIS posts report periodically on opinion in their countries as measured by press comment and the pronouncements of opinion leaders. Often the Agency queries its posts for reaction to specific events, and sometimes this practice is carried to extremes. Asked for press reaction to a major international development, one African post responded: "No press reaction. No press." Asked during a crisis what people in Jidda, Saudi Arabia, thought of the Berlin situation, the Public Affairs Officer cabled back: "Reaction in Jidda to situation in Berlin same as reaction in Berlin to situation in Jidda."

On the whole, however, the reports from the field—including regular analyses by PAOs of opinion trends—are pertinent and helpful. So are painstaking studies of foreign trends by Washington-based researchers. So are public opinion polls, commissioned by the Agency's Office of Policy and Research to determine attitudes on issues affecting U.S. interests.

USIA's polls have been controversial since their beginnings in the early 1950s. For nearly a decade the Agency classified their results and did not make them public. After they became an issue in the 1960

Presidential campaign, USIA redefined the purposes of its polling and agreed to make most results public after a certain lapse of time: two years for highly sensitive polls, one year for the others.

A confidential policy statement spelled out the Agency's new approach:

We use the public opinion poll abroad, in concert with other methods, to measure (1) understanding of and support for important U.S. policies and actions, (2) the standing in the public mind of the U.S. compared to the U.S.S.R. and other nations with respect to relative military power, scientific progress, economic growth and the like, (3) attitudes on questions and personalities not directly related to the U.S. but of significance to this country in the conduct of its foreign affairs, (4) the aspirations, fears and prejudices of USIA target audiences, and (5) the importance and credibility of the various communications media in different countries for different audiences.

At first, officials responsible for USIA polls were reluctant to release them, citing three areas of potential trouble: where the results would embarrass the host country, e.g., by revealing the unpopularity of local political leaders or their policies; where the release of a poll would identify and embarrass the polling organization employed by USIA, thus making it difficult for the Agency to use it for future polls; and where the results in one country would be embarrassing to another (e.g., India and Pakistan) because of the nature of the questions asked.* As it turned out, however, once the polls were no longer secret the press and public showed little interest in them, no doubt because their two-year-old findings were often obsolete.

Nonetheless, with foreign criticism of U.S. policy in Vietnam mounting, USIA Director Marks in 1966 discontinued much of the Agency's polling on policy issues, notably the multicountry surveys. He explained that he did so because they were not of sufficient value to warrant continuing. The head of his Research Division described the change as "greater concentration upon evaluation studies of Agency programs." Skeptics, however, pointed out that the results of 1966 polls would have been made public in 1968, when Johnson

* In 1965 USIA was forced to cancel a poll in Pakistan because the Pakistani Government, at the time seeking improved relations with Communist China, objected to some of the questions as constituting interference in Pakistan's internal affairs. The objectionable questions asked what foreign country was considered most friendly to Pakistan and what was thought of such men as Chou En-lai, Nasser, and Sukarno.

presumably would be seeking re-election with his Vietnam policy as a major issue.

There were those who agreed with Marks's downgrading of polls. At the annual Anglo-American talks on propaganda strategy in 1966, British officials pooh-poohed a USIA-sponsored survey showing that Britons believed the Soviet Union was ahead in the space race. "The ordinary Briton is mostly interested in beer, gambling and women," said one. "What the hell does he know about the space race?" Another commented: "We dislike these polls, and we don't trust them."[5]*

Many U.S. career diplomats feel the same way. One, while serving in a country ridden with crisis because of public turbulence, remarked: "To hell with public opinion and public opinion polls. I am here to deal with the government, not with the public." Another condescendingly admitted that "we Foreign Service Officers are not sensitized to these psychological matters." An expert in the field has sadly reported that Foreign Service Officers often display "superiority, if not contempt, when confronted with the findings of intensive public opinion pollsters."[7]

"What's Bugging People?"

If anything, too little USIA polling is done abroad, not too much—especially since Marks reduced the operation in 1966. Even before the cutback, the Agency's "World Survey" covered only twenty-one of the world's 127 countries, and in ten of those the interviewing was confined to a single city and in five others to two to four cities. Although USIA needs to know more about its audiences, particularly in crisis areas, it has never spent more than a fraction of one percent of its budget on opinion research. Fortunately, there is considerable private American polling conducted abroad, and the results are often available to the Agency.

USIA-sponsored surveys employ the same techniques as those used by American pollsters. A cross-section "sample" of the general population (or a particular group) is carefully selected for interviews, with due regard to geographic location, economic status, level of educa-

---

* Nonetheless, Britain itself has done some foreign polling. In the late 1950s the American Ambassador gingerly approached British Foreign Secretary Selwyn Lloyd for permission to do a USIA poll in the United Kingdom. Lloyd laughed and said, in effect: "Go right ahead. We've carried out several polls in the United States and never bothered to tell you."[6]

tion, occupation, and ethnic background. The belief is that a small segment of an entire population or group, if representative of the larger body, will faithfully reflect the views of the whole. The interviewers are citizens of the country, and they do not disclose (and often do not know) that the polls were commissioned by USIA, thus avoiding any bias, pro or con, because of the sponsorship.

For many years, a major weakness of Agency polling was the bureaucratic gap between those responsible for propaganda operations and those doing the polling. The former took too little interest in and made too little use of the polls, in part because they were not under their control. The latter knew too little about, or were inadequately interested in, the needs of the operators. Consequently, the pollsters often ignored Target Audiences and sometimes asked esoteric or naïve questions.* This situation improved when all research activities were put under a Deputy Director of the Agency.

There are special problems in polling overseas. In some countries it is not feasible to go into the countryside; in others, especially those with less than democratic governments, the populace is fearful—or at least guarded—in answering questions, telling interviewers what they think their governments would like them to say. Given these limitations, the polls are useful as guides to what people are thinking, but are by no means infallible.

Unfortunately, too much of USIA's foreign polling—like much domestic polling—has been superficial. As veteran pollster Lloyd Free has said, "It must go into matters deeper than 'opinions.' It must investigate 'reality worlds' in general and the assumptions, often latent or implicit, upon which attitudes and opinions are based. . . . The findings must be interpreted against a broader background of social science data: studies of the power and influence structure in particular societies; of 'national character' . . . of the 'political culture.' "[8] Or as one Director of USIA put it, the Agency needs to learn "what's bugging people."

USIA must know how people react to various words. The Agency has done some, but not nearly enough, of this kind of research. For

---

* Nigerians were asked if they would "like to see three million overseas [American] blacks return to settle here in Nigeria." Slum dwellers in Rio de Janeiro were asked if U.S. astronaut Gordon Cooper's space flight was "a great accomplishment or just a moderate accomplishment." Illiterate peasants in Nicaragua and El Salvador were asked if they knew "who has been the President of the United States for the last two years."

example, in one revealing series of surveys in Latin America, Africa, and Asia, USIA found a highly favorable reaction to the word *socialism,* particularly among students. *Communism* elicited a strongly unfavorable reaction, and the response to the word *capitalism* was mixed, but disapproval clearly predominated.

Further questions revealed that those who reacted favorably to *socialism* mostly thought of a socialist society as a democracy with social justice, equality under the law, social security protection for the very old, the very young, the ill, and the unemployed, minimum wage laws and a progressive income tax—in other words, an economic system much like that in the United States. Yet most of them characterized the U.S. economy as capitalistic, and a high percentage identified *capitalism* with economic exploitation and social insecurity.

Or take the word *Negro.* Certainly, all know what the word means. Or do they? An astonishing survey conducted for USIA by Market Research (Nigeria), Ltd. showed that 40 percent of uneducated or little-educated respondents in the Nigerian capital of Lagos had no idea what the word meant. Of those more knowledgeable, four out of five said it referred only to "black Americans," while a mere 17 percent declared that it referred to "blacks the world over."[9] The poll was an eye-opener for the Agency.

Sometimes the polls reveal answers to questions that were not asked. Sub-Saharan African students in French universities during De Gaulle's administration were revealed to be intensely anti-American and often pro-Soviet. In terms of general esteem, the United States ranked sixth on a list of seven nations, trailed only by Communist China.[10] A poll of students from the same countries in universities in West Germany, where the government was warmly allied with Washington, found them highly pro-American and anti-Soviet.[11] Ergo: the climate of opinion in which African students were living in France was unfavorable to the United States, but just the opposite was true in Germany.

Whatever the results of USIA polls, they are more often than not important: as a guide to policy-making or execution and as a clue to USIA's problems and effectiveness. Our propagandists have fared best when they have listened before speaking, and taken heed of what they heard.

4 *Hard Sell and Soft Sell*

Now let us return to the mid-1950s when Streibert, to make the new U.S. Information Agency an effective instrument of American foreign policy, sought to engage the interest and support of President Eisenhower. In this he was only partly successful. Eisenhower believed in the information program, ordered several studies to improve it, and had a "psychological" adviser on his immediate staff. Yet when he wrote his memoirs on eight years in the White House, the two massive volumes contained almost no mention of USIA.

Nonetheless, both before and after his Presidency, Eisenhower had more to say publicly about American propaganda than any other chief executive. Five years after his return to private life, he recalled that, despite the contrast between the enormous defense budgets and the relatively small appropriations for USIA, "I cannot recall a single instance during my years as President when my recommendations for the support of USIA were not seriously reduced in Congress." Though Eisenhower showed little inclination to fight for USIA when he was in the White House, he later recommended spending "whatever is necessary—a half billion or even a billion a year, if it takes that much."[1]

How, then, do we reconcile this vigorous advocacy with his relative indifference while President? Part of the answer may be found in Eisenhower's view of the Agency's role. Unlike Kennedy, for example, he did not feel USIA was an immediately useful tool for furthering U.S. objectives, but rather a secondary agency (which it was) of peripheral value (which it was not). Consequently, he demonstrated no interest in its day-to-day operations and dealt with the

Agency mostly through his Secretary of State.

But Dulles did not want to be bothered with USIA. When Lyndon Johnson and other Senators suggested in 1957 that USIA be put back into the State Department and Eisenhower was inclined to go along, Dulles strongly protested to the President, saying State "should confine itself to foreign policy formulation, advice and execution" and "not become a collection of operating agencies."[2]

Dulles saw no connection between public attitudes abroad and the conduct of U.S. foreign affairs. "If I so much as took into account what people in other countries are thinking or feeling," he remarked on one occasion, "I would be derelict in my duty."[3] And he was concerned about USIA "acting behind the backs" of foreign governments in talking to their people.

More importantly, however, Dulles was proud of being, as he put it, the *only* (not just the principal) foreign policy adviser to Eisenhower. "There has never been any question of anyone else being able to influence the President in foreign policy," he told an aide. "There could be nothing more frustrating than to feel that the President . . . was counseling with other people on foreign affairs. I'd have to resign if that were the case."[4] He did not have to resign.

Dulles did not object to USIA operations (as opposed to its advisory role), however, so long as they did not interfere with what he considered State Department prerogatives. He acquiesced when Eisenhower, after urging greater Congressional support for USIA in his 1955 State of the Union Message, invited Streibert to attend meetings of the National Security Council as an observer and made him a full member of the Operations Coordinating Board. These steps had only limited significance, however. Streibert did not sit at the table with NSC members, and, like other lesser staff officials seated around the room, remained mute except in the rare instances he was called upon to speak. All of Streibert's speeches had to be cleared by the State Department, whatever the subject matter, and when Dulles overruled him he seldom chose to argue.

With others, however, Streibert was quick to speak up for USIA. He dealt effectively with one persistent critic, feisty Roy Howard of United Press International, who was carrying on a feud with USIA that he had begun more than thirty-five years earlier with the Creel Committee. Howard claimed that USIA was unfairly competing with his wire service, and he badgered people all over Washington about it. The charge was absurd; USIA did not provide a full news service to foreign newspapers, merely texts and other supplementary material. Streibert prepared a forceful rebuttal, recruited powerful friends in the government and the press, and the aging Howard retreated.*

Within the Agency, an important step forward was the creation of an Office of Research to analyze foreign issues, attitudes, audiences, and media. Although Dulles disapproved of polls, and for a time had them stopped, an expanded series of periodic public opinion surveys was begun. (Occasionally, after Dulles had briefed the NSC, Eisenhower would say, "But, Foster, you forgot the human side," and pull out a report based on a USIA poll.[5]) The Agency's researchers also conducted regular studies of Communist propaganda which proved useful to both USIA and State Department officers.

Prompted by a vastly expanded program of Soviet exhibitions in underdeveloped countries, Congress approved a "President's Emergency Fund" to finance U.S. participation in international trade fairs abroad, fairs which often had more of a propaganda than a commercial flavor. The U.S. program, which later was financed through regular annual appropriations, was administered by the Commerce Department under USIA policy direction. Although it is questionable whether the costly exhibits were as productive as other propaganda activities, they were great crowd pleasers, especially where they involved motion pictures.

Much publicity was given to a concerted Agency campaign on "people's capitalism," an effort to persuade the world that the American economic system was not the evil machine described by Communist and socialist critics abroad. Although America's material affluence was widely envied, many foreigners—including many who had no sympathy for Communism—saw the U.S. economic system in nineteenth-century terms of arrogant, greedy capitalists exploiting the masses. This view was reinforced by the fact that the most pro-American elements in many countries were also the wealthiest, most reactionary, and least democratic.

In cooperation with the Advertising Council, USIA produced a

* The accusation was revived in 1957 by Senator Lyndon Johnson as part of a general attack on USIA's budget. It has been raised since from time to time, but never very seriously.

"People's Capitalism" exhibit, showing a pioneer home in 1776, a typical worker's home in the 1950s, and a series of panels illustrating how progress had been achieved. Films, press features, photographs, broadcasts, and pamphlets, all featuring the theme of American capitalism, were produced in great numbers. Eisenhower predictably lauded the effort; equally predictably, *Pravda* called it "as senseless as fried ice."

Although USIA would not admit it, the campaign was not a success. The word *capitalism* had been so thoroughly if unfairly discredited that its use as a label was unfortunate. More serious, the campaign emphasized the already well-known material wealth of America while putting little stress where it was needed: on the broad public and private programs for social welfare, education, health, and recreation in the U.S. system. The importance of the government's role in America's mixed economy was played down. Consequently, few foreign skeptics were converted.

The Agency's expanded Motion Picture Service sent abroad complete films of all Eisenhower press conferences, doubtless pleasing White House aides (if not the more modest General himself) but perplexing USIS posts, which had no market for them. Documentary films were produced on Vice President Nixon's various trips abroad, and on the visits to the United States of foreign dignitaries. Inexpensive book packets were widely distributed by USIA and CARE; in some countries USIS posts organized local "book-of-the-month" clubs.

Television activities continued to grow. Although some new programs, such as *The World Through Stamps,* were of doubtful value, others were successful from the start. *Report from America,* an unpretentious monthly review of everyday life in the United States, was a hit on the BBC. "What is finest about these fascinating reports," commented the London *Sunday Times,* "is the integrity that is written all over them. America speaks for herself, through undoctored pictures of her streets and the untrained voices of men in them."

In 1956, with President Eisenhower's enthusiastic support, the People-to-People Program was launched. Its purpose (never fully realized) was to encourage private American citizens who traveled, worked, or had contacts abroad to supplement USIA efforts "by helping convey the truth about our country and its peaceful aims."

Under a People-to-People Committee of prominent private citizens, numerous activities were undertaken, guided by USIA's Office of Private Cooperation. Some of the activities were useful; others were either irrelevant or never really got under way.

Among the more useful activities were those carried on by a newly established Business Council for International Understanding comprised of U.S. business firms with overseas operations; the World Affairs Council's "Books Abroad" campaign, which flooded USIS posts with secondhand books; and the "affiliations" of American cities and universities with their counterparts abroad, with the resultant exchanges of ideas, visitors, exhibits, radio programs, and newsletters.

Summit and Suez

In 1955 Malenkov, who had succeeded Stalin, was replaced by Nikita Khrushchev and Nikolai Bulganin. In contrast with the Chinese Communists' increased belligerence, the new Soviet leaders put their emphasis on political and economic competition and greatly increased their trade and aid in the Middle East and South Asia. Not only "cultural" delegations but Khrushchev and Bulganin themselves made unprecedented visits abroad. In Europe they withdrew Soviet forces from Austria, restored normal relations with the renegade Marshal Tito, and even established diplomatic relations with West Germany.

The Soviet "peace offensive" offered new opportunities, but also new perils. The impetus of European political and economic unity slackened perceptibly as the danger from the East appeared to lessen. The underdeveloped countries welcomed the new Soviet overtures, and some of them saw a chance to profit by playing Washington against Moscow in a competition for aid. Public and press demands swelled for a "summit" meeting of the world's principal leaders, but the United States, wounded at Yalta and fearful of contributing to what Dulles called "a false euphoria," remained cautious. USIA warned its audiences that no summit conference could produce miracles, but the cry for a meeting only intensified.

USIA polls in Western Europe showed that large majorities believed a conference would be worthwhile even if no solutions were reached, as long as there was some relaxation of tensions. Except in Italy, a plurality of respondents believed the danger, if any, was that the United States would make too few, rather than too many, concessions.[6]

Finally, the United States acquiesced. The "big four"—Eisenhower, Bulganin (with Khrushchev at his elbow), British Prime Minister Anthony Eden, and French Premier Edgar Faure—met in Geneva in July, 1955. American skepticism was largely justified; nothing concrete came out of the meeting. The occasion did provide grist for propaganda mills of both sides, however. (Although Streibert was not included in the U.S. delegation, Nelson Rockefeller, the White House propaganda adviser, was.)

USIA, while warning against unrealistic expectations, waged a global campaign on behalf of Eisenhower's imaginative "open skies" proposal, which Rockefeller had urged the President to offer. The idea was simple: let American and Soviet airplanes regularly inspect each other's countries to seek out preparations for surprise aggression. A USIA exhibit, "Mutual Inspection for Peace," a brochure, and two documentary movies convincingly depicted how the concept would work. Additionally, USIA distributed a great torrent of news releases, features, and photographs on the scheme. Reaction around the world was favorable, more so than for the Soviets' counterproposal for a limited number of fixed inspection points. But in the weeks that followed, and at a foreign ministers' meeting in October, the Russians continued to say *nyet* to "open skies," and the proposal finally died.

One constructive result of the conference was a cautious beginning of cultural exchanges between the U.S. and the U.S.S.R. At first, the suspicious Soviets were flatly opposed; Foreign Minister Molotov charged that a USIS post in Moscow would be nothing more than a cover for espionage. Eventually, however, the Russians did agree to the resumption of *Amerika* magazine in the Soviet Union in return for the sale in the United States of a similar Soviet publication, *USSR*. Distribution of each was handled by the host government, and it quickly became clear that many more copies of *Amerika* than the authorized 52,000 could have been sold had the Soviet Government permitted it.

Though the price was relatively high (fifty-five cents at the official rate of exchange), the magazine usually sold out within a few hours —to the dismay of Soviet officials, whose magazine did less well in this country. *Amerika* had no political propaganda as such, concentrating on straightforward presentations of U.S. cities, schools, farms, factories, and homes, with emphasis on progress in science, medicine, education, and culture.

Subsequent negotiations led to a formal agreement in January, 1958, for exchanges of technical and other delegations, students, scholars, radio and television programs, and motion pictures.

But the summit meeting's principal product was the euphoria that Dulles had feared. USIA public opinion polls, taken in Western Europe in mid-August, 1955, revealed that the conference had reduced the public's fear of war to a new low point. At the same time, there was a marked drop in the number of recipients who believed their countries should take sides in the Cold War and a lesser but significant decline in the number who favored their countries entering the conflict if the U.S. and the U.S.S.R. got into a shooting war. Eisenhower's prestige rose sharply, but so did Bulganin's.[7]

The decline in tension was good, but the decline in vigilance was not, and Moscow was quick to exploit the situation. There was a sharp increase in the number of Soviet cultural and trade-and-aid delegations sent to woo the underdeveloped new nations. Then, in the autumn of 1955, the euphoria was rudely shattered by news of massive Communist military assistance to Egypt, a political jump past pro-Western Turkey and Iraq into the heart of the Arab world.

Prompted by an Israeli retaliatory raid in February, 1955, on the Egyptian-controlled Gaza Strip, Egyptian President Gamal Abdel Nasser had sought unsuccessfully to obtain $27 million in arms from the United States. After another Israeli raid in late summer, Egypt mortgaged its cotton production for five times that much military assistance from Czechoslovakia, acting on behalf of the Soviet Union. The arms deal was a bombshell in the Middle East, an anti-Western bombshell. Nasser's stock soared; as Arabs saw it, he had challenged the long-dominant West and won.

Nasser stepped up his propaganda campaigns against the unpopular Dulles-sponsored Baghdad Pact, and against pro-Western regimes in Iraq and Jordan. The United States, alarmed, joined Britain in offering Egypt a grant of $70 million and a loan of $200 million to help build a high dam at Aswan. USIA widely publicized the American offer, and it was well received throughout the area, for the dam was the leading symbol of Egyptian economic independence.

Nonetheless, Egypt appeared to draw closer to the Communists, or so thought Secretary Dulles, who insisted on interpreting every Egyptian move as either pro-U.S. or pro-Communist. In May, 1956, Nasser recognized Communist China. Britain and others had done so years before, but the U.S. Government was outraged and said so. USIS-Cairo, saddled with justifying the Baghdad Pact and explaining American support of Israel and apparent U.S. opposition to Egypt's getting arms from anybody, found itself largely impotent.

In June, after a visit to Cairo by Soviet Foreign Minister Shepilov, the Egyptian Government raised new questions about the terms of the U.S. assistance for the Aswan Dam. Infuriated, Dulles abruptly informed the Egyptian Ambassador in mid-July that the U.S. offer was withdrawn; equally infuriated, Nasser a week later bitterly condemned the United States, nationalized the Suez Canal Company (which was principally British and French owned), and proclaimed that canal revenues would go toward building the dam.

Throughout Africa and Asia, as well as in Egypt itself, the U.S. aid withdrawal was denounced and Nasser's seizure of the canal hailed. USIA efforts to justify the American position were lost in the wind. Ever sensitive of their dignity, the people of the new nations were especially indignant at what they considered the arrogant manner of the withdrawal. But Western Europe was frightened; its economies were in large measure dependent on Middle Eastern oil and other trade through the canal. While diplomats toiled to find some satisfactory formula, London and Paris secretly plotted with Israel to recover the canal and rid themselves of Nasser once and for all.

On October 27 U.S. intelligence indicated that Israel was mobilizing its forces, and the State Department and USIA began the evacuation to Italy of dependents and some employees from Israel and Jordan. On the night of October 29 Israeli forces crossed the border and raced to within twenty-five miles of the Suez Canal. The next day Britain and France demanded that both sides withdraw ten miles from the canal and permit Anglo-French forces to occupy key positions along it. Egypt rejected the ultimatum, the United States denounced the Israeli attack, and the British began bombing key targets in Egypt. Shortly thereafter, British and French forces parachuted into the canal area.

Despite the historic political, military, and cultural ties between the United States and Britain and France, despite the need for Western unity in the face of the concurrent anti-Soviet revolution in Hungary, and despite the fact that America was in the last days of a Presidential election campaign, Eisenhower and Dulles acted courageously and decisively to oppose the Anglo-French-Israeli invasion. USIA proclaimed the U.S. position around the world, and the Voice of America increased its Arabic broadcasts from one and one-half hours daily to fourteen and one-half hours.

Nonetheless, the outcome probably would have been the same had the United States supported its allies in the United Nations, for the invasion was doomed from the start. The year was 1956, not 1856, and world public opinion—that elusive and much maligned force—proved stronger than the combined military forces of Britain, France, and Israel. The invaders won a military victory (Israel's performance was a classic of its kind), but they suffered a major political-propaganda defeat when the United Nations, led by the United States, demanded and got a cease-fire and an unconditional withdrawal of their forces.

As a result of the firm U.S. stand, confidence in America soared throughout Africa and Asia. It was a classic example of propaganda of the deed: the United States had demonstrated that it applied the same standards to its friends that it applied to others. In the Arab world and elsewhere, USIA moved to exploit America's heightened prestige. And then Eisenhower and Dulles threw it all away.

Encouraged to act by pro-Israel sentiment in the United States and concerned that the Soviet Union and Nasser might move into what appeared to be a "political vacuum" in the Middle East caused by the departure of Anglo-French influence, the Administration in January, 1957, proposed the "Eisenhower Doctrine." By means of a Congressional resolution, it offered economic and military aid to those Middle Eastern nations willing to collaborate with the United States and authorized the President to use military force, if necessary, to protect their independence. After much debate, Congress approved the Doctrine in March.

The result was further polarization of political forces in the Middle East. Those already committed to the United States embraced the Doctrine; the neutrals, led by Egypt, bitterly opposed it as an unacceptable substitute for British-French influence. Nehru of India warned Eisenhower that the Doctrine would excite "passions and create divisions among the Arab countries." Many USIA and State Department experts agreed, but their advice was not sought. So the Agency did its best to sell the Doctrine, although without much success. In Egypt copies of the joint Congressional resolution and a pamphlet entitled *Is There a Vacuum?*, justifying the doctrine, were distributed in the biggest mailing in Egypt's history—more than a million pieces—but the more Egyptians knew about the Doctrine, the less they liked it.

Hungary: The Credibility Gap

While Suez and its aftermath were raising, then dropping, American prestige in the Middle East, other significant events were having a major impact on both U.S. prestige and U.S. propaganda. These events took place in Eastern Europe on the very days (in a rare coincidence of history) that the Middle Eastern crisis came to its climax.

In mid-October of 1956, the Polish Communist Party, increasingly independent since Stalin's death, moved to break out from under Moscow's domination. The instrument was Wladyslaw Gomulka; the issue was his demand for the ouster of Russian Marshal Konstantin Rokossovsky as Poland's Minister of Defense. Khrushchev flew to Warsaw, and though he raged at Gomulka the Poles stood firm. Gomulka was in, Rokossovsky was out, and Poland headed on a new course. One consequence of the change was the ending of Polish jamming of the Voice of America.*

The freedom infection quickly spread to Hungary, where students, intellectuals, and workers in Budapest began to demonstrate for the withdrawal of Soviet forces and the restoration to power of the moderate former Premier, Imre Nagy. Demonstrations turned into riots and riots into insurrection, fired by the repressive measures taken by political police and Soviet forces. Nagy became Premier, but the rebels fought on, fed up after a decade of Russian domination

---

* Debating the matter in Parliament, Polish legislators revealed that Poland had been spending seventy million zlotys ($17.5 million) a year for jamming, a figure roughly equal to the total cost of VOA operations world-wide at that time.

and hopeful of help from the West after all the talk in Washington of "rolling back the Iron Curtain." Large elements of the Hungarian Army defected to the rebel side.

Excited Hungarian-born broadcasters in the Voice of America and Radio Free Europe wanted to proclaim the beginnings of a holy war to drive Soviet forces from Eastern Europe once and for all. They were not allowed to do so, later charges to the contrary notwithstanding. Nonetheless, it is understandable that the buoyant Hungarian "freedom fighters" misread the message from the West. Had not Dulles spoken repeatedly of freeing the Eastern European satellites? On October 25 Eisenhower proclaimed that "the United States deplores the intervention of Soviet military forces," and six days later announced U.S. willingness to give economic aid to new and independent governments in Eastern Europe.

The following day, Nagy renounced the Warsaw Pact, declared Hungarian neutrality, and appealed to the UN for help. A U.S. resolution calling on the Soviets to withdraw their troops from Hungary was introduced in the UN Security Council and vetoed by the Soviet delegate. On November 4 the Soviets moved troops and tanks into Budapest and the rebels, issuing pitiful last cries for American help, were crushed. VOA urged the Hungarian people to be brave, and Eisenhower asked Bulganin "in the name of humanity and in the cause of peace" to withdraw Soviet forces. But words could not move the Soviets, and weapons would have moved them—and us—into a world war.

Hungary was a classic example of the confusion between *aspiration* and *action*. We wanted Hungary to be free, and so our statesmen and our propaganda repeatedly proclaimed. But U.S. vital interests were not at stake in Hungary, and we were not prepared to launch World War III in Budapest. The vital interests of the Soviet Union were involved; Khrushchev and Bulganin acted because they had to. Eisenhower and Dulles did not act because they did not have to, and because they could not have justified the resulting war to their people, to the world, or to history.

Under these circumstances, did Western broadcasts mislead the people of Hungary? An examination of scripts indicates not, at least not intentionally, but that is not the way some Hungarians heard it. In late November, USIA commissioned a private Austrian survey organization to poll 410 Hungarian refugees:

• Half of the respondents said without qualification that Western broadcasts "give the impression the West would give military help in case of an uprising." Another fourth made the same statement but with qualifications suggesting that the promise was not explicit.

• Only a third, however, believed the United States should have intervened if it involved the risk of world war.[8]

It was a hard but useful lesson for USIA, which thereafter put greater emphasis on the credibility of its output and less on the "hard sell." Seven months later, in its semiannual report to Congress, the Agency stressed "the necessity of sticking to the truth, of avoiding at all costs the twisting or perversion of fact, a heavily propagandistic or argumentative line." Such an approach "is not only inappropriate to the official voice of the United States Government," the report continued; "it also simply does not work."

Taking indirect note of the criticism of international broadcasters in connection with the Hungarian affair, the Agency reported: "In the Voice of America, after intensive studies of past programs, tighter controls were established and language broadcasts were submitted to even more rigorous review before they went on the air. The process extended also to the other communications media and to the local output of USIA posts overseas."[9]

Insofar as American propagandists and politicians misled the people of Hungary prior to and during October, 1956, they were guilty of being provocative and irresponsible. Men and women may have died who today would be alive. Certainly the credibility of America's willingness to use its military power in defense of freedom was damaged. In some quarters American prestige suffered, although there was no evidence that most or even much of the world preferred nuclear war to the defeat of the Hungarian rebels.

In retrospect, however, the consequences of the Hungarian revolt look far different from the way they did in the gloomy days of late 1956. USIA found that the reputation of the Soviet Union was badly damaged everywhere, and there were widespread defections from the Communist Party. Moscow was forced to loosen its grip on the nations of Eastern Europe, and since the blood bath in Budapest not one of them has been a "satellite" in the sense that it was before Hungary. Janos Kadar, who succeeded Nagy as Premier, introduced many of the reforms that the rebels had sought. It can be argued that, just as Britain and France found defeat in victory at Suez, so the Hungarian "freedom fighters" achieved victory in defeat at Budapest.

In the months and years after the Hungarian revolt, USIA kept the story alive. When the United Nations issued its Special Report on Hungary, the Agency blanketed the world with the text and commentary. USIA's book operation produced thousands of copies in many languages of James Michener's *The Bridge at Andau*, George Shuster's *In Silence I Speak*, and Laszlo Beke's *A Student's Diary: Budapest, October 16–November 1, 1956*, among others. Agency motion pictures—*Hungarian Fight for Freedom, A Nation in Torment*, and *Now We Are Free*—were widely shown abroad. Thousands of dramatic photographs were distributed, as were copies of a special *Life* magazine supplement on the revolt. American aid to those who fled Hungary, and the success stories of those who resettled in the United States, were publicized.

Larson and Lyndon

The notable week that brought war to the Middle East and an end to the short-lived Hungarian rebellion saw still another major event in America: the re-election of President Eisenhower over Adlai Stevenson by an even greater margin than in 1952. Streibert felt that his four years of government service were enough, and he resigned after the election to join the business staff of the Rockefeller brothers in New York. By any standard, Streibert had done a good job as Director of USIA. The new organization had been soundly and firmly established, and morale largely restored after its shattering during the McCarthy period.

When Streibert came in, the Agency was defensively self-centered, more concerned with survival than achievement. Its field posts were so completely under the thumb of headquarters that initiative had a dubious odor. To do nothing seemed to many employees to be preferable than doing something; it certainly was thought to be safer. Streibert changed the tone and style of the Agency, and encouraged ideas and initiative from his field officers—although he did not always accept them.

The growing importance and respectability of the Agency were confirmed by Eisenhower's selection of a man he considered one of his most promising protégés to succeed Streibert as Director. The President's choice was Arthur Larson.

A Rhodes Scholar who had resigned as dean of the University of Pittsburgh School of Law in 1954 to become Under Secretary of Labor, Larson in 1956 wrote a book entitled *A Republican Looks at His Party* which described and defended what the President called "modern Republicanism." Democrats and conservative Republicans not unexpectedly derided the book, but Eisenhower was delighted with it. Publicly and privately, he warmly praised the volume and its author, and even suggested Larson as a possible Republican candidate for President in 1960.

Looking around for a spot to give Larson greater visibility and broader experience, Eisenhower hit upon USIA and named him the Agency's second Director. Although he had no experience in communications or foreign affairs (except for a brief wartime stint with the Foreign Economic Administration), Larson was a man of considerable ability and had the all-important qualification (for USIA) of being close to the President. He should have been a great success in the job, but he never had a chance. Admittedly, the undoing of Arthur Larson was largely his own fault, but he had help.

In early 1957 the President asked Congress for $144 million for USIA, a $31 million increase. But the House Appropriations Subcommittee under Representative John J. Rooney refused to support the increase. The full House backed up its subcommittee, cutting the figure to $105 million. It was not, however, unusual for the Senate to restore cuts made by the House, and the Agency was hopeful that the Senate would do just that.

But it was not to be. On April 16 Larson threw away any chance that the Democratically controlled Congress would see it his way. Speaking before a partisan Republican crowd in Hawaii,* Larson's enthusiasm outran his judgment when he proclaimed in passing that "throughout the New and Fair Deals, this country was in the grip of a somewhat alien philosophy, imported from Europe."

---

* Larson's first mistake was to accept partisan speaking engagements while serving as Director of USIA, a mistake which Streibert and Larson's successors carefully avoided.

The remark was prominently reported in the Washington press, and Larson returned to a storm of criticism. His defense, that he was talking about the Democratic Party of Roosevelt and Truman rather than the party of 1957, helped not at all. One man in particular took special note of Larson's words, a man whose admiration of Roosevelt and Truman was exceeded only by his skill as the chief strategist of the Democratic Party in Congress. That man was the chairman of the Senate Appropriations Subcommittee that would consider USIA's budget, and also the Majority Leader of the upper house: Lyndon B. Johnson of Texas.

The Senate hearings on USIA's budget opened on May 2. Joe [1957] McCarthy, a member of the subcommittee who had persecuted the information program four years earlier, was not present; he died that very day. But Johnson was waiting for Larson, and he was no McCarthy; he had everything going his way. Conservative Southern Democrats were looking for ways to cut Eisenhower's budget, and Northern liberal Democrats—who had regularly defended USIA— were infuriated by Larson's remark, which they interpreted as being directed at them. With one stroke Johnson could unite the quarrelling wings of his party, champion economy in government, and scuttle Eisenhower's pet apostle of "modern Republicanism." It was too good an opportunity to miss, and Johnson didn't miss it—with the help of Senators Fulbright, Mike Mansfield, and Allen Ellender, among others.

His voice heavy with sarcasm, Johnson opened the hearings by telling Larson, "Of all the agency heads . . . you are asking for the most money to be restored. . . . We look to you as the distinguished author and spokesman for your party to enlighen us."

From that moment on, Johnson kept it up. When Larson praised USIA's motion pictures, Johnson asked him: "Do you screen them carefully for any 'alien philosophy'?" And later: "I would gather from the little I know about you that you are an adventurous fellow— imaginative and modern. So I am going to rely on you to help me establish a moderate balance between the modern and old guard so that we can win the propaganda war." And still later: "We realize that you are one of the 'modern Republicans' . . . [but] instead of giving us glittering generalities . . . tell us why the House was unwise in reducing 193 jobs from the budget. . . . This agency does not know what it is doing."

At one point, when Larson became especially agitated, Johnson barked: "Let us do it quietly now. . . . We do not have to be loud about it." When Larson ticked off eight reasons to justify the Agency's budget request, Johnson replied: "The Director has given me an excellent recital of the discovery of new ways and means of spending money. What I want to do is to discover why we have to greatly increase this. I do not think we have that justification."

When Larson, asked about USIA activities of earlier years, said he was "not competent to go back and reconstruct history," Johnson reminded him that "you went all through the Fair Deal and New Deal and their 'alien philosophy,' and reconstructed history back to 1932."

Larson was not the best of witnesses. He was often uninformed, which was not surprising in light of his newness to the job. But he also annoyed the Senators by making extravagant claims of Agency successes. For example, when he boasted of the impact made by a USIA exhibit on Eisenhower's "open skies" proposal, Fulbright asked disbelievingly: "Is it your theory that because of your activities the Kremlin is now changing its view?" When Larson answered with a "flat 'Yes,'" the incredulous Fulbright could only respond in amazement: "That is your view?"

Johnson repeatedly pressed Larson for detailed justifications, but the Director answered mostly in generalities, prompting even the moderate Republican Saltonstall to tell him, "I think the statements made by the chairman should be specifically answered by you—not in the way you have answered them . . . because you have not given us anything." And finally Johnson told Larson: "Never before have I experienced as much difficulty and have I spent as much time getting the facts and been shown so few facts in regard to any program as I have with the USIA. . . . There is no point in telling this committee that you must combat Communist ideas. There is no point in telling this committee that we must have greater mutual understanding. These are glittering generalities. . . . What we want to know is: How? . . . I implore you to spend your time today on specifics."

When Mansfield asked Larson about his Hawaiian speech, the Director turned to Johnson and inquired if "this comes under the category of specific justification for items under this budget?" Johnson angrily replied: "It does not make any difference to the committee what it comes under. . . . We do not want to be lectured on how to ask questions. You are here to answer the questions that the Senator chooses to ask and in whatever category he wants to."[10]

Johnson Wins, Larson Leaves

"Nobody but nobody loves the USIA," concluded the *New York Times* as the hearings ended.

As the up-and-coming apologist for the Republican Administration, [Larson] has recently made political statements that the Congressional Democrats are determined to repay with compound interest. But as a "modern Republican" of the Eisenhower brand, he can expect no support from the conservative Republicans who dominate his party in Congress. And as the petitioner for an unpopular agency that wants a big increase in spending money, he is an affront to all the Senators and Representatives who are crying out for economy.[11]

On May 14 the Senate Committee recommended $90.2 million, and pointedly suggested that USIA should "concentrate on improving its personnel" and return to the State Department.

The next day, the matter went to the Senate floor for debate, where Johnson showed little enthusiasm even for the emasculated budget bill that bore his mark. "There is not one scintilla of evidence," he told his colleagues, "which would justify the assertion by a judicious, prudent man that the $90 million we have recommended will be wisely spent."* He recalled that when Taft and Knowland had been Majority Leaders of the Republican Senate, USIA had received only $79 million and $84 million respectively.

Johnson apologized for his vote the previous year in upping USIA's appropriation. "What did the Agency do? It added 200 employees, in defiance of the most generous friend the Agency has had"—none other than Lyndon Johnson himself. "We tried to find out whether the programs of the USIA were effective. The reply was that this year will offer a glorious opportunity to combat Communist imperialism. . . . The only thing that became clear is that the USIA never abandons an activity, but only increases its personnel and

---

* Only a month later, Johnson annoyed Eisenhower by blandly recommending that the Administration support a Congressional resolution encouraging the President to "make every effort" to increase the international exchange of information.

spending, unless an abrupt halt is ordered by an outside authority."*

Asked by Senator Douglas of Illinois, who defended USIA, about Larson's competence, Johnson replied: "I am not prepared to pass judgment on the gentleman's I.Q. I must say, in all frankness, that he was a very poor witness."

Senator Aiken, the kindly Vermonter, tried to get the debate off Larson. "If he chose to emulate the sitting duck, and received the treatment usually accorded sitting ducks, that was his privilege. But . . . we ought not to consider the Director. We should consider the purpose for which the money is being appropriated." But only a few Republicans (among them, Jacob Javits and John Sherman Cooper) spoke up for the Agency; even many of the "modern Republicans" were silent or supported Johnson.

Several liberal Democrats, however, concerned that partisanship was being carried too far, felt that the national interest should take precedence. One of them was John F. Kennedy of Massachusetts. Wouldn't Johnson believe it wise, he asked, "in view of the activities being undertaken by the Russians, the Chinese, the Egyptians, and others, that we should at least continue the program on the level at which it is maintained today?"

When Johnson demurred, Kennedy pressed his point. "I believe in this program," he said. "It is difficult for me to believe that the program is so hopelessly conducted that it is not able to spend as much as it spent last year wisely and well." Democratic Senators Joseph Clark of Pennsylvania and Richard Neuberger of Oregon joined Kennedy in defending Eisenhower's program against the bipartisan criticism. But Johnson had the last word: "If Mr. Larson and Mr. Washburn will spend a little of their time fighting Communism, and not so much of their time fighting the Committees on Appropriations of the respective bodies, I think they will be more successful with the information program."[12]

The bill was not amended. Kennedy and Clark told Johnson privately that they might try to restore some of the money. But Johnson was adamant, informing them that "this is a leadership matter."[13] In the end, Neuberger was the only Democrat to vote against the cut and only fourteen Republicans supported Eisenhower. John-

* Under President Lyndon Johnson ten years later, the budget of USIA was twice what it was in 1957.

son's version of the USIA budget was approved, with a larger cut than was imposed on any other agency that year. Although House-Senate conferees later raised the figure to $96 million, it was still nearly $10 million less than the House had originally voted and nearly $50 million below what Eisenhower had asked. The President, furious with Johnson, subsequently described it as an "irresponsible diminution of an agency on the front line in the cold war."[14]

Although hurt, USIA survived, but Larson did not. It would have been unthinkable to send him back up to the Hill the following year, and after his ordeal Larson had no stomach for the job. In late 1957 he was "kicked upstairs" to the White House, where for a short time he served as a special assistant to Eisenhower.*

Meanwhile, the Agency took stock of what and how it was doing, conducting what Larson called "an entire reappraisal of our program throughout the world." A "USIA Basic Guidance Paper" was issued, and it made good sense. "Drawing obvious morals" was banned, as were "all kinds of polemics and denunciation" and output which was "sarcastic or boastful or self-righteous."

At the same time, USIA officers were reminded that "our material should always be purposeful. We are not in the business of news or art or literature or entertainment or education for their own sake. Our output should in fact form the basis of conclusions that support our foreign policy and objectives." Emphasis was put on "the factual approach" which "makes the information service both believed and welcome. . . . [But] this does not mean the Agency has the obligation, as might a commercial news service, to carry news merely because it is news. However, our standards may on occasion require us to relate facts which are unfavorable to us, when failure to do so would damage our believability."[15]

During that autumn of 1957 there occurred two events "unfavorable to us" that the Agency struggled, without much success, to put into a perspective not damaging to the reputation of the United States abroad. Those events put new words into the common vocabulary of people around the world: *Little Rock* and *sputnik*.

---

* Seven years later, Larson demonstrated that he was able to forgive and forget. When ultraconservative Barry Goldwater was the Republican nominee for President in 1964, Larson bolted his party and worked on behalf of Johnson's candidacy.

ye gods !

Little Rock and Sputnik

Following the 1954 Supreme Court ruling, a Federal District Court in 1956 approved a plan for integration prepared by the school authorities of Little Rock, Arkansas. But the Governor of Arkansas, Orval Faubus, backed by extremist White Citizens Councils, declared he would resist. He followed up his words in early September, 1957, by ordering the Arkansas National Guard to surround Central High School in Little Rock and keep a handful of Negro students from entering. His official rationale was that the troops were needed to prevent violence.

A shocked world, which had assumed (partly from what it had been told by USIA) that the Supreme Court had dealt with the matter once and for all, watched with fascinated horror. USIA, which had not prepared its audiences for trouble, was tongue-tied.

A Federal judge ordered integration to proceed, but Faubus refused to back down. A Federal court injunction then forced Faubus to remove the National Guard, but racist mobs assembled in Little Rock to do unofficially what the Guard could not do officially. Delighted Soviet propagandists proclaimed that racial violence was being "committed with the clear connivance of the United States Government."

School opened on Monday morning, September 23, and although eight frightened Negro children managed to enter Central High unhurt, a noisy mob demonstrated outside for three hours while reporters and television cameramen from all over the world watched and photographed. The mob finally had its way, and Little Rock's Mayor ordered the police to remove the Negro students.

But events at Little Rock had not only damaged America's prestige abroad; they had also outraged law-abiding citizenry in this country. When on Tuesday morning the mob surrounding the school was larger and uglier, Eisenhower federalized the Arkansas National Guard and sent a thousand U.S. paratroopers to secure admittance of the Negro students.

Overseas, nothing could undo the damage done to America by the strutting Faubus and the snarling, spitting mob outside Central High. But the dispatch of U.S. troops made it clear that the American Government, speaking for a majority of the American people, would not tolerate this sort of thing—and that was a plus. Nonetheless, there were few abroad who were reassured when USIA told them (in the words of its semiannual report that winter) "that isolated events like those at Little Rock . . . must be put in the perspective of the solid advance of the Negro in our democratic society."

For months Little Rock was a principal topic of Communist and other unfriendly foreign propaganda. USIA countered with facts and photographs on integrated schools, and stressed positive stories of Negro progress. A number of distinguished Negro Americans, though dismayed by Little Rock, helped by writing articles and doing broadcasts for the Agency. Notable Negroes traveling abroad, such as famed contralto Marian Anderson, spoke to USIA-arranged gatherings and press conferences on the American racial situation.

In the end, the Agency claimed publicly that its "consistent, factual handling of the racial question contributed substantially to the generally restrained and well-balanced reaction to the Little Rock story overseas."[16] But that was not what its private polls showed. A week after the events at Little Rock, the Agency commissioned "flash" public opinion surveys in thirteen major cities abroad. The results, not released to the public, revealed that the United States suffered a stunning defeat at Little Rock.

In half the cities polled, a plurality believed that "the majority of the American people disapprove of Negroes and whites attending the same schools." In all the cities, large pluralities believed that Negroes were badly treated throughout the United States. Everywhere except in Scandinavia and Holland, pluralities believed that relations between Negroes and whites in the U.S. had worsened over the previous several years.

Respondents in all thirteen cities expressed the view that, "all things considered, current developments with regard to Negro-white relations in the United States" had tended to "lower American standing in the world," and most thought the lowering had been "considerable." In every city except Tokyo, a plurality of respondents said their own opinion of America had declined, although there remained more good opinions than bad in all of the cities except Paris and New Delhi.[17]

Then, ten days after the crisis at Central High, there occurred a second event that did lasting damage to American prestige abroad. America's scientific pre-eminence had long been a primary ingredient in USIA's message, and widely accepted abroad. The Russians had, of course, claimed during Stalin's heyday to have invented the airplane, the telephone, the automobile, and just about everything else, but no one really believed them. Few knew of any Soviet counterparts to Eli Whitney, Samuel F. B. Morse, Thomas Edison, or Henry Ford. Soviet science was widely considered to be politicized, managed by incompetent Lysenkos. True, the Soviets did build an atom bomb, but everyone "knew" that was because their spies stole the secret from American scientists.

In the mid-1950s USIA put great stress on American scientific achievements. Although the principal emphasis was on "atoms for peace," no aspect of U.S. science, from anthropology to zoology, was ignored. While the United States had not yet gone into outer space, it would soon; a dramatic USIA exhibit, "Space Unlimited," literally promised the moon in describing the U.S. "Vanguard" program which would soon put a man-made satellite into orbit around the earth.

Americans were shocked, and people around the world deeply impressed, when on October 4, 1957, the Soviet Union put its sputnik into orbit first, thereby demonstrating an astonishing scientific sophistication. The immediate reaction in many parts of the world was: if Communism can do this, it can't be all bad; and even if it is bad, it is powerful and successful, outdoing even the rich Americans. A wave of apprehension engulfed America's allies and friends. Little Rock, they thought, had exposed America's grave internal problems; now sputnik revealed a lag in power, for the rocket thrust that put the beeping satellite into orbit could also be used to shower any spot on earth with nuclear bombs.

In its efforts to put sputnik "into perspective," USIA was not helped by the strong odor of sour grapes emanating from Washington. Eisenhower proclaimed that he had never felt space exploration should be "considered as a race" and blandly reassured the American public that sputnik "does not raise my apprehensions, not one iota." Former Secretary of Defense Charles E. Wilson dismissed it as "a nice technical trick," while Eisenhower's aide Sherman Adams saw no reason for concern over "an outer-space basketball game." Dulles privately discounted the Soviet propaganda advantage.[18]

Not all American statesmen felt the same. Senator Lyndon Johnson warned that Rome once controlled the world "because it could build roads" and Britain because it had ships. "Now the Communists have established a foothold in outer space. It is not very reassuring to be told that next year we will put a 'better' satellite into the air. Perhaps it will even have chrome trim—and automatic windshield wipers."[19]

But that is just about what USIA did tell the world: that America had a "better balanced" space program that in the end would produce more scientific knowledge of greater value to humanity. "No effort was made to belittle this amazing [Soviet] scientific advance," the Agency explained later, "but the dramatic breakthrough was treated in Agency reports as one—and only one—of many notable achievements in current scientific and technological progress, in which the United States continues to be a leader."

And so while the world exclaimed in wonder, admiration, and some fear over sputnik, USIA proudly opened an innocuous exhibit in Europe entitled "Kalamazoo—and How It Grew." The new Director of USIA said: "I am convinced that the overseas information program can best serve the United States by continuing to present overseas a balanced picture of American aims and policies with confidence and dignity, and by refusing to be thrown off stride by the sputniks and other big and little crises that arise."[20]

The U.S. Advisory Commission on Information, however, took a gloomier view:

The United States may be a year behind the Soviets in missiles. It may be five years behind in mass technological education. But it is thirty years behind in competition with Communist propaganda. . . . Each year sees the Communists increase their hours of broadcasting, their production and distribution of books, their motion pictures and cultural exchanges and every other type of propaganda and information activity. . . . We should start planning to close the gap in this field before it widens further.

The Commission called for a greatly stepped-up effort.[21]

Secret USIA public opinion polls, taken in Western Europe during the last two weeks of November, 1957, gave substance to the Advisory Commission's concern as they revealed almost universal awareness of the Soviet triumphs and equally universal concern over their consequences. In every country except Germany, a plurality of respondents believed that, "all things considered, Russia is ahead of the United States in scientific development at the present time." Although a majority believed Russia's lead was only temporary, opinion was evenly divided as to which would be ahead after twenty years. Even more ominous were the opinions on which of the two great powers was "ahead in total military strength at the present time"; in Britain more than twice as many respondents believed the U.S.S.R. was ahead as thought the U.S. was.[22]

George V. Allen: The Soft Sell

After the Larson debacle and the propaganda crisis caused by sputnik, Eisenhower looked for a Director of USIA who had a proven capability of getting along with Congress (especially Southern Democrats like Lyndon Johnson), who could also work well with the professional diplomats in the State Department, and who had more than a casual acquaintance with the problems of international information. He found his man in George V. Allen, a North Carolina-born career Foreign Service Officer who had headed the program in the late 1940s when it was in the State Department and who since had served as Assistant Secretary of State for the Near East and South Asia and as Ambassador to Yugoslavia, India, and Greece. Allen reluctantly gave up his duties in Athens and returned to Washington.*

Because of fears raised in the American press about the U.S. "image" in the wake of sputnik, the White House made Allen's appointment something of an event. The *New York Times* reported:

The Eisenhower Administration, jolted by the propaganda effect of the Soviet satellites, is arranging for closer teamwork between the top policy makers and the United States Information Agency. Officials disclosed tonight a new, "open door" program on the part of President Eisenhower and Secretary of State Dulles toward the agency. . . . [Allen] was invited to participate in Secretary Dulles' policy making conferences every Tuesday and Thursday. President Eisenhower told Mr. Allen he was always welcome at the White House, and agreed to a monthly meeting with him.[23]

Policy, of course, was not being made at fixed meetings on Tuesday and Thursday mornings, and Eisenhower's offer of a monthly meeting

---

* "It wasn't a job that I wanted," Allen recalled later. "I tried to get out of it both times. But I was needed to 'defuse' the operation after Larson, and make it professional, if possible."

was no more than what Streibert had been given, and something less than Larson's special relationship with the President. But it was a useful gesture, reaffirming the Administration's interest in the much-criticized Agency.

("Eisenhower," Allen recalled later, "had a soft spot for the information program. He was a sentimentalist; he thought of it as people-to-people togetherness. Ike had a naïve belief in people-to-people diplomacy.")

With this send-off, Allen settled in as the nation's chief propagandist—but that is not the label he applied to himself. Whereas Streibert depended perhaps too heavily on the "hard sell," Allen's approach was the "soft sell," perhaps too much so. He believed the Information Agency should inform, but no more than that. He did not believe that USIA should attempt to persuade its audiences of anything.

Allen relaxed the tight grip that Streibert had held over the organization. His area assistant directors found that decision-making was diffused, and not as hasty as under Streibert. Allen generally wanted a consensus of his top officials before taking any major step.

The new Director probably underestimated USIA's potential. "Ninety percent of the impression which the United States makes abroad depends on our policies and not more than 10 percent, to make a rough estimate, is how we explain it," he told the Agency staff upon taking office. True enough, but what he failed to say was that the 10 percent sometimes is decisive and almost always is significant. Allen was, however, quite right when he pointed out that "we can work our hearts out for years building up goodwill for the United States in a given country when suddenly one little policy action is taken which does more to destroy our position than the USIA can rebuild in a very long time."

Allen was skeptical of USIA being on too intimate terms with the White House, where it could be drawn into foreign problems and domestic political crises of the moment. He felt the Agency should be "detached" (his word) and objective—"an independent, reputable news agency with stories that could be published by anyone."

Given his way, Allen would have preferred the Voice of America to be separated from the government entirely and operated by a nonpartisan board of distinguished Americans. Then, he thought, the rest of USIA might as well be in the State Department. As a practical matter, however, he opposed efforts in the late 1950s to return USIA to State on the grounds that "since it is already an independent agency there is no point in pulling the potatoes out of the ground to see how they are growing." When Dulles reversed his earlier views and decided USIA should come back to the department, Allen dragged out discussions until the election of 1960 made the matter academic.

Meanwhile, Allen aggressively promoted a plan, first proposed by his predecessors, to create a professional Foreign Service Officer Corps within USIA which would give Agency officers equal status with State Department Foreign Service Officers. When Congress failed to act on the measure, Allen used his administrative authority to appoint Foreign Service "Reserve" Officers to establish a professional career corps identical in most respects to the State service. State Department standards were applied, and joint State-USIA examining boards were created to select and promote members of the new corps.

Allen got along well personally with Dulles, though he often disagreed with him privately on policy. Dulles listened to Allen's views, but he did not want USIA participating in policy-making. Although Allen dutifully told a Congressional committee, in response to a leading question, that "I have a better opportunity to speak out more effectively in connection with the formulation of foreign policy at present than when I was an Assistant Secretary of State in charge of this operation," he had no illusions about his role.

Senator Mansfield and some others feared that USIA would not follow State's advice. But that was no danger under Allen, who later said his big problem was *getting* policy guidance from State. "And I never felt we at USIA had any particular expertise on matters dealing with foreign opinion," he recalled. "We never claimed we knew more than Dulles or anyone else." His modesty was becoming, if not wholly accurate.

The only time USIA under Allen ever deliberately ignored State Department guidance was when a revolution in Turkey resulted in the execution of former Prime Minister Adnan Menderes. The new Turkish Government did not want its people to know for the time being, and asked the United States and Britain not to report the execution. The State Department suggested that VOA not use the item, but the Voice did anyway—to protect its credibility.

An early dispute between Allen and Dulles was over USIA polls abroad, which Dulles had banned just prior to Allen's appointment. "Dulles," Allen recalled later, "felt he knew what foreign opinion would be—if he cared. When he was doing something he thought right, he didn't want to be told it was unpopular abroad. If he felt it was right, he should do it whatever people might think." Also, Allen recalled, "the polls often showed that Dulles himself was not popular overseas, and that just added to his skepticism about their usefulness."

Allen quietly eased USIA back into the polling business, first by "piggybacking" on polls done by others, and later by commissioning private polling organizations to conduct surveys abroad for USIA, as the Agency had done in the past.

The new Director sought to make USIA an instrument for relaxing international tensions, rather than for making Cold War points. With Henry Loomis, the new chief of the Voice of America, Allen sought to calm down VOA's more excitable scriptwriters and announcers and to obtain a quieter tone, "even flat, if possible." To enhance the Voice's credibility, he encouraged the recruitment of native American, instead of foreign-born, announcers, even if they did not have as good a command of the languages they were broadcasting in. Allen believed that émigré announcers were often disliked or distrusted in the countries from which they had come.

He increased VOA's English-language service on the grounds that people were more likely to believe what we said in our language than what we said in theirs, and by late 1958 the Voice was on the air in English around the clock. He dreamed of an international agreement whereby nations would broadcast only in their own languages (a step which the United States, Britain, and possibly France would favor, because of the widespread use of their languages abroad, but one to which the Soviets would never agree).

In line with his emphasis on long-range activities, Allen put great stress on cultural programs, particularly English-teaching, which he felt could provide foreigners with a ready access to American ideals and concepts in a noncontroversial fashion. He strengthened USIA libraries and promoted—with mixed success—the Agency's book translation program. *The Autobiography of Benjamin Franklin* was published in nineteen languages, Emil Ludwig's *Abraham Lincoln* in fourteen languages, and John Dewey's *Freedom and Culture* in thirteen, among others.

A USIS Youth Center was opened up on the Left Bank in Paris; *The New Yorker* magazine described is as "a clear, encouraging answer for American taxpayers who wish to know what is done with that thin fraction of their money that goes into overseas intellectual propaganda." In an increasing number of cities from Florence to Saigon, USIA sponsored university courses on American history and literature, and provided the necessary textbooks. One especially readable and attractive Agency book, *USA—Its Geography and Growth,* was produced in great numbers and in many languages; a member of the British Parliament noted that "today the United States textbook is a familiar sight in university libraries everywhere . . . due largely to the aid and information program of the United States Government."

Although the Agency had sought to minimize the significance of sputnik, it went all out when the American Explorer satellite was put into orbit. Four days after the event, a ten-minute USIA motion picture, *The Explorer in Space,* was sent abroad, where it was viewed in eighty-three countries. Live VOA coverage of the launchings of Explorer and the later Vanguard contrasted sharply with the U.S.S.R.'s secrecy in its space program. *Exploring Space,* a pamphlet produced in twelve languages, went to 800,000 persons in thirty-two countries. Agency models of the two satellites, included in two hundred space exhibits, attracted great crowds. Although polls still showed that the world continued to believe (correctly) that the Soviets were ahead in space, at least the United States had entered the race—and everyone knew it.

Castro to Camp David

Allen's three years as Director of USIA were far from trouble-free. Although the Agency had reported to Congress that, quoting one Havana newspaper during the Batista regime, "USIS in Cuba in doing a real job of winning friends and influencing people," Fidel Castro came to power and relations with the United States deteriorated rapidly. A book on Washington Irving by the Agency's Cultural Officer in Havana was widely praised by the literati there, but their acclaim did not drown out the drums of revolution.

Elsewhere in Latin America, the long-neglected USIA program was strengthened some. New binational cultural centers were opened, and efforts were begun to reach labor, university students, and intellectuals. The low-price-book program was expanded, and labor periodicals were launched in Argentina and Chile.

The Agency gave broad coverage to Communist Chinese verbal and artillery attacks on the offshore islands of Quemoy and Matsu, although it was unable to generate much support for the notion that the islands were worth risking a war. USIA publicized Peking's repressive measures in Tibet and the flight of the Dalai Lama. Khrushchev began his campaign to take over Berlin, and USIA stressed the determination of the United States and its allies to guarantee the security of West Berlin. An Agency picture story, "A Tale of Two Cities," contrasted life in East and West Berlin.

In the spring of 1958, a pro-Nasser and largely Muslim insurrection broke out in Lebanon against the government of President Camille Chamoun, a Christian Arab who had taken his country into the Western camp by embracing the Eisenhower Doctrine. Washington watched the situation nervously until mid-July, then acted after a bloody revolution in nearby Iraq overthrew the pro-Western King and Prime Minister. The U.S. Sixth Fleet was dispatched to the eastern Mediterranean and Marines and other U.S. forces were landed at Beirut to separate the combatants.

USIA played an active—and highly successful—role both within and outside Lebanon in justifying the U.S. action. The Pentagon's psychological warriors were put under the direction of USIS-Beirut, and an intensive campaign was waged to convince Lebanese of all political and religious faiths that the Americans were there only to help restore peace and would leave when the need was over. Ducking stray bullets, the USIS staff produced pamphlets, newspaper articles, and radio broadcasts for internal use, and generated columns of copy for dissemination abroad. U.S. Air Force planes dropped a million USIS leaflets over isolated Lebanese villages.

The Agency brought in newspapermen from all over Asia and the Middle East to see the situation for themselves; one originally hostile Indian editor went home converted and headlined his editorial "U.S. in Lebanon: By Invitation, Not Intervention." As it would later in Vietnam, USIS handled press relations for the military and held twice-daily press briefings.

The Voice of America tripled its broadcasts to the Middle East, carrying thirty minutes of news in Arabic on the half-hour and in English on the hour, twenty-four hours a day. VOA broadcast UN General Assembly sessions on the crisis, canceling all other programs during the debate. When Soviet jamming of the UN broadcasts became intense, the Voice let the world hear, through recordings of VOA as it was received in Moscow, how the Russians were keeping their people from learning what was going on. The U.S. Army supplied a transmitter and USIA supplied the programs for a strengthened Radio Beirut.

With the insurrection ended and a new Lebanese President peacefully chosen, U.S. forces departed in October. Thanks in part to USIA, it was one of the few military interventions in modern history that was not widely denounced.

The U.S.-Soviet cultural exchanges agreement was renewed, and in the summer of 1959 there was a dramatic "first" in American-Russian relations: the U.S. National Exhibition in Moscow, which, in the Agency's words, "transported ten acres of America to the heart of the Russian capital for six weeks." It was a counterpart to a Soviet exhibition in New York. Three million Russians toured the display at Sokolniki Park.

Allen was coordinator of the exhibition, and USIA helped plan and staff it. The Agency provided a Walt Disney film, *Circarama,* which was the most popular attraction. USIA also prepared three thousand questions and answers in Russian for Ramac, an electronic "brain" which visitors plied with questions. It was in a model home at the exhibit that Nixon had his famous "kitchen debate" with Khrushchev; although there was some question as to who came out ahead, the Agency sent verbatim texts of the exchange to all its field posts.

When Khrushchev came to the United States in 1959, the Soviets ended their jamming of the Voice of America. After he left, the jamming was resumed only selectively. And jamming was one of the topics discussed when Eisenhower, Khrushchev, and their advisers met at the Presidential retreat Camp David near Washington. Soviet Foreign Minister Gromyko proposed that each nation limit its broadcasting to the other to three hours daily, in order to reduce tensions. Allen replied that such an agreement would be contrary to America's policy of spreading information, not limiting it, and the U.S. did not care if the Soviets broadcast twenty-four hours a day.

The Soviets then indicated they would stop their jamming if VOA would eliminate its "hostile and provocative" broadcasts. Allen denied that the Voice broadcasts could be so characterized. "We just broadcast the straight news and comment on it," he explained. The Soviets were not convinced, but, for a few months at least, their jamming was greatly reduced.

The talks resulted in Eisenhower's agreeing to visit the U.S.S.R. the following spring and to go once more to the "summit" with Khrushchev. Soviet propagandists made much of what they called "the spirit of Camp David," but USIA cautiously reminded its audiences that there had been "few tangible results." Khrushchev had, for the moment, removed his threat to end the presence of Western forces in Berlin, but after he returned home the Communist-aligned Pathet Lao in Laos intensified their rebellion. "There is," the Agency concluded, "no grounds for a relaxation of the free world's vigilance in the absence of concrete Communist actions."

U-2 and the "Prestige" Polls

That vigilance was part military, part ideological, part diplomatic—and part photographic. In 1954 CIA, with the approval of the President, had begun the supersecret development of a high-altitude, special-performance photoreconnaissance aircraft, the U-2. The work was intensified after the Soviets turned down Eisenhower's "open skies" inspection scheme in 1955, and U-2 flights over the U.S.S.R. began in 1956 to gather intelligence on Soviet military capabilities. Presumably the Russians knew the planes were there, but they had no way of reaching them at their high altitudes. So Moscow fumed in private and worked on its antiaircraft capability.

The summit meeting was scheduled for May 16, 1960, in Paris. On May 1 Eisenhower was informed by his military aide that a U-2 was missing over Russia; the next morning the news was confirmed. A National Aeronautics and Space Administration information officer, unaware of the true mission of the U-2, announced that the plane, "being flown in Turkey on a joint NASA-USAF Air Weather Service mission, apparently went down in the Lake Van, Turkey, area [after] experiencing oxygen difficulties." Then on May 5 Khrushchev informed the Supreme Soviet that an American reconnaissance plane had been shot down deep within Soviet territory.

Eisenhower had been assured that a U-2 would disintegrate if it ran into trouble, either from its inherent fragility or from a self-destruction mechanism. After Khrushchev made his announcement, the President conferred with those few senior diplomatic, military, and intelligence officials who were aware of the U-2 operation—but not with Allen of USIA, who might have been able to warn him of the propaganda pitfalls. Eisenhower was persuaded that the State Department should immediately issue a statement that would reconcile the NASA release with Khrushchev's announcement by claiming that the plane may have "accidentally" drifted into Soviet air space after the pilot lost consciousness due to a failure in the oxygen equipment. The statement was issued, and America walked right into the trap that Khrushchev had set.

The next day Khrushchev angrily announced to the Supreme Soviet that America had deliberately lied, that the plane was on an espionage mission, that its pilot—Francis Gary Powers—and equipment were intact in Soviet hands, and that Powers had confessed to the real nature of his assignment. Photographs of Powers and fragments of the plane were put on public display.

That was bad enough, but then Washington made it worse. First, the State Department—still without consulting USIA—lamely stuck with the cover story, though by this time it covered nothing. Then, on May 7, with Eisenhower's approval, it issued still another statement, reversing itself. The true mission of the U-2 was admitted and Presidential responsibility acknowledged, although the statement carefully pointed out that specific missions had not been subject to Presidential authorization. This effort to take Eisenhower off the hook backfired; foreigners and Americans alike were incredulous that the CIA or the Pentagon could on its own approve espionage operations that might jeopardize the forthcoming summit meeting and possibly even world peace.

Eisenhower canceled future U-2 flights over Soviet territory and on May 14 took off for the summit meeting in Paris. Waiting when he arrived was a copy of a message from Khrushchev to De Gaulle saying he would not attend the meeting unless the American President would denounce the U-2 flights as irresponsible provocation, renounce all future flights, and punish those responsible for the operation. This was, of course, unacceptable, and Khrushchev broke up the meeting shortly after it convened with a long diatribe against the United States. He canceled his invitation to Eisenhower to visit the Soviet Union that spring.

The propaganda consequences of the U-2 affair and the abortive summit meeting were mixed. The United States in general and its President in particular were made to look silly, and that was bad. But Allied and neutral nations were impressed and relieved to know that the United States had an effective method of keeping watch over Soviet military preparations, and that was good. They hoped that we would find it possible to continue our surveillance.*

Although the United States knew from its 1955 experience that summit meetings had more impact on propaganda than on policy, USIA played no role in preparations for the 1960 meeting. A special interdepartmental committee, under the direction of a high State Department official, was established to prepare for the conference, but USIA was not included. Only a few days before everything was settled —and that at the tardy direct orders of Secretary of State Herter— was a USIA representative allowed to sit in on the discussions, "not as a participant but as a tolerated observer."24

There is no evidence that Eisenhower would have been better advised had he counseled with USIA on U-2 and the summit. But these were major psychological problems, and the Agency's expertise should have been brought to bear on them. Allen, however, with his narrow concept of USIA's role, was undisturbed. Nor was he bothered by the fact that the official Voice of America had continued to use the U-2 cover story even after Khrushchev had exposed it. "Why not?" he remarked later. "AP and UPI were also using the 'weather plane' story, and our coverage should always be the same as theirs."

When the U-2 furor broke, the Russians resumed full-scale jamming of VOA's broadcasts in Soviet-bloc languages, though not in

---

* In fact, we already had. Unpublicized space satellites were already beginning to do the U-2 job; Eisenhower gave up little or nothing when he canceled U-2 flights over the U.S.S.R. When satellites were mentioned by De Gaulle at the brief summit session, Khrushchev said he was talking about airplanes, not satellites; he had, he claimed, no objection to satellite reconnaissance over his country. Kennedy later put U.S. space reconnaissance under deep secrecy wraps, partly on the grounds that if we did not talk about it, the Russians would not feel obliged to make an issue of it—since they could do nothing about it.

English. But in the pages of USIA's *Amerika* magazine, the Russian people met Eisenhower secondhand, if not in person. Anticipating the President's trip, the May issue had been largely devoted to Eisenhower. The American Embassy in Moscow noted that it aroused more interest than any previous edition of the magazine; at the very moment that Khrushchev was denouncing Eisenhower to the Supreme Soviet, a crowd of Muscovites was seen buying copies at a kiosk in the National Hotel opposite the Kremlin.

As always, the Presidential campaign provided grist for the Agency's mills that year. Recognizing that many foreigners were apprehensive about what a change in the White House might mean, USIA played up the good qualities of both candidates—Vice President Nixon and Senator Kennedy—and stressed (without being wholly accurate) that, no matter who was elected, the basic policies and objectives of the United States would remain unchanged.

After the Larson fiasco in 1957, Allen had done a good job of keeping USIA out of partisan controversy, but through no fault of his the Agency was caught in the midst of campaign crossfire in the fall of 1960. Nixon said that American prestige was at an all-time high after eight years of Republican rule; Kennedy charged that U.S. prestige had declined and that there were USIA polls to prove it.

In mid-October, after Kennedy had repeated the charge, Senator Fulbright telephoned Oren Stephens, head of the Research and Reference Service which directed USIA's polling operations, and asked to see the Agency's recent polls. On instructions from Allen (which originated in the White House), Stephens refused. The poll results were classified, he said, and although Fulbright was cleared to receive classified data, there was also a matter of executive privilege involved.

Fulbright berated Stephens on the telephone, then called a press conference at which he recounted his conversation with Stephens and denounced him for withholding information. Fulbright then wrote Allen, asking for the poll findings, and was turned down on the same grounds. Allen told Fulbright he thought the Agency should be kept out of partisan politics and that civil servants should be able to write and report their views freely within the government without fear of publicity or adverse reactions from their superiors.

Next, Congressman John Moss of California, a crusader for freedom of information (and also a Democrat), wrote Allen demanding permission to examine the Agency's files on polls. He, too, was denied the poll results.

Since Nixon was saying that USIA polls supported his contention that American prestige had never been higher, Kennedy challenged him to prove his influence with the Administration by getting them released. Nothing happened. Then Myer Feldman, a Kennedy aide, obtained several of the Agency surveys from a friend in the State Department. Their findings generally supported Kennedy's position. So he could quote them without being charged with improperly obtaining classified information, Kennedy turned the polls over to the *New York Times,* which published them on October 27 and 29.[25]

The first of the two surveys was entitled "Post-Summit Trends in British and French Public Opinion," and it did not make pleasant reading for Administration supporters. The second, even more damaging to Nixon, was entitled "World Reaction to U.S. and Soviet Space Accomplishments," and included both polling results and foreign press comment.

The "leaked" surveys were given wide publicity, prompting Eisenhower's Special Assistant, Wilton B. (Jerry) Persons, to request—and then demand—that Allen issue a statement saying USIA polls showed American prestige had never been higher. Allen, who was already planning to depart after the election, categorically refused. Eisenhower was infuriated, but Allen would not give ground. The furor ended on election day with Kennedy's narrow victory.

The unpleasantness with the White House on the "prestige" issue left a bad taste in Allen's mouth, but it had nothing to do with his departure from USIA. A career diplomat in a job for which he had no overriding enthusiasm anyway, Allen wanted to move on to other things, and it was likely that the new President would want his own man in any case. Shortly after election day, Allen announced his resignation to become president of the Tobacco Institute and departed on November 30.

Allen was good for USIA in his three years as Director. He greatly improved relations with Congress after the Larson fiasco, and also with the State Department, which was happy to have one of its own running the Agency. He strengthened USIA's long-range cultural operations and improved the Voice of America's credibility. Inside and outside the government, USIA's reputation for professionalism had justifiably improved.

He would have been more effective had he believed that the Agency should persuade, not just inform. He was America's chief propagandist, but he did not believe in propaganda.

5 *American Propaganda Comes of Age*

In the winter of 1960-61, normally blasé Washington was charged with an air of unsuppressed excitement. The White House had changed hands many times before, and with it the leadership of the departments and agencies of the national government, but this time there seemed to be a special newness to the new.

John F. Kennedy was the first President born in this century. He was the youngest man ever elected to the job. He was the first Catholic President. And he had made clear, in his campaign speeches and in his stirring Inaugural Address, that his Administration would take a new look at the old problems of Cold War and fragile peace.

Perhaps more than any other successful politician in American history, Kennedy had taken advantage of the communications media to rise from obscurity to instant identification. Himself a onetime journalist who numbered journalists among his best friends, he understood better than most the power of the press and the potential of television for mass persuasion. He was determined to use them abroad for national purposes as he had used them at home for personal political purposes.

Kennedy inherited from Eisenhower an information agency which, although far stronger than it had been eight years before, was still troubled by uncertainty about its mission, hostility or indifference in Congress and the State Department, and a too rapid turnover of leadership. But the new President also inherited a just-completed reappraisal of the goals and requirements of American propaganda that would help him in revitalizing USIA.

117

Thirteen months before he left the White House, Eisenhower had appointed a Committee on Information Activities Abroad, headed by New York industrialist Mansfield D. Sprague. The group included the Directors of USIA and CIA, an Under Secretary of State, several other top officials, and a few prominent businessmen. They consulted experts in and out of government, and—twenty-eight days before the end of the Republican Administration—submitted their report. For the most part, it made good sense.

At the heart of the report was the recommendation that the President "reaffirm" to all departments "the importance of adequately considering foreign opinion factors in the formulation of policies and the execution of programs which have impact abroad."* But Eisenhower, in a letter to Sprague acknowledging the report, said merely that "it is my hope that all agencies and departments will continue to take appropriate organizational and training measures to this end," although in fact few if any such measures were being taken.

The committee made a number of thoughtful recommendations, among them: an expanded exchange-of-persons program tied to "advancing the foreign policy objectives of the United States"; full consideration of "the psychological potentialities of foreign aid programs"; expanded USIA programs in Latin America and Africa; more information to and contact with the Soviet bloc; more publication of American books overseas; and more and better research and training.[2]

One of the strongest Sprague recommendations, firmly endorsed by Eisenhower, was rejected almost immediately by his successor. The committee praised Eisenhower's creation of the Operations Coordinating Board in 1953 as "a major step forward" insofar "as information activities are concerned." But Kennedy abolished the OCB, vesting some of its functions in himself, some in his White House staff, some in the State Department, and some in the Director of USIA.

The Sprague Committee's approval of the OCB was due in part to

---

* Columnist Roscoe Drummond called this a "superbly heretical" notion. "The highest officials of the United States Government, especially State Department officials and career Foreign Service Officers, have been paying polite lip-service 'to the factor of public opinion in foreign policy' and have simultaneously been excluding from the councils of policy decision everybody qualified to weigh the factor of public opinion in making such decisions," he wrote. "This, the Committee finds, has been the fatal weakness of the United States Information program."[1]

enthusiasm for the OCB among most USIA officials, who saw it as the only continuing mechanism whereby the Agency was regularly consulted on policy. Some apprehension was felt in USIA when the new President wiped it out, although Kennedy's explanation was reassuring: "Insofar as the OCB—as a descendant of the old Psychological Strategy Board—was concerned with the impact of our actions on foreign opinion, on our 'image' abroad, we expect its work to be done in a number of ways: in my office, in the State Department, under Mr. Murrow of USIA, and by all who are concerned with the spirit and meaning of our actions in foreign policy."[3]

Long before the campaign debates over American prestige, Kennedy had come to appreciate the foreign information program. I first met him in 1954, while on home leave from a USIA assignment in Lebanon, and found him remarkably well informed on the Agency. During the Eisenhower Administration he was an understanding supporter of USIA, even when the Information Agency might have been —and was for some other Democrats—an easy, partisan target.

Accepting the Presidential nomination, Kennedy asked Americans: "Can we carry through in an age where we will witness not only new breakthroughs in weapons of destruction but also a race for mastery of the sky and the rain, the ocean and the tides, the far side of space and the *inside of men's minds?*" If he won, much of the answer would lie in his hands. He was determined to be prepared.

Kennedy arranged for two of Adlai Stevenson's associates to set up task forces on various aspects of foreign affairs. The teams were quickly organized after the election by the able and amiable George W. Ball, later Under Secretary of State, and John H. Sharon. Their reports covered a somewhat unrelated collection of problems and policies: Africa, disarmament, foreign economic policy, State Department operations, and the U.S. Information Agency. Lloyd Free, a former Agency official who headed the Institute for International Social Research, was put in charge of the USIA study.

There were other studies of the Agency, too. Through my brother Ted, who was Kennedy's principal aide and Special Counsel-designate, the President-elect asked me to do a "one-man task force" report. Still another survey of the Agency was done by Donald M. Wilson, the incoming Administration's "advance" man in USIA for seven weeks prior to the inauguration. The Sprague study, the Ball-Sharon report, my recommendations, and those of Don Wilson all had an impact on the shaping of USIA in the Kennedy Administration. The four reports generally agreed with each other, and in basic principles did not stray far from the recommendations of the Jackson Committee eight years earlier.

The Ball-Sharon-Free task force recommended, as did Wilson and I, that USIA remain an independent agency reporting directly to the President. We agreed that the Director of USIA should be the principal "psychological" adviser to the Executive Branch on foreign policy and continue to participate in meetings of the National Security Council.

The task force made one major recommendation that was not accepted because, like the OCB, it was contrary to Kennedy's notions of departmental responsibility. This was a proposal that the President establish under NSC a "Committee on Information and Exchange Policy" to "infuse psychological considerations . . . into the formulation and execution" of policy, "develop long-range psychological objectives" for all the foreign affairs agencies, "anticipate" Communist moves, and assess—and devise ways of increasing—U.S. prestige abroad. The task force argued that these functions could not be effectively performed by any one agency because they "require a coordinated effort by a number of agencies which can only be assured structurally through the formation of a board or committee." But in the Kennedy Administration USIA carried out these functions, or tried to.

The Ball-Sharon task force also recommended that the cultural programs of the State Department and the trade fair operations of the Commerce Department be transferred to USIA, and that the Agency be renamed the "International Exchange Agency" or the "United States Cultural Exchange Agency." Wilson and I also recommended that these functions be put into USIA, although we did not suggest a change in name.* But no changes in function or name were accepted.

The task force also urged that USIA arrange to make the commercial American wire services more available abroad; increase distribution of U.S. books and magazines overseas "at competitive

---

* The Eisenhower Administration had proposed changing the Agency's name to the "United States Information *Service*" on the grounds that this would eliminate the confusion caused by the fact that USIA's overseas offices are known as USIS, not USIA.

prices"; increase assistance to English-teaching in foreign institutions; "assume responsibility for arranging and conducting suitable Independence Day celebrations abroad"; request from Congress an "emergency contingency fund" of $100 million; double its research expenditures; and get Congress to approve a career service for USIA employees.

Recognizing that "we cannot put a good face on unsound or inadequate policies or unwise actions by information or cultural operations," the task force argued that "the decline in U.S. prestige can be arrested only by more dynamic Presidential leadership, a much clearer sense of our national purposes, sound substantive policies and better coordinated programs." Specifically, the report recommended that the U.S. "adopt a posture . . . more positive than mere anti-communism"; identify itself with the "revolution of rising expectations"; "come to terms with the spirit of nationalism (and concomitant feelings about racism)" in the Afro-Asian countries; and "do a more effective and imaginative job of waging the psychological war against Communism behind the Iron Curtain."[4]

Wilson's report was the briefest and the most quickly prepared; he had only two weeks for intensive study. Given his prior lack of knowledge about the Agency, Wilson's report to Kennedy showed considerable perception. In addition to organizational recommendations already mentioned, Wilson suggested: an increased effort in Africa, with emphasis on English-language teaching and contacts with African students in Europe; greater attention to an "inadequate" Latin-American program, with emphasis on work with student and labor groups; and a "full scale science program" to make up for "how badly we have failed in translating the great achievements of U.S. science to the world."

Wilson also noted USIA's perennial need "to recruit better people." The Agency could compete better with private industry, he said, if the President would take "official notice of USIA's most outstanding activities" and participate "occasionally . . . in some of USIA's most original and dramatic operations."[5] As it turned out, President Kennedy was the Agency's star performer for three years.

My report to the President-elect recommended that "all overseas psychological (information, cultural, educational) operations" of the government be merged into one organization which would "take its policy guidance from the State Department but . . . be independently administered. . . . This organization should be the overseas psychological instrument of the U.S. Government."

In a survey of immediate needs, I argued for greater flexibility to permit USIA "to commit resources where urgently needed without neglecting other areas." Noting the "emergence of national aspirations in Africa and nationalistic tendencies in Latin America, both with anti-American overtones," I suggested much larger programs on those two continents without neglecting the crisis areas of Southeast Asia, India, or Germany. "The requirements in one spot should not be sacrificed as the pendulum of crisis swings to another."

The most important recommendation, in my mind, dealt with the long-debated role of the Agency. I told Kennedy that I thought USIA's purpose should be to persuade, not merely to inform; that the Agency should be charged with furthering the achievement of U.S. foreign policy objectives by "promoting climates of opinion abroad that will enhance the prospects of achieving these objectives through diplomatic means" and by "advising the President and the State Department on the reactions of foreign peoples to, and the consequences of, proposed U.S. policies, programs and official statements."

Between election and inauguration, Kennedy worked part of the time at his father's winter residence in Palm Beach, Florida, and part of the time at his own home in Washington's Georgetown district. In early Jaunary I was summoned to Georgetown to discuss my recommendations.

Kennedy again demonstrated his excellent grasp of the purposes and problems of USIA. (Although he did not comment directly on my thoughts regarding the role of the Agency, when he later wrote a new Statement of Mission for USIA to replace the 1953 Eisenhower document he made clear he subscribed to the same concepts.) However, he told me flatly that, whatever the merits of the case, Senator Fulbright would not stand for USIA absorption of the State Department's educational and exchange programs and no organizational changes of that nature would be made.

Murrow and the "Troika"

The President-elect read aloud the section on the qualities I thought a new USIA Director and Deputy Director should bring to their jobs:

Experience in world affairs and knowledge of foreign peoples . . . Should comprehend the "revolution of rising expectations" throughout the world, and its impact on U.S. foreign policy . . . Pragmatic, open-minded and sensitive to international political currents, without being naïve. Understand the potentialities of propaganda while being aware of its limitations . . .

Kennedy asked if I could suggest the names of any men who met these exacting standards. I confessed to having few ideas but mentioned several names, one of which was Edward R. Murrow, the distinguished news broadcaster. I would like to claim credit for Murrow's subsequent appointment as Director of USIA, but cannot. He was an obvious choice; others who carried more weight than I with Kennedy recommended him, and the new President had a high regard for Murrow although he did not know him well.

The Southern liberal editor and author Jonathan Daniels was considered for the job, and Kennedy felt out Dr. Frank Stanton, president of the Columbia Broadcasting System, who turned it down. A few days after inauguration, he offered the post to Murrow, who promptly accepted. Kennedy then nominated Wilson to be Deputy Director.

When Wilson and I asked Murrow why he took a 90 percent cut in pay to become a $21,000-a-year bureaucrat, he replied simply: "I just figured that if this young man couldn't do it, no one could, and if he wants me to help, I have an obligation to do it." Later Murrow told another friend: "I had been criticizing bureaucrats all my adult life, and it was my turn to try."

Murrow was born in Greensboro, North Carolina, but at an early age moved with his family to the Pacific Northwest. As a teen-ager he worked for a logging company and retained a lifelong appreciation of beautiful wood. Christened Egbert Roscoe Murrow, he changed his name to Edward to avoid (as he later put it) "having to fight every lumberjack on the West Coast—not that I couldn't have licked them!" He was graduated from Washington State College in 1930, serving (from 1929 to 1932) as president of the National Student Federation. He headed the foreign offices of the Institute of International Education before joining CBS as Director of Talks and Education in 1935.

Except for Kennedy himself and Adlai Stevenson, Murrow was the best-known member of the incoming Administration. After twenty-five years of broadcasting and telecasting for CBS, his name, face, and resonant voice were familiar to nearly every American household. Murrow had rushed to Vienna in 1938 to tell the world of Hitler's annexation of Austria, and subsequently had put together in Europe one of the great reportorial teams of U.S. journalism.

He had stood among the falling bombs of the Battle of London in 1940-41 to arouse an apathetic, confused America to the challenge of Adolf Hitler. His crisp broadcasts of suppressed emotion, opening with "This [pause] is London," were unforgettable to all who heard them. Murrow became a confidant of Churchill and Roosevelt, and was at the White House on Pearl Harbor day. FDR considered naming him to head OWI. As a war correspondent, Murrow insisted on being where the action was, and hitchhiked along on some of the most dangerous bombing runs over Germany.

After the war Murrow served briefly as a CBS vice president before returning to active journalism, giving rise to the myth that he was a poor administrator. He successfully switched from radio to television and became even more celebrated with his penetrating *See It Now* and *CBS Reports* documentaries and lighter interviews on *Person to Person*. His postwar commentaries focused attention on the enemies at home: prejudice, poverty, and McCarthyism. Some called him America's conscience.

The intense, brooding Murrow was a confirmed skeptic, but no cynic. He understood communications; he understood America; he understood the world. He was known and trusted everywhere. Few Americans had his credentials of credibility.

A sensitive and sometimes sentimental man of deep but usually well-disguised emotion, Murrow suffered over important decisions but was always able to make them and, once made, live with them. In 1964, when he was awarded the Presidential Medal of Freedom, his citation summed up his life: "He has brought to all his endeavors the conviction that truth and personal integrity are the ultimate persuaders of men and nations."

Some years later, Vice President Hubert Humphrey described Murrow as "one of the most selfless celebrities of our generation. In both broadcasting and government—two public professions in which there is no surplus of modesty—he remained to the end a totally unpretentious person." Humphrey recalled that when "something close to a Murrow cult began to emerge" at CBS, a network official felt it was going too far and "announced that he was forming a 'Murrow Isn't God Club.' Ed promptly wrote to him and applied for a charter membership."

Humphrey also recalled that when a "fellow broadcaster was attacked by a group of super-patriots" and "found himself on one of TV's infamous blacklists," Murrow gave the man $7,500 to hire a lawyer, remarking, "I'm not making a personal loan to you; I am investing this money in America."[6]

In the several years prior to his appointment as USIA Director, Murrow had become increasingly restive at CBS. He took a year's "sabbatical" and went around the world, but the frustrations remained. "There had seemed to be gathering within him a searing disgust" with television and his role in it, historian Arthur Schlesinger, Jr. wrote later. "He was a harrowed, gloomy presence at New York dinners, punctuating his incessant cigarettes with brief and bitter cracks and leaving the impression that all idealism in the world had vanished with the Battle of Britain."

Murrow had a low opinion of the Eisenhower Administration, and especially of Vice President Nixon, but throughout much of 1960 he also remained skeptical of John F. Kennedy—in part because of Kennedy's ambiguous record on McCarthyism, in part because of his low regard for the Senator's father, former Ambassador to London Joseph P. Kennedy.

According to Schlesinger, Murrow "had no faith at all at this time in Kennedy," saying on one occasion that "if McCarthyism seemed to Kennedy's advantage, Kennedy would become a McCarthyite overnight." Early in the campaign, Murrow interviewed the young candidate for CBS and was not impressed. At one point, Murrow asked Kennedy why he thought at his age he was qualified to be President. Annoyed by the question, Kennedy responded in a manner Murrow thought arrogant.

As the campaign progressed, however, Murrow's confidence in Kennedy grew. He was deeply impressed by the President-elect's "farewell to Massachusetts" and Inaugural Addresses. By the time he arrived in Washington in late January, he was full of enthusiasm for Kennedy, the new Administration, and his own job. As Schlesinger put it: "Kennedy gave Murrow his full confidence; no government information chief . . . had been so close to a President; and Murrow, the professional doubter, at last had found someone since Churchill in whose intelligence and purpose he could wholeheartedly believe."[7]

Ed Murrow came to Washington three months before his fifty-third birthday. He was ten years older than the President and slightly sensitive about his age. He need not have been; Murrow worked longer and harder than most of his colleagues in a hard-working administration, and his younger subordinates had to scramble to keep up with him.

Murrow liked his office cool, kept the air conditioner going summer and winter, and even then received all visitors—from elegant foreign ministers to lowly messengers—in his shirt sleeves. A surprisingly shy man, taciturn and uncomfortable among strangers, he let his visitors do most of the talking while he sat head bowed, sucking audibly on the ever-present cigarette, an occasional brilliant smile illuminating his normally gloomy face. Murrow mostly shunned the exuberant party life of the New Frontier, finding his social pleasures in swapping yarns with old comrades over Scotch and water (but no ice).

It is not unusual for high-ranking new appointees, especially in a new administration, to bring with them their own coteries of assistants and secretaries. Murrow brought no one. Although he had known me only a few weeks, in mid-February, 1961, he appointed me Deputy Director (Policy and Plans), the third-ranking post in the Agency. (The top two positions in USIA are filled by the President.) We had worked together intensively but unofficially those few weeks, mostly discussing the implications of the various studies of USIA, and Murrow said he wanted me to continue to advise him "on policy and plans, and everything else around here for that matter," on a formal basis.

Wilson had recommended me for the job, but I had not expected to get it. I was young (not quite thirty-five) and a middle-grade Agency officer outranked in grade, years, and experience by scores of others. I told Murrow there would be some grumbling in the Agency (and there was), and some would think I was foisted on him by the White House where my brother was the President's principal aide (and some did). Murrow replied that the White House had said nothing to him about me, except to give him my study of USIA with Kennedy's general endorsement. Murrow subsequently obtained the President's approval of my appointment, and told a USIA staff meeting that "I would have chosen Sorensen even if he were *my* brother!"

Don Wilson, Kennedy's selection to be Murrow's first deputy, was also young (thirty-five) but brought to his new job broad foreign and domestic experience as a correspondent for *Time* and *Life* magazines. He took a leave of absence as head of *Life*'s Washington bureau to be a press aide in the Kennedy campaign, and came to USIA with the confidence and high esteem of the new President, an invaluable asset to an agency long the stepchild of the Executive Branch. Wilson was well known and trusted by the Washington press corps, and this, too, proved to be an important asset.

Murrow called the three of us the "troika" (the Russians, at the time, were trying to impose a three-man "troika" rule on the UN Secretariat), although some less reverent staff members used less charitable descriptions such as "the unholy trinity." Murrow ran the Agency and we never forgot it, but he liked to discuss all major problems and decisions with Wilson and me, and he preferred to have us direct the staff work that formed the basis for his decisions. The three of us soon developed a warm personal relationship which lasted throughout the Murrow years.

Murrow and the Kennedys

As Director of USIA, Murrow had to operate in four arenas: in his own twelve-thousand-man Agency; in the Executive Branch (mostly the White House, the Bureau of the Budget, and the Departments of State, Defense, and Commerce, but also the National Aeronautics and Space Agency, the Labor Department, and others); in the Congress, particularly the Appropriations Committees; and in American public opinion. There were long-standing difficulties and potential pitfalls in each of them, and Murrow moved cautiously but firmly to improve the Agency's position and the effectiveness of its operations.

Fortunately, Kennedy had a realistic idea of what could and could not be accomplished through propaganda. He believed in the tool, but he recognized, as he said in one speech, that "it is a dangerous illusion to believe that the policies of the United States . . . can be encompassed in one slogan or adjective, hard or soft or otherwise." On another occasion he said: "If we are strong, our strength will speak for itself. If we are weak, words will be of no help."

Still, Kennedy was acutely aware of the power of words, and particularly of the power of words uttered by the President of the United States and heard around the world. He came increasingly to depend on advice from his Director of USIA. By nature reticent, Murrow often had to be pressed for his views. Mary McGrory of the Washington *Star,* in a perceptive essay after his death, noted that "at the White House, this quality was prized. In a field of rampaging egos, Murrow was conspicuously self-effacing." She quoted McGeorge Bundy, the White House foreign policy adviser, as recalling "that Murrow never once asked to go to a meeting. In time he never had to ask. President Kennedy increasingly said: 'Let's find out what Ed thinks' or 'Be sure Murrow is here.' "

Miss McGrory wrote that

Kennedy's regard for Murrow's always solicited advice began during the period of the Bay of Pigs. Too late to stop that fatal course, Murrow heard what was afoot and compellingly and eloquently spoke out against it. "Yet," says one witness, "no one ever heard him say he had tried to prevent it. He worked harder than anyone to pick up the broken china." . . . "He never fought a problem," says Bundy. "He never tried to impose himself on it."[8]

Much better known than his colleagues in the Administration, and with an already established reputation, Murrow could have—and perhaps in some instances should have—imposed himself. In retrospect, Wilson and I believe he should have spoken up more often. But he did not, and it would have been contrary to his nature had he done so.

As the months passed, Kennedy's appreciation of both Murrow and USIA grew. The President required all government agencies to report to him weekly in writing; he did not read every agency's report every week (although someone in the White House did), but a special telephone on Murrow's desk (he called it the "blowtorch") rang increasingly often with Presidential queries about items in USIA's report or some other matter. Kennedy was particularly interested in

Agency surveys of foreign opinion, and often asked for full texts of the studies, or information on what people in Country X were thinking about Problem Y. The President's calls and other signs of interest were welcomed throughout the Agency as evidence that USIA was at last in the mainstream of American foreign affairs.

Kennedy's and Murrow's mutual respect grew into mutual affection. In 1962, at a private dinner at the White House, Kennedy suggested that Murrow consider seeking the New York Democratic gubernatorial nomination. Although he had little enthusiasm for incumbent Republican Nelson Rockefeller and no fear of a hard fight, Murrow demurred on two counts: he wanted to finish the job at USIA, which had been plagued by a too rapid turnover of directors; and he believed (possibly correctly) that his shyness would make him a disaster on the back-slapping, handshaking campaign circuit. Kennedy did not press the matter.

Murrow's relationship with the President's brother and principal adviser, Attorney General Robert F. Kennedy, was equally cordial, but it took longer to develop. Murrow's original doubts about John Kennedy, stemming from the McCarthy period, were even more applicable to brother Bobby, who had been on the McCarthy committee staff and who had publicly defended the Wisconsin Senator. In 1955, when Bob Kennedy was picked by the Junior Chamber of Commerce as one of "the nation's ten outstanding young men," Murrow spoke at the award dinner in Louisville on the abuses of Congressional investigations—and young Kennedy left the room during the speech. Bobby, in 1961, still wondered whether Murrow was one of those "reflex" liberals whom—in those days, particularly—he distrusted and disliked.

As the two observed each other in the new Administration, however, they developed a healthy mutual respect. Murrow attended sessions of the "Hickory Hill Seminar," the informal discussion group held at Kennedy's home with Cabinet members and other New Frontier eminences as participants. Don Wilson's close relations with both men also helped bridge the gap. Murrow was impressed by the soundness of Bobby's advice to his brother and liked his impatience with mediocrity. The younger Kennedy appreciated Murrow's loyalty and good judgment.

Normally it would not matter what the relations were between the

Attorney General and the Director of USIA. In this instance, however, they were important. As a Presidential confidant and trouble-shooter, Robert Kennedy played an important role in foreign policy. His trips abroad contributed much to foreign understanding of the United States, particularly among young people, whom Kennedy deliberately sought out. The Attorney General and Murrow worked together in developing programs of youth activity and counterinsurgency. They found themselves allied against the apathetic, cynical, or overly conventional elements in the State Department that automatically reacted negatively to new ideas. Unquestionably, Robert Kennedy's support helped make possible Murrow's success.*

But, despite the Kennedy brothers' understanding of the uses of the Agency (an understanding that was shared by most of the White House staff), there was little more comprehension of USIA's role in the departments and agencies than there had been under Eisenhower or Truman. Kennedy's view of USIA was nominally accepted, in some cases grudgingly, elsewhere in the Executive Branch. But real interest and understanding were lacking. Secretary of State Dean Rusk was no exception. He liked and respected Murrow, partly because USIA never gave him any trouble, but he never really understood or much cared what Murrow and his Agency were trying to do. In turn, Rusk often puzzled Murrow. "I don't understand that man; I just don't understand him," Murrow would occasionally mutter to Wilson and me. But Rusk's Assistant Secretaries for Public Affairs were usually understanding and always helpful.

Murrow sometimes found it necessary to go over departmental heads to the White House. On those occasions Bundy was unfailingly helpful, whether he agreed with USIA's position or not. One such discussion in June, 1963, was recorded by Murrow in a memorandum to Wilson and me:

. . . I opened by saying I did not believe the Agency could operate effectively or efficiently unless we were able to plan by participating in policy-making decisions, and I instanced troop reduction in western Europe, arms

---

* Nonetheless, in the summer of 1964 the dying Murrow declined to endorse Robert Kennedy's bid for the Democratic Senatorial nomination in New York. Murrow thought it truly was "carpetbagging," and he was influenced also by his friendship with incumbent Republican Kenneth Keating and an instinctive sympathy for the underdog.

aid to India and Pakistan, and our lack of information regarding planning in connection with Haiti, as examples.

Bundy said . . . the best way to solve the problem regarding not only State but ACDA and AID was for him to act as the pivot, and that I should feel entirely free to query him at any hour. . . . He urged me not to be reluctant to bother him, again insisting that he recognized the importance of our job, its difficulties, and the skill with which it was being done.

Adlai Stevenson was less understanding. Murrow and Stevenson were old friends, and the latter had no quarrel with the Agency, but he never really grasped how USIA could help him at the United Nations. As a forum of world opinion the UN offered unparalleled opportunities for USIA exploitation, and Murrow assigned several men full time to the U.S. Mission to keep the Agency advised on what would happen next in the Security Council, the General Assembly, and the several committees. Stevenson, however, had his own public affairs adviser—the able Clayton Fritchey—and did not bother to take the USIA people into his confidence even though Fritchey's attention was devoted almost entirely to the American press.

Murrow and Johnson

Vice President Lyndon B. Johnson's skepticism about the Agency dated back to when he was chairman of the Senate Appropriations Subcommittee that considered USIA budgets. Although he and Murrow shared a roughly common political philosophy, they otherwise were as different as two men could be. Unlike Johnson, Murrow was shy, given to understatement, thick-skinned to criticism, and uninterested in bureaucratic perquisites. The two had never been particularly fond of each other, and the lack of mutual esteem came to the surface when they were thrown together in the Kennedy Administration.

Murrow was vexed by what he (and others) considered thoughtless if not arrogant behavior by the restless, underemployed Vice President on his several trips abroad: Johnson's special demands for a particular brand of Scotch, a particular type of shower fixture, and a particular size of bed; his sudden rages at aides and U.S. Embassy personnel; his haggling over purchases; his erection of a plywood partition in the Istanbul Hilton to separate him from others in his party; his vocal preoccupation with the size of crowds; and many more incidents that were quickly reported back to Washington by word of mouth.

Johnson, for his part, was understandably concerned with the foreign and domestic press coverage he was getting on the trips, and blamed USIA because there was not enough of it. After a visit to the Far East in early 1962, Johnson peppered his friends with complaints about the alleged failure of USIS posts to publicize him adequately and provide him with the services he required.

Consequently, on two subsequent Vice Presidential trips abroad, USIA sent high-ranking officers on the Johnson plane to supervise the Agency's coverage and support. Johnson was pleased with their efforts, and particularly with the work of the Agency's chief photographer, Yoichi Okamoto, who also went along. "Okie" was not only a superb craftsman; he also quickly picked up the Johnson rules, such as only photographing the Vice President from the left side.

But Okamoto was a source of friction: Johnson wanted him to be his personal photographer, accompanying him on all trips at home and abroad and on other occasions; Murrow, who had no suitable replacement for Okamoto, demurred. The Vice President needled Murrow constantly—even at a memorial service for House Speaker Rayburn—but the more he needled, the stiffer Murrow's resistance became.*

The head of the newly established Peace Corps, Kennedy brother-in-law Sargent Shriver, was so afraid his volunteers would be labeled "propagandists" that he kept his agency at arm's length from USIA, and as a result the volunteers were less able than they should have been to discuss American policy intelligently. The top brass of the new Arms Control and Disarmament Agency would have profited by more attention to foreign opinion factors, but ACDA's public affairs chief—former USIA officer Ned Nordness—worked closely and successfully with his old agency.

---

* When Johnson became President, he summoned Okamoto to the White House, and USIA was happy to acquiesce. The President, of course, has first call on the services of anyone in the Executive Branch, and the needs of the President are considerably more important than the needs of the Vice President. However, after a short period, the press called attention to the ever-present Okamoto and his camera, and the President angrily sent him back to USIA. Some months later, when the fuss had died down, Okamoto quietly rejoined the White House staff.

USIA also established friendly relations with the Central Intelligence Agency. Like Allen, Murrow insisted that USIA not be used as a cover for CIA operations—and it was not—but he also believed that the Information Agency should be better informed about CIA's limited operations in the information field and that CIA should be kept abreast of what USIA was doing. CIA Director Allen W. Dulles called on Murrow and, in Dulles' words, offered to "open a new chapter" in relations between the two agencies. The ensuing cooperation did not compromise USIA's integrity, but it did permit both agencies to avoid duplicating or contradictory activities.

Some officials of the Agency for International Development had never fully accepted Eisenhower's 1953 decision to put into USIA all foreign public affairs activities related to the aid program. They thought the Information Agency did not adequately publicize AID's efforts, and in some instances they were right. What many of them failed to recognize, however, was that straight "publicity" of AID activities was not always in the national interest; indeed, too much publicity about American largess often irritated its recipients. The proper USIA role, as Murrow saw it, was to help explain the modernization process, build an understanding of the role of U.S. assistance in economic development, and clarify the effect this assistance had on a recipient country's relations with us and its neighbors.

This was a more sophisticated and difficult task than straight publicity, and it was never fully understood in either AID or USIA. But Murrow pressed this concept with the support of Fowler Hamilton and Hamilton's successor as AID Administrator, David E. Bell. An attempt by subordinates of Teodoro Moscoso, U.S. Coordinator of the Alliance for Progress, to take over all information activities in Latin America related to the *Alianza* was rebuffed. Some jurisdictional disputes between AID and USIA, however, particularly over English-teaching and book programs, were never fully resolved.

In the Defense Department, McNamara's general cooperativeness —even if not based on interest or understanding of foreign opinion factors—engendered a healthy degree of support for USIA's efforts, especially from Assistant Secretary Arthur Sylvester, McNamara's controversial press officer. The Pentagon's "state department," the Bureau of International Security Affairs, was not obstructionist, but neither did it work with USIA as it should have. As a result, several propaganda blunders occurred that might have been avoided. For example, the reasons for U.S. troop reductions in Europe and apparently related U.S. military exercises in Franco Spain were inadequately explained to Western Europeans, who, then as now, were extremely sensitive to any indication of a possible lessening of the U.S. commitment to their defense.

Recognition and Reform

With the American people as a whole, as with Congress, Murrow's reputation for integrity and his quiet modesty were great assets to his Agency. Despite occasional flurries of well-publicized controversy, USIA had never been well known to the public at large. Agency officers often found that if they identified themselves as USIA employees, they got blank stares in return, whereas if they said, "I work for Ed Murrow," there was instant recognition. Murrow was deluged with requests to speak, but accepted only those in which, as he put it privately, "I can do the Agency some good. After all," he added, "I personally have had all the exposure I need, after a quarter-century in broadcasting." Some of Murrow's prestige rubbed off on the Agency, giving it more stature than it ever had. More important, Murrow brought new recognition to the function of international persuasion.

Only days after his appointment, an incident occurred that caused Murrow some public embarrassment. He had produced a television documentary for CBS entitled *Harvest of Shame,* a crusading piece pointing up the deplorable conditions of migrant farm workers in America. The BBC had paid a goodly sum of money to CBS for it, but Murrow was not eager for the film to be shown abroad, now that he was the official U.S. spokesman overseas. He unwisely asked his old friend, BBC Director General Hugh Carleton-Greene, not to use it. The word got out, and Murrow was chided in the press for attempting "censorship."

Murrow's most important relationships were, of course, with the people in his own Agency. He was surprised at the amount of talent he found. "I could staff any commercial media outfit in the country with people from this Agency," he remarked "and it would be as good as or better than any of its competitors." Murrow brought in a few able outsiders, but only a few. Most USIA employees took great satisfaction in his appointment as his Executive Assistant of Reed Harris, who had been hounded out of the information program by McCarthy eight years earlier.

Murrow did find weaknesses in the Agency. A few of the senior officers with the longest experience were tired, in a rut, and not performing at the level of excellence demanded by the Kennedy Administration—if they ever had. Unlike some bureaucrats, Murrow was more concerned with performance than seniority, and he did not hesitate to promote junior and middle-grade officers into positions of major responsibility if he thought they were better able to handle the big jobs than anyone else.

He had no illusions about his ability to overhaul the Agency's personnel structure; trying in 1961 to fire several incompetents, Murrow was thwarted by Civil Service regulations and Congressional pressures. Thereafter he took a more practical approach, trying to put men into jobs where their abilities would be used to the fullest and their weaknesses least likely to do damage, and then give them the maximum support and inspiration possible. In this he had much success, assisted by two extraordinarily effective personnel officers —William H. Weathersby and, later, Lionel Mosley.

Murrow's concept of managerial responsibility was much like Kennedy's. He knew the decisions were his, but he wanted to be exposed to all the issues before making up his mind. Also like Kennedy, he was generous in sharing the credit for what went well while taking the blame for what went badly. This endeared him to subordinates, although some Agency officials were not entirely pleased with his leadership at first. They were accustomed to operating without too much attention from the Director's office. But Murrow was interested in everything they did. He abolished the Agency's Operating Committee, a group of senior officers that had been making major decisions, for he no more needed an Operating Committee than Kennedy needed an OCB.

The various studies of USIA had urged greater coordination among the Agency's media services, with common themes and emphases in their output. I pressed Murrow to undertake this reform, and after study he agreed it was needed. Each of USIA's media services was independently deciding the subjects it would cover, and it was only a coincidence—or special circumstances—when the output of, say, the Voice of America reinforced the output of the Motion Picture or Press Service. Murrow created a new position, that of Director of Media Content, and appointed an experienced USIA Foreign Service Officer, Edgar D. Brooke, to fill it.

Brooke's task was to coordinate the output of the media services in Washington, ensure joint planning by them, and see that they all gave priority attention to matters that, in the judgment of the President and the Director, required sustained, comprehensive treatment. Murrow said the five media services must "work together as five fingers in a fist" if they were to have maximum impact and if their output was to be most useful to USIS field posts. Accustomed to going their separate ways, the media services were less than enthusiastic. But the new approach worked well, for the most part.

Abroad, USIA was strengthened by being made more a part of the regular embassy operation in every country. In May, 1961, Under Secretary of State Bowles drafted, and the President sent to every American ambassador, a letter defining the ambassador's responsibilities. Although Eisenhower had made ambassadors "chiefs of mission," Kennedy's letter went further and was more explicit: every ambassador would be responsible and accountable for all U.S. Government employees and programs in his country. As a result, USIA Public Affairs Officers sought more guidance from their ambassadors, and involved them more deeply in the USIS operations; the ambassadors, for their part (although not all of them), made increasing use of USIS to achieve U.S. purposes in their countries.

One of Murrow's favorite quotations was Edmund Burke's axiom, "The only thing necessary for the triumph of evil is for good men to do nothing." Murrow gave up fame and fortune in television so he could do something in government. There was much to do.

Busy with a rash of new Administration appointments, the Senate did not get around to confirming Murrow's nomination until mid-March; like other appointees, however, he took up the job as soon as the President called him to Washington. Murrow worked himself and his senior colleagues well into the night, and he treated Saturdays like any other working day—a marked departure from bureaucratic custom.* He had to update the previous Administration's USIA budget

---

* It took a while for Murrow to become accustomed to being a government official. Returning from his first meeting of the National Security Council, he told

and defend it before Congress. He had to develop a new and meaningful philosophy for USIA's global operations. He had to assess the pluses and minuses of American prestige in a rapidly changing world.

Called before the Senate Foreign Relations Committee which was considering his nomination, Murrow promised the Senators that USIA would "attempt to make United States policy, as designed by the President, everywhere intelligible and wherever possible palatable. . . . We will not be content to counter [Communist] lies and distortions. We shall constantly reiterate our faith in freedom. To the emerging nations . . . we shall try to make it clear that we as a nation are not allergic to change and have no desire to sanctify the *status quo.*"

With Churchillian eloquence, Murrow said: "The voice of this country should at all times be steady—firm but not bellicose—carrying the conviction that we will not flinch or falter in the face of threats or provocations. In the end of the day it may well be that the example of this nation will be more important than its dollars or its words. If we, in this generous and capacious land, can demonstrate increasing equality of opportunity, social justice, a reasoned concern for the edution, health, and equality under law of all our citizens, we will powerfully affect, and probably determine, the destiny of the free world— and that freedom may be contagious. . . .

"We cannot threaten," Murrow warned, "we must persuade. . . . Our task is formidable and difficult, but difficulty is one excuse history has never accepted."[9]

The Senate confirmed him without dissent.

Murrow's was not the only eloquent voice in the new Administration. "Let the word go forth," proclaimed Kennedy in his Inaugural Address, and a flood of rhetoric began to flow from Washington, articulating new goals, new approaches, and new programs of the New Frontier. McNamara, Rusk, Ribicoff, and others joined in the chorus. USIA's Public Affairs Officer in Morocco half-facetiously

---

Wilson and me: "I took detailed notes until, halfway through, I suddenly realized I didn't have to prepare a broadcast from them!" Then as subsequently, he gave us a superb debriefing (as the government calls it) on what took place at the meeting. Finished, he tossed his notes into the wastebasket. I fished them out, remarking, "You can't do that. This material is 'top secret' and must be burned." He laughed, but never did it again—not only for security reasons but because temperamentally he was one of the most discreet men in often indiscreet Washington.

cabled the Agency: "Arabic and French translation operations crushed under sheer weight of magnificent prose of new Administration. . . . Running about two-and-a-half four-thousand word speeches behind now and losing ground daily."

Within weeks after Murrow took over, a new spirit began to spread in USIA in Washington and abroad. At last the Agency, under Kennedy and Murrow, was finding its proper place in the conduct of American foreign affairs. Confidence in themselves and in their Agency grew among the ranks as employees saw evidences of Murrow's leadership and were inspired by his presence. Of no little importance was the fact that some State Department officers and others who had previously viewed USIA with scarcely disguised contempt now saw it in a new light.

The millennium had not arrived. The problems were greater than ever, and USIA had to prove that it could undertake greater responsibilities with good judgment and wise programs. But now there was a golden opportunity for the Agency to contribute as never before. After a painful birth, a troubled childhood, and an uncertain adolescence, American propaganda had come of age.

6 The Murrow Years: Hot Words in the Cold War

The Kennedy Administration was less than the proverbial hundred days old when USIA nearly choked on all its fine words. It helped not at all to know that the President himself was similarly stricken.

Deputy Director Donald Wilson was home shaving on the early morning of April 16 when he was urgently summoned by telephone to breakfast with an old friend, Tad Szulc, a Washington correspondent of the *New York Times* with long Latin-American experience. Szulc, just back from a three-day visit to Florida, told Wilson that he was certain that an invasion of Cuba would take place in the next few days, fully supported by the U.S. Government. Szulc urged that a briefing center be established for correspondents in Miami or some nearby spot once the invasion started; otherwise, he said, correspondents would not be able to get authoritative information on the progress of the fighting.

Nonplused, Wilson, who knew nothing of any invasion plan, said he would carry Szulc's request to higher authority. He rushed to his office and reported the conversation to Murrow, who telephoned CIA Director Allen W. Dulles requesting an immediate appointment. In Dulles' office, Murrow gently asked what was going on. Dulles talked at length on Cuba, but admitted nothing. Murrow, realizing that Dulles was under oath of secrecy, did not press him. McGeorge Bundy learned of the conversation, and called Murrow to the White House, where he filled him in. Murrow strongly opposed the scheme in his conversations with Bundy and Wilson, but otherwise suffered in loyal silence. At that point, it was too late to do anything else.

Early on the morning after Murrow saw Dulles, a brigade of Cuban refugees landed at the Bay of Pigs with the announced intention of overthrowing Fidel Castro. It quickly became apparent that the United States Government was behind the invasion, and soon the word was out that the Central Intelligence Agency had devised the scheme and trained the invasion force.

Not surprisingly, great cries of protest sounded around the world from both friend and foe. The invasion violated the cherished Latin-American doctrine of nonintervention, appeared to pit a great power against a weak one (although no U.S. troops participated), involved the United States in the kind of sudden aggression we had so often criticized, and—worst of all—was unsuccessful. Like the British-French-Israeli attack on Egypt four and a half years before, it was wretchedly conceived and clumsily executed, and could not and did not succeed before world opinion was aroused against it.

Kennedy had inherited the project from the Eisenhower Administration and, after repeated assurances from CIA, authorized it to proceed despite some misgivings on his part. Recognizing that secrecy was essential, he consulted few of his advisers. Murrow was not among them, although the degree and direction of Cuban and foreign public reaction to the invasion obviously would be significant factors in the scheme's outcome.

We can only speculate on what might have happened had Murrow been brought into the preinvasion discussions. His opposition might have reinforced the President's own doubts and resulted in the attack being called off. Or, as he did on some other occasions, Murrow might have merely spoken his piece and then remained silent. But at least Kennedy would have known that one of the major premises of the operation was false.

A year earlier, just before the Iron Curtain clanged down on Cuba, the Institute for International Social Research of Princeton, New Jersey, had taken a last public opinion poll on the island. It found that Castro was popular among the Cuban people, with a small opposition confined almost entirely to Havana. The study was made available to USIA, which presumably sent it to the State Department and CIA (though it may not have reached those in charge of the secret Cuban project).

Not knowing of the invasion plan, USIA did not send the months-old study to the White House after Kennedy became President, and Kennedy had no way of knowing that CIA assurances of a popular uprising against Castro once the refugees landed were unfounded. Arthur Schlesinger, Jr., a Kennedy adviser on Latin America, came across the Cuban survey later, and wrote Lloyd Free, Director of the Institute, that he wished "we had had it earlier."[1] They might have, had Murrow been cut in on the planning.

Though caught unprepared, the Agency quickly began broadcasting around-the-clock to Latin America. VOA had little in the way of justification to offer, but its comprehensive, objective newscasts helped dispel some of the more sensational rumors afloat. Kennedy's assumption of all responsibility cut off most of the usual Washington post-mortem bickering, and tempers abroad gradually cooled.

Nonetheless, the Bay of Pigs marred American prestige for months to come, and our prestige was none too good in the spring of 1961 anyway. Since sputnik in 1957, foreign confidence in the United States had been on the downgrade. The U-2 incident and the subsequent humiliation of Eisenhower by Khrushchev at the abortive Paris "summit" in 1960 had speeded the process. The Bay of Pigs, coming only five days after the Soviets put the first man into orbit, brought American prestige to a postwar low.

More than words were required, but words would help. Murrow mobilized the Information Agency to do its part. By this time he had developed his own ideas on the proper role of USIA. Unlike Allen, he believed the Agency should persuade, not just inform, and that it should aggressively and expertly advise the Executive Branch on the foreign opinion implications of policies and programs.

In shaping the Agency, Murrow soon learned that enunciating an operating philosophy was one thing, but getting USIA's twelve thousand employees to understand and carry it out was something else again—especially when the new philosophy differed sharply from that of his predecessor. Murrow had spent his entire life in communications, but at USIA he was plagued with the same problem that afflicted his counterparts around Washington: inadequate internal communication.

"How the hell can we expect to persuade foreigners," he said to me one day, "if we can't get our own people to understand what we are doing, why we are doing it, and what is expected of them?" On another occasion he complained: "I'm talking into a 'dead mike.' I make a decision, everybody says 'fine,' and then I find six months later that nothing has happened!"

Although a few USIA staff members obstructed, delayed, or deliberately misinterpreted Murrow's wishes when they did not agree with him,* most were ready to reshape the Agency's operations according to the Director's desires. But Murrow's views were often unwittingly garbled in transmission down the chain of command. Many employees were imbued with the philosophy of the Eisenhower Statement of Mission as interpreted by Allen, and thought their job was limited to "telling America's story to the world," a much less complicated task than was called for. Others simply did not care.

Kennedy's "Statement of Mission"

Finally, Murrow and the White House agreed that a formal, written redefinition of the Agency's mission was required. Although the new philosophy had been put into practice in early 1961, Kennedy did not actually issue a new directive until January, 1963.

"The mission of the United States Information Agency," it said plainly and without qualification, "is to help achieve United States foreign policy objectives." This was to be done in two ways: By "*influencing* public attitudes in other nations" (not just disseminating information), and by "*advising* the President, his representatives abroad," and the various departments "on the implications of foreign opinion for present and contemplated" U.S. policies and programs— a clear indication that Kennedy welcomed USIA participation in the policy-making process.

While the Director of USIA "shall take the initiative in offering counsel when he deems it advisable," Kennedy continued, "the various departments and agencies should seek such counsel when considering policies and programs which may substantially affect or be affected by foreign opinion." This was an important step forward,

---

* A shocking example of willful obstruction occurred when Murrow, shortly before his resignation, sent an instruction to a highly placed Agency official which would have had the effect of downgrading his position. Instead of acting on it, this man waited for Murrow's departure and then either buried it in his files or destroyed the memorandum. Carbon copies existed, however, and the instruction was subsequently carried out by Murrow's successor.

although of course it did not bind other agencies to follow the advice they were required to seek.

In USIA operations abroad, said the President, "individual country programs should specifically and directly support country and regional objectives determined by the President"—not individual USIA officers' ideas as to what our objectives are or should be, as so often had been true in the past.

The Agency was directed to: encourage support abroad "for the goal of a 'peaceful world community of free and independent states, free to choose their own future and their own system so long as it does not threaten the freedom of others';* identify the United States as a strong, dynamic nation qualified for its leadership of world efforts toward this goal; and unmask and counter hostile attempts to distort or frustrate" U.S. objectives and policies. In language similar to that used in the Eisenhower Statement of Mission, USIA was instructed to "emphasize the ways in which United States policies harmonize with those of other peoples and governments, and those aspects of American life and culture which facilitate sympathetic understanding" of U.S. policies. The Kennedy directive, however, made these emphases means toward persuasion rather than ends.

The new Statement of Mission, though not entirely successful, was helpful in getting other agencies to consider the foreign opinion implications of what they were doing. Some in the State Department continued to believe (and still do) that they knew all they needed to know about foreign opinion, or that it was not really important (the Dulles view), or that their own information office (the Bureau of Public Affairs) could supply specialized advice if needed. Some in other departments held similar views. But the new directive undoubtedly helped.

Even more important, Kennedy's instruction explicitly tied USIA activities to specific U.S. objectives abroad. Henceforth, in preparing their Country Plans of operation, Public Affairs Officers were required to start with the official U.S. objectives, and then formulate activities to achieve them by directing specific messages at specific audiences in support of specific Psychological Objectives. This new approach was more sophisticated—and more difficult—than merely saying "helpful" things to "key" people. Now every PAO was re-

* A quotation from Kennedy's first State of the Union Message.

quired to justify each part of his program in terms of its contribution to the achievement of specific objectives.

Not all USIA officers welcomed the new approach. Some had built reputations by being busy, without giving much thought to the purpose of their activity. Others were so wedded to a particular medium of communication that they had lost sight—if they had ever had it—of the message being communicated. Some others thought each USIS post should have a "balanced" program, equally divided among the various media without regard for the nature of the messages to be conveyed, the audiences to be reached, or the objectives to be furthered. Still others, accustomed to thinking of themselves as journalists or educators rather than persuaders, could not or would not understand the new approach.

One Public Affairs Officer, in Washington on home leave, told me in glowing terms of "the best USIS post anywhere"—his. He described his staff's numerous activities and high morale. Impressed, I asked him what his post's Psychological Objectives were, and what progress had been made toward achieving them. His face fell. "I should have known you policy boys would ask a question like that," he replied. Finally, he explained vaguely that his objectives were to "promote U.S. policies and fight Communism." Perhaps he did have an effective program, but if he did it was wholly accidental, for he had no idea whom he was trying to persuade of what.

The great majority, however, welcomed USIA's enhanced role and was delighted to follow Murrow's leadership. In 1963 he took advantage of House Foreign Affairs Committee hearings to define again his philosophy of propaganda, and he made certain that every Agency employee received a copy of his remarks.

"Ten years ago," Murrow reminded the legislators, the Jackson Committee "stated that 'any program established by government funds can only be justified to the extent that it assists in the achievement of national objectives,' I agree—and that *is* the purpose, the sole purpose, of USIA today." Murrow made particular note of the Agency's policy advisory function, recalling that "experts have repeatedly urged that there be greater consideration of psychological factors" in policy-making. "Today," he said, "these factors are usually given appropriate consideration."

Murrow noted that "there has been confusion about the role of 'truth' in a government information program. But there is no confusion within USIA. . . . We operate on the basis of truth. . . . We emphasize those aspects of American life and policy which are of greatest significance in furthering our foreign policy objectives. We report events in context; we explain why things happen. But we do not lie, we do not cheat, we do not suppress—and as a result, we are able to obtain a high degree of believability and persuasiveness."

Admitting that "it is very difficult to measure success in our business," Murrow pointed out that "no computer clicks, no cash register rings when a man changes his mind or opts for freedom. And . . . above all, it is what we do—not what we say—that has the greatest impact overseas. USIA can explain, interpret, clarify, synthesize and project, but we cannot change the unchangeable or do the undoable."

Nonetheless, he said, "persuasion is one of the most important" instruments of American power. "Our arsenal of persuasion must be as ready as our nuclear arsenal, and used as never before."[2]

One of Murrow's first actions to improve "our arsenal of persuasion" was to make USIA's media output "more responsive to policy direction and emphasis." For the first time, the Agency's media services were told which subjects to emphasize. In July, 1961, for example, the media services were told to give priority in their output to materials that would help field posts persuade their audiences that:

1. Despite Soviet intransigence, the United States is doing everything in its power to obtain a treaty banning nuclear testing. . . .

2. Soviet efforts to abrogate their agreements and deprive West Berliners of their freedom threaten the security and freedom of people everywhere. Under no circumstances, therefore, will the U.S. abandon free Berlin.

3. An effective United Nations which has sufficient authority to act in crisis situations is indispensable to the security of small nations. . . .

4. The Sino-Soviet Bloc, despite lip-service support to emerging nationalism, is implacably opposed to independent nationalist movements and genuine neutrality. Man's best hope is in a "world of free choice." . . .

5. Modernization of newly developing nations can best be achieved through democratic, pragmatic political and economic development consistent with the traditions, character and aspirations of a people.

Murrow did not want to substitute Washington control for initiative and flexibility in the field, as long as that initiative was in support of established objectives. Nor did he want or expect "universal and equal emphasis, either by all Media or in all countries." But he did want to require the media services to give priority attention to priority matters. And he noted that "I have been specifically charged by the President with the task of undertaking efforts on items one and two."[3]

Those two items—nuclear testing and Berlin—occupied much of Murrow's attention during his three years in office.

The Bomb and Berlin

Since October, 1958, the United States had been negotiating at Geneva with the Soviet Union and other powers in a fruitless attempt to reach agreement on a treaty banning nuclear testing. During that time an informal, unenforced moratorium on testing was observed by both the U.S. and the U.S.S.R.; however, as the negotiations dragged on and the Soviets continued to balk at adequate on-site inspection, pressure for resumption of testing began to build up within the American Government and in the press. The Pentagon was understandably concerned over the possibility that the Soviets would improve their nuclear capability vis-à-vis the United States, or already had, by resorting to undetectable underground testing.

But USIA was well aware, and so advised President Kennedy, that world opinion was strongly opposed to a resumption of testing, and whichever nation that did it first would be subjected to violent criticism which would damage not only its "image" but its position on other key issues as well (in our case, Berlin and Laos, among others). USIA did not, of course, suggest that the United States desist from testing solely because of foreign opinion; it did urge, however, that the U.S. resume testing not merely because of vague fears or frustrations but only if a military necessity was clearly established.

Recognizing that we might be forced by such necessity to test, USIA set out to prepare world opinion by emphasizing that the United States was doing everything in its power to obtain a workable test ban treaty, and would not resume testing unless the security of the free world absolutely required it. Murrow and I pressed home the urgency of the problem in a series of "operations conferences" held on four continents by Under Secretary Bowles to acquaint American ambassadors and their principal aides with the new emphases of the Kennedy Administration.

Then, on August 30, 1961, the U.S.S.R. abruptly announced resumption of atmospheric testing. Kennedy was shocked and angered, and even more by the mild reaction from the neutrals who had been the most vociferous opponents of testing. A Conference of Non-Aligned Nations, coincidentally in session in Belgrade, criticized the Soviet action—but only cautiously.

When the National Security Council met the next morning, some wanted the United States to resume testing immediately, and Rusk had a draft statement announcing resumption for the President to issue. But Kennedy was not to be panicked into resuming atmospheric testing until it was absolutely necessary (although underground testing was begun almost immediately).

The President changed Rusk's statement to announce preparations for testing, not testing itself. But Murrow still objected, cautioning that "if we issue that statement, we destroy the advantages of the greatest propaganda gift we have had for a long time."[4] He urged "no precipitate action that might throw away this opportunity to consolidate our leadership of the non-Communist world and isolate the Communist bloc. The voices on the right 'who today urge you to resume testing immediately,' he said, 'will tomorrow contend that the decision to do so was merely another belated reaction to Soviet action.' "[5]

Rusk then switched to support Murrow, and his view prevailed. As issued, the statement was a "controlled and deliberate response that made the most of world-wide antagonisms toward the Soviets without compromising our own freedom to test."[6] And, despite the reaction from Belgrade, public opinion in the nonaligned countries and elsewhere was sharply critical of the Kremlin. A USIA survey of foreign press and radio comment revealed the greatest surge of anti-Soviet sentiment since the repression of the Hungarian rebellion in 1956.

In its voluminous output during the weeks that followed, USIA pointed to the health and peace hazards of the Soviet act, noted American restraint, reviewed the history of U.S. efforts to obtain a treaty, and renewed the demand for one before it was too late. On Sunday, November 5, fifty-two Voice of America transmitters, operating on eighty frequencies backed by 4,300 kilowatts of power, were turned toward the U.S.S.R. for eight hours of special broadcasting to the Soviet people on the nuclear issue. The unprecedented concentration of transmitters blasted through the jamming curtain; Murrow called it his "Sunday punch." When the United States finally did resume atmospheric testing eight months later, after first giving the Soviets still another chance at a treaty, there were few protests.

The problem of Berlin was fraught with more immediate dangers. Emboldened by Soviet successes since sputnik, embarrassed by the growing defections of East Germans through Berlin, and pressed by the Chinese to prove himself properly militant, Khrushchev became more and more determined to drive the Western powers from the city. He set several deadlines (and then postponed them), threatening to sign a peace treaty with the Soviet-controlled "German Democratic Republic" which would unilaterally wipe out Allied occupation rights in West Berlin and absorb the city into East Germany. Acheson warned Kennedy in April that a major crisis was likely in 1961.

There were major psychological aspects to the problem. One was the widespread feeling among Europeans that, having suffered catastrophic losses from two world wars caused by Germany, they were not obliged to risk a third (and this time atomic) war for the sake of Germany. Another was the not unrelated feeling in much of the world that the Berlin problem was of concern only to Germany, had originated in a clumsy, temporary postwar arrangement, and in any case was not worth the risk of world war.

USIA launched a major campaign to persuade its audiences that the fate of all free men was linked to Berlin, that Communist success there would ignite similar pressures in other parts of the world, and that no alliance of free nations would mean very much if the West reneged on its commitments to the people of West Berlin. The campaign was stepped up after Khrushchev told Kennedy at Vienna in June that come what might he would sign the peace treaty with East Germany before the end of 1961.

A USIA "Potomac Cable,"* radioed to all USIS posts, restated

---

* The "Potomac Cable" was—and is—one of the Agency's most useful forms of providing fast policy guidance to field posts. An unclassified commentary on current developments, it differs from other USIA output in that it is specifically cleared by the State Department as an authoritative policy statement. Thus in the field it can be used simultaneously as policy guidance for embassy staffs and also as an article or commentary to be placed in local newspapers or on local radio stations.

the American position, emphasizing that there was no need for a Berlin crisis ("If one develops it will be of Soviet making") and pointing to the Soviet refusal to permit East Berlin and East Germany to exercise self-determination. Berlin "may seem a remote problem to countries far removed," but the Western powers "cannot and will not abdicate their responsibility to protect the freedom of the people of Berlin," the Agency proclaimed. Otherwise, "the security of all peoples would suffer."[7]

USIS posts around the globe pressed the Allied case. Other Potomac Cables followed. On August 9, through the same channel, USIA told the world that the developing crisis over the German city was

no more a "Berlin" crisis than that of 1938 was a "Czech" crisis or that of 1939 a "Polish" crisis. The latter were Hitler's crises; this is Khrushchev's crisis. . . . The question is not: "Why die for Berlin?" It is: "Will Khrushchev kill for Berlin?" . . . East Germany exists as a regime imposed by force. Twenty-two Soviet divisions hold its people in bondage. A thousand refugees flee East Germany every day.[8]

It was this last fact, as much as any, that galled the Communists. Not only was East Germany losing the cream of its citizenry, but each man who fled was "voting with his feet" against the system that Moscow was trying to sell to other nations. Daily the exodus grew, rising to twelve thousand during August 12-14, as the whole world watched. Alarmed by the damage being done to Communist prestige but afraid to risk nuclear war, Khrushchev finally acted—not to settle the Berlin problem once and for all, as he had threatened, but to cut off the flow of refugees. First with barbed wire and then with bricks and mortar, the East Germans began in the early hours of August 13 to erect a wall along their Berlin frontier.

The West was caught by surprise. The swift Communist action, and the lack of any effective counteraction, gave the Allies a propaganda black eye—for the moment. Kennedy sent Vice President Johnson to reaffirm the American commitment to West Berlin, and later sent the popular General Lucius Clay as his personal representative. These moves, essentially psychological, helped. Then it dawned on USIA that the Wall could be turned into a propaganda defeat for the Communists.

VOA devoted much of its broadcasting to the Berlin story. Four

Agency motion pictures were quickly produced and shown to millions abroad: *Journey Across Berlin* described the flow of refugees from the East; *Promise to History* reviewed the Allied commitment to the people of Berlin; *Day of Denial* depicted erection of the Wall; and *They Are Not Alone* featured Johnson's visit. Two television documentaries, *Anatomy of Aggression* and *Focus: Berlin,* were produced. Nine hundred prints of film versions of Kennedy's address to the nation on the crisis, and a subsequent speech to the UN General Assembly, were circulated overseas. A USIA cartoon strip described the Wall for 100 million readers of twelve hundred foreign newspapers. Three million copies of an illustrated pamphlet were distributed in eleven languages.

Working with Berlin's city government, the Agency helped bring more than 750 journalists from eighty countries to see Berlin for themselves. Eyewitness accounts by Asian, African, and Latin-American visitors to the city were cross-reported from one continent to another, all expressing support for the U.S. position.

Stark, brutal, and visible, the Wall became a symbol of Communist failure at home and Communism's disregard for its agreements abroad. The Communists did solve their desperate problem of East German defections, but they suffered a major propaganda setback in doing so.

During the 1962 campaign Republican leaders in Congress thought there might be political capital in charging that the Administration had not done enough to rouse world opinion against the Wall. Senator Dirksen and Representative Halleck so wrote the President, and Kennedy asked me to prepare a memorandum on what USIA had done. When he transmitted the memo to the Republican leaders, the President wrote them: "I am sure you will agree that it shows an energetic effort and a gratifying response."[9] Apparently they did, or at least it ended the correspondence on the matter.

Europe: West and East

The recurrent crises over Berlin provided USIA with a rationale for a propaganda program in Western Europe at a time when one was sorely needed. Some members of Congress wanted to cut operations way back on the grounds that there were too many activities at too many USIS posts staffed by too many people, a legacy of the gigantic programs of the occupation and Marshall Plan eras. Moreover, many of the Agency's old European hands had never served elsewhere, were too committed to old ways of meeting old problems, and often were of lesser caliber than their colleagues on other continents. Within USIA itself, as well as in Congress, there was grumbling about the "European club" and the proclivity of its members to promote each other up the career ladder while holding onto the poshest assignments. ("My God, do they all live like this?" Murrow asked, upon seeing the luxurious villa of one European PAO.)

The critics were wrong, however, in asserting that little or no U.S. propaganda was required in Western Europe where we were best known and presumably best loved. Despite all that had occurred elsewhere, NATO was still the keystone of our foreign policy. Its members had far more power—economic and military, if not always political—than the underdeveloped countries of the Southern Hemisphere. Even more than enemies and neutrals, our European friends constantly wanted to know exactly where we stood and often required reassurances on our intentions.

Murrow set out to refine and redefine his West European program, reducing the numbers of objectives, operations, and people. This required effective leadership and fresh talent, but in Europe USIA was short on both. A succession of assistant directors for Europe did not work out as well as Murrow had hoped, and he did not change them as fast as he should have. A "task force" of high-ranking Agency officers identified many of the problems in an intensive 1963 study, but was not very successful in devising solutions.

Toward the close of the Murrow administration, a new Assistant Director was selected who had never served in Europe and had no sentimental or vested interests in USIA programs there. The choice —Robert A. Lincoln—proved to be a good one. Lincoln had demonstrated imagination and skill as Assistant Director for the Near East and South Asia; in Europe he was a breath of fresh air. Some called it brashness (and some of it was), but standards were raised, old ways of doing things questioned, and new faces brought in. Many "European club" members reacted with suspicion and anxiety, and others never quite grasped what Lincoln was trying to do. But the program improved.

Lincoln quickly reduced the staff in Europe and eliminated a third of all branch installations. In media activities, the emphasis was changed from distributing news to providing background information which put the news into perspective. Ten second-rate USIS periodicals were dropped. Library collections were refined to provide research rather than mass reading facilities. Seminars and press tours were employed to publicize U.S. support for European unity and to increase European support for NATO. USIS posts promoted American disarmament proposals, expanded trade with the United States, and the Administration's scheme for a multilateral force (MLF) to give U.S. allies a voice in the use of nuclear weapons.

MLF, which was quietly buried in 1965 after failing to win acceptance, was only part of a larger problem: the relationship of the new Europe with the United States. Rapid economic growth, widespread prosperity, and a decline in fear of the Soviet Union fueled European desires for more independence. President De Gaulle of France repeatedly urged Europeans to send the Americans packing. USIA made much of Kennedy's "declaration of interdependence" speech on July 4, 1962, in which the President proclaimed this country's desire to have an "Atlantic partnership" on equal terms with a united Europe, with Europeans determining what form that unity would take and at what pace it would proceed.

A year later, Kennedy's visit to Western Europe did what no amount of USIA propaganda could ever do. The President's reception was the warmest given any American on the continent since Wilson in 1919. In Frankfurt, Kennedy answered the Gaullists: "The United States will risk its cities to defend yours because we need your freedom to protect ours. . . . The choice of paths to the unity of Europe is a choice which Europe must make." In Berlin the President capped American efforts to make the Wall a Communist liability with one of the toughest speeches of his Administration. As the crowd roared its approval, Kennedy said free men everywhere identified themselves with Berlin, and he, too, was proud to say, *"Ich bin ein Berliner"* ("I am a Berliner"). The Agency commissioned a talented young film maker, Bruce Herschensohn, to produce a magnificent color film, *The Five Cities of June,* which made the most of the Berlin speech.*

---

* Kennedy was delighted with the film. It included a moving sequence on the death of Pope John and the coronation of Pope Paul, both of which had taken place in June, 1963, and Kennedy had USIA send a print of the film to the new Pope with his compliments.

The Kennedy Administration's interest in Europe was not limited to this side of the Iron Curtain, however, nor was its concern with Communism reflected exclusively in direct attacks on the Soviet system. Recognizing that Eastern Europe was growing restless, the Administration set out to encourage a loosening of ties between the Kremlin and its satellites. A great wave of Western European prosperity, prompted in large measure by the Common Market, aroused both envy and hope in Eastern Europe, and USIA encouraged Eastern Europeans to draw closer to and take heart from their cousins in the West.

The opportunities for reaching the people of Eastern Europe were few, but various USIA programs, operating under the aegis of formal "cultural agreements" and informal understandings, afforded one avenue. USIA was convinced that reciprocal exchanges of any kind were to America's advantage. True, a USIA magazine or exhibit in Leningrad meant a Communist magazine or exhibit in Chicago. But the free American press conveyed every public word of top Communist officials to all the citizens of this country anyway, whereas the Communist governments decided what their people should see and hear, and it was not always factual and never comprehensive.

In the summer of 1961, a USIA exhibit, "Plastics USA," was seen in Kiev, Moscow, and Tbilisi by 375,000 people, and the following year in Warsaw and Zagreb by another million and a half. "Transportation USA," the second in the series, was viewed in the autumn of 1961 by 172,000 in Volgograd (Stalingrad) and Kharkov, and by another 390,000 the following summer in Belgrade and Ljubljana. Similar crowds toured "Medicine USA" in Moscow, Kiev, Leningrad, Zagreb, and Belgrade during 1962. "Technical Books USA" was seen by more than 140,000 people in early 1963 in Moscow, Leningrad, and Kiev. "Graphic Arts USA," "Communications USA," and others followed. In three years, more than seven million people visited American exhibits in the U.S.S.R. and Eastern Europe.

The crowds were interested and friendly. USIA recruited guides who spoke the local language to explain and answer questions about the exhibits, and they had as much impact as the exhibits themselves. The guides, mostly enthusiastic second-generation Americans in their twenties and thirties, skillfully handled thousands of questions which ranged far beyond the exhibits, covering topics from everyday American life to U.S. policy on Cuba. Some of these temporary employees later became full-fledged USIA officers.

Among the questions asked most often at one exhibit in Leningrad were: How much do you earn a month? How much does a new car cost? How much does a kilogram of butter cost? Of sugar? Of bread? Of meat? Why do you have so many unemployed in America? How do the unemployed live and where do they get money to live on? How do you pay for medical service? Higher education? Do you jam Radio Moscow? How much monthly rent do you pay for an apartment? How long must you wait to buy a new car? A house? A telephone? Can a worker really save enough to start his own business? Are there a lot of gangsters in America? What will you do when your workers revolt? Why don't you want to disarm? Why don't you like Castro and Cuba?

The guides were such a success that some of them were subjected to various forms of harassment, including charges of espionage. Visitors who toured the exhibits were invited to sign guest books and add whatever comments they cared to make. One brave Russian wrote in 1962: "Khrushchev says we will soon pass the United States. Please let me off when we go by."

Other means of communication were useful, too. Russian- and Polish-language editions of USIA's *Amerika* magazine were sell-outs in those two countries, and many more copies would have been sold had the Moscow and Warsaw governments permitted it. Cultural and scientific bulletins were published for direct mailing to interested citizens. The USIA-operated Information Media Guaranty program made it possible for American producers of books, periodicals, newspapers, TV films, motion pictures, and records to sell millions of dollars' worth of their products in Poland, and be reimbursed in dollars by the U.S. Government for the Polish zlotys they received in payment.

Some exchanges of news and views were unprecedented. Aleksei Adzhubei, Khrushchev's cocky son-in-law and editor of *Izvestia,* came to the United States in 1961 and was granted an exclusive interview with Kennedy, which he published in full on the front page of his newspaper. Kennedy was courteous but candid, explaining U.S. policy in words which USIA on its own could never have distributed in its Russian-language publications. Technically, Adzhubei was here as a guest of Presidential Press Secretary Pierre Salinger, and a few months later he invited Mr. and Mrs. Salinger to pay a return visit.

Because of Berlin, Cuba, and other major differences between the two countries, Kennedy wanted Salinger's visit to be strictly business. So Mrs. Salinger stayed home and I accompanied the gregarious Press Secretary to Moscow. During our first two days in the Soviet Union we spent thirteen hours with Khrushchev, some of it in fast-paced hikes around the grounds of a government-owned *dacha* on the banks of the Moscow River. The Soviet Premier alternated between affability to us personally and hostility to American policy generally. He put on a good show: exhibiting his wife, children, and grandchildren; guzzling brandy at every meal; spouting Russian proverbs; talking nostalgically of the good old days with Bulganin; and demonstrating his prowess as a trapshooter. On serious matters, though, he was very serious indeed.

Germany and Soviet agriculture dominated his serious conversation, although he also touched on many other topics including a nuclear test ban treaty and what he considered America's unreasonable demand for on-site inspection of seismic events. At lunch one day, in what must have been the twentieth toast, I raised my brandy glass to my lips but did not drink. Khrushchev, who was doing the pouring, observed this and accused me of "cheating." We had been discussing the test ban, and I confessed to not drinking the toast but added: "You caught me with your on-site inspection; it's the best way of preventing cheating."

Later, annoyed by a passionate Khrushchev monologue on "wars of liberation," I not so innocently asked if such wars could take place "in developed areas such as Europe, or were they limited to Asia, Africa, and Latin America." In one of his quick changes of humor, Khrushchev snapped: "I know what you are talking about; I know what you mean! And the answer is no, never. The countries of Eastern Europe have already been liberated!"

A few months earlier, Khrushchev had agreed to an exchange of televised speeches with Kennedy, but then reneged at the last minute, claiming to be offended by the President's resumption of nuclear testing. Now, Salinger sought to win agreement for regular radio, television, and book exchanges between the two nations. He was forceful and persuasive, but the Russians did not budge. Nonetheless, Salinger's visit was useful in reinforcing a personal relationship with the abrasive Adzhubei. The Press Secretary addressed a luncheon meeting of the Moscow press corps and fielded malicious questions with skill and good humor. His presence, if not his point of view, was widely advertised on Moscow radio and television.*

Top Soviet propagandists were also present at the Moscow meetings, and one of them, Yuri Zhukov, took it upon himself to needle me incessantly about USIA and particularly the Voice of America. He asserted that Radio Moscow's broadcasts to the United States were not provocative or hostile, but that VOA's were. In turn, I needled him about Soviet jamming of our broadcasts, a subject on which Soviet brass were obviously sensitive. Zhukov insisted the jamming would continue until the Voice changed its tune.

I was unperturbed by Zhukov's criticism, reflecting as it did Soviet concern over USIA's effectiveness. Not long after Murrow became Director, Soviet slurs on the Agency increased. Party journals repeatedly attacked USIA, and similar articles and broadcasts were directed to foreign audiences, particularly in Africa where the thirst for knowledge had made USIS libraries important intellectual centers.

A favorite Soviet trick was to forge a letter or pamphlet containing outrageous sentiments (usually racist or imperialist), make it look as if it originated with USIS, and then give it wide circulation. Although the "black propaganda" forgeries were believed by some, the device backfired with others, who saw through the forgeries, sympathized with USIS, and blamed the Communists for making trouble.

Communist attacks on USIA notwithstanding, the decline in thought control after Stalin opened new opportunities for the Agency behind the Iron Curtain. Although Communist governments—with the exception of renegade Yugoslavia—refused to permit full-scale

---

* After our return to Washington, an amusing incident revealed that not everyone in the Russian capital knew of his visit. I was invited to cocktails by Presidential Assistant Schlesinger to meet a recently arrived delegation of Soviet writers. Schlesinger identified me by saying I had "been in Moscow with Salinger." The dour-faced leader of the Soviet group replied abruptly, "Salinger has never been to Moscow." Startled, Schlesinger politely replied that Salinger had indeed been there in May of 1962, and that I had been with him. The Soviet writer repeated: "Salinger has never been to Moscow." Recalling the great popularity in Russia of J. D. Salinger's *Catcher in the Rye*, the light dawned and I interjected: "It was Pierre Salinger, not J. D. Salinger." Fixing beady blue eyes on me, the Russian asked: "And *who* is Pierre Salinger?"

libraries and other standard USIS operations, some information and cultural activities were allowed, and they expanded as the rules relaxed. These programs were supervised by USIA officers assigned as cultural attachés to our embassies.

Organizationally, USIA had traditionally administered activities for the Soviet Union and Eastern Europe as part of its European division. But Murrow found that the Agency's radio, publications, cultural, and policy people dealing with that part of the world had little contact with each other, and that the European experts devoted most of their thought and effort to USIS programs in Western Europe. He established a separate geographic division, the Office of the Assistant Director for Soviet and East European Affairs, to give full attention to Agency activities directed at the no longer so closed Communist societies.

Alianza para el Progreso

New leadership also strengthened USIA's Latin-American program, which long had been given low priority. Castro's revolution in Cuba had helped awaken Americans to the critical problems of their own hemisphere, but these problems were not caused solely by Castro and Communism. Economic growth had failed to keep pace with rapid population growth. The people of Latin America, caught up in what Adlai Stevenson had called the "revolution of rising expectations," were no longer willing to put up with economic domination by a few oligarchic families. They resented U.S. support of Latin dictators and the fact that most American aid went to the Middle and Far East and relatively little to our own neighbors. Kennedy made Latin America an issue in the 1960 campaign and launched an *Alianza para el Progreso,* an "Alliance for Progress," when he became President.

Kennedy was the most popular U.S. President in Latin America since Franklin D. Roosevelt, but USIA's job was not easy. Many in the area saw the Alliance for Progress not as a joint program, requiring considerable effort and sacrifice on their part, but as a straight U.S. aid scheme. While it was important for USIA to win support for the Alliance, it was equally important not to oversell it, for that could only (and in some cases did) lead to frustration and disillusionment when results were not immediately forthcoming. Moreover, many

Latin Americans agreed with Castro's objective of independence from "Yankee imperialism" even if they disapproved of his methods and his ties with the Soviet Union.

USIA increased both the volume and quality of its activities, and so did the Communists. By late 1963 Cuban shortwave radio stations were beaming 109 hours of Spanish-language broadcasts to Latin America every week, and an hour a day in Portuguese to Brazil. Added to 120 hours broadcast from the Soviet Union, slightly more than that from the East European Communist nations, and 38 from Communist China, this made a total of 415 hours of Communist broadcasts weekly to Latin America. Against this VOA was broadcasting only 63 hours weekly in Spanish (although that was three times as much as when Murrow took over) and 21 hours in Portuguese. However, many Latin-American radio stations rebroadcast VOA programs, and USIS posts were placing more than two thousand hours of recorded programs weekly on 2,100 local Latin-American stations.

While the Communist nations had 170 "cultural" institutes and "friendship" societies through which they channeled tons of printed materials to Latin-American audiences, USIA increased its installations to 22 posts and 23 branch offices, staffed by 215 Americans—most of them Spanish-speaking—and four times that many foreign employees. Thirty specialists in student affairs and nine labor experts were assigned to USIS posts to work with those two key audiences.

The Agency's field staffs paid particular attention to personal contact, devoting time not only to leaders of the "in" groups, but the discontented and radical (but non-Communist) left as well. During the Murrow years more than ten million cartoon books promoting the Alliance for Progress were distributed, and more than thirteen million anti-Castro cartoon books. A weekly television newsreel *Panorama Panamericano* (for placement in local stations) and a monthly film magazine *Horizons* (for use in local movie theaters) were supplemented by other films designed especially for Latin audiences. Kennedy himself proved to be the best propaganda vehicle, and USIA made the most of his three trips to the area: Venezuela and Colombia in 1961, Mexico in 1962, and Costa Rica in 1963.

The President took a personal interest in USIA's book activities in Latin America, and his prodding encouraged the Agency to move faster than it would have otherwise. In early 1961 the Agency's new leadership recognized that there was a "book gap" south of the border: pro-Communist and other anti-American books were being distributed in ever larger numbers, while U.S. book programs were losing ground. We were especially dismayed to learn that an Argentine publisher with whom USIA had been working was feeding the Agency false figures. More money was pumped into the effort, but progress was slow; those who managed USIA's book operations in Washington seemed to lack the will and the ability to overhaul the Latin-American program.

In the spring of 1962 Kennedy asked me a series of questions about the operation. The answers I received from USIA's book officials were confused if not evasive. It quickly became clear that we did not really know exactly what and how we were doing. Murrow decided to circumvent the regular channels and appoint a "czar" for Latin-American book activities who would be directly responsible to top Agency officials.

The biggest problem was marketing. The demand was there, as were publishers capable of filling it, but great distances, a shortage of retail outlets, the lack of specialists in area-wide distribution, import controls and high interest rates kept most editions down to five thousand copies or less. USIA was not, of course, publishing or selling the books itself; rather, it supported Latin-American publishers in bringing out editions of U.S. books translated into Spanish and Portuguese. To handle negotiations with these publishers and help them expand their marketing outlets, full-time USIA Book Officers were given special training by the American Book Publishers Council and assigned to Mexico City, Buenos Aires, and Rio de Janeiro.

More than three and one-half million copies of 323 titles were contracted for publication in Spanish and Portuguese during Murrow's last year in office, compared to a half-million copies of sixty titles in 1960-61. Among the best-sellers which went through several printings were Kennedy's *Profiles in Courage* and *The Strategy of Peace,* Joel Dean's *Managerial Economics,* Theodore Draper's *Castro's Revolution,* Dorothy Gordon's *You and Democracy,* and William Shelton's *The Story of Cape Canaveral.*

The improved USIA effort in Latin America bore some fruit, but the Alliance for Progress moved more slowly than many had hoped. In some countries military coups took place. In others, oligarchs blocked progress at every turn. Inevitably, there were some in Congress and in the Agency for International Development (which was in charge of U.S. programs for the *Alianza*) who blamed USIA for not immediately transforming years of Latin animosities into love for the United States. But USIA did a creditable job in Latin America during this period, certainly a better job than had been done for many years.

In the autumn of 1962, USIA surveyed public opinion in Argentina, Bolivia, Brazil, Colombia, Chile, Ecuador, and Venezuela. The results were encouraging. Except in Argentina, as many favored U.S. influence in Latin America as opposed it. Two-thirds expressed confidence in U.S. world leadership. Although most believed the United States had given too much support to Latin dictators in the past, they also thought that was no longer the case. Awareness of the Alliance for Progress ranged from 31 percent in Argentina to 81 percent in Colombia, and most who were aware of it also were able to cite at least one of its objectives. While respondents viewed past American aid as "selfishly motivated, beneficial mainly to government officials and the economically privileged, and inequitably distributed among the various recipient countries," a large majority of those who knew of the Alliance approved of it.

A majority of those interviewed were dissatisfied with their living standards but had "extremely optimistic expectations for improvement in the near future"—an unrealistic view almost certain to lead to disillusionment and frustration. Surprisingly, only a few, averaging 6 percent, recommended radical changes in their country's political or economic systems; most pleaded simply for more jobs, higher wages, and lower living costs. The United States was more frequently identified as a champion of land reform than the Communists. Only 8 percent, on the average, had a good opinion of Castro. Although many felt Communism's influence was substantial, 77 percent wanted it reduced or eliminated.

"Free Choice"

The goals of the Alliance for Progress made the Kennedy Administration immediately popular in Latin America, but it took longer to win the confidence of the uncommitted, underdeveloped nations of

Africa and Asia.* Most of them were pleased by Kennedy's friendly words in his Inaugural Address, and even more pleased by remarks in his first State of the Union Message (stressed in USIA output) which they interpreted as acceptance of neutralism or "nonalignment," as it was now called. While some of these countries were neutral "in our favor," more of them leaned the other way and accepted Communist jargon about "imperialism" and "neo-colonialism," though not Communist ideology. But all of them had resented the Eisenhower Administration's view of nonalignment as "immoral."

The Kennedy Administration sought to cajole no one into a military alliance. It reaffirmed its support for the Dulles-sponsored SEATO and CENTO, but downgraded the importance of these pacts. While it courted the support of the nonaligned nations, it was also prepared to see them remain neutral—particularly if they dealt firmly with their internal Communist and other totalitarian elements, as many did.

Kennedy occasionally lost his patience with the more blatant hypocrisies of Sukarno, Sihanouk, Nkrumah, and Company. After the neutrals failed to protest vigorously the Soviet resumption of atmospheric nuclear testing in 1961, Kennedy had some pointed remarks for them when he signed the aid bill. The President's words were given a too harsh interpretation abroad, so at USIA's suggestion he restated his basic position at his press conference: "We are not attempting to use our aid in order to secure agreement by these countries with all of our policies. . . . Our view of the world crisis is that countries are entitled to national sovereignty and independence. That is the purpose of our aid—to make it more possible. Now," Kennedy continued, "if a country has ceased to choose national sovereignty or ceased to choose national independence, then of course our aid becomes less useful." USIA made certain that his words were heard in the right places.

In 1962 Kennedy expanded on this theme. "The revolution of national independence is a fundamental fact of our era. . . . As new nations emerge from the oblivion of centuries, their first aspiration is to affirm their national identity." This "diversity and independence," he continued, "far from being opposed to the American conception of

* USIA and other government agencies generally refer to them as "developing" and "newly developing" rather than "underdeveloped" nations to avoid bruising their egos, some of which are sensitive to an extreme.

world order," in fact expressed "the very essence of our view of the future." In 1963 Kennedy began referring in his speeches to U.S. hopes for "a world made safe for diversity."

All this was great grist for USIA's mill, and Kennedy's words were printed and reprinted, broadcast and rebroadcast, for increasingly receptive audiences in Africa and Asia. Many of these countries lacked developed communications media, and their people were hungry for news and ideas. Consequently, Agency pamphlets, news bulletins, periodicals, and films had an impact far greater than in Western Europe, where USIA output was often lost in the great volume and variety of the indigenous media.

USIA put more emphasis on the problems and purposes of modernization and less on trying to get new nations, wrapped up in their own problems and interests, involved in the major Cold War disputes. The Agency's message in essence was: "We want you to be truly independent. We want you to develop your resources, natural and human, to the fullest extent possible. The purpose of American aid is to help you do that."

In USIA shorthand, these themes were referred to as "free choice" and "modernization." For the first time, the Agency's media services began to turn out quantities of material useful in Africa and Asia. USIA encouraged, then made good use of, public statements by Administration figures repeating and reinforcing the Kennedy view. The feeling was not, however, unanimous. Some in the government clung to Dulles' view that those who are not for us are against us. Others feared that too much encouragement of the former colonies would alienate our chief allies, their ex-masters.

In the late summer of 1961, leaders of the "nonaligned" nations met in Belgrade. Murrow and I thought the United States should try to make the best of the situation, recognizing that there would be the usual denunciations of "imperialism." At the least, we thought, there should be a Presidential message to the conference (Khrushchev certainly would send one) reaffirming Kennedy's constructive view of neutralism. The State Department was generally opposed, and finally prepared a cable—which I learned about from a friend in CIA—advising our Embassy in Belgrade that there would be no message. I complained to the White House, and a meeting was called. The State Department representatives urged "caution," i.e., no message, but this time we prevailed. An American observer at Belgrade subsequently reported that Kennedy's message "had been a success and its omission would have been a serious error."[10]

India was the recognized leader of the neutrals, but USIA could find little good to say about Prime Minister Jawaharlal Nehru's unfruitful visit late that autumn to the United States. A few weeks later, when Nehru seized the Portuguese colony of Goa on India's west coast, the clumsy U.S. reaction brought us brickbats from both parties to the quarrel. In March, 1962, however, Kennedy's wife Jacqueline visited India (and Pakistan), and the trip was a great success. USIA's Motion Picture Service made appealing films on each visit which were widely shown abroad. (The films later were combined into one and—under the questionable mandate of a Congressional resolution which passed the Senate but failed, in the rush of last-minute business, to clear the House—shown in theaters throughout the United States.*)

When the Chinese Communists attacked India on October 20, 1962, public opinion there underwent a rapid and radical change in its view of the United States. Opinion in Delhi was sampled by the Indian Institute of Public Opinion on behalf of USIA one week before, and again five weeks after, the Chinese assault. In this six-week period, esteem for the United States rose from 34 to 89 percent (and for Britain from 22 to 76 percent). A favorable view of the Soviet Union dropped from 47 to 33 percent, and unfavorable views rose from 7 to 25 percent.

USIA took advantage of the new situation to strengthen the ties between the two nations, now stronger than they had been for more than a decade. Under the leadership of USIA's exceptionally able Minister-Counselor for Public Affairs, William H. Weathersby, USIS-India stepped up its activities, avoiding the natural temptation to say, "We told you so." The Agency's program in India was larger and more costly than in any other country, though not costly to the American taxpayer. Most USIA operations there were financed by Indian rupees taken in payment for U.S. surplus food sales, and the United States had more rupees than it could possibly use.

With both sides emboldened by the new atmosphere, Weathersby

* Prompted by a Republican Congressman, the General Accounting Office later complained that USIA exceeded its authority in showing the film in this country.

and an official of the Indian Ministry of Information and Broadcasting —acting with Nehru's approval—signed an agreement in July, 1963, which would give both All India Radio and the Voice of America a medium-wave signal in South and Southeast Asia. Technically, the deal was a "sale" of a $2 million 1,000-kilowatt transmitter by the United States to the Indian Government. But the cash price was only one rupee (twenty-one cents); the real price was Indian authorization for VOA to use the Calcutta-based facility three hours daily during peak listening time for five years.

It was a good deal for USIA, which badly needed a broadcast band (medium-wave) signal into South and Southeast Asia. It was also good for India, which was getting a means of broadcasting to its neighbors without dipping into foreign exchange. But when the agreement was announced, there was an uproar in New Delhi. Communist members of Parliament, joined by some non-Communist leftists, attacked it on the grounds that India's nonalignment was compromised. There were angry editorials and a few demonstrations in the streets. Unable or unwilling to ignore the outcry, the tired, old Nehru reneged, claiming that the agreement had been made without his being aware of the details.*

The improvement in Indian-American relations also caused trouble for the United States in Pakistan, which since partition had hated and feared India more than any other nation. Dulles had brought Pakistan into both CENTO and SEATO (the only Asian nation so honored), and the country was supposed to be a bulwark against Communist aggression. But the Pakistanis made no secret of the fact that their seeming devotion to the pacts was due to their usefulness as sources of military and economic aid, and perhaps allies, in their quarrel with India.

Now, in the early 1960s, the Pakistanis overlooked the past outpouring of American aid to them and became sharply critical of the new American warmth toward India. When the United States, with Britain and India, sponsored a joint air defense exercise and provided other military assistance to India after the Chinese invasion in

---

* In late 1965 the Soviet Union agreed to sell a 1,000-kilowatt transmitter to India for the equivalent in rupees of $1,771,140. The Russians did not need, did not ask, and did not get air time on the transmitter, which will go on the air in 1968.

1962, many Pakistanis were outraged and cheered the Chinese on. USIS had to share in the blame; its large program in Pakistan had been poorly administered, vague, and ineffectual. Changes were made, and the new Public Affairs Officer—William B. King—brought about considerable improvement in the Agency's operations if not much immediate bettering of U.S.-Pakistan relations.

The Build-up in Africa

Except for experts on Africa, few Americans realized in the late 1950s that a great "independence explosion" was coming on that continent —and there were few experts on Africa, and few Americans who would listen to them. Most Foreign Service Officers in the State Department and USIA avoided assignment to Africa, not because of racial prejudice (although some were afflicted with it) but because they believed it would hurt their careers. They were right. Sub-Saharan Africa had often been used as dumping ground for men unable to make the grade elsewhere, and few had been able to build their careers on African specialization.

In 1959 the State Department tardily created a separate African Bureau, and USIA followed suit. Edward V. Roberts was named Assistant Director for Africa, but his new status solved few problems. His staff was too small (and not adequately competent), his budget was undernourished, and the top management of USIA was not much interested in Africa. Kennedy's election changed all that. Deeply concerned about the continent for some time, he had been chairman of the African subcommittee of the Senate Foreign Relations Committee and during the Presidential campaign had made repeated references to Africa.

After his election, Kennedy selected Michigan's liberal Governor G. Mennen Williams to be Assistant Secretary of State for Africa. Williams made more trips to the continent than any of his predecessors, and on several occasions Kennedy sent his brother Robert and his brother-in-law Sargent Shriver on special visits. African leaders were invited to Washington in unprecedented numbers, twenty-eight making the trip during Kennedy's brief Administration. The visits proved a perfect vehicle for USIA to tell Africans about America while reporting and filming their leaders' activities.

The Sprague Committee had recommended a major step-up in information activities in Africa, as had the Ball-Sharon task force, Wilson, and I in our separate reports to Kennedy. I had noted that

the new countries of Africa want our help and sympathy; if they don't obtain them from us they will get them elsewhere—from the Communist Bloc or the U.A.R. or both. We must make our sympathetic presence felt, and quickly, with textbooks for their schools, English teaching programs, useful materials for their infant press and radios, libraries, periodicals and newspapers. . . . The Communists have increased broadcasting to Africa from three hours to more than 100 hours per week; we must step up Voice of America broadcasts.

The greatest impetus to USIA came from events themselves. In July, 1960, Belgium agreed to independence for the Congo, and the nation plunged into civil war which soon embroiled the U.S., the U.S.S.R., and the United Nations in heated controversy. In the fall sixteen new African states were admitted to the UN. In December Britain talked Eisenhower into abstaining on an anticolonial resolution sponsored by Afro-Asian nations; nonetheless it passed 89-0, and USIA found itself tongue-tied in two-thirds of the world. Hardly two months later, with Kennedy in the White House and Stevenson at the UN, another African resolution—on the Portuguese colony of Angola—came before the United Nations; this time the U.S. voted on the side of the anticolonialists.

Like it or not, the United States could no longer ignore Africa, and Africa was no longer ignoring the United States. A rioter in front of a USIS library in Africa justified his violence with an American quotation: "The tree of liberty must be refreshed from time to time with the blood of patriots and tyrants." He had read it in a book borrowed from the USIS library. Its author was Thomas Jefferson.

Murrow understood what was happening, remarking that "one need only recall the heady wine of our own independence in 1776 to appreciate the new intoxication of Africa." He gave Roberts the support he had not previously had. Murrow asked Congress for more men, money, and facilities for Africa. He made it clear that successful performance in an African assignment was one of the best ways for a USIA officer to improve his career prospects. He instructed his personnel staff to give Africa priority over other areas in the competition for talent. He called for an "Africa Corps" of first-rate USIA officers who would specialize in the continent.

It still was not easy to fill assignments in tropical Africa, where living conditions, schools for children, health facilities, and cultural opportunities were far below those in other parts of the world. Many USIA officers (and their wives, especially) preferred more comfortable posts where the living and the job were easier. In theory, all USIA officers were supposed to be available for assignment anywhere; in fact, it was difficult and not always wise to send a man where he did not want to go.

But the build-up proceeded. Comparative statistics point up the change: In 1959 there were 10 independent nations in Africa, and USIA had 24 posts in 13 countries staffed by 63 Americans and 254 local employees. By 1963 USIA had 174 Americans and 542 local employees at work in 55 posts located in 33 countries. The combined operating budgets of these posts more than tripled between 1959 and 1963.

Men and money were important, but they were not the only problems. The people whom USIA was seeking to persuade, and the cultures in which it was operating, were far different from any the Agency had dealt with before, and the transition to new approaches was not easy—especially since USIA knew less about its audiences in Africa than anywhere else. In 1962 Chairman J. Leonard Reinsch of the Advisory Commission on Information spent five weeks inspecting USIS posts in ten African countries. Some of his findings were disturbing:

The basic problem in Africa for USIA appears to be the erroneous application of European techniques to a continent . . . where the people are not well informed about the United States or Russia and appear to be not much concerned about either. . . . Film, print, and photographic material should contain a more balanced presentation of whites and Negroes in the United States. . . . Many [USIS] programs are too somber, heavy and textual.[11]

Reinsch's report was useful in goading USIA's management into giving more personal attention to Africa. Murrow visited several African countries, receiving a warm reception from leaders and intellectuals who knew he was one of their best friends in Washington.

They spoke to him with candor. "I found a simple formula which would earn me an hour's rest at any time," Murrow said on his return. "I would just turn to the group and say, 'Tell me, what is the United States doing that is wrong?'"

The Agency paid close attention to the answers, for in them were clues to a better operation. USIA media products were developed which were more meaningful for Africans. By 1963 USIA was distributing 150,000 copies of a monthly newspaper in English and 100,000 copies of a similar newspaper in French to present the American point of view to literate Africans in positions of importance. A USIA-produced newsreel, *Africa Today,* was seen every month by more than thirty million Africans. A million and a half American books were published in French and sold at low prices. USIA English-teaching classes in nineteen African countries (up from six only two years before) numbered prime ministers, foreign ministers, parliamentarians, army officers, civil servants, and educators among their students.

USIS libraries were crowded as soon as they opened. In several African countries the first borrower's card went to the prime minister or president. In Morocco the sheer weight of numbers forced a USIS librarian to issue cards of seven different colors, one for each day of the week, and to restrict use of the library to once a week for each card holder. One small USIS library in Africa had more requests for *The Federalist* papers in four weeks than the New York Public Library had in a year. Newly thrust into positions of responsibility, thousands of Africans hungered for information to help them form their own views of the world. Quietly, and—hopefully—persuasively, USIA sought to provide that information.

Murrow had high hopes for the new VOA African relay station, then under construction near Monrovia, Liberia. He wanted its programs to have a truly African flavor, reporting Africa to the Africans by informing those in one country of the progress and good works of another. The United States wanted stable, independent nations in Africa, and VOA could best promote that objective not by exhortations from Washington but by encouraging and publicizing the efforts of constructive forces in the new nations. A program center was established in Monrovia, and VOA correspondents were stationed in key cities throughout the continent.

USIA also sought to influence development of friendly African media, but in this it had less success. Press, radio, television, all were in their infant stages. The Africans wanted help, but the U.S. Government provided little, despite the Agency's prodding.

Efforts failed to get the American news services to expand their limited coverage of Africa and, especially, their limited service to African clients at a price they could afford. On a straight commercial basis, independent AP and UPI could not compete with Tass and the New China News Agency services which Moscow and Peking provided all media at little or no cost. USIA's giveaway Wireless File, prepared especially for Africa and transmitted daily in French and English, did its best to fill the gap.

But the growing USIA effort could hardly keep pace with the rapidly changing scene in Africa. Two weeks after Kennedy's inauguration, pro-Communist Premier Patrice Lumumba was murdered by his opponents in the Congo, and Communist propagandists blamed the United States. Apartheid in South Africa provided the Communists with another stick with which to beat the West. Newly independent countries found that freedom increased, not lessened, their problems. The Soviet Union and—increasingly—Communist China exploited the situation, stepping up their subversion and propaganda. Some African nationalists worked with the Communists against men and ideas they labeled "neo-colonial."

Fortunately, the Communists overplayed their hands in several countries, notably Guinea, and suffered setbacks. USIA's silent ally against Communist ambitions was the African's unwillingness to be dominated by a new master so soon after getting rid of the old.

Particularly embarrassing to the Kremlin were accusations by demonstrating African students in Moscow and other East European cities that they had been subjected to discrimination. As one Kenyan student at the University of Baku described it: "Because we were black they hated us. . . . We were told we could not go out with Russian girls. There was no law against it, but they said it was just local custom. We soon discovered it was unsafe to go out alone with a Russian girl because there was a good chance of being beaten up." In Moscow the Soviets established Lumumba University for African and Asian students, but the students quickly realized that the institution existed primarily to separate Russian and nonwhite foreign students.

Such experiences brought hundreds of disillusioned African students in the Iron Curtain capitals to the doors of American embassies; others went to West Germany. Most of them wanted visas and scholarships for study in America, which posed a problem for the United States: Should we refuse to become involved? Should we encourage the students to return home, where they would spread the truth about life under Communism? Or should we bring them to the United States to study, thereby encouraging the notion that the shortest route to America is via Moscow? The problem was compounded by the fact that many of the students were academically or linguistically unqualified for college study in this country. At one point Murrow leaned toward the idea of encouraging a mass exodus of African students to embarrass the Communists. But that still left us with the problem of what to do with the students after they came out, and in the end not very much was done at all.

The disaffection of African students behind the Iron Curtain blunted the principal theme of Communist anti-American propaganda in Africa: the plight of the Negro in the United States. But Africans needed no reminders from the Russians; they followed the civil rights struggle in America with intense interest. The informed African's view of the United States was shaped primarily by what the U.S. did in Africa and its attitude on such issues as South Africa, Angola, and the Congo. But he also felt that if America could not afford its colored citizens the protection and opportunity it gave its whites, then it could not be trusted in a world whose three billion people were more pigmented than pale.

As time passed, it became increasingly clear to USIA that the credibility of America's leadership of the forces of freedom in Africa and Asia depended to a significant degree on how the United States faced its domestic racial problems. By good fortune, both the President of the United States and the Director of the U.S. Information Agency were committed champions of freedom at home as well as stalwart defenders of freedom abroad.

7 *The Murrow Years: Successes and Failures*

Before Murrow, American propagandists gave little thought to the subject of U.S. race relations. USIA would have liked to avoid the matter, but that was often impossible: the Communists exploited it at every opportunity. When required to discuss the issue, USIA usually did so defensively and in terms of "Negro progress." All but a fraction of the Agency's officers were white, and most of them believed with most other American whites that the Negro was indeed making good progress and that existing inequities were gradually being removed. USIA output on race relations regularly cited the school desegregation decision, but almost never mentioned that integration was painfully slow and in many places nonexistent. The increase in Negro educational and job opportunities was emphasized; the widespread limitations on these opportunities were not. Marian Anderson, Booker T. Washington, and Louis Armstrong were featured along with other Negro artists, musicians, athletes, and educators; militant civil rights leaders were mostly ignored.

The pre-Murrow management of USIA employed many Negroes, but none at upper levels in Washington and only a few abroad, mostly in Africa. At his first senior staff meeting Murrow looked around the crowded conference room and saw not one non-Caucasian face (as he noted to Wilson and me afterward). True, several prominent Negroes had traveled abroad before 1961 under the auspices of the USIS-administered exchange-of-persons program.* And there were

* One was Carl Rowan, who later became Director of USIA; another was Thurgood Marshall, who had argued the school desegregation case before the

171

many in the Agency who recognized the significance of race relations in the world's view of America. But there was little top-level interest. That changed with Murrow.

"There is no other single subject, month in and month out, that so consistently occupies the cares and curiosities of other peoples about the United States," he said. "Events here plague us over there." He would tell American audiences of the African official who interrupted an American diplomat's eulogy of U.S. policy with the cutting query: "Why are you trying to kill my people in Mississippi?" And Murrow described his frustration upon seeing a USIA magazine, a Negro on its cover and a favorable story on American race relations inside, appear on foreign newsstands next to local papers with the headline, "BIRMINGHAM CHURCH BOMBING KILLS FOUR NEGRO CHILDREN."

The facts were difficult enough to deal with; worse yet were the exaggerations. One nonwhite diplomat, arriving in this country for the first time, greeted his host at the airport with eyes fixed firmly on the ground. Asked why, he replied: "I am afraid I shall see a white woman, and when a man of color looks at a white woman in America, mobs of white people may tear him to pieces." That was a diplomat speaking; not an uninformed villager from the backwoods of nowhere, but an educated government official, arriving at Washington's National Airport.

Murrow did not, of course, believe that adverse foreign opinion was in itself an argument for seeking an end to discrimination. "We do it because it is right," he said. And because it was right, Murrow made changes in, and put new emphasis on, the Agency's handling of the racial issue.

First, the Agency began to face the problem head on, rather than skip over it lightly as had been done so often in the past. "The prob-

---

Supreme Court. As the distinguished counsel for the NAACP, Marshall was as credible a spokesman for the American Negro as could be found. This credibility permitted him to be far more blunt and candid, and far more effective, than any white. At one African appearance Marshall was heckled by a Communist student until the tall Negro lawyer, thoroughly exasperated, barked: "I've answered your questions. Now what do you want?" The student replied: "Take a message to the Supreme Court. Tell them to take their responsibilities in race relations seriously!" Marshall thundered back: "Good. And now take a message to yourself. Tell yourself to go straight to hell!" In 1967 Marshall himself was appointed to the high court.

lem will not go away just because we don't talk about it," Murrow said. "Indeed, it will only get worse." The Agency became more candid in reporting racial developments, noting the bad as well as the good. Some members of Congress, particularly Southerners, were highly critical of this approach. But USIA persisted, because a basic law of propaganda was involved: foreigners, hearing the bad news from others if not from us, would be unlikely to believe USIA's good news if unpleasant developments were ignored or shrugged off.

Second, the Agency began to report race relations in depth, instead of merely following the headlines. Developments were put in perspective. In effect the world was told: racial violence is bad, but don't forget that (as Murrow put it) "controversy and disorder are inevitable by-products of our national concern over equal rights for all"—in other words, a price worth paying.

Third, the Agency began to treat Negroes not as a special group worthy of occasional "up from slavery" stories but as equal participants in a multiracial American society. Stories about Negro writers emphasized their prose, not their pigmentation; those on Negro physicians stressed their skill, not the color of their skins. Photographs illustrating USIA press releases and exhibits showed Negroes in all walks of life acting and reacting no differently than other Americans.

Murrow conceded that "we shall not be able to undo wholly" the damage done to America abroad by lurid reports of discrimination and violence. But, as he explained to a group of lawyers on one occasion, there is much USIA can do. "We detail the full and active Administration support of all measures required to solve the problem. . . . We seek out and use sources which give a continuing flow of news about significant constructive developments—however unspectacular. . . . We explain the peculiar nature of the U.S. Federal system, making it clear that local officials are locally elected and local police are locally directed. They are not, as in many other countries, under control of the national government."[1]

That last point was one of the most difficult to convey. America's system of autonomous local government is contrary to most foreign practice. Thus it was not surprising for USIS officers in foreign lands to be told, as they so often were: "If your President really believed in desegregation, he would order discrimination stopped and send the Army to enforce it." Over and over again, at newspaper offices, lecture halls, diplomatic receptions, and private homes, USIS officers patiently explained: "President Kennedy, Federal law, and a majority of the American people oppose discrimination and segregation. Kennedy is determined to enforce Federal law. Until recently, however, local custom and local law prevailed. Now Federal law is covering much that had previously been considered purely local. But still, everywhere in America, law enforcement is local. We do not have a national police force; we do not want one."

Slowly the new approach began to pay off. For example, the Ghanaian newspaper *Ashanti Pioneer,* basing a story on candid USIS press coverage of "freedom riders" who were seeking to end discrimination in Southern bus terminals, commented: "We have said many unkind things about America each time we heard about race problems in that country. Now we know that the trouble constitutes a problem which many Americans are honestly and sincerely trying to solve."

The demonstrations and disturbances increased in number and intensity in 1962 and 1963, but so did foreign understanding. Many sophisticated Africans came to realize they should sympathize with the American Government, not denounce all Americans indiscriminately for the sins of a relatively few, especially since the government was not trying to cover up what was happening. President Kennedy's warm receptions for visiting African leaders, and his candid talks with them, helped mightily. The increase in the number of Negro officers in USIA was also helpful; the number of Negroes holding executive rank went from eighteen in 1961 to thirty-six in 1962.

Mississippi, Alabama, and "The March"

The University of Mississippi riots over the enrollment of Negro student James Meredith in the autumn of 1962 provided a field day for Communist propagandists. Although Kennedy acted decisively, sending in troops and explaining in a nationwide broadcast why he did so, Radio Moscow nonetheless asserted that "the President devoted most of his speech to praising the State of Mississippi. The President's party is facing the November Congressional election and it has no interest in worsening relations with the strong racist groups of the Southern states."

Not only the Communists misrepresented, misunderstood, or exaggerated the story. Some actual headlines, collected by the Agency, included: "AMERICAN POLICE ALERTED IN MISSISSIPPI TO PREVENT NEGRO FROM ENTERING UNIVERSITY" (Tunisia); "REVOLUTION IN U.S." (Mexico); and "WASHINGTON FEARS CIVIL WAR IN MISSISSIPPI" (Germany). USIA countered by quietly and repeatedly telling the full story, making certain the positive aspects were heard, too. Subsequent headlines reflected this effort, among them: "KENNEDY OPENS WAR ON COLOR BAR" (Nigeria); "U.S.A. DETERMINED TO PUT AN END TO RACIAL DISCRIMINATION" (Tunisia), and "FEDERAL AUTHORITY TO PREVAIL" (Norway). *The Daily Nation* of Kenya considered the Meredith case "a vindication of American democracy." Burma's *Yuwadi* told its readers: "The U.S. Government is trying to suppress racial discrimination and it is only a handful of American reactionaries who . . . are defying the law."

Negro civil rights leaders such as James Farmer of CORE and Roy Wilkins of the NAACP spoke on the Voice of America, as did the Attorney General. Head of the Federal Government's civil rights effort and the President's brother and confidant, Robert Kennedy was an authoritative witness. His message laid down the themes that USIA reiterated in all media:

Those who are unfriendly toward the United States rejoiced over the conflict in Mississippi. But most people rejoiced over James Meredith's entry into the University, and over the protection of his basic rights by the courts and by the Federal Government. . . . His enrollment was (at first) prevented by the direct intervention of the Governor . . . [who] held that local traditions and state laws had priority over the national Constitution and the courts. This was an open challenge to the law of the land. It was in support of law, and in pursuance of peaceable enforcement of law, that the United States Government placed Federal peace officers and troops in the town of Oxford.

Then a key theme: "What the world saw in Mississippi was a democratic nation putting its house in order. It was proof of our intent to live not by rule of men but by rule of law." With candor, the President's brother added: "We do not pretend that we are perfect. . . . Segregation remains a problem . . . but we are striving hard to solve it—and we are making progress. . . . Where it still persists—as in the Meredith case—we are determined to bring racism to an end."[2]

A USIA pamphlet, *Success Stories from America,* differed from its predecessors in that it frankly admitted that "widespread publicity given comparatively few celebrities . . . is apt to give almost as distorted an image of the Negro's participation in American life as overemphasis on the occasional incidents of racism." Distributed in ninety-two countries, the pamphlet contained biographical sketches and photographs of both well- and lesser-known successful Negroes. Negro magazines such as *Ebony, Phylon,* and *Negro History* appeared on many USIS library shelves for the first time.

All was not advance, however. In the spring of 1963, repressive measures by the Birmingham, Alabama, police resulted in widely publicized violence. News photographs of a police dog attacking a Negro picket and a policeman pinning a Negro woman to the ground appeared on front pages around the world. The reaction from the foreign press and radio was harsh: "The United States does not practice the freedom it preaches." "Whoever heard of such barbarous acts in the twentieth century by people who claim to be civilized because their skin is white?" "Since the dark days of the Nazi Gestapo, no such barbaric and merciless repression has been seen as in Birmingham."

USIA answered with essentially the same themes used nine months earlier on the Meredith case. But there were limits to how much understanding we could expect from abroad, and to how long we could expect it. Moreover, the situations were different.

"It was easy for the world to understand that in Mississippi twenty thousand Federal troops enforced the enrollment of one Negro," Don Wilson pointed out a few days later. But "it was difficult for the world to understand why Federal troops were not used in Birmingham because there was no violation of a Federal statute. . . . It is difficult to explain that President Kennedy has no direct control over 'Bull' Connor and the police of Birmingham. . . . The peak of understanding was probably reached after the Oxford, Mississippi, crisis. Birmingham may have reversed the trend."

Why? Because, said Wilson, "we no longer can claim that the incidents are isolated, for they are increasingly national in scope. . . . Words will not enlist the world's confidence in this country as a bastion of democracy. Only action can do this."[3]

As it turned out, Wilson was overly pessimistic. Only one day later, on June 11, a combination of words and deeds by the President had a powerful effect in increasing foreign confidence. Again it was Alabama; again it was a recalcitrant Governor, this time George Wallace, who stood in a doorway and tried to stop the admittance of two Negroes to the University of Alabama at Tuscaloosa. Kennedy federalized the Alabama National Guard, and Wallace backed down. There was no violence. That evening the President, speaking to the nation on radio and television, committed the United States "to the proposition that race has no place in American life or law."

We are, said Kennedy, "confronted with a moral issue. . . . Now the time has come for this nation to fulfill its promise. . . . We face a moral crisis as a country and as a people. It cannot be met by repressive police action. It cannot be left to increased demonstrations in the streets. It cannot be quieted by token moves or talk. It is a time to act." He said he would send new and forceful civil rights legislation to Congress.

The speech, hastily prepared but deeply felt, had great impact on foreign opinion, particularly African. Here, in plain words devoid of legalisms and circumlocutions, was a commitment to make real the American dream of equal opportunity and equal protection for all. Kennedy's message was understood and applauded everywhere. USIA broadcast and rebroadcast it, reproduced it as a pamphlet in several languages, and reprinted it in Agency publications.

Not all USIA output on American race relations was as inspiring or effective as Kennedy's speech. Under the pressure of events, USIA's media services fell into disarray in their handling of civil rights during the summer of 1963. Some Voice of America writers, accustomed to following the headlines and the commercial wire services, and armed with Murrow's instruction to "be candid," emphasized the sensational and mostly negative developments at the expense of the less exciting but more helpful signs of progress. Murrow appointed a committee to study the Agency's handling of "racial problems and progress"; its report on July 2 was not reassuring:

> The . . . hectic, incomplete and therefore inaccurate [view abroad of the racial issue] is in large measure being re-enforced by USIA's output. . . . It is the responsibility of the fast news output to go behind the daily headlines to put the bad event into perspective by incorporating the less spectacular but positive developments which are taking place every day. . . .

Commentaries and analyses excessively discuss and rediscuss Supreme Court decisions and Federal efforts (or their lack). Too often the net effect is dull generalization. . . . There is an abysmal failure to tell the powerful story at our disposal.

Murrow read the report aloud, in his best voice of doom, at a staff meeting. The media directors, outraged, submitted lengthy rebuttals. In fact, the committee's report was exaggerated, but it served its purpose: thereafter there was a pronounced improvement in the tone and quality of USIA's handling of the racial issue.

On August 28, 1963, came the long-promised "March on Washington" in support of President Kennedy's civil rights bill, then pending in Congress. By bus, train, plane, and private car more than 200,000 people poured into Washington. Some Americans, not all of them racists, feared violence, but there was none. The crowd, moving with a great dignity, was completely orderly. In the shadow of the Washington Monument and at the feet of the brooding marble Lincoln, the assembled people—black and white, young and old, rich and poor— were symbol of and witness to the vitality of democracy. President Kennedy spoke for most Americans when he told the leaders of the march that evening: "This nation can properly be proud."

If the message of the march was not understood in every corner of this land, or in every office on Capitol Hill, it was well understood abroad. Everywhere there was a new appreciation of American democracy. In Africa the criticism which had become so intense after Birmingham began to taper off. In the Soviet Union, Radio Moscow began to speak of other things. After all, there would never be permitted any protest marches on Moscow or Peking. The civil rights bill became law the following year, and though the march had little effect on its passage, it did have a great impact abroad. Not planned as such, it was a master propaganda stroke.

USIA produced a powerful motion picture on the march. When the film was completed, however, several members of Congress demanded its suppression on the grounds it would "air our dirty linen abroad" and "not tell the full story." Special showings were staged for House and Senate committees, and the furor abated after the Agency added an explanatory introduction and agreed not to "force" any USIS post to show the movie where in the judgment of the PAO it would not be advisable. Subsequently the film received several international honors, including the Grand Prize of the Netherlands National Film Festival and awards from the Cannes International Youth Film Festival and Philippine and Australian film festivals.

American race relations would continue to be a problem for USIA for long years to come, and the problem would grow worse. But, in the autumn of 1963, there was a lifting again of foreign confidence in America. Men of goodwill recognized that the civil rights anthem *We Shall Overcome* was more than a song, a slogan, or a hope. It was a prediction.

Exploiting Space Exploits

Racial problems were not the only cause of wavering foreign confidence in the United States in the early sixties. America's space achievements—or lack of them—were another. The impact was enormous because, rightly or not, our lag in space led foreigners to believe that we were also behind the U.S.S.R. in science and technology generally, and—even more ominous—behind in over-all military strength. Confidential USIA polls showed that in Britain 81 percent thought the U.S.S.R. was ahead of the U.S. in space development; in France the figure was 74 percent; in West Germany 53 percent. Six times as many Britons believed the Soviets had "the most dependable rockets for launching missiles and satellites" as believed the U.S. had; twice as many thought the U.S.S.R. had "the most effective military missiles" as thought the U.S. had.

Kennedy and Murrow set out to remedy the problem. A chronicler of the Kennedy Administration reports that the President

was convinced that Americans did not yet fully grasp the world-wide political and psychological impact of the space race. With East and West competing to convince the new and undecided nations which way to turn, which wave was the future, the dramatic Soviet achievements, he feared, were helping to build a dangerous impression of unchallenged world leadership generally and scientific pre-eminence particularly.[4]

Less than a week before the 1961 Bay of Pigs debacle, Soviet cosmonaut Yuri Gagarin became the first man to orbit the earth in space, and American prestige that April suffered a telling one-two punch. Kennedy pressed the experts to come up with a plan for competing in the space race, and soon USIA had much to talk about. In a second State of the Union Message in May, the President promised that the United States would send a man to the moon and back "before this decade is out."

In early May the United States had its first manned space flight. Astronaut Alan Shepard did not go into orbit, only up from Cape Canaveral and down in the nearby Atlantic. But USIA capitalized on another important difference between the Gagarin and Shepard flights: Gagarin's exploit was conducted in deep Soviet secrecy and announced only after its success was assured, whereas Shepard left the pad in full view of television cameras and hundreds of correspondents. Had the Russian flight failed, no one would have been the wiser; had the U.S. effort failed, American prestige would have suffered another damaging blow. But ours was a risk inherent in an open society, and Shepard's flight dramatically illustrated the difference between the American and Soviet systems. The lesson was not lost on the world.

A month later, for example, the Turkish newspaper *Milliyet* reported that journalists who had attended a USIS-Istanbul film showing on Shepard's flight

were pleased when the Russian Consulate invited them to a film showing Gagarin's flight, as they thought they could make a comparison between the two. After a long propaganda film, Gagarin was at last seen on the screen, roaming through the streets of Moscow with people cheering him. . . . There was nothing in the film about the space flight. . . . Gagarin may have gone into space and the Russians may be far superior in the space race but this was the impression of the journalists who saw both films: Shepard really went into space, not Gagarin, and in front of the whole world, too.

A seventy-eight-year-old Greek peasant wrote the Voice of America:

Tonight's broadcast: what a joy! . . . I began to dance around and to sing. My dear old wife rushed from the kitchen fearing that something had gone wrong with me. "Don't you worry," I tell her. "Go to the cellar and fill my canteen with wine for we shall drink tonight to President Kennedy's health." . . . Long live the Astronaut Shepard and all those who contributed to this great American feat.

USIA kept the story alive with features and photographs. Many foreign publications carried an Agency-distributed article under Shepard's by-line. (One of them, *Al Gumhuriya* of Cairo, claimed that its editors had cabled the astronaut and received the article in response.) A USIA film, *Shadow of Infinity,* prepared in advance, was shown on television stations in forty-nine countries on the day of the launch. A film shot on the day of the flight was shown by Vice President Johnson on his trip to South Asia and by Secretary Rusk to a NATO conference in Oslo. Full-size models of Shepard's spacecraft were exhibited in Europe and the Far East.

The all-out USIA coverage of this first American manned space flight set the pattern for subsequent flights. In February, 1962, John Glenn orbited the earth, and Scott Carpenter's successful flight followed two months later. VOA covered the flights "live" from the predawn countdowns to the landings in the Atlantic. USIS posts were provided in advance with films, backgrounders, photographs, and TV interviews with the astronauts for use on the days of their flights.

A week after Glenn's orbit, thirteen hundred prints of a ten-minute documentary went out to 106 countries. Buenos Aires reported that three million Argentines saw the film; Beirut said 200,000 Lebanese saw it in two weeks; a million and a half viewed it in Turkey, and there were special showings for the Turkish parliament. A NASA color film, distributed by USIA in eleven languages, was seen in Italy by ten million television viewers; in Warsaw the film was shown six times a day to standing-room-only audiences at the Museum of Technology. USIA distributed seventy thousand first-day covers of a stamp commemorating the flight. With a bow to the Agency, an Italian newspaper summed it up: "Never in history have so many people followed in all its details such an event of such proportions."

To capitalize on the world-wide excitement, USIA proposed that Glenn's space capsule be exhibited abroad. NASA said no; it was "needed" in this country. USIA appealed to the White House, and NASA was overruled. The capsule toured twenty-two countries between April and August, and was seen by millions. Bill Davis of USIS-Accra collaborated with Cab Kaye, a popular Ghanaian entertainer, to write a catchy tune, "Everything Is Go" ("Go, go, go—John Glenn, he said it so"); after fifty thousand Ghanaians saw the capsule during its three days in Accra, the local *Sunday Mirror* acidly commented: "Khrushchev regards [his] spaceship as top-secret which must not be seen by people who are not Russians."

The Glenn and Carpenter flights gave American prestige a healthy boost, but world opinion continued (probably correctly) to consider the United States behind the U.S.S.R. in space. In June, 1962, for example, a USIA poll in Britain showed 50 percent still believed the Soviets ahead, while only 20 percent thought the U.S. was leading. This was, however, an American gain over the Soviet lead of 78-7 percent a year earlier.

A few weeks later, the U.S. position was further strengthened by the successful launching of the communications satellite Telstar. In socialist Burma, Rangoon's *The Nation* said: "Communists the world over must be staying up late these nights pondering the strange contradiction of Marxist dogma created by the success of Telstar. . . . [Its] dramatic success was a product of the capitalistic West." *Dagbladet* of Oslo thought Telstar "as revolutionary as the invention of printing." A USIA-commissioned poll in Britain found that 82 percent were able to identify Telstar by name, compared to 78 percent who could name sputnik in 1957.

However, the American triumph was short-lived. That summer the Soviets launched their twin Vostok flights, and the world marveled. A typical comment was that of the conservative, influential *Corriere della Sera* of Milan: "Without doubt the flight gives the U.S.S.R. great prestige, and politically and psychologically increases its strength. Nikolaiev [the cosmonaut] fires the popular imagination and confirms the strength and scientific leadership of Russia." *Figaro* of Paris believed Russia "intended to make us prudent and to calm any desire of resistance on our part."

USIA responded by making even more of the next American space spectacular, Gordon Cooper's orbital flight in May, 1963. The Voice of America's English-language service put on a marathon forty-hour broadcast employing the largest radio network ever put together: fifty-five transmitters with a total output of 5,673 kilowatts. VOA reporters at Cape Canaveral provided "live" coverage and recapitulations in many languages for foreign listeners. Dozens of radio stations rebroadcast the VOA programs. Crowds gathered at USIA exhibits where loudspeakers announced the latest details. Jordan's King Hussein telephoned USIS in Amman to ask that his congratulations be relayed to Kennedy. USIS-India's switchboard broke down under a deluge of calls.

Despite such triumphs, foreign opinion continued to view the Soviet Union as the leader in space, and did so until the summer of 1965 when America's Gemini flights finally pushed the United States into the lead. Much of the prestige-in-space gap was closed during the early 1960s, however, and this was in part due to the sustained effort of USIA.

Molding the Media

One factor in the improved performance of the Agency was the time and attention Murrow devoted to scripts and manuscripts. He had been more responsible than any other man for setting the tone and direction of American radio and TV public affairs programs; now he sought to do the same with the government's media. It was a frustrating and time-consuming job, and he was not wholly successful.

Murrow moved first to reform the Agency's Motion Picture Service. It was responsible for producing documentaries and newsreels for USIS use and theatrical placement abroad. Outside film makers were contracted to do most of the work, although the service retained control over each stage of production. It also acquired from Hollywood and industry short films which would be useful for USIA purposes. Unfortunately, the service's Washington staff of several hundred included few innovative minds, not excepting the head of the service, and the contractors—mostly old-line newsreel producers—were equally uninspired.

Murrow looked for a bright, imaginative, fearless young film maker to head the service and stir it up. After unsuccessfully trying to hire Sam Goldwyn, Jr., he found his man in George Stevens, Jr., scion of another great Hollywood family. Still in his twenties, Stevens was just what was needed: he cajoled the ablest of the nation's young producers into making movies for USIA, and he obtained the cooperation of the film industry as none of his predecessors had been able to do.

Stevens often exasperated his Foreign Service colleagues with his insistence that an audience in London or Paris was no different, really, from an audience in Cochabamba or Ouagadougou, and therefore a film that appealed to sophisticated Europeans would have equal appeal for, and be just as easily understood by, unsophisticated Africans. To some, Stevens also appeared on occasion to be more concerned about method than message. But he made interesting, persuasive films, better than those produced by his predecessors, and they were invariably well received abroad.

Particularly pertinent and persuasive were films on the visits of prominent foreign visitors to the United States, designed for showing in their home countries; in his early months on the job, Stevens produced motion pictures on visits here by four African leaders, the Shah of Iran, and Cypriot President Archbishop Makarios. Other good films followed in 1962, among them: *Gateway to Peace* and *Search for a Treaty*, on U.S. efforts to obtain a nuclear test ban treaty; *Harvest of Learning*, marking the centennial of America's land-grant colleges; *A Threat to the Peace*, on the growing war in Vietnam; and *A Day of Hope*, showing the United Nations at work around the world.

The best production in 1963 was the previously mentioned *The Five Cities of June*, a low-key documentary which won its audiences with colorful reportage on death and coronation in the Vatican, then moved on to a "strategic hamlet" in Vietnam, American and Soviet space spectaculars (making the point, without actually saying so, that Russian space exploration was conducted in secrecy), the successful enrollment of a Negro at the University of Alabama, and finally Kennedy's triumphal appearance in Berlin.

Murrow was less successful in improving USIA's Television Service, which also sorely needed help. It was poorly led, ridden with internal dissension, and underfinanced. Yet Murrow was uncharacteristically reluctant to interfere (as he had also been unwilling to interfere with VOA), perhaps because he had so disliked front-office intervention when he was in commercial television. Finally, however, Murrow tried a new approach, putting at the head of the Television Service a trusted Agency field officer with no professional TV experience. The new chief, Alan Carter, restored harmony in the ranks and greatly improved the quality of the service's output.

The brightest and most persuasive television productions of this period included *Blueprint for Terror*, a story of Cuban subversion in Venezuela prompted by the discovery of a large arms cache there; *Nuestro Barrio (Our Community)*, a series of "soap opera" dramas on a Latin-American village; and a film on the importance of music and religion in American life, based on the Mormon Tabernacle Choir. Less happy were clumsy TV productions on the March on Washington and on Cuban refugees.

Murrow had even less success in improving the quality of the Agency's Press Service. It turned out a great torrent of material for use by USIS posts abroad, and its abundance of output was part of the trouble: there was insufficient discrimination in deciding what to send overseas, and much of the material was too lengthy, requiring extensive editing abroad. Too much of the writing was pedestrian at best, prompting the acidulous Professor John Kenneth Galbraith, Kennedy's Ambassador to India, to inquire: "Why it is that the agency whose business is to communicate manages to employ so many people who can't write?" Galbraith periodically needled USIA in tart telegrams that Murrow found both amusing and helpful—particularly one which demolished both the style and substance of an Agency commentary on economics, the professor's specialty.

There were also problems with the Center Service, the catch-all division that supports the cultural and book programs. The holdover head of this service, William J. Handley, was one of the Agency's ablest officers—so able that Murrow nominated him to be the first Ambassador chosen from USIA ranks. But Handley's successors were unable to make the Center Service a wholly responsive instrument of Agency policy, as Handley himself had been unable to do.

Like Allen, Murrow put great emphasis on English-teaching. The popularity of the Agency's English classes created a problem, however. USIS could not teach English to every foreigner who wanted to learn, not even to every foreigner who was willing to pay. The custom had been to take students on a first-come, first-served basis. This was changed; USIS posts were told to avoid any outward appearance of discrimination but to assure that applicants from USIS Target Audiences would get priority over others. The content of teaching materials was changed, not to inject an obvious propagandistic message but to assure that students of the language simultaneously learned something affirmative about American values and institutions.

In 1961 the Agency began to teach English via television. *Let's Learn English,* during its first two years, appeared on nearly sixty TV stations in thirty-five countries; its estimated daily audience was 25 million, far more than could be reached in the classrooms. In Japan there were twice-daily showings over eleven stations. A network executive in Vienna called the series "the most popular television show in Austria"; fan mail also disclosed a broad following in Czechoslovakia, Hungary, and Yugoslavia where Austrian TV can be received.

186 | THE WORD WAR

Two years later, the Agency started a second series of sixty-five programs, *Let's Speak English*. It was equally successful. Programs in both series consisted of two parts: a serialized story filmed in USIA's Washington studios, followed by "live" instruction by an overseas teacher.

The USIS libraries were, of course, the heart of all USIS operations abroad in Murrow's time, as before and since. While he was Director of USIA, more than thirty million people visited the USIS libraries annually, borrowing eight million books to take home and reading twice that many on the premises.

Murrow wanted the libraries to be free, open, and representative of all shades of American thought. But, as with the English-teaching and other cultural programs, he wanted them to concentrate on USIS Target Audiences. He understood that high patronage did not necessarily mean high effectiveness; it might mean that a USIS library was the only air-conditioned spot in town open to the public without charge. He was more interested in how well the books and magazines were used than in how well they were catalogued. Under his direction many (though not all) USIS libraries became more used and more useful.

One important innovation in the media field during the Murrow administration was establishment of a Foreign Correspondents Center in New York. The motivation was simple: foreign newspapers, magazines, and radio and TV stations understandably use more of their own correspondents' material than they do "handouts" from USIS, and their readers, listeners, and viewers naturally give greater credibility to their own journalists than to foreign propagandists. It was, therefore, important that USIA make every effort to assist and influence the 550 foreign newsmen who cover this country.

The Center was opened in October, 1961, a block from United Nations headquarters. It was jointly sponsored by USIA, the White House, and the State Department, and staffed and operated by USIA. Although representatives of the big foreign newspapers and periodicals have made little use of it, a hundred or more who have fewer high-level contacts and operate on limited budgets have welcomed and patronized the Center.

The Center assists in arranging interviews with government officials and newsworthy private citizens, provides background information on a regular basis, organizes trips around the United States for correspondents who otherwise would be tied to New York, provides a convenient location where American newsmakers who are not easily accessible to foreign journalists can hold press conferences, and provides a reference library (including daily newspapers from thirty-five American cities) and a recording booth.

White House Press Secretary Pierre Salinger took considerable interest in the Center, and on opening day was there to greet foreign newsmen and to read them a letter from President Kennedy: "We want to make it as easy as possible for you to cover this large, complex and many-sided country. . . . Truth is often elusive and rarely simple; if our Center helps you in the pursuit of truth, we shall feel adequately rewarded."

Although the Center did not live up to early expectations, Salinger later wrote that he considered its establishment "one of the most important single acts of the Kennedy administration in the field of press relations."[5]

In the White House itself, Kennedy added a second Assistant Press Secretary, whose primary task was to work with foreign journalists in Washington, arranging special briefings by top U.S. officials and undertaking related chores. The job was filled for a time by Jay W. Gildner, a young USIA officer who had impressed Salinger and the President during Kennedy's 1961 visit to Canada, where Gildner was serving.

White House interest in making the most effective use of the Agency was demonstrated in other ways, too. Recognizing that Presidential pronouncements had great impact abroad as well as in this country, Salinger invited Wilson or me to attend meetings of government information officials which preceded every Kennedy press conference; likely questions, and the best ways of handling them, were discussed. One of us also attended McGeorge Bundy's staff meetings.

Salinger assisted Agency efforts to coordinate its activities with the foreign information operations of America's allies. Beginning in 1957, USIA and the State Department held periodic meetings with British Government information officials to exchange views, ideas, and techniques. In 1961 similar talks were begun with the German Government. Although his predecessor had not, Salinger attended several of these meetings and made useful contributions. He also arranged to make Camp David, the Presidential retreat in the nearby Catoctin Mountains, available for some of the meetings, a gesture much appreciated by our foreign visitors.

Laos and Vietnam

One of the subjects brought up repeatedly at the meetings with the British and the Germans was Southeast Asia, where the United States needed all the support, psychological as well as military and economic, that it could get from its European friends. Our allies were sympathetic but guarded in their responses.

Early in his Administration Kennedy recognized that Lao neutrality was the only realistic alternative to a Communist takeover or full-scale American intervention, neither of which was considered acceptable. Reversing the Eisenhower policy, the U.S. Government sought a coalition regime that would take Laos out of the big-power struggle. In neighboring Vietnam, however, the problem was more complicated. Sporadic Communist-led guerrilla warfare against the government of Ngo Dinh Diem was developing into what Khrushchev had called a "war of national liberation," and the U.S. commitment to Diem was such that Washington could not, at that late date, switch to a policy of favoring neutrality—or so the Administration believed.

In Laos USIS did its best to follow the change in U.S. policy from all-out backing of faltering Premier Phoumi Nosavan to support for a neutralist coalition headed by Prince Sovanna Phouma. Radio and leaflet operations aimed at undermining the Communist Pathet Lao, and anti-Communist propaganda directed at friendly audiences, were continued. But the greatest emphasis was now put on building support for the throne, the Lao constitution, and "national reconciliation," i.e., the coalition government.

USIA had posts in the administrative capital of Vientiane, the royal capital of Luang Prabang, and the provincial cities of Savannakhet and Pakse. USIS officers worked closely with their counterparts in the Lao Government, traveled throughout the country, and as a consequence took many personal risks. One of them, Francis P. Corrigan, Jr., was killed.

Elsewhere in the world, USIA sought to clarify the issues of Southeast Asia. A Potomac Cable in the autumn of 1961 presented the prevailing U.S. position in favor of "a truly neutral Lao government" and "an International Control Commission armed with sufficient authority and mobility to enable it to safeguard the neutrality, independence and sovereignty of Laos." On Vietnam, once again a matter of world interest, the cable noted that "infiltration from Communist North Vietnam since the first of the year has increased the Viet Cong force in South Vietnam from nine to fifteen thousand men— probably the largest guerrilla force in the world today. Its activities include ambushes, kidnappings, assassinations and other forms of terror. The Vietnamese Army is fighting courageously and with increasing success. . . . However, it is important to recognize that major battles are yet to be fought."[6]

The truth of that last sentence became more stark as the months passed.

In early 1961 USIA participated in a White House task force on Vietnam which recommended that U.S. forces fight there, not merely "advise" the local forces. Vice President Johnson, and later Presidential advisers Maxwell Taylor and Walt Rostow, went to Saigon and returned urging a greatly stepped-up effort, including the use of American combat forces. Despite the increasing pressure to commit troops, Kennedy refused—although he did order sizable increases in advisory forces and authorized them to fire if fired upon.

While the President recognized that there were major political, psychological, and economic factors in the Vietnam struggle, military considerations dominated most meetings on the subject. Perhaps they should have. But the U.S. problem there, as in any guerrilla insurrection, was heavily psychological. There was little chance of Saigon defeating the Vietcong and pacifying the countryside if the villagers of South Vietnam fed, sheltered, and assisted the rebels, whether because of sympathy or intimidation.

"Defoliation" was one military problem with major psychological overtones on which the White House did listen carefully to USIA. South Vietnamese trains and trucks were being ambushed by guerrillas operating with relative safety from the jungle which surrounded roads and rail lines; also, there were areas where the Vietcong were living off crops grown by local villagers. The Pentagon wanted authority to use chemicals to kill brush, trees, and crops where necessary. USIA understood the military necessities but, remembering the

Communist "germ warfare" charges of the Korean conflict, warned that our use of defoliants could give us a propaganda black eye. After much discussion it was decided that defoliants would be used, but only sparingly and only with prior Washington approval in each instance.

As the war escalated (the word was just becoming popular), so did the USIS effort. More men, more mobile film units, more projectors, and more presses were sent to Saigon and a growing number of provincial USIS posts. Murrow and his top staff began to devote more of their time to Vietnam, and particularly to getting good people assigned there; USIS had been handicapped by the relatively low quality of some of its staff.

Another handicap to effective propaganda operations in Vietnam was a running—and time-consuming—quarrel with American correspondents stationed there. In Saigon as in other foreign posts, USIS handled relations with American journalists as well as with the local press. Most places this arrangement worked smoothly, but Saigon was different.

Essentially, the problem stemmed from the fact that the American reporters in Saigon had a better feel for what was happening than did officials of the American Embassy, even though the latter of course had more complete information.

Arthur Schlesinger, Jr. wrote later that

the Administration in Washington was systematically misinformed by senior American officials in Saigon in 1962-63 regarding the progress of the war, the popularity of Diem, the effectiveness of the "strategic hamlet" program and other vital matters. It was not that these officials were deliberately deceiving their President; it was that they deceived themselves first. Ordinary citizens restricted to reading the American press were better informed in 1963 than officials who took top-secret cables seriously.[7]

Most of the correspondents disliked President Diem and hated his brother Nhu and his wife, who pushed them around; they were certain the war was not going as well as was claimed; and they resented what they considered deliberately dishonest reports from the embassy, particularly those regarding combat and the extent of U.S. participation in it. In a vain effort to bring the correspondents and the embassy together, President Kennedy sent a series of troubleshooters to

Saigon. The State Department drafted a new press relations policy which was approved by USIA and the White House and sent to our embassy in Saigon on February 21, 1962. Shortly thereafter John Mecklin, a former *Time* foreign correspondent, was made the new head of USIS in Vietnam.

Mecklin knew several of the correspondents there personally, had covered the French defeat in Indochina eight years earlier, and had a good sense of propaganda. But he was in trouble from the start. The February press policy proved to be of little help; as Mecklin noted later, "It recognized the right of American newsmen to cover the war in Vietnam, but it was otherwise little more than a codification of the errors the mission was already committing."[8] Some in the embassy viewed with suspicion Mecklin's close personal relations with American newsmen, yet the newsmen no longer considered him one of their own. Mecklin himself found it hard to accept the embassy's sanguine views of the war and Diem, and even harder to accept the policy of inadequately informing, if not misleading, the press.

"Those responsible for the information policies of the government were therefore squeezed hard," Salinger wrote later, "between the desire of the administration to downplay the war for a whole variety of military and political reasons and the desire of the reporters on the ground to tell all to the American people. . . . The solution may have well been reached in a middle position, but the hardening of attitudes by both press and government never allowed us to reach that compromise."[9]

In the spring of 1963, Mecklin returned to Washington for a throat operation; before he went into the hospital I took him to see President Kennedy. Mecklin made a hoarse, fervent plea for greater candor with the press, and the President did agree to instruct embassy officers to take American correspondents more into their confidence. The new policy was drafted by Salinger and hand-delivered to Ambassador Nolting and the U.S. military commander in Vietnam, General Harkins. But it did little good, for the situation by then was moving fast—and mostly downhill.

Many of USIS-Saigon's activities were in direct support of, if not in actual collaboration with, the Diem Government, and growing Vietnamese disaffection with that government added to Mecklin's woes. But the elusive Vietcong were, of course, USIS's greatest problem. In an awards ceremony honoring Vietnamese employees (one posthumously), Mecklin noted: "This is an unusual occasion—to my knowledge the first time such awards for courage in combat conditions have been made by USIS-Vietnam, and perhaps by USIS worldwide. . . . I would also like to point out that the risks and hazards which you face in USIS field work are not endured for USIS nor for the United States but for your own country."[10]

But courage was not enough. The United States began to pressure Diem to reform or else, and reform meant getting rid of, or at least putting under wraps, Diem's brother Nhu and his powerful, beautiful wife (who promptly flew to the United States to arouse American opinion against the new U.S. policy). The reforms did not come, and on November 1, 1963, a military coup overthrew the regime and Diem and his brother were murdered. USIA, in Saigon and elsewhere, emphasized that the basic issues of Vietnam were unchanged, whatever the government in power. But the subsequent short life of successor regimes, and the worsening of the war picture, exacerbated the problems of USIA as well as of the American Government as a whole.

Counterinsurgency and the "Emphasis on Youth"

At the outset of his Administration, Kennedy was greatly concerned with the lack of U.S. preparedness for dealing with Communist-sponsored guerrilla warfare, from doctrine to "hardware." Our unmatched nuclear strength, an awesome weapon in all-out war, was of no use in the jungle. Attorney General Kennedy, a kind of Presidential special agent within the foreign affairs bureaucracy, began to devote much of his time to seeking remedies.

A Special Group (Counter-Insurgency) was established to advise the President and goad the departments. Chaired by General Maxwell Taylor (and later by Under Secretary of State Harriman), its membership included the Deputy Secretary of Defense, the Chairman of the Joint Chiefs of Staff, the Attorney General (who served as the group's conscience and gadfly), the Deputy Under Secretary of State, the Administrator of AID, and the Directors of USIA and CIA. The Special Group (C-I) kept an eye on countries where insurgency was a present or potential threat, sponsored a series of four-week training seminars on insurgency at the State Department's Foreign Service Institute (making attendance compulsory for middle- and senior-grade officers of all agencies who were being assigned to underdeveloped countries), and prodded the agencies to improve their anti-insurgency capabilities.

Within the Special Group (C-I), USIA pushed for more attention to situations where insurgency had not yet developed but might, urging greater use of psychological, political, and economic means to "immunize" these countries from the disease that had struck Vietnam. President Kennedy approved of this emphasis, telling the first training seminar that "this is not merely a military effort; it also requires . . . a broad knowledge of the whole development effort of a country, the whole technique of the national government to identify itself with the aspirations of [its] people."

Unfortunately, inadequate attention was given to developing methods for removing the causes of insurgency. USIA established its own training program on counterinsurgency with the emphasis on "immunization" and put a former Saigon PAO in charge of it. In eighteen months a thousand USIA officers, including many desk-bound Washington employees, attended the course. Because much of the impetus for the counterinsurgency programs came from the Kennedy brothers (and in USIA from Murrow), the special effort declined or was incorporated into regular operations after the Kennedys and Murrow left the scene.

There was another special effort in which Robert Kennedy and USIA played key roles. In most underdeveloped countries, many young people—particularly university students—are susceptible to frustrations that lead to a desire (often with good reason) to overturn or radically change the *status quo*. The youth then become emotionally anti-American because they think the U.S. always favors the *status quo*. Often hostile to their own governments, these young men and women subscribe to a vague "socialism." They are hard to reach, for they avoid embassy cocktail parties and USIS libraries, and are deeply suspicious of "imperialist" propaganda. With the emergence of a score of new nations in the early 1960s, many of this type were thrust into positions of importance; some quickly became cabinet ministers. Others, less fortunate, found it difficult to find jobs, and economic frustrations added to other anxieties led them into noisy politics.

If for no other reason, sheer numbers made young people important. In India and Pakistan, 60 percent of the population was under twenty-five; in Brazil 64 percent; in Venezuela 72 percent; in Indonesia 61 percent. Two-thirds of the people of Iraq, Egypt, and South Korea were under thirty. Even those still in school were making their mark in the political life of their countries. Students had participated in the Hungarian revolt of 1956; student riots in Japan had forced the resignation of the Prime Minister and prevented President Eisenhower's 1960 visit; students brought down the Syngman Rhee government in Korea, and helped topple the Menderes regime in Turkey.

America's adversaries were not overlooking this audience. The Soviets brought 25,000 young men and women from all over the world, but especially from the underdeveloped countries, to study (and be indoctrinated) in the U.S.S.R. Russian teachers were in the classrooms of thirty countries. The Kremlin sponsored costly World Youth Festivals in Moscow, Vienna, and Helsinki.

After several trips abroad, where he proved particularly adroit in discussions with students, Robert Kennedy returned convinced that not only USIA but the government as a whole had to do more to reach and persuade young leaders, potential leaders, and potential troublemakers. At his instigation an Interagency Youth Committee was set up under the chairmanship of the able Assistant Secretary of State for Educational and Cultural Affairs, Lucius D. Battle, with representatives from State, AID, USIA, Defense, and other agencies. The committee's efforts were given a strong endorsement by the President and Secretary Rusk, and Attorney General Kennedy religiously attended all its meetings. Ambassadors and their staff abroad were instructed to get busy devising new ways of reaching politically active young people.

Some U.S. diplomats welcomed the new "emphasis on youth" policy, held seminars for university student leaders, invited them to their receptions, and sought out speaking engagements on campuses. Others believed the policy was contrary to traditional diplomatic procedure and not likely to succeed anyway. They dragged their feet, even after being goaded into action by an interdepartmental inspection team which paid lightning visits abroad to see how the effort was going. AID was slow in getting the word; it took desk pounding by Robert Kennedy and some personnel changes before that agency participated wholeheartedly.

The Attorney General was perplexed by the bureaucratic backsliding. "Why," he asked, "do they resist even after the President has made clear what he wants?" The answer was that the "emphasis on youth" policy was new, different, difficult, and lacking full support from many upper- and middle-level officials—civil servants who were more concerned with pleasing their immediate bosses than a remote President or Attorney General. And some old-timers, lacking enthusiasm for the Administration, felt that the new approach was just a whim of the Kennedys and should be resisted.

The Attorney General persisted, however, and much was accomplished. Some of the best work was done by the youngest Foreign Service Officers, who spent long hours conversing with young foreigners in coffeehouses and on campuses. USIA's top management was strongly behind the new approach, and James R. Echols, appointed Youth and Student Affairs Adviser, was a vigorous and articulate exponent. Still, the Agency's response was spotty. Some in USIA, noting that many VOA listeners and USIS library patrons were under twenty-five years of age, concluded that the Agency was already doing its job. But they missed the point: the "emphasis on youth" policy sought to reach the heretofore unreachable, the young man who came to the USIS library to throw a rock, not read a book.

Despite the laggards, by 1963 USIA's new emphasis on youth began to have an impact on operations. Some examples:

• The Voice of America inaugurated two new programs, *Young World Viewpoint,* broadcast daily in English, and *The World We Live In,* aired fifty times a month in eighteen languages.

• *American Outlook,* the Agency's widely distributed African periodical, added a four-page insert describing the life of African students in American universities.

• Twenty-eight Student Affairs Officers were assigned to work with Latin-American students in USIS posts and binational centers.

• In Venezuela young intellectuals participated in a USIA-sponsored week-long seminar on democratic thought; in Japan seminars on America were arranged for professors and students from fifty-three universities throughout the country.

• In a six-month period, USIS-India presented cultural programs in ten major cities, reaching students of eight universities and twenty-five colleges; a two-week program at the University of Calcutta, for example, attracted 20,000 students, and an American Cultural Week in Andhra Pradesh was attended by 22,750 students and faculty from Andhra University.

• In Italy the role of youth was stressed in a seminar on "Europe and the Atlantic Community" organized by USIS at the University of Florence; a USIS-organized Youth Week in Palermo brought students together from all NATO countries to discuss "problems of a united Europe."

When Johnson succeeded Kennedy in the White House, he re-affirmed his support for the "emphasis on youth" policy. But, gradually, much of the steam went out of the effort. Some bureaucrats who had never cared for the policy, or who had been annoyed by Robert Kennedy's prodding, took their cue from newspaper stories of tension between him and the new President. When Johnson ruled Kennedy out of the Vice Presidential race in mid-1964 and the Attorney General resigned to run for the Senate, there was a further decline of interest in the youth effort.

Meetings of the Interagency Youth Committee became fewer and further between. Its chairman departed to become Ambassador to Egypt. The new Assistant Secretay of State, Harry McPherson, was able and interested, but in a few months Johnson moved him over to the White House staff. Like some other governmental operations, the youth effort was never killed; it merely withered.

8 The Murrow Years: Triumph and Tragedy

In the autumn of 1962, there occurred an event far more menacing to the security of the United States and the world than anything wild-eyed students could foment. The place was Cuba, but the danger was Soviet, nuclear, and considerably deadlier than Castro subversion. It was the supreme test of the Kennedy Administration: a sudden confrontation of American and Soviet nuclear power. For USIA it was a unique challenge, and a unique opportunity to play an unprecedented role.

After the Bay of Pigs, Fidel Castro drew closer to Communism. Although in 1959 Castro had denounced "ignoramuses" who called him a Communist, in late 1961 he proclaimed: "I am a Marxist-Leninist until the day I die!" In early 1962 the Organization of American States expelled Cuba and denounced Communist penetration of the hemisphere. That summer, Soviet aid to Cuba increased sharply, and five thousand Soviet "technicians" swarmed onto the island. In August surface-to-air missiles were installed; the Kremlin went out of its way to assure the United States that all arms supplied Cuba were exclusively defensive in character. Nonetheless, Kennedy ordered intense surveillance of the island.

On September 11 the Soviet news agency Tass distributed a harsh statement. It proclaimed that Russian missiles were so powerful that there was no need to locate them outside the U.S.S.R., charged that the United States was "preparing for aggression against Cuba," and threatened "aggressors" with "a crushing retaliatory blow." In an

197

unusual move, USIA replied directly to the Tass statement; even more unusual, Murrow wrote the reply himself:

The Soviet statement . . . reflects a lust for power and disregard for truth. The Government of the United States threatens no nation and no people. . . . The Soviet statement regarding Cuba appears to say "Stop doing what you have no intention of doing, or terrible things will happen to you."[1]

Terrible things were exactly what the Soviets had in mind.

Swiftly and secretly, they shipped to Cuba forty-two medium-range ballistic missiles of the type using atomic warheads and began construction of twenty-four reusable launch pads for medium-range missiles and sixteen launching sites for intermediate-range rockets. Had construction of these sites been completed, Soviet nuclear striking power against the United States would have nearly doubled, the credibility of America's willingness to use its nuclear deterrent would have been damaged, and Moscow would have been given a powerful bargaining tool on Berlin, overseas bases, and other issues.

Early Sunday morning, October 14, a U-2 plane flew a routine reconnaissance mission over western Cuba. Photo interpreters late Monday spotted the telltale signs of a medium-range missile site, and the President was informed the first thing Tuesday. Three hours later his top advisers were convened to consider what should be done. There was not much time; construction was being carried forward so rapidly that in two weeks the missiles would be targeted on American cities and defense installations. The President called for absolute secrecy, so the Soviets would not know a minute sooner than necessary that they had been found out. A group of advisers, later designated the Executive Committee or "Ex Com" (of the National Security Council), met at least once, and often several times, daily from then until the end of the crisis.

The complete story of the Cuban missile crisis has been told elsewhere. This is an account of USIA's role, one of the most important in the Agency's history.

It quickly became clear that communication was a key element of the crisis. The U.S. Government had to consider several foreign audiences: the men in the Kremlin, the Cuban Government and people, the governments and people of Latin America, allies, and the nonaligned nations. It was essential that the United States not tip its hand prematurely and not mislead the Soviets into making a miscalculation that could lead to nuclear war. Once the U.S. response was announced, it would be essential that the government's intentions and its will and ability to carry them out be understood by all. Persuasiveness, accuracy, and speed were paramount. If this was "news management," as some journalists later charged, so be it.

USIA was not immediately brought into the deliberations. On Wednesday morning, after a routine Cabinet meeting, Robert Kennedy asked Wilson if Murrow would be "available" on the weekend. Wilson said no, Murrow was in the hospital with pneumonia and would be away for some time. "Too bad," said Bobby. "Will you be available?" Again Wilson replied no; he was planning to visit his mother in New Jersey. "Please don't leave town this weekend," asked the Attorney General, and Wilson said he would not. That noon I lunched with my brother Ted at the White House. He obviously was deeply preoccupied, but refused to tell me why or to comment on my speculations.

On Friday morning Robert Kennedy telephoned Wilson and asked him to see Under Secretary of State George Ball and Latin American Assistant Secretary Edwin Martin "on a secret matter of urgent importance." That evening Ball and Martin briefed Wilson on what was happening and told him to work out means of keeping the Cuban people informed throughout the crisis. McGeorge Bundy amplified the instructions on Saturday morning, and Wilson brought Latin American Assistant Director Hewson Ryan, VOA chief Henry Loomis, and me in on the planning shortly thereafter.

Although Robert Kennedy was working closely with his brother on the crisis, there apparently was a breakdown in their communication. The President seemingly had not wanted to bring USIA in that soon, and was momentarily annoyed when he learned of the Bundy briefing, instructing my brother Ted to enjoin us to secrecy. (Kennedy apparently never was aware of Wilson's session with Ball and Martin.) But on Sunday morning he welcomed Wilson to the latter's first meeting of the Executive Committee, and a day later officially designated him a member of the group.

While "Ex Com" was deciding what course of action to recommend to the President, USIA organized its effort. The Agency's first task was to improve its broadcast capability to Cuba. VOA transmitted to Cuba and Latin America only by shortwave, whereas most Cubans had radio sets that could receive only medium-wave broadcasts. USIA had no one to blame but itself for this gap; so far as I know, it had never seriously considered building facilities for medium-wave broadcasting to Castro's island. A USIA mobile medium-wave transmitter, under construction in Texas, was rushed to a Florida key and hastily installed. A second transmitter was supplied by the Navy. But that was not enough; we quickly came to the conclusion that we would need the help of private American radio stations. VOA had a list of nine that would blanket Cuba.

On Sunday President Kennedy approved our plan. The White House communications director was instructed to arrange for direct, continuously open telephone lines to the radio stations involved. Salinger was briefed on the crisis Sunday, and he and Wilson agreed that Federal Communications Commission Chairman Newton Minow was essential in gaining the cooperation of the stations. Minow had left for New York that night and could not be found, but Wilson located him early Monday morning and told him cryptically that he must fly back to Washington at once. Minow did so, abandoning a luncheon speech and arriving about noon.

The three men met in Salinger's office and agreed on the following: Minow would immediately investigate the legal aspects. Salinger would schedule telephone calls to the owners of the stations for 6 P. M., one hour before the President was to address the nation and disclose the crisis and the U.S. response. USIA would draft a statement for Salinger to read to the owners, and as each one agreed to cooperate, the White House communications experts would tie the Voice of America into his station.

The plan worked perfectly. At the appointed hour Salinger called the owners in rapid succession (alerted in advance, they were standing by). All agreed to relay VOA nighttime broadcasts to Cuba from the President's Monday evening, October 22, speech until the end of the crisis. The VOA rebroadcasts were limited to the hours from dusk to dawn because, due to atmospheric conditions, that was the only time the stations could be heard in Cuba. The cooperating medium-wave "broadcast band" stations were WGBS, WMIE and WCKR in Miami; WSB in Atlanta; WCKY, Cincinnati; WKWF, Key West; and

WWL, New Orleans. Also adding their facilities were two private shortwave stations, WRUL of New York and KGEI in San Carlos, California.

The use of commercial radio stations was unprecedented, but so was the crisis. Six weeks later President Kennedy honored the stations in a ceremony at the White House. "We were anxious," he said, "that medium wave be used and the only device that we could use was the radio stations. We went to all of them. They immediately volunteered their assistance. None of them put forward all of the objections which they could have. . . . I think they showed two things: first, how significant radio is in getting across a message beyond national boundaries, and secondly, how patriotic were those men who ran these stations."

While the radio plans were being worked out, Salinger met with the press officers of State and Defense to work out a policy of news coordination. To avoid contradictory statements which might mislead friend or enemy, they decided nothing should come out of either department without prior White House approval. Meanwhile, the President and the State Department laid plans to notify our allies—and the Soviets—at the appropriate moment. U.S. ambassadors were instructed to brief the highest officials of their host governments.*

Salinger took one more step to make certain the Soviets got the message. In arranging the limited "pool" of reporters from the large Washington press corps who would be in Kennedy's office while he broadcast, he deliberately chose Mike Sagatelyan of Tass. When the surprised Russian asked why, Salinger told him: "I want to be sure that you read the President loud and clear."[2]

---

* No matter how carefully American ambassadors or USIS officers explain the issues, however, there is always a question as to how much of the message is heard and understood. The Chinese Communist attack on India occurred the same week as the missile crisis, and many American ambassadors explained the U.S. position on both matters when they called upon high government officials of the nations to which they were accredited. One African Foreign Minister listened with apparent great interest to what our ambassador was telling him, clucking sympathetically at the right moments. When the ambassador was leaving, feeling he had done a most persuasive job, the Foreign Minister escorted him to the door and then remarked heatedly: "But why would Chiang Kai-shek want to attack India?" The disillusioned ambassador went home, took a long cold shower, and reflected on the mysteries of intercultural communication.

The Case for America

But neither Tass nor foreign statesmen could be expected to argue America's case before the bar of world opinion. A major share of this task was borne by USIA. It had to convince the world that the Soviets were actually doing what Kennedy said they were doing, that the danger to the peace and security of America and the world was real and imminent, and that the U.S. response—initially a blockade of Cuba, until the missiles and bombers were removed—was necessary and appropriate, neither more nor less than the situation required. USIA sought to convey the picture of an unpanicked but determined America, unflinching in the face of intimidation but avoiding war unless Moscow made it necessary.

The President's speech, calm, measured, but determined, was the best weapon in the Agency's arsenal. When Kennedy's text was ready, Russian, Spanish, and French translators were summoned to put it into those languages for immediate transmission abroad once he started speaking. The translators were given their assignments Monday morning, put into adjacent rooms, and told to speak to no one. I wrote a "lead" story, to be used by VOA and the Agency's Press Service. I also wrote a classified policy guidance, to be transmitted to all posts in code as soon as the President went on the air, and an unclassified Potomac Cable to go out on the Wireless File. The Potomac Cable laid down our line:

The United States has acted swiftly, firmly and decisively to protect the security of the Western Hemisphere and the peace of the world. . . . The issue was simple: Secretly and under cover of fervent protestations to the contrary . . . the Soviet Union has swiftly been constructing offensive nuclear missile sites in Cuba. . . . These new, clearly offensive, mass destruction weapons threaten the safety of the entire hemisphere and the peace of the entire world.

The response of the United States to this grave threat clearly indicates the U.S. desire to keep the peace—and equally clearly indicates that the U.S. cannot accept this "deliberately provocative and unjustified" act by the Soviets. . . .

No shots need be fired; no blood need be shed. This is not an act of war but an act to prevent war. . . .[3]

Late that afternoon I asked the Policy Application Officers of the media services and the geographic areas to come to my office at 6:30 P.M., where copies of the English and foreign-language texts of the President's speech, the Potomac Cable, the classified guidance, and the official news story were piled high. Within USIA, at least, the secret had been well kept; my colleagues by that time knew from the press that a crisis was brewing, probably about Cuba, but they did not know its nature. After being briefed they picked up their copies of the documents and soberly hurried back to their offices. For many in USIA that week, each working day extended far into the night.

The Voice of America carried the President's address "live" from the White House; it was followed by Spanish and Portuguese translations to Latin America and repeats in other languages at peak listening hours. The Latin-American service stayed on the air around the clock for the duration of the crisis. As had been true in other times of crisis, the Voice's audience mushroomed enormously. People everywhere wanted to know what the United States was doing and saying. The British Embassy reported massive listening in Havana.

Two special Russian-language programs were beamed daily by VOA to the Soviet "technicians" in Cuba. These broadcasts were largely identical to those transmitted to the U.S.S.R. itself, but they also made it clear—mostly by implication—that if hostilities erupted, the Russians manning the missile installations would be the first to pay for Khrushchev's folly. However, the Agency never learned whether these broadcasts were listened to or whether they had any impact.

As the President was speaking to the nation, USIA's Wireless File radio teletypes were transmitting the text of his address, in English, French, and Spanish, to all USIS posts around the world. Within hours these posts delivered translations of the address to hundreds of foreign newspapers and radio stations and thousands of government officials and diplomats. Drawing on the classified policy guidance and the Potomac Cable, USIS posts prepared and distributed their own news releases and "backgrounders" to support the American position.

Within a week, the Agency's regional printing centers in Mexico City, Beirut, and Manila published illustrated pamphlets with the text of the President's address in several languages, as did many individual USIS posts. Two hundred prints of a film of Kennedy's speech, dubbed in many languages, were sent abroad. A film clip of highlights was produced for foreign newsreels. A ten-minute motion picture on the Cuban situation was sent overseas in forty languages. USIA's TV service quickly produced documentaries based on proceedings at the UN and interviews with Cuban refugees. One hundred copies of a photo exhibit were rushed to Latin America.

There was some discussion within the Executive Committee on whether the U-2 photographs should be made public to bolster the American case. The longest discussion took place the day after Kennedy's speech, when world reaction—not all of it favorable—began to come in. Wilson, supported by Salinger, argued strongly in favor of releasing the pictures. CIA, supported by the Pentagon, was opposed, arguing that it would compromise their operation if the Soviets knew how sharply we were able to determine each little detail on the ground. Kennedy reluctantly decided not to release the photographs, but he was concerned by the skepticism of several important British newspapers, some of which even questioned whether in fact there were any offensive missiles in Cuba.

Then, within hours, USIS-London inadvertently released the photographs to the BBC, which promptly showed them on television. Kennedy was surprised but not too disturbed; British Ambassador Ormsby-Gore had been urging him to release the pictures, and he had been reconsidering the matter. Stevenson used the photos in a scathing attack on the Soviets at the United Nations, and USIA—working its limited photographic laboratory around the clock—sent out over the next few days 64,215 photographs of the missile sites and related matters. The pictures proved indispensable in convincing the world of the presence of offensive missiles in Cuba.

Latin-American expert Hewson Ryan and I prepared a one-page leaflet in Spanish, featuring the best of the missile site photographs, for dropping by plane over Cuba. Press Service Director Ray Mackland flew secretly to the Army's Psychological Warfare Headquarters at Fort Bragg and arranged for the printing of six million copies. Four airplanes, armed with canisters of the leaflets, moved to an advance base in Florida. Kennedy, however, never gave the order to drop —possibly because he did not want to be accused of unnecessary provocation. (After the crisis was over, Wilson asked the President, at a meeting of the Executive Committee, for permission to cancel the leaflet operation. Kennedy asked how many had been printed, and when Wilson replied "six million" there was a gale of laughter around the table. Although several inelegant uses for them were suggested, the leaflets were subsequently destroyed.)

USIA also briefly considered, then discarded for technical reasons, putting a television transmitter on a plane circling between Florida and Cuba. The idea was to relay television broadcasts of the UN proceedings on the crisis to the Cuban people.

Within the Executive Committee, discussions of USIA operations dealt mostly with radio, photographs, and leaflets, and such schemes as the airborne TV transmission. But there also was constant consideration of the effects of possible U.S. moves on foreign opinion—a far cry from the deliberations that led to the Bay of Pigs, when world opinion was ignored. Throughout the missile crisis USIA compiled a twice-daily bulletin of foreign editorial comment which went to the President, members of the Executive Committee, and other senior government officials.

Khrushchev had hoped to surprise the United States with the missiles in Cuba; instead, the U.S. response caught him off guard. Moscow newspapers waited fourteen hours before reporting Kennedy's speech, and then made no mention of its conciliatory passages or even of the Cuban missile bases. Nor did they mention the President's statement that "it shall be the policy of this nation to regard any nuclear missile launched from Cuba against any nation in the Western Hemisphere as an attack by the Soviet Union on the United States, requiring a full retaliatory response upon the Soviet Union." Radio Havana did not tell its listeners that the Organization of American States had unanimously endorsed the U.S. blockade, merely quoting Castro as saying that OAS acceptance of U.S. leadership was an "act of betrayal." VOA, of course, put heavy and repeated emphasis on the hemisphere's support of the blockade.

On Wednesday the Voice began alerting listeners behind the Iron Curtain to stand by for a saturation broadcast the next day that was designed to penetrate Communist jamming with the truth about the U.S. quarantine of Cuba. Fifty-two VOA transmitters totaling 4,-331,000 watts of power—the equivalent of more than eighty-six of America's strongest commercial radio stations broadcasting simultaneously—were used on eighty frequencies in an eight-and-a-half-hour-long radio barrage. The audience was alerted in advance because Communist jamming was so flexible that only three un-jammed minutes could be gained by a surprise move, and the alert would assure a much greater audience than normal.

Suspense—Then Triumph

In the days between the President's address (October 22) and Khrushchev's backdown (October 28), the reaction abroad was mixed. De Gaulle of France and Adenauer of Germany were un-stinting in their support of the United States. British Prime Minister Macmillan was less sure, and he was joined in his doubts by Labour Party Leader Gaitskell. The usually sensible Manchester *Guardian* thought the U.S. had "done its cause, its friends and its own true interests little good." But generally, friends and neutrals believed the United States had acted prudently and with necessary firmness in the face of great provocation. Stevenson's acid eloquence in the UN ("This is the first time that I ever heard it said that the crime is not the burglary but the discovery of the burglar") helped. The logic and necessity of the American position, as disseminated by USIA and the private news media, began to have their effect.

The *Daily Express* of London said: "The full extent of the menace which Cuba has become is dramatically exposed by the American photographs. These enormously strengthen the American case." *Asahi,* Japan's leading daily, commented: "We can understand the fears of America over the construction of Soviet missile bases in Cuba as tantamount to jabbing a pistol in your side." The Nairobi *Daily Nation* concluded that "if the American information is correct, then it is impossible to condemn President Kennedy's action, however dangerous the consequences may be." *La Nación* of Buenos Aires noted approvingly that Kennedy had "refused to act drastically . . . until evidence warranted."

Another Potomac Cable sought to answer those who equated Soviet missiles in Cuba with NATO missiles in Europe:

The secretly built Soviet rocket bases in Cuba . . . are totally different in conception and purpose from the NATO bases in Turkey and Italy. . . . At a meeting of the fifteen NATO heads of government in December,

1957 . . . they agreed that, as long as the Soviet Union persisted in its saber-rattling, NATO had to mount the most modern and effective defenses it could devise. . . . Agreements were concluded with the Italian and Turkish Governments to establish missile bases in their countries, and the world was told about it. The bases were built neither secretly nor with extraordinary speed. Mr. Khrushchev knew about them. He knew that they were purely defensive. . . .[4]

The President's calm courage gave strength to the Executive Committee and hundreds elsewhere in the government. I saw Kennedy once during that week. I was in his outer office Saturday morning, October 27, when he joined a handful of his aides to discuss the latest developments. He appeared tired, but in complete control. Suddenly Roger Hilsman, State Department Intelligence chief, burst into the room with the news that an American U-2 had accidentally strayed over Soviet territory and had been pursued but not caught by Soviet planes. Bundy uttered a short expletive. The President gazed out the window at the vast green of the White House lawn, silent for a long moment. Then he said calmly: "We must let Khrushchev know it was a mistake, so they won't make something of it."

That Saturday night was the gloomiest of all. Soviet ships appeared likely once again to challenge the U.S. blockade and Khrushchev's messages to Kennedy alternated between belligerency and conciliation. One American U-2 had been shot down and its pilot killed; another such incident could bring us to the brink. Wilson telephoned me at a not very cheerful party to convey the latest instructions for USIA; his remarks were guarded over the phone, but his pessimism was evident. Later, I was awakened just after 2 A.M. by the howl of fire sirens; for a moment I thought that war had come.

Sunday morning Wilson and I were considering the USIA's next move when at 9 o'clock the Reuters ticker began chattering out the report of a Moscow broadcast on Khrushchev's latest letter to Kennedy. Half unbelieving, we read the good news: the missile sites would be dismantled, and offensive weapons shipped back to the Soviet Union. The great confrontation was over. Kennedy's strategy, to stand firm but to give the Soviets a chance to back down without losing too much face, had worked.

There was jubilation in Washington, but USIA was careful not to let it show in pronouncements lest the hard-liners in the Kremlin use it as an excuse to reverse Khrushchev. The Agency took its line from Kennedy's response to the Soviet Premier; a Potomac Cable sent to all posts that sunny afternoon sought to avoid euphoria in the aftermath of crisis:

Crucial problems—both short-run and long-range—remain with us. Short-run problems include the prompt and verified removal of the offensive Soviet missile installations in Cuba, the continuing threat of indirect aggression based in Cuba and directed against other nations of the Western Hemisphere, and the threat to the freedom of the people of West Berlin. Among the longer-range problems are the proliferation of nuclear weapons to other nations and in outer space, the related need for an effective treaty banning nuclear testing, and wider measures of disarmament. . . . The removal of these bases will be no cause for complacency.[5]

But victory it was, and the accolades properly belonged to President Kennedy. Within USIA, it was Donald Wilson's finest hour. His effective leadership of the Agency and his useful counseling within "Ex Com" had helped make USIA a meaningful and responsive tool of American foreign policy in that policy's greatest test in recent years. From Murrow's hospital bed came a message to all in USIA: "Well done. You have handled the emergency like the dedicated pros I know you to be."

There was one sharp dissent. Writing on USIA a few months later, former Director George V. Allen charged that Agency efforts "actually did more harm than good" because they enabled Castro "to pose, with convincing evidence, as the target for the largest concentration of propaganda effort unleashed against an individual since Stalin tried to purge Tito by radio in 1948." The fault, he said, was "in thinking of USIA as a propaganda agency," whereas if its functions were "properly conceived and executed," it would act no different from "the Associated Press or the Rockefeller Foundation." But "nothing has served to label USIA more indelibly than the anti-Castro campaign," he concluded, "and nothing could have helped Castro more."

There was no way for USIA—or Allen—to test Cuban opinion, but his view was not borne out by postcrisis samplings of attitudes elsewhere in Latin America. Even before the missile confrontation, Castro had been losing support in the hemisphere, and the crisis speeded the process. In Latin America and elsewhere, American prestige was given a big boost, based in equal parts on the restrained use of power by the United States and on the solid indication that in a test we could be relied upon. No doubt the world would have taken a different view had the United States rather than the Russians backed down, or had the crisis been resolved in some less satisfactory fashion. But the U.S. blockade *was* successful, and the British newspapers, for example, that had been frightened and querulous after Kennedy's speech, subsequently lavished praise on his leadership.

Interestingly enough, Soviet prestige—and specifically that of Khrushchev—also rose. Soviet propaganda took the line that it was the restraint of the Kremlin that had saved the peace, and the line found wide acceptance in Europe and elsewhere. In addition, the successful resolution of the crisis permitted increased restlessness within the Atlantic Alliance because some of its members, notably France, believed that the Soviets, having been turned back in a major effort at nuclear blackmail, no longer posed so great a threat to European security.

In early 1963 USIA sponsored public opinion polls in Britain, West Germany, France, and Italy. In all four countries the net favorable impression of "what the American Government has been doing in international affairs recently" was sharply higher than the readings taken in each of the three previous years. "U.S. actions in the Cuban crisis were the major factor in the high level of approval for U.S. foreign policy . . . particularly in West Germany," the Agency's Office of Research reported. "In Britain and France, belief that America is basically trustworthy, reliable and firm in its intentions is widespread."

In Britain, for the first time in four years, a solid majority believed that America was "doing all it should to prevent a new world war." A plurality was achieved for the first time in France on the same question, and in Germany the net favorable view of the United States was quadrupled. American credibility ("what the United States does in world affairs" compared with "what it says") rose sharply, as did confidence "in the ability of the U.S. to provide wise leadership for the West."

At the same time, the polls showed a considerable increase in favorable impressions of Moscow. While few thought the Soviets had gained from the Cuban crisis, about one-fourth believed that the two powers had come out "about even." Except in Germany, where opinion was evenly divided, Western Europeans generally favored the removal of American nuclear missiles from bases near the Soviet Union. (About the time the poll was being taken, the United States —as it had long planned—did remove its missiles from Italy and Turkey, substituting Mediterranean-based Polaris submarines.)

What the polls could not show was the most important consequence of the autumn confrontation: both great powers had looked into the abyss of nuclear war, and they did not like what they saw. For the first time since the beginning of the Cold War, a new atmosphere paved the way—and governments had the will—to take some meaningful if hesitant and partial steps toward real peace. The changing political climate required changes in the tone of American propaganda.

"Peace for All Men"

In the months following the missile crisis, the talents of USIA were enlisted in the Administration's push for solutions to the outstanding problems that Kennedy had enumerated in his October 28 letter to Khrushchev. Murrow, who returned to his desk in mid-November after his illness, believed that the United States should clarify what kind of government it would encourage in Cuba after Castro. Kennedy was interested, agreed that the U.S. should make known its support for the aims of a non-Communist, non-Castro liberal revolution, and declared in a speech that "we will be ready and anxious to work with the Cuban people in pursuit of those progressive goals which a few short years ago stirred their hopes."

The details of getting the Soviet missiles and bombers out of Cuba occupied much of the President's time, and much public attention. But Kennedy recognized, as one aide put it, that "the new fluidity in the post-Cuban Communist camp . . . presented opportunities which seventeen years of cold war rigidities had never made possible before."[6] Murrow felt the same way. The Administration had not given up its fight for a ban on nuclear testing, and when Khrushchev indicated after Cuba that he was ready to talk of new agreements, a test ban topped Kennedy's list.

Disarmament talks were reconvened but continued to founder on the Soviet refusal to accept an adequate number of on-site inspections of suspicious seismic events. Nonetheless, the Administration persisted. Kennedy and Macmillan proposed high-level negotiations in Moscow on a test ban treaty, and the President decided to announce the offer publicly in a commencement address at American University in Washington on June 10, 1963. At the same time, he proposed to pledge that, once the current series of American nuclear tests was completed, the United States would not be the first to resume testing in the atmosphere.

The speech was prepared with some secrecy. Desiring to break away from the usual clichés of the Cold War, the President did not work from the customary State Department draft, although some of us from the foreign affairs agencies contributed material and participated in a meeting called by Bundy to review Ted Sorensen's draft.

June 10 was a Monday, and the President was in Honolulu the previous weekend to speak at a conference of U.S. mayors. While he was there, putting finishing touches on the speech, Khrushchev cabled his acceptance of the Kennedy-Macmillan offer of nuclear talks in Moscow, and it was incorporated into the speech. Bundy's able deputy, Carl T. Kaysen, obtained clearances and last-minute suggestions from the departments and had the final version typed. I went to Kaysen's home Sunday night to pick up copies of the speech and deliver them to Voice of America Russian translators. VOA would carry the speech "live" in English, but we wanted to broadcast it in Russian to the Soviet Union as quickly as possibly thereafter.

Kennedy's speech was powerful and persuasive, going far beyond what USIA or any department might have thought of proposing on its own. War, said the President, "makes no sense in an age when a single nuclear weapon contains almost ten times the explosive force delivered by all of the allied air forces in the Second World War. . . . I speak of peace, therefore, as the necessary rational end of rational men."

Recognizing that some say such talk is "useless until the leaders of the Soviet Union adopt a more enlightened attitude," Kennedy said he also believed that "we must re-examine our own attitude" for "our attitude is as essential as theirs. . . . Every thoughtful citizen who despairs of war and wishes to bring peace" should begin "by examining his own attitude toward the possibilities of peace, toward the Soviet Union, toward the course of the Cold War and toward freedom and peace here at home." The world's problems "are man-made; therefore they can be solved by man."

He was not, said Kennedy, referring to some "absolute, infinite concept of universal peace and goodwill" but to "a more practical, more attainable peace—based . . . on a series of concrete actions and effective agreements which are in the interest of all concerned." A test ban treaty, ending the poisoning of the atmosphere and inhibiting the spread of nuclear weapons, would be just such an agreement. "It is an ironical but accurate fact that the two strongest powers are the two in the most danger of devastation," he pointed out. "In short, both the United States and its allies, and the Soviet Union and its allies, have a mutually deep interest in a just and genuine peace, and in halting the arms race."

So, he went on, "let us not be blind to our differences—but let us also direct attention to our common interests and to the means by which those differences can be resolved." (This was a theme that USIA had never touched upon in three administrations, as was his next point.) Americans should remember, said Kennedy, "that we are not engaged in a debate, seeking to pile up debating points. . . . We must deal with the world as it is, and not as it might have been," persevering in the search for peace "in the hope that constructive changes within the Communist bloc might bring within reach solutions which now seem beyond us." And he announced the Moscow talks, and his decision not to resume atmospheric nuclear testing if others did not.

For USIA, Kennedy's address was the most useful Presidential pronouncement in years. The Agency broadcast the speech or a summary of it in many languages, and sent abroad film and video-tape coverage. The full text was supplied to thousands of foreign newspapers and radio stations. Although it received surprisingly little attention in the United States, the speech's impact abroad was impressive. Thousands of individuals asked USIS for copies. In India alone the printed text went to more than 35,000 who requested it

—an unprecedented response. Most important of all was the Soviet reaction: Moscow stopped jamming VOA broadcasts, three weeks later announced its willingness to accept a ban on atmospheric testing, and six weeks later initialed the long-sought treaty.

Other steps of *détente* followed. That autumn Kennedy approved the sale of wheat to Russia. Over the years, USIA had produced— for distribution in underdeveloped countries that might be tempted to follow Soviet practices—great amounts of literature on the weaknesses of Soviet agriculture. The propaganda was more or less persuasive, but not nearly as persuasive as the news that Communist Russia had to come to capitalist America to buy grain because Soviet farmers could not produce enough. USIA reported every step of the transaction. It was not necessary to comment on the story; it spoke for itself, and the lesson was not lost on such countries as hungry India.

The lessening of tensions was enormously popular throughout the world, and the United States was given its deserved share of the credit. The Agency's media priorities were revised, with themes on "the pursuit of peace," "strength and reliability," and the "rule of law" added. The emphasis on rule of law applied to both domestic and international relations. Some foreigners still clung to the notion, nurtured by Hollywood films, that lawlessness prevailed in the American West. "We will continue to work toward perfecting the rule of law at home and encourage its extension to and among all nations," proclaimed the USIA theme. But it had not yet been perfected in this country, as soon was to be demonstrated in the Southwestern city of Dallas.

The Kennedy Phenomenon

Friday the twenty-second of November, 1963, was quieter than usual at USIA headquarters in Washington. Murrow was out ill and the President was out of town, and when Kennedy was away the bureaucracy's pace was always more relaxed. Then, at lunchtime, came the awful news: the President had been shot while riding in his motorcade in Dallas. Frantic calls to a dozen restaurants finally located me, and I ran three blocks back to my office. Anguished and unbelieving, a group of colleagues and I sat silently before a television set. Throughout the building typewriters slowed, then stopped. Everyone watched, listened, and waited. Some prayed.

Finally the irrevocable news came that Kennedy was dead. A stunned city, a bewildered nation, and a frightened world dissolved in grief, excitement, and uncertainty. It was early evening in London when BBC told its listeners. Russians heard Radio Moscow blame the killing on "racist reactionaries." In Saigon, where President Diem had been murdered three weeks earlier, U.S. military advisers heard the news at breakfast. In Washington work came to a halt in dozens of government buildings. But not at the Pentagon, which alerted American armed forces around the world, and not at USIA.

The Agency had a big job to do, and it had to be done immediately. The world needed to be reassured that, in Garfield's words when Lincoln was shot, "God reigns, and the Government in Washington lives" —to be reassured that the assassination was not the beginning of World War III—to be reassured that Lyndon B. Johnson, Kennedy's constitutional successor, would carry on Kennedy's policies—and to be reassured that while the nation, and indeed the world, had suffered a terrible loss, they would recover.

From the assassination Friday through Johnson's address to Congress the following Wednesday, USIA put all its energies into reporting and interpreting the transition from one President to another, with the aim of building foreign confidence in Johnson. The new President cooperated fully in the effort. VOA provided "feed" relay broadcasts to hundreds of foreign radio stations. The Wireless File transmitted a pamphlet text on the new President, and it was quickly published in many languages. Inserts were prepared for the current Russian and Polish editions of *Amerika* magazine. Several hundred prints of motion picture coverage of Johnson's Congressional address were sent abroad; language versions were produced in Spanish, Portuguese, French, and Arabic. A brief biographical film on Johnson and a longer documentary on Kennedy and his successor were produced for television. A short color movie and two thousand copies of an eight-panel exhibit on Johnson were sent to the field. Five thousand copies of *The Lyndon Johnson Story*, a campaign biography by Booth Mooney, were bought and air-pouched to USIA libraries.*

---

* Though not much of a book, Johnson loved it. Mooney had taken a leave of absence from Johnson's staff to write it, and one Texan who knew them both

The private media, as always, did the lion's share of the job. But thanks in part to the intensive Agency effort, Johnson—who, a month earlier, had like most Vice Presidents been relatively unknown abroad —soon became one of the best-known men in the world. USIA sought to dispel speculation about the circumstances of Kennedy's death. The Warren Commission Report and summaries of it were distributed overseas in vast numbers. Agency efforts were not completely successful, however. The fact that Johnson came from Texas, scene of the assassination, aroused some unwarranted skepticism. Johnson's totally different manner and his small-town Texas background were not as understood or as appreciated as Kennedy's had been. But Johnson was quickly accepted overseas, if grudgingly in some quarters, and a share of the credit belonged to USIA.

Abroad as well as in this country, Johnson was both helped and handicapped by following an enormously appealing President. America was, of course, politically divided over Kennedy and his policies, but the domestic differences were unimportant overseas. In the months preceding November, 1963, it had become increasingly apparent that USIA's greatest asset in building foreign confidence in the United States was President Kennedy himself. Programs, policies, and statements that could be identified with the President personally found a much more receptive audience than run-of-the-mill USIA output.

During the 1960 campaign, columnist Murray Kempton had written that Kennedy was a man at whose funeral no stranger would weep. The prediction could not have been more wrong. When Kennedy was killed, more strangers wept honest tears of grief and despair than had done so on all similar occasions in man's history. From La Paz to Lagos, from London to Leningrad, the great and the lowly were shocked, tearful, and disbelieving. A storekeeper at a remote Sudanese oasis cried: "The greatest man in all the world is dead today." It was, as an Egyptian editor told me later, as if there had been a death in the family—everyone's family.

---

called it "a hymn of praise from invocation to benediction." Johnson's friends, wrote Larry L. King, "were forever having gift copies show up in the mail, lovingly autographed not by the author but by the subject. Congressmen, critics, or even casual office visitors might suddenly find LBJ pressing a copy of Mooney's book on them." By late 1966, according to King, USIA had bought and distributed 214,000 copies.[7]

In Athens, traffic was halted for two minutes as the President's funeral began in Washington. Streets and public squares all over the world were renamed in his honor, notably the main square in front of Berlin's City Hall where Kennedy had delivered his famous speech five months earlier. Thousands lined up at American embassies and consulates to sign condolence books. Two thousand Vietnamese students marched in his honor, and four thousand Egyptians jammed into a Cairo memorial service. The Peruvian Chamber of Deputies unanimously recommended that Kennedy be awarded the Nobel Peace Prize, and the Argentine Government ordered flags at half-mast for eight days. Nina Khrushchev, wife of the Soviet Premier, was weeping as she called at our embassy to offer condolences. A young Japanese said, "I wish I could have died instead." A Senegalese secretary summed it up for millions when she said: "He was the only important world leader who wasn't out of date. He was different."

And it continued. Sixteen months after the President's death, I was riding over a bumpy road in the backwoods of India with three Indian businessmen. Kennedy's name was mentioned, and one of them promptly recited from memory the entire Inaugural Address. In Indian cities merchants still sell cheap portraits of Kennedy and calendars carrying his picture, some showing him (like the sainted Gandhi) surrounded by happy Indian children.

This great tide of affection and respect for Kennedy had—and still has—an immeasurable effect on the world's view of the United States, diminished only slightly by the violent suddenness of the assassination, its sordid aftermath, and the passage of time. In death even more than in life, he became a prime asset to USIA, a persuasive symbol of the goodness and greatness of America.

Why this Kennedy phenomenon? What set him apart from other rulers, other celebrities, in the minds of people everywhere? The sudden, senseless nature of his death shocked millions, but in many parts of the world life is usually uncertain and death often violent. Kennedy was seen as someone special. Four reasons stand out:

First, he was a man of his times, young, vigorous, and full of hope. The great majority of the world's people, also young and hopeful as never before, identified with him as he had identified with them.

Second, he was one of the few world statesmen since World War II to talk of peace as an achievable goal, not a pious platitude. His American University speech, discarding the clichés of the Cold War, had more impact on more people than was recognized at the time.

Third, he was the first American President to see civil rights as a great moral issue, not merely a discomforting political problem. His stance was understood and appreciated in the remotest villages of Africa and Asia.

Fourth, his obviously heartfelt determination to help other peoples and nations as well as his own break the cycle of poverty, ignorance, and disease restored many a skeptical foreigner's confidence in the essential humanity and good faith of America.

Nonetheless, the world would not have reacted as it did had not the mass media of communications, with a large assist from USIA, made the man and his message better known than any other political figure in the postwar era. Hundreds of millions in all corners of the globe felt they knew John Kennedy well, and believed he measured up to their ideal of what a President of the United States ought to be.

There were others in Kennedy's Administration who enhanced American prestige and made USIA's job easier. Adlai Stevenson was widely admired for his ideals and integrity. Professor Edwin O. Reischauer and his Japanese-born wife restored the tarnished image of the American Embassy in Tokyo, where he served as Ambassador. Chester Bowles, the most popular American in India, returned to New Delhi for a second tour as U.S. Ambassador. A new breed of diplomat—some of them career Foreign Service Officers, others not; some very young, all empathic—filled many U.S. embassies abroad: Kenneth Galbraith (who preceded Bowles in India), William Attwood in Guinea, James Wine in Luxembourg and the Ivory Coast, Lincoln Gordon in Brazil, Edmund Gullion in the Congo, Armin Meyer in Lebanon, Taylor Belcher in Cyprus, Philip Kaiser in Senegal, William Blair in Denmark, William Handley in Mali, and others.

Not the least of those who added new luster to American prestige was the nation's chief propagandist, Ed Murrow. His credentials of character, sympathy, and goodwill were widely known to the literate of countries big and small. They trusted Murrow, therefore they believed him. And they liked his personality, his style.

"Good-bye, and Good Luck . . ."

A Murrow trademark was the ever-present cigarette. It was no affectation; he was addicted to it, and smoked constantly, day and

night. He suffered from "smoker's hack," yet when he awoke cough-
ing at night would light still another cigarette. His daily consumption
averaged seventy Camels. "Maybe they cause cancer and maybe they
don't," he said, "but I've been smoking too long to stop now." Like
many heavy smokers, Murrow was susceptible to respiratory ailments,
and fought two bouts with pneumonia. In late September of 1963, a
sudden attack of what he thought was laryngitis forced him to miss
a speaking engagement. A medical examination showed an ominous
spot on his left lung, and exploratory surgery proved it cancerous.
The lung was removed. Murrow never smoked again.

Victims of cancer face long odds, but Murrow had faced long odds
before and won. He knew his chances were slight but, as usual, he
faced the future with equanimity. "I relish danger," he said in an
effort to cheer me, "but I would just as soon face it some other way."
The lung operation was followed by a series of cobalt radiation treat-
ments, unpleasant and debilitating. Murrow's doctors were cautiously
optimistic, but he was realistic. He told President Kennedy that he
would resign if he could not handle the job in the manner he thought
it required.

On that grim November day when John Kennedy was assassinated,
part of Ed Murrow died with him. On a rainy Saturday morning the
President's body lay in state in the East Room of the White House,
and Murrow left his bed to pay his respects with other senior officials
of the Administration. By mistake, the USIA driver took Murrow
to the wrong entrance, and he had to climb steep stairs. Gasping for
breath on every step, he was barely able to complete the pilgrimage.
Returning to the car, he was silent, somber, and dry-eyed—and more
determined than ever to finish the job Kennedy had given him.

But his convalescence was slow, much slower than had been hoped
for, although he seemed to improve. He was helped considerably by
the loving care of his brave and capable wife Janet, who had seen
him through other crises. President Johnson asked him to stay on,
along with other top Administration officials. Murrow began coming
to the office for two or three hours a day, drawn by his Puritan sense
of responsibility. By mid-December, however, it was clear that he
would not be restored to full health for months, if ever, and that same
Puritan conscience compelled him to submit his resignation.

He called in Wilson and me, and showed us a draft of his letter to the President. We protested and pleaded. His departure so soon after Kennedy's death would be a grievous blow to USIA. But he had made up his mind, and that was that.

"I deem it my duty to ask you to accept my resignation," he wrote Johnson.

As you know, I was separated from a cancerous lung in early October. The doctors assure me the operation was successful and the recovery to date has been normal. However, it will be several months before I can resume full-time duty. Were I to continue as Director of this Agency during that period it would mean that I could not direct its affairs as I would wish, as I have tried to do, or as you are entitled to expect it to be directed. . . . After [Kennedy's] tragic death, it had been my hope to continue to serve my country under your leadership. My inability to do so is deeply disappointing.

In the last speech of his career, Murrow had said, "I today am a propagandist." He said it without apology, indeed with pride. He was a propagandist for hardly three years, but in that short time made a lasting mark on USIA and American propaganda. Under his leadership the Agency:

• Put confidence, excitement, and new hope into America's message to the world.

• Built up its operations in Latin America and Africa, two areas previously neglected.

• Ended the diffusion of effort and output that had previously characterized USIA, and concentrated on persuading the most important foreign audiences on the most important aspects of American policy.

• Began to participate significantly in the formulation and execution of American foreign policy.

Murrow gave the much-battered, oft-confused Information Agency new inspired leadership, new direction, new competence, new pride, and new stature. He gave his President honest and sound advice. He gave Congress a look at the realities of American propaganda that it had never before been given. And he gave the American people a spokesman to the world whose courage, intelligence, and integrity contributed importantly to the restoration of American prestige in the early 1960s.

Early that September, congratulating USIA on its tenth anniversary, Kennedy had written Murrow: "In the critical times of the last two years, the Agency under your leadership has demonstrated an imagination, skill and maturity that would do justice to an organization with many decades of experience rather than one." Murrow's administration had not been wholly successful, however. While the quality of USIA's media products was markedly improved, they still were not as good as he thought they should and could be. Weaknesses remained in the staff. The State and Defense departments still sometimes by-passed the Agency. And he had been unable to get Congress to vote USIA as much money as he thought it—and the national interest—required. It was this failure that galled Murrow the most.

In the months just prior to his last illness, Murrow broke with precedent to challenge openly the decision of the Appropriations Committees to deny USIA funds it had requested. To the annoyance of some legislators, he took his case to the people. "Most people in this country never know of our Agency unless it gets into trouble," he told a group of advertisers in Georgia. "Learn of us now, because we're in trouble now." In a cutting voice, he said: "Either the House of Representatives believes in the potency of ideas and the importance of information or it does not. On the record it does not so believe. . . . We are a first-rate power. We must speak with a first-rate voice abroad."[8]

A few weeks later he admitted in a Detroit speech to "deep dismay" that Congress "does not appear to share the urgency of the [Communist] challenge and our nation's response to it. . . . Not to recognize an opportunity is a shame; to recognize it but fail to respond in full measure is dangerous." More money alone, he conceded, "will not promise us success, but inadequate money may well threaten failure." And he drew headlines when he proclaimed: "If it is the decision of the Congress that we should continue to be outspent, out-published and out-broadcast, then that is the way it will be. I do not believe that is the way the American people want it to be."[9]

Shortly before cancer struck him down, Murrow spoke at USIA's Seventh Annual Honor Awards Ceremony. Unknown to him and his audience of Agency employees, it was his swan song.

"We cannot know what the future holds," Murrow said. "We do know, however, that change is the only constant in world affairs. And we know our Agency is charged with helping to fashion that change. The mandate we have from the President clearly tells us what it is he wants of us on behalf of the American people: He wants specific effort in specific areas, both geographical and conceptual. He expects us to do the things that diplomacy and force alone cannot: to change the minds of men in their best interests and ours. . . .

"The coalition of Communism is not our only adversary," Murrow continued. "Even were its energies dissipated and its voice mute, this Agency would continue to be charged with a great responsibility. We would still have the mission abroad of combating ignorance and fear, suspicion and prejudice. This struggle, as you well know, will not be won in a single day or a single decade. It is long-term indeed, perhaps permanent."[10]

When President Johnson received Murrow's letter of resignation, he called him over to the White House and urged him to remain, but to no avail. Murrow was pleased by Johnson's cordiality but mystified by what followed. In early January, his physicians recommended that he enter a clinic immediately for further treatment. The dying USIA Director attempted to see the President again, so that his resignation could be announced promptly. But Murrow could neither get an appointment with Johnson nor reach him on the telephone. He tried daily for a week, meanwhile making and then canceling airline reservations.

In retrospect it appears Johnson was not being deliberately rude or difficult; in this sensitive period of Presidential transition he wanted to have a successor to announce before releasing Murrow. Murrow had strongly recommended that he be succeeded by Don Wilson, but the President turned thumbs down. Johnson's attitude was understandable. This would be his first major appointment, a situation quite different from merely carrying over Kennedy appointees. Wilson was very much a Kennedy man, and known to be a close friend of Robert Kennedy, whereas it was no secret even then that Johnson and Bobby were not on the best of terms. The new President was agreeable to keeping Wilson as Deputy Director, but not to putting him in the top job. He asked my brother Ted, still on the White House staff, for other names.

My brother turned to me, and I suggested Carl T. Rowan, a Negro former newspaperman who, during two years as Deputy Assistant

Secretary of State for Public Affairs, had earned Johnson's admiration when traveling abroad with the then Vice President. The President thought the suggestion splendid, called Rowan home from Finland, where he was serving as U.S. Ambassador, and finally accepted Murrow's resignation on January 20:

It is with the greatest reluctance that I yield to your insistence and accept your resignation. . . . I had been hoping you would find it possible to stay on. . . . You have done a magnificent job in this post. . . . You will be sorely missed.

You leave with the thanks of a grateful President and a grateful nation. I close, Ed, with a paraphrase of the words you made forever famous on radio and television: "Goodbye, and good luck!"

It was good-bye, but there was not to be good luck. Murrow rested in California, returned briefly to Washington, and then went to his 280-acre farm on the rolling hills near Pawling, New York. The long-deserved honors came. On September 14, 1964, President Johnson awarded him the Medal of Freedom, the nation's highest civilian honor. Six months later, recalling his contribution to British freedom in World War II, Queen Elizabeth made him an Honorary Knight Commander of the Order of the British Empire.

To visitors, Murrow described the great satisfaction his work at USIA had given him. "I have never worked harder in my life and never been happier. I haven't had such satisfaction since the days of covering the London blitz."[11] He spoke of all the things he wanted to do when his strength returned. He was interested in the untapped potentials of educational television. He wanted to do a network documentary on John J. Rooney, chairman of the House Appropriations Subcommittee on the State Department and USIA, "so the American people may know what power this narrow little man has over our foreign policy." He was showered with job offers, from movie actor to college president. CBS, slipping in its news competition with NBC, begged him to come back.*

But none of this was possible. His physicians had not been able to destroy all the cancerous cells, and they spread through his body. In November he had another operation, but it helped only temporarily.

---

* This particularly pleased Murrow, for he was a mite jealous of Walter Cronkite, the man who had succeeded him as the number one CBS news personality.

The doctors let him go home for the last time to the farm he loved, and three days after his fifty-seventh birthday Edward R. Murrow died there quietly on April 27, 1965.

The tributes poured in from everywhere. President Johnson took note of his "unrelenting search for the truth." Murrow's friend, "Scotty" Reston of the *New York Times,* accurately observed that "those who knew him best admired him most." Not surprisingly, the eulogies dealt mostly with his contributions to broadcasting: "The first man of heroic stature to emerge in the new medium," wrote John Grigg in the Manchester *Guardian Weekly.* "The Murrow imprint on electronic journalism is indelible and will last as long as the medium itself," said Leonard Goldenson, head of the ABC network. "Unique . . . in broadcasting . . . [he] set standards of excellence that remain unsurpassed," said his old boss, William Paley of CBS.

There was some recognition of his government service. The Washington *Daily News* noted that, "despite his asserted aversion to a brass hat, he reorganized and reoriented the USIA and developed, largely by perseverance, into a top-grade administrator." And Grigg in the *Guardian* thought "his appointment [to USIA] was a signal to the world that the United States was not afraid of the truth, and under his direction American propaganda was effective because it was widely believed." Yet most commentators skipped over Murrow's USIA years because they knew little about them. That was too bad.

Historian Arthur Schlesinger, Jr., who had watched Murrow's performance from the White House, wrote of him: "He revitalized USIA, imbued it with his own bravery and honesty and directed its efforts especially to the developing nations. . . . Murrow himself was a new man, cheerful, amused, contented, committed. When his fatal illness began, he must have had the consolation, after those glittering years of meaningless success, that at the end he had fulfilled himself as never before."[12]

When former Vice President Alben Barkley died in 1956, Murrow in his broadcast tribute harkened back to his days in the lumber fields of the Pacific Northwest: "In the woods, when a great and ancient tree that has weathered many storms suddenly comes crashing down, there is the noise of smaller trees snapping back into position, the rustle and the cries of small creatures, and the descending noise of twigs, branches and bits of moss falling to the ground. And then there is silence, more complete and oppressive than any silence that went before."[13] Nine years later, the same words could have been applied to the death of the man who spoke them.

An old friend, David E. Lilienthal, who had fought many of the good fights with him, understood better than most what Ed Murrow's life had meant to us all. "He stands with Churchill," said Lilienthal, "as proof that only one man, be he brave enough, can turn the tide against tyranny and fear."

9 *The Voice of America: Contribution and Controversy*

Let us pause in our historical narrative to take a long look at the medium of communication that gave both Murrow and Rowan some of their finest successes—and some of their worst headaches.

First, fastest, and—once, if perhaps not now—foremost in modern propaganda is radio.

The Voice of America speaks. Today America has been at war for seventy-nine days. Daily at this time we shall speak to you about America and the war. The news may be good or bad. We shall tell you the truth.

The day was February 24, 1942, eleven weeks and two days after the United States entered World War II. It was the first broadcast labeled the "Voice of America," and the Voice has never been still since. Wars and crises have come and gone; the news has continued to be sometimes good and sometimes bad. Today as then, the Voice of America tells the truth, or tries to.

VOA is the best-known and the most controversial of the nation's propaganda activities. Although it came perilously close to being shut down in the late 1940s, it has since grown rapidly under the impetus of the Cold War. The Voice has been the radio arm of the U.S. Information Agency since the Agency's creation and its director is subordinate to the Director of USIA, yet the much-publicized VOA is better known to the American people than its parent agency.

Despite its being well known, the Voice is often confused in this country with another foreign broadcaster, Radio Free Europe (RFE).

225

RFE and similar stations—Radio Liberty and the much-newer Radio Free Asia—are ostensibly private, nonprofit organizations supported by contributions from the American people. Those stations, and VOA, were embarrassed in 1967 when the press disclosed that the former were financed primarily by the Central Intelligence Agency.

Why the need for both overt and covert government-financed broadcasting abroad? The fact is that VOA and the "private" stations perform different functions, both necessary.

RFE broadcasts only to the smaller Communist nations of Eastern Europe; Radio Liberty broadcasts to the Soviet Union; and Radio Free Asia to North Korea, Communist China, North Vietnam, and neighboring countries. These stations are mostly staffed, though not directed, by émigrés from the listening countries, and provide an alternative to the party-line broadcasts emanating from the Communist capitals. Their announcers speak not for America, as do their counterparts at VOA, but for the homelands they left. It is Czechs speaking to Czechs, Russians to Russians, and Koreans to Koreans.

VOA, on the other hand, is the Voice of America, not the voice of other countries. It also broadcasts to Eastern Europe and the Far East (as well as to every other part of the world), but it does so in the name of the American Government and people, not in the name of foreigners. It is not always appropriate for the U.S. Government's official radio station to comment on internal matters in these countries, but the "private" broadcasters are free to do so.

Now that CIA's role has been disclosed, there probably is no reason why the U.S. Government cannot overtly provide financial support to Radio Free Europe, Radio Liberty, and Radio Free Asia, so long as both the American people and listeners abroad understand that what these stations say does not always represent the official views of the U.S. Government. Whatever the financial arrangements and ostensible attribution, there has been and continues to be a need for both one official and several unofficial radio voices abroad.

The Voice of America differs from other USIA media in that its programs go directly from this country to audiences abroad, free from interference (unless jammed) or censorship by foreign governments. VOA now broadcasts directly in thirty-eight languages (including English) for a total of 850 hours every week. VOA ranks fourth among international broadcasters, if measured by air-time hours. First is the Soviet Union, which broadcasts 1,555 hours per week in sixty-seven languages; Communist China is second with 1,131 hours. In third place is the United Arab Republic (Egypt) with 910 hours; fifth is Britain's BBC with 731. Sixth, and coming up fast, is West Germany with 721 hours.

From VOA's Washington studios, broadcasts are transmitted by telephone land lines to forty-two transmitters at seven locations in the continental United States, and by radio to two transmitters in Hawaii. The U.S. transmitters broadcast programs directly, and some of them also beam programs to VOA's fifty-six relay transmitters abroad. In its overcrowded Washington headquarters, VOA houses two-thirds of its 2,300 employees and an impressive physical plant, including nineteen studios with multiple transcription facilities and a master control capable of selecting program material from a hundred sources.

The U.S.-based VOA transmitters are located at Bethany, Ohio; Bound Brook, New Jersey; Delano and Dixon, California; Marathon and Sugar Loaf, Florida; Greenville, North Carolina; and Honolulu. Although the stations in Ohio and California will be doubled in power by the end of 1968, the Greenville complex, containing eighteen transmitters, is by far the largest. On the air since 1963, this 4,800-kilowatt-powered station beams programs across the Atlantic and to Latin America.

The foreign-based transmitters are in Liberia, Morocco, Germany, mainland Greece, the Greek island of Rhodes, Britain, the Philippines, Ceylon, and Okinawa. When the 1,500-kilowatt transmitter complex near Monrovia, Liberia, began broadcasting in 1964, it gave VOA a good signal in sub-Saharan Africa for the first time. Additional 2,500-kilowatt transmitters are going up in the Philippines and Greece to give the Voice its first adequate signal in Central Asia. New transmitters planned for Thailand will put VOA loud and clear into Communist China.

In 1961 USIA invested in an air-transportable radio-relay station, and subsequently asked Congress for several more. The first mobile facility—containing four 50-kilowatt transmitters, three of them shortwave and the other medium-wave—was used during the 1962 Cuban missile crisis, and later in Monrovia while VOA's African station was being built.

Because the United States is flanked by oceans, VOA must have permanent foreign-based relay transmitters if it is to reach its desired audiences. The Soviet Union, situated in the center of the Eurasian land mass, has no such problem. The National Aeronautics and Space Administration is studying the transmission of radio programs via satellite directly to receivers in the home rather than through ground stations. In addition to eliminating the need for foreign-based transmitters, satellites could also assure a more reliable signal through the ionosphere for shortwave and frequency-modulation (FM) broadcasts, if not for amplitude-modulation (AM) transmission.*

But, until now, obtaining permission from foreign governments to locate transmitters on their soil has been one of VOA's most time-consuming and frustrating tasks. Unfriendly countries, of course, will not do business at all. Neutral and even allied governments are concerned that they may be criticized at home and abroad for assisting in the dissemination of American propaganda. Consequently, negotiations for a transmitter site often last for years, and failure is more common than success.

Once a transmitter goes into operation, only jamming can prevent those within its range from hearing. But jamming is only partially effective at best, and in any case has not been a significant factor for VOA since the Soviet Union and most East European countries discontinued their jamming in 1963. (Bulgaria, East Germany, Cuba, and Communist China still try to jam the Voice, but they are not as effective as the Russians were.) The United States has never seriously contemplated jamming, although it has been suggested by the military from time to time.

The relatively free movement of radio across national boundaries has made it a particularly important means of communication with closed societies whose governments prevent conventional USIA operations on the spot. Thus 22 percent of all VOA broadcast hours are now directed to Communist Eastern Europe.

The Communists well understand the threat from Western broad-

* The prospect of using communications satellites for international broadcasting and telecasting caused some nervousness abroad. In March, 1966, Britain and other European countries joined the American-dominated Intelsat consortium to announce that they would launch a world-wide system of communications satellites by 1968. Three days later, Eurospace, an organization of 160 European industrial firms engaged in aerospace work, warned that global television, relayed by Soviet and American satellites, could be used as a political instrument that might threaten the independence of other countries "without similar means of expression."

casting, and periodically complain about "hostile" and "provocative" VOA broadcasts. On one occasion, Murrow had the last word. After listening patiently to a long list of grievances enumerated by Mikhail Kharlamov, then head of Soviet radio and television, Murrow shut him off by saying, "I want you to come over and testify before the Congressional committees that pass on appropriations for USIA. With your testimonial to our effectiveness, I think they might give me twice as much money!"[1]

Currently the Voice broadcasts eight hours daily in Russian and lesser amounts in other Soviet languages ranging down to a half-hour of Slovene and Ukrainian. Broadcasts to the other Communist countries of Europe total one to two hours each. Six and a half hours in Mandarin are directed daily to mainland China. Communist Cuba hears VOA's regular Latin-American service on shortwave, and can also tune it in on two medium-wave frequencies relayed from transmitters on the Florida Keys.

A unique USIA broadcasting station is RIAS (Radio in the American Sector), which the Agency has operated since 1946 for listeners in East Germany. From West Berlin the station beams news, public affairs, music, and entertainment to an audience estimated at 75 percent of East Germany's adult population. Although tensions in divided Germany have eased in recent years, the Communist regime continues to jam RIAS and to exhort its people not to listen—but without much success in either instance.

Of course, audience statistics are hard to come by, in East Germany and elsewhere. If one is skeptical of the accuracy of Nielsen and other measurements of domestic radio and TV audiences (and I am), then one must also be skeptical of measurements of foreign audiences that are based largely on guesswork. And when USIA itself is doing the guessing, it is unlikely that its figures err on the low side. Basing its claims on scattered public opinion polls and fan mail "projections," VOA estimates that world-wide 20 to 25 million people hear its broadcasts every day, with the figure increasing to around 80 million in times of crisis. Listening varies from country to country; VOA believes it has 23 percent of the total potential audiences in Communist East Europe, but only 3 percent in Red China.

Whatever the exact total figure, it must be impressive, and it probably is growing. In 1950 there were eighty million radio receivers in the world; today there are well over 300 million in use outside the

United States and Canada, and the figure is rising rapidly. The competition for these listeners is growing, too. In 1950 there were about five thousand hours of international broadcasting per week; today there are over 25,000 hours. Those who cannot read can listen; those who lack roads, telephones, newspapers, and even electricity can tune in the outside world on their battery-operated transistor radios.

Nonetheless, the rapid development of domestic radio networks by the new nations, and the accompanying "explosion" of medium-wave-only small transistor receivers, could make the mostly shortwave VOA an anachronism unless it expands its medium-wave transmissions more rapidly than it has. Unfortunately, there is little evidence that either USIA or Congress fully appreciates this danger.

VOA programs emphasize news and information; most listeners tune to their local stations for entertainment. VOA newscasts are followed by commentaries on the news, or fuller explanations of particular items, or excerpts from what the Voice calls "responsible American editorial opinion." Some programs are picked up from the American commercial networks and local stations. VOA's entertainment programs feature various aspects of American life and culture, although some—for example, "soap opera" dramas beamed to Latin America—have a political bite.

In fact, there is no hard line between "political" and "entertainment" programs. One of the most popular of the latter has more political impact than many of the former. This is *Music USA*, a twice-daily forty-five-minute program featuring quality popular music in one segment and jazz in the other. Presiding over this program since 1955 is a New Yorker named Willis Conover, who, though virtually unknown in this country, is a celebrated figure abroad. A survey taken in Poland in the 1950s indicated Conover was the "best-known living American." Many credit the great popularity of jazz among young Russians to Conover's broadcasts. His program has fourteen hundred fan clubs in ninety countries. The effect of all this on the foreign view of America may not be subject to measurement, but undeniably it is considerable.

"Neither Conscience Nor Morality"

Superlatives are required to describe the Voice of America. It is the biggest single element of USIA, and the most costly. With Congress, it is the most popular. And within USIA itself it has been the most controversial, for building new transmitters has only increased the problem of what to say on them. As Murrow once noted: "Communications systems are neutral. They have neither conscience nor morality, only a history. They will broadcast truth or falsehood with equal facility. Man communicating with man poses not the problem of how to say it but, more fundamentally, what is he to say?"[2]

For no Director of USIA has the question been merely rhetorical. No one disputes that VOA should be truthful.* But should the Voice of America be the voice of American Government policy? Or should it reflect the many divergent and often contradictory voices of our pluralistic society? Or should it do some of both?

Should the Voice be exclusively "strategic," seeking over the long run to build confidence in the American people and nation? Or should it also be a short-range "tactical" instrument, seeking to influence foreign attitudes on current developments?

Should VOA concentrate on what is of prime interest to the United States Government? Or should it emphasize what is of prime interest to its listeners? Or should it emphasize both?

These philosophical questions quickly translate into difficult operational questions: Should the Voice be subject to State Department and USIA policy guidance to the degree that other Agency media are, or should VOA emulate the independence of private American broadcasters? If there is State Department and USIA policy control over VOA, does that control apply just to commentary, or is it applicable to all VOA programs including newscasts?

Within the Agency—as in Congress, the State Department, and elsewhere—there is considerable difference of opinion on these questions, and this difference has resulted in what one observer, Albert Bermel, described as the "split personality" of USIA. "There is," he wrote, "a certain ambivalence in the role of the agency which in theory purveys 'objective' information but in practice is an arm of the Amer-

---

* From the beginning, VOA has adhered faithfully to the truth. Edward W. Barrett, a top U.S. propagandist during World War II, tells how the Voice, "over considerable opposition," broadcast General Stilwell's 1943 remark that "we took a hell of a beating" in Burma. When the war was over, says Barrett, the Allies learned it had been "a singularly happy decision. Germans, Italians and Japanese testified that they had come really to believe the Voice of America first when they heard it carry Stilwell's statement. 'We felt if the Americans made such admissions to the world,' said one, 'they must be telling the truth.'"[3]

ican Government."⁴ This ambivalence has created deep, long-standing differences within USIA ranks.

• Most top officials in USIA, and certainly the great majority of its field officers, believe that radio should be used by the Agency as other media are used: to influence foreign attitudes for the purpose of furthering American objectives.

• Many in VOA (and a few elsewhere in the Agency) believe that the Voice's primary goals are to attract an audience and achieve credibility with it, and that doing so in itself furthers American interests.

The first group says: "Fine. Win an audience. Be truthful. Be credible. Be interesting. But always have specific policy objectives in mind, especially in commentary on the news." The second group says: "Oh, no. We cannot be both propagandists and honest broadcasters. Propagandists are liars; we tell the truth. If we follow a government 'line,' we lose our credibility as a purveyor of the truth."

The key word here is *credibility*. The VOA group argues that credibility can be maintained only through "objective, balanced, comprehensive" programming, which in turn can only be accomplished through a minimum of policy guidance. Their critics argue that credibility and purposeful broadcasting are not incompatible.

There are several reasons why many VOA employees feel the way they do. One is the physical separation of the Voice from other USIA operations; since moving to Washington from New York in 1954 at the insistence of Congress, VOA studios have been in the Health, Education, and Welfare Department building, two miles from USIA headquarters. Off by themselves, VOA broadcasters are not exposed to the propaganda problems that daily preoccupy those who work at USIA headquarters. Second, most VOA employees are part of the domestic Civil Service personnel system, rather than the Foreign Service; most have never served USIA abroad and have never been in direct contact with their audiences.

Finally, many Voice employees are overreacting to the situation that prevailed in the early years of the Cold War when VOA was more interested in polemics than persuasion and engaged in what were called "hard-hitting, anti-Communist" broadcasts that for the most part were convincing only to the already convinced. Although time has thinned the ranks of Voice employees who fled to this country when the Communists seized their homelands, at one time they comprised the bulk of VOA's foreign-language staff. Not surprisingly, many of them were more interested in the nations they left behind than in U.S. policy.

To balance VOA's output and make it credible, Voice officials in the late 1950s pushed the pendulum hard in the direction of objectivity. Unfortunately, they pushed too hard and too far; in the name of objectivity and credibility, too much VOA broadcasting became merely pointless.

Although some in the Voice assert that, once the 1953 McCarthy ordeal was over, they had no real policy problems until the Kennedy Administration, in fact there developed in the late fifties a running dispute between the policy desks and the broadcasters. President Eisenhower intervened in one instance. As he later related it,

I had been told that a representative of the Voice of America had tried to obtain from a senator a statement opposing our landing of troops in Lebanon. In a state of some pique I informed Secretary Dulles that this was carrying the policy of "free broadcasting" too far. The Voice of America should, I said, employ truth as a weapon in support of free world objectives, but it had no mandate or license to seek evidence of lack of domestic support of America's foreign policies and actions.[5]

"Credibility" and the "VOA Charter"

Audience credibility is, of course, more than just a shibboleth of the broadcasters. It is essential to effective propaganda: if listeners do not believe, they cannot be persuaded. But persuaded to do what? The real question is not the merit but the meaning of credibility in propaganda. For credibility is not, or should not be, an end in itself but a means to achieving deliberate goals. It is the definition and imposition of these goals that many VOA people object to, prompting one experienced Agency official to warn in the early 1960s that "objectivity, credibility, comprehensiveness, balance have become mumbo-jumbo inhibiting judgment. . . . We are falling into the old trap: equating popularity, acceptance [and] listenership with effectiveness."

The U.S. Government monitors and analyzes all foreign government broadcasting of news and comment. This task is carried on at considerable expense by a little-known agency, the Foreign Broadcast

Information Service. The United States does this because it knows that such broadcasts often reveal the intentions of foreign governments. VOA broadcasts are similarly monitored and analyzed by the Soviets and by many lesser powers. (Soviet propagandist Yuri Zhukov once told me: "I know more about what your Voice of America is saying in Russian than you do." I denied it, but he was right. I did not have time to follow every VOA language service every day, but the Russians were listening carefully to every word on our Russian-language service—as our monitoring service was listening carefully to them.)

Foreign governments monitor VOA broadcasts for precisely the same reason we monitor theirs: for clues to our intentions and for authoritative presentations of our views. They do not monitor CBS or NBC except as part of their surveys of private American opinion. They do monitor VOA because it *is* the Voice of America, the U.S. Government's only official radio station and presumed to present the U.S. Government's views.

VOA credibility, therefore, must be considered in this context. It is not, and cannot be, the same context in which Huntley and Brinkley operate at NBC or Cronkite at CBS. If Voice of America newscasts say, "The crisis has eased," (because that is what the commercial wire services are saying) when in fact the President is planning to take steps which—in Soviet or Chinese eyes—will exacerbate the situation, then VOA is not being credible; it is being misleading. With the general audience, this is undesirable but not fatal. Much more dangerous is the possibility that Soviet or Chinese leaders will misread the American President's intentions on the basis of what they hear on the American Government's official radio.

Similarly, VOA is not being credible when it misleads or confuses its listeners with commentaries heavy on speculative interpretation and light on facts. There are occasions when it may be desirable to mask or obfuscate our intentions, but the decision to do so should be a calculated one made only by the President or his responsible subordinates.

Whether we like it or not, the Voice of America is viewed abroad as the voice of the American Government. Moreover, the listener makes little if any distinction between what is attributed to the Voice's own commentators and what is attributed to nongovernmental sources of opinion.

This is not to say that VOA should be a pale American copy of Radio Moscow, parroting only the official line on its newscasts, as distinguished from its commentaries. It most emphatically should not, and if that sad day ever comes, VOA will lose whatever credibility and persuasiveness it now has. But it is an arm of the American Government, and its authoritativeness should be taken no more lightly by VOA broadcasters than by their listeners.

To be credible the news must be presented honestly; to be meaningful it must be presented in perspective—which private broadcasters may or may not do. If there is a race riot in Detroit, the Voice must broadcast the story, but it should also broadcast stories of genuine progress in American race relations, even though the wire services may not think they are sufficiently "newsworthy" to report. If a Soviet spokesman distorts the facts in commenting on the American economy, a wire service will carry the story straight, but the VOA has no obligation to disseminate Soviet misrepresentations without correction simply because it is "news."

Although many VOA officials consider the Voice exclusively "strategic" or long-term in its impact, radio also has a short-term "tactical" impact. News and timely commentary are obviously "tactical"; people and governments react to them now, tonight, tomorrow—not just in five or ten years—and these immediate reactions often are important to the U.S. national interest. Applying policy considerations skillfully and subtly in the preparation of VOA programs serves to enhance, not diminish, the Voice's credibility and effectiveness in both the short and long runs.

Those at the Voice of America who oppose this view fall back on what they call the "charter" of the VOA to sustain their argument. This "charter" was written by VOA officials and approved by George Allen in his final days as Director of USIA in late 1960. The document never received Presidential sanction, contains no reference to the Presidential Statement of Mission for USIA, and in fact makes no reference to USIA at all:

The long-range interests of the United States are served by communicating directly with the peoples of the world by radio. To be effective, the Voice of America must win the attention and respect of listeners. These principles will govern VOA broadcasts:

1. VOA will establish itself as a consistently reliable and authoritative

source of news. VOA news will be accurate, objective, and comprehensive.

2. VOA will represent America, not any single segment of American society. It will therefore present a balanced and comprehensive projection of significant American thought and institutions.

3. As an official radio, VOA will present the policies of the United States clearly and effectively. VOA will also present responsible discussion and opinion on these policies.[6]

After reading a draft of the "charter" in October, 1960, Allen commented: "My own view has always been that we should be in this field only to the extent responsible private networks . . . cannot or will not do the job. I'm not quite certain I'm yet ready to go along with the notion that it's good per se for the government to have an official radio for news broadcasts. . . . Secondly, is our purpose to present the government's foreign policy persuasively, or just present it and let people make up their minds about it? The President and the Secretary of State should of course be persuasive, and when we report them we'll presumably be persuasive too, but should VOA itself try to persuade? If so, it becomes an advocate, not a reporter."

Allen's comments reveal the paradox of his position: he was the head of the government's propaganda agency, but did not believe its radio outlet should attempt to persuade or even advocate. In my judgment the "charter," while generally unobjectionable as far as it goes, does not go far enough, and is ambiguous and vague.

The three "principles" are unobjectionable, but no purposes or goals are cited. While VOA is finally identified as "an official radio" and instructed to "present the policies of the United States clearly and effectively," this function is given no special emphasis and indeed is conditioned by the final sentence: "VOA will also present responsible discussion and opinion on these policies."

VOA officials wanted the "charter" promulgated by the National Security Council, if not the President, to give it more force than a directive from the Director of USIA. But Eisenhower refused, noting that he had already provided USIA with a Statement of Mission. The Sprague Committee report, the high-level study of America's foreign propaganda operations which went to President Eisenhower about six weeks after VOA published its "charter," agreed:

VOA should be the official radio presenting the policies of our Government to foreign audiences clearly and persuasively. Its broadcasts should present a balanced and comprehensive picture of American society, thought and institutions. VOA should build its credibility through consistently reliable, accurate, objective presentation of the news. . . .

Recommendation: The Voice of America as a component of USIA should continue to be guided by the Presidential directive . . . to USIA. Any additional guidance which is necessary to clarify and stabilize the program policies of VOA within this framework should be issued by the Director of USIA.

Crisis Over Cuba

When the information program was taken out of the State Department in 1953 and put into a newly created U.S. Information Agency, the State Department was instructed to continue to exercise policy control over USIA. While the State Department's authority over USIA output is virtually unlimited, in practice State provides general policy guidance but leaves to the Agency's discretion how to present the U.S. position most persuasively.

The Agency's Office of Policy supplements the political guidance from State (and the White House) with what it calls "information policy guidance," advising the media services and field outposts on how to treat various stories directed at various audiences. The guidance does more than merely insert the government "line" into broadcasts and other USIA output. It also assures that the Agency's facts are correct and, equally important, keeps the views of individual officials from dominating VOA's airwaves and USIA publications—restraining the "hawks" as well as curbing the "doves." Over the years the guidance has served as much to restrain those who would overstate U.S. policy as those who would emphasize criticism of it.

Restless under restraints that do not exist in private broadcasting, many VOA broadcasters in past years refused to accept, or simply ignored, much of the guidance, falling back on the 1960 "charter" to support their independence.

During the Cuban missile crisis of October, 1962, the Voice was not adequately responsive to policy guidance at a time when Soviet misreading of U.S. intentions could have been disastrous. To assure tight policy control, Don Wilson—in Murrow's absence—dispatched to VOA a ranking policy official to supervise personally all broadcasts touching on the crisis. He was told to keep the news and commentary truthful, but at the same time to assure that neither the situation nor the U.S. Government's views were misrepresented or presented in any way that could lead the Soviets or our allies into dangerous miscalculations.

There was one slip, which was immediately corrected: when Moscow capitulated and agreed to remove Soviet offensive missiles from Cuba, the Voice reported "jubilation" in Washington despite President Kennedy's insistence that there be no crowing or self-congratulating by U.S. officials so that Khrushchev would not be forced by his more militant Kremlin colleagues to reverse himself.

During the days of peril, VOA officials dutifully accepted the supervision, but after the crisis had passed they exploded in anger. Their "charter" had been violated, the "news judgment" of their editors second-guessed. VOA Director Henry Loomis wrote Murrow that the Voice "failed to sound convincing because of our monolithic tone"— although it is hard to understand why it would have been more convincing to provide listeners with an indiscriminate mixture of fact, speculation, official positions, and unofficial views.

"The charter states the operating philosophy which we believe to be most effective in convincing the skeptical," Loomis wrote.

We see no reason to change this philosophy no matter how severe the crisis—including armed conflict. . . . During the Cuban crisis, in our judgment, we were required to distort and concentrate our program at the expense of credibility and relevance to our audience. . . . If [a news] analysis restricts itself to merely repeating in different words what the President or Secretary of State says, it becomes, as time passes, increasingly dull, and it reveals, increasingly, a propaganda motivation.

To me the Loomis arguments were unpersuasive, and I told Murrow so. What could have more "relevance to our audience" than the most dangerous big-power confrontation in history? What evidence was there that VOA writers would have been more lively, or at least less "dull," than President Kennedy? And even if these scriptwriters had been more lively or less "monolithic" than the nation's highest officials, is it not likely that the frightened peoples of the world were, at least for the moment, more interested in the official views of the U.S. Government than in the unofficial speculations of VOA broadcasters? Finally, Loomis' assumption that Kennedy and Rusk had in this supreme crisis a "propaganda motivation" while VOA did not is unsupported by evidence available then or since.

Nonetheless, Loomis found Murrow not entirely unsympathetic. As an active and interested Director of USIA, Murrow never hesitated to second-guess his subordinates; he alone, after all, was responsible to the President and the Congress for what USIA did. But Murrow was clearly reluctant to countermand decisions made by the Voice of America, and he displayed toward his broadcasters a tolerance of mistakes and poor judgment that he did not extend to other divisions of the Agency.

There were, I believe, two reasons for Murrow's double standard:

First, he had spent most of his life as a working broadcaster, quarreling with *his* front office more than once, especially when it tried to influence what he said. Now he found it hard to be in the front office himself, issuing orders to radio newsmen and commentators. Second, also a result of his own experience in radio, he had an emotional—and admirable—attachment to the principle of free speech for broadcasters. But this caused him to agree on occasion with those in VOA who felt that the Voice was less a part of government than the rest of USIA.

So Murrow agonized over the VOA problem, sometimes siding with his policy experts and sometimes with the Voice's position, usually trying to compromise the two. After the blow-up over VOA's handling of the Cuban crisis, he formally reaffirmed the "charter," but added:

It is vital that our broadcasts not mislead either our enemies or our friends about the nature, intent, and implications of our actions and purposes. Therefore, VOA commentaries and analyses on foreign affairs should at all times, and especially on subjects involving vital U.S. interests, reflect the nuances and special emphases, as well as the main thrust, of the policies and intentions of the U.S. Government. Commentaries should give as accurate a picture of U.S. public policy as can most persuasively be presented up to air time.[7]

Murrow then wrote Loomis a memorandum reaffirming existing guidance procedures, and pointedly added that he wanted VOA to follow instructions issued directly by "the Agency Director, Deputy Director, and Deputy Director (Policy and Plans) . . . particularly when guidance and information are received directly from the highest levels of the Government," meaning the White House.[8]

Thereafter the situation did improve, yet in too many instances the Voice went along largely as before, with VOA officials citing the "charter" but not the Murrow memoranda when it suited their purposes. Commentaries were exempted from Murrow's instructions by the simple device of renaming them "backgrounders" or something else.

Seven months later, for example, when President Kennedy radically changed the direction of America's Cold War policies in his historic American University peace speech, Loomis declined to instruct his commentators to interpret the speech along the lines laid down in a memorandum to USIA from White House Assistant McGeorge Bundy, or even to say much about it at all. Loomis, a holdover from the Eisenhower-Dulles Administration, apparently did not think the speech was particularly important. When the world's leaders and press subsequently greeted the speech with glowing enthusiasm and attached great significance to it, VOA finally went to work and did a good job —but did it four days late.

When Carl Rowan succeeded Murrow in 1964, the VOA situation improved. The new Director imposed no new restrictions on the Voice, but he did insist that the established procedures for policy guidance be followed. And, despite press allegations to the contrary, President Johnson imposed no new controls on the Voice. As Rowan followed the Murrow policies and procedures (admittedly sometimes ignored during the Murrow years), so Johnson saw the VOA much as his predecessor had.

Kennedy's view had been expounded in 1962 when he spoke at ceremonies marking the Voice's twentieth birthday. "What we do here in this country, and what we are, what we want to be," he told the broadcasters, "represents really a great experiment in a most difficult kind of self-discipline, and that is the organization and maintenance and development of the process of free government. And it is your task . . . to tell that story around the world. This is," Kennedy admitted, "an extremely difficult and sensitive task. On the one hand you are an arm of the Government . . . and it is your task to bring our story around the world in a way which serves to represent democracy and the United States in its most favorable light. But on the other hand, as part of the cause of freedom . . . you are obliged to tell our story in a truthful way, to tell it, as Oliver Cromwell said about his portrait, 'Paint us with all our blemishes and warts.' "[9]

VOA and LBJ

Johnson felt the same way. When Rowan was sworn in, Johnson gave him one commandment: to tell the truth. But both Kennedy and Johnson wanted the truth in context; it is no more honest to emphasize the "blemishes and warts" than it is to pretend they do not exist—and it is certainly not good propaganda.

Rowan brought the Voice in line, and Loomis became increasingly restive. In March, 1965, after seven years as Director of VOA, Loomis resigned to become Deputy Commissioner of Education. In a farewell speech to his staff, he not surprisingly cited the "charter" and asserted that "during these seven years, *we at the Voice* have largely reached a consensus on how best to apply this charter to our day-to-day programming." Although conceding that the "charter" is "not a substitute for judgment," Loomis said, "it is my hope—my belief— that the charter, like the Constitution, is so fundamental and so represents the realities of the world and the moral principles that undergird this nation, that the charter will endure for the life of the Voice. . . .

"Perhaps most fundamental of all," Loomis continued, "we believe our audience judges us as a radio, while some of our colleagues assume that the audience considers a commentary on the Voice as authoritative a statement of United States policy as a statement by the Secretary of State or the President. . . . To sweep under the rug what we don't like, what does not serve our tactical purpose, is a sign of weakness."[10]

Mary McGrory of the Washington *Star* was invited to hear Loomis' speech, and was "briefed" on its significance. Ignoring Loomis' comment (as everyone did) that "our credibility is equal to the best," she wrote the next day that "everyone present . . . knew what he meant when he said 'the Voice of America is not the Voice of the Administration.' Old-timers in the Voice say they are going through a period almost as bad as the McCarthy era. . . . No dispute over handling of the news has arisen, but every commentary must be cleared with the policy department of the Voice's parent agency, the U.S. Information Agency, before broadcast."[11] Obviously Miss McGrory was unaware of the Murrow memoranda, and not surprisingly was not told about them by the Voice people with whom she talked.

Top USIA officials were furious—about Loomis' speech and about the publicity it got. So was President Johnson. Rowan was on a trip to Vietnam, so the full force of White House wrath fell on Acting Director Donald M. Wilson, who was wholly sympathetic with the President's view. Johnson was surprised and annoyed to learn for the first time that Loomis was going to be Deputy Commissioner of Education. He decided, however, that the Loomis appointment was probably so widely known that to recall it would create more of a furor than it was worth.*

It was sad that Loomis' departure was marked by so much acrimony. In many ways he had done an excellent job as chief of VOA. He aggressively directed the building of the Voice's massive new network of transmitters, won the loyalty of the VOA staff as none of his predecessors had, and improved the quality of its key personnel. His weaknesses were important, but so were his strengths.

After Loomis left, the public fuss abated for a few months and then flared anew in mid-1965, when the *New York Times* front-paged a report that "policy differences and charges of censorship are ruffling relations between the Voice of America and its parent agency. . . . Longtime [VOA] staff members . . . complain their most valued asset, credibility with the listeners, is being sacrificed in favor of putting a high polish on the Johnson Administration's policy lines."

Rowan replied: "There has been no interference with the content of news programs, and . . . editorial control of commentaries is no more rigid than it has been in the past." Agreeing that "our news report must be accurate and honest," he added: "But our commentaries on the news have the same purpose an editorial in a newspaper has. They express opinion, and it is the official opinion of the United States Government. It is my responsibility to see to it that these expressions of opinion by the Voice of America accurately reflect the policies of the Government. . . . We simply cannot afford to have the intentions and objectives of the United States misunderstood by other governments."[12]

Nonetheless, the *Times* subsequently editorialized: "The White

---

* But the shadow followed Loomis to his new job. After only a year at HEW, he departed after twenty years in government to join his brother in business.

House and the State Department have always tried to exert pressure upon the VOA to some extent, but in this Administration the situation has materially worsened."[13]

Then *Newsweek* charged that "under direct and restrictive order from above, the news broadcasts carried by VOA present an almost unrelieved picture of U.S. righteousness in foreign affairs." The magazine blamed both Johnson and Rowan, calling the latter "hamhanded." But it also quoted Rowan as saying: "I do not think that the Voice of America should be ruled by some vague intellectual notion of 'impartiality.' I think that its news programs should be honest, and they are. But I insist that these people at the Voice realize that its fundamental purpose is the same as the rest of the USIA— to further the foreign policy objectives of the U.S. Government."[14]

Rowan subsequently wired *Newsweek,* asserting that

neither the President nor anyone speaking for him has given a single order that the Voice be restricted or censored in any way. Such guidance as has been given the Voice was given by me,* consonant with my judgment as to what constituted the national interest, and based on my participation in meetings of the National Security Council and the Cabinet. This guidance has related entirely to that part of the Voice's programming where it reflects policy and serves as the official radio of this country, not to its news programs. I hope that you will agree that I might justifiably be called "ham-headed" and not "ham-handed" were I to permit the Voice to air policy statements that misled friend and foe.[15]

But the controversy continued. Another critic charged that during crises VOA news "is more vigorously vetted" by top USIA officials than the "slow" media, which consequently are "more balanced, convincing, and therefore palatable."[16] In fact, the contrary is true: USIA's deputy and area assistant directors carefully scrutinize before release all motion picture, television, and publication products, but these officials almost never see the VOA news output until after it is broadcast, if then.

In a nationwide television interview, Rowan defended his position and said it was shared by most Voice employees. He admitted, however, that "in any element that large" there are bound to be some who "think they ought to be airing *their* foreign policy instead of that of

---

* It would have been more accurate had he added "or in my name."

the United States Government, and I think they've been a little un-happy when I tell them that's not their function." Repeating that the only instruction the President had given him was "to tell the truth . . . to tell the good and bad," Rowan said, "the best propaganda is the *wisest* use of the truth.

"What makes the VOA a difficult medium," he continued, "is that there are a great many truths in this field of foreign policy. For exam-ple, it is true that on a given day, a number of pickets may be in front of the White House saying 'Get out of Vietnam,' and the Voice could report that at some length, and it would be reporting the truth. But if the sum of their reports indicated that the great majority of the American people wanted the President to turn tail and run out of Southeast Asia, then those programs would add up to an untruth, and what we try to do is to insure that the Voice's programming is so balanced that the overseas listener lines up with a total understanding that adds up to the truth about what Americans stand for, what their intentions are, what their objectives are."

VOA commentaries, said Rowan, "must accurately reflect the pol-icy of the United States Government. This is why on occasion I have said, 'I want to see this commentary on Vietnam before it goes on the air.' Well, I'm the man in the Agency who sits on the National Security Council. I'm the one who sits in the Cabinet meetings. Thus I'm the one who has the best knowledge of anybody in the Agency as to what U.S. policy and U.S. intentions are. I feel that it is my responsibility to the American people to insure that the Voice is not broadcasting erroneous reports."

The interviewer put the all-important question: "To sum up, [VOA] is to be thought of not as a dispenser of truth, primarily, but as an instrument of propaganda?" And Rowan replied, for what must have seemed the thousandth time: "It is both, but in dispensing the truth and the facts—this winds up as our best medium of propa-ganda."[17]

Changes with Chancellor and Daly

In July, 1965, President Johnson persuaded an experienced and clear-headed thirty-eight-year-old NBC news correspondent, John Chancel-lor, to take on the job of running the Voice. He was the first working newsman to hold the job.

The most sensible comment on Chancellor's appointment came from the Washington *Star*. "One trouble with the Voice of America," said a *Star* editorial,

has been that some of its directors—including Henry Loomis—have pretended it could be a wholly objective, detached observer of the world scene, independent of the policy of the United States Government. In theory this is jim-dandy, but in practice it is nonsense. . . .

This does not mean, of course, that the VOA is a mere propaganda apparatus; the best information policy remains to report the truth and comment on it. It does mean, however, that the VOA cannot expect to operate separately from the government which has created it, which finances it and which depends upon it—wholly apart from our free press—to give foreigners an official version of what is going on among us. Mr. Loomis apparently could not adjust himself to such an operation. We hope Mr. Chancellor does.[18]

Mr. Chancellor did.

When his appointment was announced, Chancellor told newsmen: "I am satisfied the President wants the Voice to tell the truth."[19] On September 1, 1965, upon taking the oath of office from the new Director of USIA, Leonard Marks, the incoming VOA chief had more to say to his new colleagues at the Voice, and it differed not at all from the Murrow and Rowan philosophies of government broadcasting.

"We regard sensible opposition as an American sacrament," said Chancellor. "When it becomes news, we report it . . . with balance and perspective and with a sense of the purpose or thrust of our society. Truth is incomprehensible out of context. Context will be our preoccupation. . . . We will send no false signals to enemies or spectators." Chancellor pointedly noted that "we do not serve the needs of an American audience. . . . Our task is to make the policies of the Government of the United States clearly and explicitly understood around the world, with no chance for any misunderstandings." Neither Murrow nor Rowan could have said it more clearly.

Chancellor also promised a new tone and tempo for VOA. "Under my stewardship," he said, "the Voice of America will not drift into arcane intellectualism or academic pedantry. We will be vigorous, amusing, avant-garde; we will be first with the latest, we will be current and contemporary. . . . It is my intent that we 'swing' a little."[20]

With the full support of Marks, Chancellor moved to end the running quarrel between his broadcasters and the policy-makers. He told the VOA staff that the acrimony must end—and it did. Chancellor agreed that the Policy Office should clear all commentaries. ("He is stricter about following the policy line than we are," exclaimed one pleased policy official.) His good judgment made it less necessary for the policy officers to intervene on news stories, which suited everyone at VOA just fine. The broadcasters stopped using the Loomis "charter" as their bible, which suited the policy people just fine. One policy official summed it up: "We still can't lay down the law on what VOA says on its newscasts, but we don't have to any more."

A year to the day after Chancellor was sworn in, James Reston of the *New York Times* returned from abroad with high praise for the Voice. "With due respect for the commercial radio and television networks in the United States," he wrote, "this Government news service to the world must be the most detailed and accurate account of American and world news out of the United States today. It is not peddling political propaganda. It is telling not only what the President and his associates say, but what the opposition says."[21] And Loomis himself wrote President Johnson that he now found truth and policy "once more" in balance."[22]

Not everyone agreed. Senator Robert Kennedy returned from a 1966 tour of Africa with the charge that VOA broadcasts were "propaganda." Chancellor was unruffled. "The Senator was quoting Peace Corps volunteers," he said, "but the VOA is not directed" to them. "We are fashioning programs for Africans. We have ample proof we are reaching them." Chancellor explained anew that the Voice does not ignore criticism of U.S. policies but tries to "show that people can disagree with policy here without necessarily planning a coup."[23]

Late in 1966, after more than a year of study and experimentation, Chancellor introduced what he called a "new sound" for VOA. "Our broadcasts must not only be American, they must sound American," he said.[24] In place of the standard fifteen-minute and half-hour broadcast, he substituted for an hour or two each day a greater variety of shorter items in the English-language service. On the first day with the new format, the longest single item was a four-minute interview with Secretary of State Rusk. The new approach was similar to NBC Radio's *Monitor* show, and not unlike NBC Television's *Today* program in which Chancellor had once starred.

A lighthearted version of "Yankee Doodle" replaced the more somber "Columbia, Gem of the Ocean" as VOA's station-break theme song. Short interviews with writers, film stars, musicians, and sports figures were interspersed with the more solemn pronouncements of political leaders. Impressed, *Time* magazine described the "swinging" new format as "almost as far out as a piccolo solo by Lyndon Johnson."[25] Others were impressed, too. The Communist nations followed suit, brightening their radio programs with more popular music, brief interviews, and fewer dreary political diatribes.

There were other signs of progress that VOA could view with pride. High school students in Moscow danced to VOA music at a graduation party in Red Square. Chen Yi, the Foreign Minister of Communist China, admitted publicly that he listened to VOA newscasts. Vietcong posters, in an unintentional tribute, warned Vietnamese villagers that "listening to the Voice of America is like letting a thief in your house who will steal your soul."

Chancellor described VOA's Russian service as the best foreign-language program offered by any international broadcaster. Under the direction of Terry Catherman, a first-rate USIA Foreign Service Officer with experience in Moscow, it became lively and experimental. For example, Catherman eliminated the staid English-teaching program in favor of what he called "mini-lessons," e.g., Frank Sinatra singing, "Jeepers, creepers, where'd ya get those peepers?" followed by an attractive-voiced woman announcer explaining the meaning of the slang. (In Moscow the next day the young people's catchwords were "jeepers, creepers.")

Most important of all, the harsh language of the Cold War, downgraded by Murrow after the Soviets stopped jamming in 1963, disappeared almost entirely, a recognition of greater sophistication on the part not only of VOA broadcasters but also of their Russian listeners. Heavy policy programs were reduced to about a fourth of the eight-hour daily transmission (6 to 8 A.M., and 6 P.M. to midnight, Moscow time). The aim now was to satisfy the growing, constructive curiosity of the Soviet people about America, rather than a futile effort to turn them against their leaders.

In February, 1967, the Voice celebrated its twenty-fifth birthday. "The miracles of modern mass media of communication have at last made it possible to create and nurture mutual understanding," President Johnson wrote in a congratulatory message. And Chancellor, looking proudly at the new VOA, said it reflected the "many-colored canvas of American life" while paying special attention to "the arts of advocacy and persuasion."

Like Murrow, Chancellor took a great cut in pay when he came to USIA. Unlike Murrow, he could not indefinitely meet, on a government salary, the commitments he had made while earning far more in private broadcasting. Besieged by numerous offers from industry, education, and commercial broadcasting, he resigned with some reluctance in the spring of 1967 to return to NBC. He assured the press there had been no friction with Johnson or Marks, as in Loomis' case: "Both men have supported me and the Voice all the way down the line. My relationship with Mr. Marks has been remarkably serene."[26]

As he did two years earlier, President Johnson himself took a hand in selecting a new Voice chief. Before long the White House let it be known that the field had been narrowed to three candidates: John Charles Daly, a former radio-TV newsman who for seventeen years had been moderator of the television show *What's My Line?*, scheduled to leave the air because of declining audience ratings; Howard K. Smith, a Murrow protégé, now the chief Washington commentator for the American Broadcasting Company; and Nancy Dickerson, an NBC Washington correspondent and long-time friend of the President. The appointment went to Daly.

A son-in-law of Chief Justice Earl Warren, the elegant, South African-born Daly was a pioneer in radio news reporting abroad. As White House correspondent for CBS, he had announced President Roosevelt's death to a stunned nation in 1945, and had been ABC's chief newsman in the 1950s until parting company with that network in 1960. Although news was his "first love," he was most widely known as moderator of the panel show, and on announcement of his appointment to VOA said happily: "I'm tickled to death. I'm going back to where I belong."

Not everyone agreed. Although Walter Cronkite of CBS described Daly as a "conscientious newsman," another well-known reporter said he was "basically a showman, and we certainly don't need a showman in this job."[27] Most of his new colleagues at VOA were prepared to give him every chance, however, and they were impressed by Daly's willingness, like Murrow and Chancellor before him, to take a great cut in pay, in Daly's case from about $250,000 annually to $24,500.

Daly promised no change in Voice policy, including that of airing dissent. "All we can do is fully and fairly put down the divisions within the country and the divisions internationally," he said. "I feel that our policy in Vietnam is right, but we have an obligation to give a hearing to those who don't." Two Congressional Democrats immediately disagreed. One of them, ominously, was Representative John J. Rooney of Brooklyn, who heads the House subcommittee that passes on VOA's appropriations; he said Daly's job "is to promote our way of thinking."

The Congressmen's comments promise that, despite Chancellor's restoration of harmony, controversy over the Voice will continue. Congress, the White House, top USIA executives, and VOA broadcasters themselves still have no common understanding of VOA's purposes. Consequently, its programs continue to be developed mostly by a combination of intuitions and stylistic preferences—and compromise. The basic question of policy control is still unresolved, and could result once more in open warfare within USIA.

"There are no national boundaries to intelligence, wit, wisdom and humor," Chancellor once said. "It is our intent that the signals we send out to the world reflect this attitude."[28] Perhaps, in the end, the Voice of America can find no better "charter" than these wise words.

10 *Carl Rowan:*
A Time of Transition

The departures of Kennedy and Murrow in the gloomy winter of 1963-64 brought USIA a new President and a new Director. Both were very different from their predecessors. Whereas Kennedy saw USIA as a tool of some importance in the conduct of America's foreign affairs, Johnson had a largely mechanical view of the Agency. The new President tended to look upon USIA as an oversized "mimeograph machine" spewing out information, rather than as a source of expert counsel in Washington and a means of persuasion abroad. Moreover, Johnson had a low regard for the Agency's staff, a view carried over from his days as a Senate critic of USIA's budget. He was not very discreet about keeping his negative opinions to himself; derogatory comments dropped here and there were quickly noted by newsmen and government officials, and the Agency's reputation suffered.

Carl Rowan shared Kennedy's (and Murrow's) view of the role of the Agency, but he did not get the support from the White House that had worked to Murrow's advantage. Rowan also was handicapped by a lack of interest and skill in the intricacies of administration, and USIA's far-flung operations required constant and sophisticated managerial attention. The administrative burden, consequently, fell increasingly on his subordinates' shoulders, while Rowan devoted a large share of his time to preparing and delivering public addresses around the country, at which he excelled.

Following Murrow had its advantages and disadvantages. It would not have been easy for anyone; it was not easy for Rowan, a proud and sensitive man eager to make his own mark on the government and the world. Shortly after becoming Director, Rowan noted publicly that he was "indebted" to Murrow for leaving "an organization with a better staff, higher morale and higher prestige at home and abroad than he found."[1] But, through no fault of his own, Rowan lacked the personal prestige that Murrow had exploited with great effectiveness in the Kennedy Administration.

If the Murrow legacy was both a help and hindrance to Rowan, so was the color of his skin. As the highest-ranking Negro in the Federal Government (not only in the Johnson Administration, but the highest ever, up to that point), he was sometimes thought of—by the press and public, and by some of his colleagues in government—as an official Negro rather than as a Negro official. On the other hand, as a Negro he could and did speak with special authority to Africa and Asia on America's civil rights problems. Murrow had privately voiced qualms about the appointment, fearing Rowan might feel it necessary to soft-pedal civil rights, but the fears proved groundless.

Asked about the matter by a reporter, Rowan replied sensibly: "I consider my race to be incidental. . . . I don't intend to be especially timid for fear that somebody will think I have done something because I am a Negro, and I don't see any need for me to go out and make any special efforts to push this question of race because I am a Negro." Rowan felt the colored peoples of the world may "sense . . . some kind of extra credibility . . . but I don't intend to rely on that."[2]

The new Director believed racial progress could be achieved within the law. On one occasion he recalled that while in college he participated in "one of the first sit-ins ever staged—in a Columbus, Ohio, dining room." And later he "spent a few chilly nights on the picket line in front of a Baltimore theater." So, said Rowan, "I have not forgotten that a dining room insult burns especially hot in an empty stomach, or that anger and frustration can rise to fever pitch" when people cross your picket line, "but we can ill afford to forget that the whole framework of justice under our Bill of Rights rests on an assumption of man's ability to control the heat in his stomach."[3]

Counseling moderation was one thing; trying to explain to the world the police mistreatment of civil rights marchers in Selma, Alabama, in March of 1965 was something else again. USIA fell back on the line it had used many times before: that "under the American Constitution police powers belong to the authorities of the individual states"; therefore the Federal Government could not "intervene directly and at once to prevent the police brutality in Selma or subsequently to reassure against its recurrence."

The Agency somewhat weakly argued that "in most of the United States, the full realization of equal rights . . . is proceeding progressively, peacefully, and without incident. Such instances of hard-core resistance and intimidation as the events in Selma represent are exceptional." USIA called attention to the various legal steps being taken by Federal authorities, including prosecution of Alabama police officials.[4]

Rowan was not naïve about the pace or extent of progress, but he felt that the press, both at home and abroad, was inadequately reporting the affirmative side of the story. Where civil rights were concerned, he said, "Bad news is halfway around the world before the good news gets its boots on." Therefore it is USIA's job to put the story "into its true and total dimensions of a society struggling as no other in history to tear down the barricades of distrust and prejudice." The Agency has not "denied our racial *problems,*" explained Rowan, "but what we have done is to underscore the racial *progress.*"[5]

There were signs that the USIA effort was having some impact. Reviewing foreign comment on the events in Selma, the Agency's Research Office reported that reaction was markedly better than it had been in earlier crises. "In the past, editorials condemned brutality and condemned the United States for permitting it," said the report. "Today they condemn the brutality but not the U.S."

This was more a result of long hours of friendly persuasion by unsung USIA officers in the field than of any Washington policy line. Happily not all of them were unsung; for example, when Information Officer William Gordon, a Negro, was transferred from Lagos, the *Daily Telegraph* there editorialized: "He came to Nigeria when there were shadows of doubt about U.S. intentions in Africa. . . . By dint of hard work and a true understanding of the people, Mr. Gordon has helped tremendously to cement U.S.-Nigerian relations."

Rowan was blessed with a sense of humor, and his jokes about the status of the Negro, delivered in a wry, dry voice, helped win over audiences both white and black. He delighted in telling an apocryphal story on himself, describing an alleged conversation with a wealthy white woman. As Rowan told it, he was mowing his lawn one hot August day, in the mostly white neighborhood where he had moved upon joining the Kennedy Administration, when a long, chauffeur-driven car pulled up to the curb. The back window was rolled down, and the woman in the car called out: "Boy, come over here." Mopping his brow, Rowan walked over. "I live nearby," said the woman. "How much do you get for mowing the lawn here?" According to Rowan he replied, "Well, ma'am, the lady of the house lets me sleep with her."

Carl T. Rowan was himself living proof that some Negro Americans could overcome the barriers of racial prejudice even before the civil rights movement began to make it possible for the many instead of the few. Only thirty-eight years old when he became Director of USIA, the moon-faced, soft-spoken Rowan had been born in a small town in Tennessee, served as a lieutenant, jg, in the Navy during World War II, earned a bachelor's degree from Oberlin College, and obtained his master's from the University of Minnesota. From 1948 to 1961 he was a prize-winning reporter and foreign correspondent for the Minneapolis *Tribune.*

Kennedy named him Deputy Assistant Secretary of State for Public Affairs in 1961, and in 1962 Rowan served as a U.S. delegate to the UN General Assembly. Kennedy appointed him Ambassador to Finland in 1963, where he served a year before Johnson brought him home to head USIA. While in the State Department he attracted public attention with his barbed criticisms of Congolese secessionist Moïse Tshombé and Tshombé's propagandist in this country, Michael Struelens.

In Murrow's Footsteps

As Director of USIA, Rowan proved to be a careful and skillful writer and speaker, if less dramatic than Murrow. In an early interview he said: "I intend to have the Agency tell the truth and put it in perspective. . . . To talk about an incident that happens today may be to tell the truth, but [simply] to talk about that incident may not be to tell the whole truth. You may have to talk a bit about the past and what the hopes are for the future and what the role of the Federal Government is and what the attitude of Congress is; and when you have said all these things you have put that event in the kind of perspective that constitutes the whole truth."[6]

In words public and private, Rowan made it clear that he subscribed to the philosophy of propaganda put into practice by Murrow. Rowan's job, as he saw it, was to perfect that practice. In so doing he depended heavily on those men in USIA in whom Murrow had shown most confidence. Wilson and I offered to resign so that Rowan could have a free hand in shaping the Agency, but he asked us to stay on.

After his confirmation by the Senate, Rowan called a meeting of Washington employees of the Agency. "I want you to know," he told them, "that I can think of no ideal that Ed Murrow clung to that I'm not willing to espouse." Calling for a greater vitality in the Agency's work, he said it could "not succeed if we rely solely on sterile pronouncements and press releases. We've got to tell our story in such a way as to touch the heartstrings of people. . . . We're going to have to have the courage to try some things that are new."

To those who still questioned the propaganda objectives of the Agency, Rowan addressed pointed words: "Our mission . . . is to inform the outside world as to what we are and what our policies are, and to do it in such a way as to enhance the foreign policy objectives of the United States. That, pure and simple, is our reason for existence. I say this knowing that there are many areas where the pride, the artistic inclinations, the professional egos of many of us are involved. . . . We aren't going to ask anybody . . . to surrender any part of his integrity. But we've got to remember that it is U.S. foreign policy that we are pushing, and not individual egos."

Rowan had equally pointed words for the "European club" and other USIA officers who resisted assignment to unpleasant places: "Any Foreign Service Officer who has a sense of mission, and is worthy to work in this Agency, should long ago have dropped the notion that assignment to any but one or two areas is an affront to him. . . . There aren't going to be any areas that constitute special preserves or any special groups or any special individuals in this Agency."[7]

Rowan's speech raised the spirits of the better USIA employees and aroused apprehensions among the mediocrities. That is exactly what he had intended. Nonetheless, the morale of many good officers remained low. This was partly a consequence of the sudden departures within a few weeks of Kennedy and Murrow, and the inevitable difficulties of the transition to new leadership. But it also stemmed in part from Rowan's methods of operation. He had far less contact with subordinates and was much less accessible than Murrow. He sometimes acted without consulting or informing his staff, and delegated too many important matters to a personal aide of limited talent.

Wilson and I in mid-March urged Rowan to meet more frequently with his subordinates and to brief them, as Murrow had done, on meetings he attended at the White House, the State Department, and the Pentagon, so they would be adequately informed. Rowan agreed, and the situation improved slightly. On matters in which he was particularly interested—chiefly Vietnam, the Congo, the Dominican Republic, coverage of the Presidential election, and civil rights—Rowan was attentive, articulate, and skillful. Concerning many other matters, especially administrative problems and routine (though important) operations, he was plainly bored.

There was, however, no question about Rowan's clear vision of the purpose of USIA or his determination that the Agency be heard in the making of foreign policy and its execution. "Today's struggle has become a struggle of ideas," he told one audience. "Even as we retain sufficient military might to meet any aggressor . . . we must also muster our resources so as to deal with the psychological challenge."[8] Rowan also recognized the limitations of propaganda, commenting on another occasion that "we in USIA are the purveyors of the American image abroad, but not its manufacturers. The image of the United States cannot be concocted in some propaganda factory."[9]

Rowan had more success in articulating the purposes of USIA than he did in maintaining its voice in the councils of the Administration. Secretary of State Rusk was more influential with Johnson than he had been with Kennedy, and—as noted previously—neither Johnson nor Rusk had much appreciation of the uses of propaganda. It was a constant fight to be heard, a fight Rowan often lost. But he persisted, and before long Johnson was complaining that he was too aggressive, reportedly telling him on one occasion, "Mr. Rowan, I already *have* a Secretary of State."

Johnson and the Future—Kennedy and the Past

Appreciated or not, the Agency had much to do. The cessation of jamming by the Soviet Union and most East European countries—plus greater Voice of America transmitting power in England, the Greek island of Rhodes, and Liberia—improved VOA's audibility and increased its audience. Student riots in Panama drew attention to that last vestige of American imperialism, the Panama Canal Zone, and the United States was embarrassed not only in Latin America but throughout Africa and Asia as well. The push for more tension-reducing agreements with the Soviet Union slowed with the widening war in Vietnam.

On the brighter side, Kennedy's civil rights bill was guided through Congress by the former Senate Majority Leader who now sat in the White House. Passage of the measure was greeted by widespread approval abroad; in Guinea, often unfriendly President Sékou Touré called it a "great victory." Johnson's proposals for a Great Society also struck a responsive chord, although there was some puzzlement about the "war on poverty"; the $3,000 annual income set as the poverty line seemed affluent to millions abroad whose incomes were below that figure. On the other hand, the Administration's pointing up of living conditions in the big-city racial ghettos and Appalachia seemed to support Communist allegations about the inadequacies of American capitalism.

USIA sought to put the Johnson program into the perspective of an expanding but imperfect American economy and explained in a "Talking Paper" (for use by USIS officers abroad) that the Great Society was not "merely a political campaign slogan" but "Johnson's vision and expression of the peaceful goals the United States must strive for in the second half of the twentieth century."[10]

Explaining the new American President to the world was a priority task all through 1964. In the winter and spring the Agency's film *The President* was seen by record numbers, estimated at 750 million or nearly four times the population of the United States. In the summer and autumn, USIA, as in the past, gave extensive coverage to the Presidential campaign. The Agency's coverage was scrupulously balanced, giving the Republican nominee, Senator Barry Goldwater, no less space or sympathy than was given President Johnson.

The election campaign helped to accomplish abroad what USIA propaganda could not do on its own: it made Johnson popular with millions who still mourned for Kennedy. Goldwater assisted in this task by taking, or appearing to take, various positions that were thoroughly unpopular overseas, notably his demands for escalating the war in Vietnam and reducing social programs (such as Social Security and the Tennessee Valley Authority) at home.

On election night, many USIS posts held open-house receptions to watch the returns. In New Delhi seven thousand persons jammed into USIS "election headquarters," among them the Soviet Ambassador. Three thousand attended a similar reception in Rio de Janeiro, four thousand in Paris, and five thousand in Vientiane (Laos). With few exceptions, foreigners greeted Johnson's landslide victory with enthusiasm.

Also in the fall of 1964, the Agency completed and sent abroad its first full-length feature film, *John F. Kennedy: Years of Lightning, Day of Drums.* Sentimental and dramatic, the film portrayed what it called "the six faces of the New Frontier"—civil rights, the Peace Corps, the Alliance for Progress, disarmament and the search for peace, freedom, and exploration of space—interspersed with heartbreaking scenes of Kennedy's funeral. Narrated by Gregory Peck and produced by George Stevens, Jr. and Bruce Herschensohn, the film was an enormous success abroad, where it was distributed commercially in sixty-seven countries and shown without charge in fifty others.

The tributes were, perhaps, as much for Kennedy as for the film. In the remote African city of Asmara, showings of the movie were promoted with a poster that featured a photograph of the late President. Within hours after the posters were hung, most of the portraits disappeared. They had been cut out for display in hundreds of huts. In Addis Ababa one newspaper called the film "the most beautiful testimonial to the memory of President Kennedy that the United States could possibly have made." A New Zealand critic called it "first-class journalism . . . as rewarding as any of the best movies of 1964." A reviewer in Johannesburg wrote: "This film makes one want to be an American." The Speaker of the Icelandic Parliament spoke for many: "This is the only picture I have ever seen during which I wanted to cry."

In Washington USIA showed the film to standing-room-only audiences at the National Press Club and to gatherings of foreign and American diplomats in the State Department auditorium. Some Congressmen saw it, and others wanted to. Many private groups asked to borrow the film, but the Agency was reluctant to loan it: Congress had repeatedly made it clear that it did not want USIA to distribute its material in this country. Prompted by public demand, resolutions were introduced in both houses of Congress to authorize domestic showings of the film.

Support for the resolutions was bipartisan but not unanimous. The White House had little enthusiasm for showings in the United States of a film glorifying Johnson's predecessor. Some Republicans feared the film might be politically helpful to Democrats in general and the surviving Kennedys in particular. "USIA is frankly a propaganda agency; this is frankly a propaganda film," cautioned the New York Herald Tribune. "The question is whether USIA should be allowed to become . . . an agency for the persuasion of the American people. . . . President Kennedy, however much his memory is respected, was a political leader whose programs are still in current controversy, whose brothers are senators seeking political support."

It was a reasonable argument, but it did not prevail. The Senate Foreign Relations Committee passed the resolution without dissent after revising it to make clear that the showing in the United States would be a special exception, not a precedent. As revised, the resolution permitted USIA to sell six prints of the film to the John F. Kennedy Center for the Performing Arts (the new name for the projected Washington Cultural Center) for $122,000, which went into the general funds of the Treasury. The Kennedy Center, in turn, was authorized to rent the film to a commercial distributor for theatrical showings in this country, with proceeds going to the Center.

There were, however, problems with some Democrats who wanted to use the film to make money for Kennedy's party rather than his cultural interests. When party officials in Milwaukee proposed to use proceeds from the film's premiere there to finance the campaign of a Congressional candidate, the White House asked the Attorney General for an opinion. The Justice Department ruled that it would be against the intent of Congress to show the film for political fund-raising purposes. Subsequently, similar "depredations" (as one indignant columnist called them) were headed off in Cuyahoga Falls, Ohio, Des Moines, and—of all places—Dallas.

But USIA's real problems as always were abroad, not in this country, and in 1964 the United States suffered a propaganda setback in Africa. Somewhat to the embarrassment of the United States, the Katanga rebel Moïse Tshombé had returned to the Congo as Premier.* The problem this time was not Katangan rebels of the right but fierce tribal rebels of the left, supported by Communist China, Algeria, and Nasser's United Arab Republic.

By August, 1964, the rebels controlled much territory, including the important city of Stanleyville, and were moving slowly toward the capital city of Leopoldville, killing great numbers of Congolese along the way and seizing foreign hostages. The Congo Government's army was ineffective during this period, but Tshombé recruited mercenary forces who succeeded in halting the rebel advance. By November they were driving the rebel forces back toward Stanleyville.

The United States deplored the Communist penetration of the Congo and the killings but, except for diplomatic overtures, made no overt move until Americans held hostage by the retreating rebels were publicly threatened with death. Apprehension and outrage spread across America during Thanksgiving week, and the U.S. Government moved decisively, in concert with the Belgian Government, to save the hostages. A five-day air-rescue operation was successful, although one American missionary was killed before he could be reached. Americans, Belgians, some Congolese, and civilians from eighteen other countries were rescued.

Instead of being pleased, many Africans were highly critical of the rescue operation. They still did not like Tshombé, whom they considered a white man's puppet, and it seemed to them that the United States had intervened to defeat the rebels and rescue whites whose lives, apparently, were more valuable than the lives of Africans. U.S. embassies or libraries were attacked at Bujumbura, Nairobi, and Cairo, while the police stood by watching. Tshombé invited other African states to send newsmen to cover the story on the spot, but few did despite USIS encouragement.

---

* Among those most embarrassed was Rowan, who, as a Deputy Assistant Secretary of State, had been particularly outspoken in his criticism of Tshombé three years earlier.

In Africa and elsewhere USIA pointed out that the rescue mission had been authorized by the legitimate government of the Congo, unlike the aid being given the rebels, and that the binational force was not sent to help Tshombé capture Stanleyville but in fact withdrew after only five days when its rescue mission was completed. At the UN Adlai Stevenson was indignantly effective, and USIA flashed his words abroad. "Never before have I heard such irrational, irresponsible, insulting and repugnant language . . . to contemptuously impugn and slander a gallant and successful effort to save human lives of many nationalities and colors," said Stevenson, his face flushed with anger. "But even such a torrent of abuse of my country is of no consequence compared to the specter of racial antagonism and conflict raised in this chamber."

In the end, after USIA subtly but persistently publicized the rebel atrocities, Communist involvement with the rebels turned out to be a liability for them. The idea spread in Africa that Communists, particularly the Chinese, were intent on provoking revolution everywhere and that no independent African government was safe so long as the Chinese Communists were allowed to supply guns to dissidents. Nonetheless, there remained a lingering suspicion of the United States in Africa, even among its friends, because of the Congo rescue mission.

People and Personnel

Still and all, the prestige of America—and of President Johnson— was high in the winter of 1964–65. There was a lull between crises, and Washington settled down to enjoy an inauguration, Texas-style. For me it was a time of change. I had spent thirteen years as a government propagandist; if I were to have new challenges and new experiences, now was the time to move on. After the election was over I accepted an offer and resigned from the Agency on January 2, 1965.

Departure was bittersweet. I left without regrets, but with some sadness in breaking professional ties with the finest group of men and women I had ever known. I lunched for the last time at the White House "mess," said my farewells at a round of parties, and cleaned out my desk. Asked by Rowan to recommend a successor, I nominated my deputy, Burnett Anderson, without hesitation. He was one of the Agency's finest officers, a loyal and dedicated counselor who was my deputy in fact as well as in name. Two weeks after my departure Rowan appointed Anderson to succeed me, and named Hewson A. Ryan, who had done an excellent job as Assistant Director for Latin America, to succeed Anderson as Associate Director.*

Within a few months another Associate Director was added under somewhat curious circumstances. Howard B. Woods was editor of a Negro newspaper, the *Argus,* and a civic leader in St. Louis. But more than that, he was one of the few Negroes of any note to support Johnson for President in 1960, and Johnson did not forget. One day in early 1965 Woods received a cryptic message to report to the LBJ ranch, and next morning was summoned to Johnson's bedroom where the President was shaving.

Johnson came right to the point. He had wanted to appoint Woods to a "neutral" vacancy on the Federal Communications Commission, but had just learned from a check with Senator Dirksen's office that Capitol Republicans did not think he was sufficiently nonpartisan. "So," said Johnson, "how about USIA?" Woods liked the idea.

The President telephoned Rowan in Washington, asking what high-ranking vacant position could be offered to Woods. None was immediately apparent. Johnson pressed for an answer; he wanted to announce Woods's appointment at a noon press conference. Rowan hastily consulted Anderson and they decided the best out was to create a second associate directorship—and worry about specific duties later. Johnson agreed and announced the appointment a few minutes later to TV cameras and the White House press corps.

Not surprisingly, USIA received Woods with some skepticism when he reported for work. But he proved such a gentle, amiable man that he soon won a wide circle of friends in the Agency. His responsibilities never were clarified, however, and he was given no meaningful assignments. Frustrated by his inactivity, Woods resigned at the end of 1966 to become editor-in-chief of a string of Negro newspapers.

In the late summer of 1965, Don Wilson resigned as Deputy Director to become a general manager of Time-Life International.† His departure was a major loss to USIA. He had been a key figure in

---

* In August, 1966, Ryan succeeded Anderson as a Deputy Director.
† Wilson became associate publisher of *Life* magazine in 1968.

the achievements of the Agency since early 1961, and had contributed much to Murrow's success. The frequent absences of Murrow and Rowan had given him greater responsibility than normally carried by number two men. Johnson, accepting his resignation, noted that "your demonstration of leadership during the Cuban missile crisis and your tenure as Acting Director from the hours of my accession to the Presidency until [Rowan's appointment] were both visible examples of the kind of competence you continually exhibited."

Back in the mid-1950s the Agency had asked Congress for legislation that would permit USIA to create a career Foreign Service corps similar to but separate from the Foreign Service Officer corps of the State Department. When Congress failed to act on the proposal, USIA in 1960 set up a career service on a temporary basis, using powers it already had. But it was clearly a temporary arrangement, and equally clearly not a satisfactory one.

Murrow, Wilson, and I had strongly supported the career service concept for the Agency. But we also believed that USIA should be a separate agency in all respects, taking policy guidance from the State Department but reporting to the President. We favored an independent USIA not for reasons of bureaucratic pride but because we remembered how badly the nation's foreign information program had been administered when it was a neglected stepchild of the State Department. We wanted USIA officers to be career Foreign Service Officers, no different in rank, privileges, or obligations from State Department employees, but we also wanted the USIA Foreign Service Officers to be appointed, promoted, disciplined, and retired by the Agency, not the State Department.

Rusk apparently did not care one way or another, but the Deputy Under Secretary of State for Administration, William J. Crockett, did. A skilled bureaucratic infighter whose bland demeanor covered a driving ambition and considerable ability, Crockett believed strongly in the concept of one inclusive Foreign Service corps that would take in personnel of all the foreign affairs agencies and be under State Department control. In December, 1963, with Murrow ill and Kennedy dead, Crockett abruptly unveiled his plan.

USIA Foreign Service employees would be appointed by the President to the State Department's Foreign Service on the recommendation of the Secretary of State and the Director of USIA. The Service's governing machinery would be broadened to include USIA officials, but the State Department would have the predominant voice in the appointment and promotion of all Foreign Service Officers, whether of State or USIA origin. Wilson and I took the plan to Murrow at his home where he was convalescing from lung cancer. Murrow's answer was a firm no.

But a month later, when Rowan succeeded Murrow, the matter was pursued with him. Rowan saw merit in the plan and, after several months of negotiations, President Johnson announced in the early autumn of 1964 that State and USIA had agreed that the vast majority of USIA field officers could, after evaluations of their competence, be appointed to the State Department's Foreign Service. Rowan called it "a significant milestone in the history of USIA."

In April, 1965, the evaluations completed, President Johnson sent to the Senate the nominations of 760 USIA officers (about 80 percent of the USIA career reserve corps) to be members of the Foreign Service. "By bringing into the Foreign Service a group of career officers of proven ability and experience," said Johnson, "we take a step forward toward that unity of outlook and purpose which is so important to the efficient conduct of our relationships with the other nations of the world." Crockett testified that it would "eliminate the invidious differences that have existed between people who have been doing essentially the same work under the same conditions."

Rowan, Rusk, Crockett—and Johnson—had counted on prompt Congressional approval, but it was not forthcoming. The obstacle was the Senate Foreign Relations Committee, where Chairman Fulbright was doubtful, ranking Republican Hickenlooper more doubtful, and Democratic Senator Claiborne Pell (a former Foreign Service Officer) flatly opposed. The committee did not reject the President's nominations; it simply did not act on them. USIA persisted through two sessions of Congress, but without success. The scheme was finally abandoned in 1966. (The Agency then returned to its earlier concept of a separate career Foreign Service Information Officer corps, and a bill establishing such a corps was introduced by Senator Pell and passed by the Senate in late 1967. The House was expected to act favorably on the measure in 1968.)

There were budgetary as well as personnel problems. Shortly after 5 P.M. on the last day of 1964, the Agency received an unexpected order from the LBJ ranch where the President was spending the holidays: cut USIA's budget request for the next fiscal year by $15 million (about 10 percent) and report back to the Bureau of the Budget with a revised request within twenty-four hours. (The deadline subsequently was extended a couple of days, and the amount to cut was increased to $17.4 million.)

"Gunboat Diplomacy" Again

From Johnson's point of view, it appeared to be a good time to cut back USIA. As previously noted, there was a lull in crises, and American—and Johnsonian—prestige was high around the world. Yet within four months the United States—and President Johnson—were under mounting criticism. Within five months Walter Lippmann returned from abroad to report "a swelling tide of dissent and doubt and anxiety about the wisdom and competence with which United States foreign policy is being conducted."

What happened?

Lippmann gave three reasons: (1) Europeans had been "unanimous in their fear of and opposition to Barry Goldwater, and they have been stupefied to see President Johnson . . . doing in Vietnam what Goldwater recommended and Johnson denounced in the campaign"; (2) the "cumulative effect" of Johnson's military intervention in the Dominican Republic "on top of the expanded Vietnamese war" had "struck at the basis of confidence in his Administration"; and (3) Europeans were "deeply shocked by the manner and the style in which these two operations, especially the Dominican, have been conducted," and by "the unlimited globalism and the rough unilateralism to which the President has resorted in explaining his decisions."[11]

On April 25, 1965, a revolt had broken out in the Dominican Republic with the stated purpose of restoring Juan Bosch to the presidency. After the long tyrannical reign of the Trujillos, Bosch had been the first popularly elected head of the nation. The U.S. Government had held high hopes for him, but Bosch proved to be a talker not a doer, and an ineffectual administrator. When the military tired of him and threw him out, Washington was only mildly disturbed. But Washington was very much disturbed by the latest revolt, and by word from the American Ambassador that Communists were taking over the revolution.

One Castro in the Caribbean was all any politically sensitive Administration could afford to tolerate. The President decided to send troops to Santo Domingo, with the announced justification of "protecting American lives and property." Evidence of Communist control of the revolution was so thin, and the "protection" rationale so reminiscent of the era of "gunboat diplomacy," that neither the President at home nor USIA abroad had much success in getting people to believe it. An Agency policy statement was long on adjectives and short on persuasion:

"When you see a friend—or a total stranger—drowning, you don't stop to consult a lawyer before plunging in. . . . There was no time for deliberate consultation." Yankee interventionism? Certainly not. "Increased U.S. manpower on Dominican soil halted a spreading contagion of death by murder, disease and starvation. It permitted wider distribution of medical help and foodstuffs."[12]

The Communists, of course, attacked the U.S. intervention, but they always attacked any use of American troops abroad. More serious was the severe criticism from our allies in Latin America and Western Europe. The former did not like American intervention in Latin affairs for any reason, and the latter were appalled by what they considered an impulsive, unnecessary use of American military power without their consent or even knowledge (except at the last moment).

In Washington the Voice of America and the Agency's Press Service went on around-the-clock transmission schedules, explaining the U.S. position with statements by the President and other officials. A team of USIA senior officers was attached to the Dominican task force in the State Department's supersecret Operations Center. The offices of top Agency officials were manned twenty-four hours a day.

With Johnson's approval, Rowan rushed ten officials, writers, and broadcasters to Santo Domingo to beef up the small USIS staff. Their job was to convince the populace that American forces had come not to wage war but to make peace, not to thwart the will of the Dominican people but to protect their fragile democracy, and not to impose an American puppet leader but to ensure that a stooge of Castro or the Kremlin was not forced on the country.

The team was headed by Associate Director Hewson Ryan, who found he had to start almost from scratch. Inasmuch as the USIS building was in rebel territory, provisional offices were set up at the home of the Public Affairs Officer. Most newspapers and printing facilities also were in rebel territory, as was—most serious of all—Radio Santo Domingo.

U.S. military and diplomatic officials, failing to recognize the importance of the radio station, had not extended their "safety zone" to include it. Don Wilson was a member of a special committee, chaired by McGeorge Bundy, that met once and sometimes two or three times daily during the crisis. From the outset Wilson warned that whoever controlled the airwaves would have a major advantage. He was listened to, but other matters seemed more important. As time went on, the wisdom of USIA's view became all too apparent, and the rebel-controlled Radio Santo Domingo was a terrible thorn in the U.S. side until it was finally silenced by American forces.

In the meantime, a Voice of America engineer, instructed to find a radio station within the U.S.-controlled area and get it on the air, found one with its transmitter equipment burned out but its antenna intact. Twenty-four hours later, the transmitter went on the air with five kilowatts of power, relaying VOA's Spanish-language Latin-America broadcasts on medium wave. Within a week the USIA team, with Army help, had four transmitters on the air, two broadcasting locally originated programs and two relaying the VOA.

Shortly after Ryan landed he had embassy mimeograph machines turning out the first copies of a crude leaflet telling the Dominican people of the reasons for American intervention. A few hours later a member of the USIA team found a small print shop in the rear of a police station. The leaflet was set in type, printed, and air-dropped in large numbers. A single-sheet newspaper, *Voice of the Security Zone,* was published in Spanish every other day, and for a time it was the only newspaper in the city.

The Army's First Psychological Warfare Battalion, complete with portable radio transmitters, mobile printing presses, and loudspeaker-equipped trucks and planes, was flown down from Fort Bragg, North Carolina. It provided most of the equipment and much of the labor for the joint military-civilian information and psychological warfare effort, although most of the planning and leadership were supplied by USIA.

Communications were a problem, partly because the rebels held the central telephone exchange and partly because torrential rains kept knocking out both civilian and military circuits. As Ryan said, "It was easier to talk to Washington than to units across the river."

USIA television and press camera crews coped with power failures, ankle-deep mud, a shortage of water, difficult communications, and intermittent sniper fire to document the benign presence of U.S. troops, the evacuation of civilians, distribution of food, care of the wounded, and the arrival of the OAS Inter-American Peace Force. Hurriedly processed in Washington, the movies and photo "stills" were distributed throughout Latin America and Europe to bolster the U.S. position.

In the early days of crisis, the U.S. propaganda operation contributed to calming the situation in Santo Domingo. In the end, though, it was not propaganda but the skillful diplomacy of a special American envoy, Ellsworth Bunker, that played the largest role in obtaining free elections and a return to democratic institutions. And regardless of what foreign critics thought of the intervention at the time, it did make possible a peaceful and free presidential election.

Trouble and Change

Rowan had a better idea than many in the Administration of the psychology of the underdeveloped world. "If we really understood how closely the ambitions of these new nations resemble our own," he remarked, "we would not be so fearful, so full of distrust, as to what they are and aspire to be." Rowan recalled that a prominent Nigerian once told him: "It sure irritates me to have these colonials talk about how they rescued us Africans from the savagery of jungle warfare. These white men won't face the fact they've devised more ways of killing more people than the African tribes ever dreamed of."[13]

Although Rowan was more tolerant than many of the double standards of some of the newer nations, his patience did have limits. In Indonesia the United States took an enormous amount of abuse from the garrulous dictator Sukarno with the hope of keeping the country from falling completely into Communist hands. In the end, after an abortive Communist *coup d'état,* the army and students tired of Sukarno, stripped him of power, and slaughtered Communists, suspected Communists, and Chinese by the thousands. But before Sukarno was removed from power, USIS offices and libraries in Indonesia took more than their share of abuse, physical as well as verbal.

After a few minor incidents, the mobs became bolder in 1964 as the tempo of Sukarno's attacks on the United States increased. In May a mob forcibly entered the USIS auditorium at Surabaya and smashed a movie projector. In August Indonesian authorities shut down the USIS library at Jogjakarta after a mob entered it and demanded its closing. On December 4 a mob broke into the main USIS library at Jakarta, smashing windows, wrecking furniture, and burning four thousand books. Three days later another mob attacked the library at Surabaya. The following February 16, a mob seized the Jakarta library. Six days later Indonesian officials took over the USIS reading room at Macassar. Then, on March 1, the USIS library at Medan was invaded by a mob of youths who took down the American flag and hoisted the Indonesian banner. *That* was the end.

Three days later Rowan closed all USIA installations in Indonesia and withdrew their staffs.* "This is a decision we take most reluctantly," he said. "That [the USIS libraries in Indonesia] were valued and appreciated is indicated by the fact that attendance . . . rose from 24,000 in 1948 to more than half a million in 1964." But, Rowan continued, "the Indonesian Government has left us no choice. . . . Not only has it failed to restrain those who have attacked the libraries periodically but it has now seized the libraries and placed the whole USIA operation under conditions we find intolerable."[14]

To some, the occasional attacks on USIS libraries abroad meant that America was hated. To the more perceptive it meant that extremists were afraid of knowledge, truth, and America, and therefore struck at the most accessible and most visible symbol of knowledge, truth, and America at hand: the USIS library. Recognizing this, Rowan could be philosophical about the attacks. He warned against "letting our indignation push us to conclusions and actions that are illogical, or are based on attitudes of defeatism."

Rowan cited several examples to demonstrate how most people abroad felt about the American libraries. Greek schoolchildren raised money to repair the bomb-damaged library in Athens. Arab revolutionary governments in Algiers and Cairo paid damages when hool-

---

* Barry Goldwater, in his humorous remarks at the annual banquet in 1965 of the Washington Gridiron Club, took note of the situation. "I thought President Johnson might offer me a post in his Administration, but all he has said so far is: 'Barry, we've got an opening for a librarian in Indonesia.'"

igans destroyed the USIS libraries in those cities. "Do not fall victim to pessimism," Rowan advised Americans, or "to this morbid psychology that causes some to weep in despair each time a midget kicks dirt at the heels of Uncle Sam."[15] It was good advice.*

Verbal attacks by America's adversaries were not unwelcome, however, being one indication that USIA's efforts were having some effect. As the intensified war in Vietnam weakened the *détente* with the Soviet Union that followed the nuclear test ban treaty, Moscow was increasingly critical of the Agency. For example, in a typical few days while Rowan was Director, Communist media took this notice of the Agency:

• "American propaganda, and in particular the vast operation of the USIA, is trying to prove in every way that American diplomacy has no other aims in Asia than to further peace and progress" (Radio Moscow).

• The Voice of America, "the most vociferous of the voices of propaganda," is attempting through "old tunes of the Cold War" to "jam out" the "righteous complaints of people everywhere" against UN operations in the Congo (*Izvestia*).

• The "American propaganda apparatus" is now more dangerous since it was "vastly expanded" during the Kennedy Administration (*Novo Vreme,* a monthly published by the Bulgarian Communist Party).

• "The widely ramified machinery of the Information Agency" is "seeking to poison the minds of Africans" (*Red Star*).

In fact, however, USIA was no longer emphasizing the wholly negative anti-Communism that featured its output during the 1950s. Instead, by increasing awareness of the West, the Agency sought to reduce the isolation and false fears of the Communist world—and this is what its leaders objected to. "We welcome the growing evidence that the countries of Eastern Europe are looking westward for a

---

* There were those who were neither philosophical nor pessimistic, merely practical. When a mob smashed the windows of the USIS library in Dacca, East Pakistan, in August of 1964, the glass was replaced by a glass company in distant Chittagong. A window was smashed again the following February, and the Public Affairs Officer asked how soon it could be replaced. "By noon tomorrow," the glass dealer replied. "In Dacca?" said the PAO, astounded. "It will take at least a week to get the glass up from Chittagong." "Yes," responded the dealer, "but when I brought the glass before I took two extra panes to Dacca. I guessed you'd lose another window or so soon."

broader range of contacts," Rowan said. "There is a great deal of curiosity about America among the peoples of Eastern Europe. We in USIA do all that we can to satisfy that curiosity."[16]

But the cautious rulers of Communism feared (with considerable justification) that satisfying that curiosity would further loosen the ties that had bound Eastern Europe to Moscow since 1945. "We Communists have never agreed, and will never agree, to the idea of peaceful coexistence in ideologies," Khrushchev had said. "In this there can be no compromise." And there was none. Cold War tensions eased, but not the word war.

USIA used straight news, rather than polemic diatribes, to keep the world informed on what the Communists were up to. The quarrel between Russia and China, which grew more heated during this period, was reported in great detail, as were industrial and agricultural failures in the U.S.S.R. and China and foreign subversive operations directed by Moscow, Peking, and Havana.

It was Vietnam, more than the Dominican intervention, that caused the sudden drop in American prestige during 1965. The war there became in the mid-sixties the Agency's biggest, most expensive, most difficult, and most enduring problem. Rowan, acting under Presidential directive, threw all his energies and an increasing proportion of USIA resources into dealing with the problem. But the Vietnam story should be told in one place, and that one place will be the next chapter.

Johnson, as we have indicated, had little confidence in the Information Agency. Rowan, as we have indicated, found no pleasure in the administrative details of running a large organization and growing frustration in USIA's declining role in the government. His early enthusiasm for Johnson had largely evaporated, as had Johnson's for him. Moreover, there were attractive job possibilities in newspaper, magazine, and TV journalism that would pay him several times his government salary.

In the spring of 1965, annoyed by Johnson's refusal to authorize a trip to Africa, Rowan indicated to the President that he would prefer to return to journalism unless USIA could play the meaningful role in foreign affairs that Rowan thought it should. Johnson, no man to take ultimatums lightly, interpreted this as an ultimatum and began casting around for a replacement. He approached several men about the job, one of them a former Kennedy assistant in the White House.

Presidential talent scouts explored the broadcasting industry "for a big name to hypnotize Congress and reassure the Agency that the President found its function . . . a vital one."[17]

Rowan's disaffection grew when the President, for no apparent good reason, refused to let him go on a trip to Thailand for which Rowan had made extensive plans. When the story leaked to the press in early July that Rowan was planning to depart, Johnson quickly found a successor and Rowan's resignation was announced July 10 at the LBJ ranch.

Rowan's sudden departure did not help the Agency's sagging morale. "An unhappy condition plaguing the USIA from its beginning has now come to the fore again," wrote columnist Marquis Childs. "The top command has been abruptly changed, leaving as several times in the past a great doubt about future direction. . . . Murrow's long illness and death were for the Agency a tragic misfortune."[18]

The fate of an agency is not really very important, of course. What matters is the fate of the function it performs, and in the summer of 1965, with Johnson under fire for his escalation of the Vietnam war, USIA's function was in real doubt. Another columnist, linking Rowan's departure with the resignation of Johnson's long-time friend and press secretary, George Reedy, noted that both jobs "call for unusually intimate relationships with the President. Both Rowan and Reedy asked to be relieved at a time when the Johnson image is suffering. . . . The image makers may be considerably removed from the centers of real power, and when they come to realize this they discover how hard it is to mold the clay in the desired form."[19]

Rowan left without apology for his stewardship. Although he had been USIA's Director for only a year and a half, he had carried forward the Murrow philosophy and program with persistence and courage, often under difficult circumstances. He had sought to give Johnson the same candid advice that Murrow had given Kennedy, and if his advice was less accepted, it was no less sincere an offering.

Although Johnson accepted Rowan's resignation with a public letter of "real regret," he was no more sorry to see him go than Rowan was to leave. The President was in trouble now, and he wanted USIA to reduce his burdens, not add to them. He needed not a gadfly but a trusted friend who would put Johnson's interests ahead of his own or his Agency's.

Perhaps, then, it was inevitable, even desirable, that there be a change. Soon it would be two years since Kennedy and Murrow had left the scene. The new President, now elected to the White House in his own right, needed and wanted a USIA management wholly of his own making.

The time of transition was over.

11 *Leonard Marks:*
A Time of War

On Friday morning, July 9, 1965, a chunky, cherubic-faced, forty-nine-year-old Washington lawyer named Leonard H. Marks was in New York City, conferring with a client, when an awed secretary interrupted to announce that the President of the United States was calling. Marks was neither awed nor surprised, for such calls were not infrequent. For nearly two decades, the firm of Cohn & Marks had represented station KTBC of Austin, Texas, and Marks and his wife Dorothy were close friends as well as advisers to the station's owner, Mrs. Lady Bird Johnson, and her husband Lyndon. Mrs. Marks had assisted Mrs. Johnson when the new First Family moved into the White House in 1963, and Marks had been Johnson's personal representative in planning the 1965 inaugural ceremonies.

But this was no ordinary telephone call. Johnson had told Marks earlier that he might like to have his old friend as Director of USIA, but Marks had not been enthusiastic. He had two teen-age sons approaching college, his law business had never been more profitable or personally satisfying, and he had no particular yen to head a troubled and sometimes troublesome government agency. Now Johnson told him he needed him, and right away. "Leonard," he said, "there's been a leak in the press about Rowan's departure. I'm going to announce his resignation and your appointment in twenty minutes."

Marks could not say no to his old friend the President, but he objected to the timing. "What will my wife say if she hears it first on the

273

radio or from a reporter?" he protested. Johnson, relieved that Marks would take the job, agreed to withhold the announcement until the following Tuesday.

Although not a journalist, as were Murrow and Rowan, Marks had, as he put it, "done nothing but work in communications" since the age of sixteen, when he had his own radio show in Pittsburgh. As an undergraduate at the University of Pittsburgh, he worked on student publications. After graduation from the law school, he taught there for four years before going to Washington to work with the Office of Price Administration.

Marks soon moved to the Foreign Broadcast Intelligence Service, then a part of the Federal Communications Commission, and by the end of the war had become assistant to the FCC's General Counsel. In 1946 Marks and his chief at FCC founded the law firm of Cohn & Marks, which specialized in communications cases. By 1965 the prosperous firm represented more than four hundred broadcast licensees. President Kennedy named Marks one of the incorporators of the Communications Satellite Corporation in 1962, and two years later he was elected a public member of Comsat's board. He served as a member or adviser of U.S. delegations to several international communications conferences.

As he was virtually unknown outside of broadcasting, legal, and Democratic Party circles, the appointment of the bubbling, effervescent Marks surprised Washington. "Nobody is sure yet" whether it means Johnson "thinks well of the U.S. Information Agency or ill of it," opined one interested observer. "Obviously he [Marks] is someone the President can talk to about the delicate matter of presenting a sympathetic view to the world of U.S. foreign policy. . . . With Marks at the head of the USIA he will at least have a friend who can give to the world a kindly interpretation of . . . Lyndon Johnson."[1]

USIA's career officials were cheered by Marks's obvious enthusiasm ("I'll stay as long as the work is exciting . . . as long as I get up in the morning with butterflies in my stomach") and, aware of the importance of the relationship between the White House and the Agency, by the prospect of a Director who had long enjoyed the President's confidence. The *New York Times* agreed, but warned that this "could be a highly negative factor if it impels Mr. Marks to view his new agency as merely an instrument of the President's personal will in telling America's story as he wants it told."[2] Another commentator noted somewhat cynically that while Marks was little known abroad, "the Presidential intimate who helped lay the foundations of the Presidential fortune has instant prestige."[3]

At Marks's oath-taking in the White House rose garden, Johnson defined USIA's mission as to be "always loyal, always faithful, always vigilant to the course of truth." He said the United States has "no propaganda to peddle" because "we are neither advocates nor defenders of any dogma so fragile or doctrine so frightened as to require it."[4]

The President's choice to succeed Don Wilson as Deputy Director was not very promising. What Marks needed to complement his own talents was a vigorous, widely experienced communicator, willing at the peak of his career to serve his country. What he got was a retired, small-city Texas newspaper editor, intelligent and amiable but with little experience pertinent to his new post.

The new Deputy Director, Robert Wood Akers, had known Johnson slightly for thirty years and was a good friend of Elizabeth Carpenter, Mrs. Johnson's press secretary, and her husband Leslie, a Washington correspondent. At twenty-six, Akers had become city editor of the Beaumont, Texas, *Enterprise,* and subsequently editor-in-chief of the *Enterprise* and *Journal,* remaining with those papers until his retirement in 1964. He and his wife were on a leisurely tour of Southern Europe and the Near East when Johnson tried to reach him. It took a week for the State Department, the FBI, and the Greek police to locate Akers. His appointment surprised Washington officialdom—including Marks.

Two days later, Marks appointed a San Diego newspaper and radio-television executive, Howard L. Chernoff, as his executive assistant. An able and aggressive administrator, Chernoff quickly became in fact if not in title the number two man in the Agency, assuming many of the responsibilities that Wilson had carried as Deputy Director. Chernoff served as Marks's right hand until illness forced his retirement in 1967, although he continued in an advisory capacity.

Marks abolished the media coordination position that Murrow had established, assigning its functions to Akers, who became a kind of "editor-in-chief" of Washington-produced output. The silver-haired Texan also represented the Agency at ceremonial functions and in

such routine but necessary matters as savings-bond and blood-dona-
tion drives. Akers was isolated from administrative and personnel
matters, as was Burnett Anderson, the Deputy Director (Policy and
Plans).*

The President reportedly told Marks that he wanted him to keep
USIA out of controversy and out of the press, avoid differences with
Congress, and concentrate on improving the efficiency and economy
of Agency operations. Marks, fully aware of his inexperience in foreign affairs, viewed himself primarily as a manager, not as an expert or
adviser on international policy.

Marks combined the Motion Picture and Television Services,
thereby eliminating duplicating activities and reducing annual operating costs by a million dollars. To assure greater pertinence in USIA's
research activities, he put them under the direct supervision of the
Deputy Director (Policy and Plans), who was retitled Deputy Director (Policy and Research). A Planning-Programming-Budgeting
System (PPBS) tied budget and program-planning more closely to
objectives. The Office of Private Cooperation was abolished and its
functions absorbed by other divisions. Printing of the Russian- and
Polish-language *Amerika* magazines, formerly done by an outside
contractor, was taken over by the Agency with annual savings of more
than $280,000.

All these moves improved USIA's efficiency. Nonetheless, Marks's
policy of avoiding differences with Congress and the State Department, and shunning controversy generally, reduced not only the
Agency's visibility but also its influence in Washington. "USIA appears
to have taken its place alongside the American Battle Monuments
Commission, the Federal Field Committee for Development Planning
in Alaska, and all those other independent federal agencies which go
their own sweet, unnoticed way in Washington," commented Douglas
Kiker in the *Atlantic Monthly.* "As a result, the Agency has lost all
the excitement and sense of purpose Kennedy and Murrow gave it; it
has become tame and dull, and everybody there is walking on eggs."[5]

Although Marks was closer to the White House than any of his
predecessors (including Murrow), there was little substantive impact

---

* Anderson was reassigned in 1966, and succeeded by his deputy, Hewson A.
Ryan. Ryan had demonstrated great ability as Murrow's Assistant Director for
Latin America and later as Associate Director (Policy and Plans).

on the Agency from this intimacy. Marks counseled with his senior subordinates even less than Rowan had, preferring to play his cards close to the chest. At the same time, most of the Kennedy-established interagency policy committees, which had provided USIA with direct opportunities for influencing policy, were either abolished or withered away or proceeded without Agency involvement.*

For all practical purposes, this left Marks as the only channel to the President, the Secretary of State, and their principal assistants, and resulted in less professional consideration of psychological factors in making and carrying out policy than there had been since Eisenhower and Dulles.

Marks considered revising Kennedy's Statement of Mission for USIA and having it reissued by Johnson. After a staff study, however, it was decided that no change was desirable. But in early 1967 Marks did produce his own interpretation of the Agency's function. It differed little from that of his two immediate predecessors, except that it lacked the Murrow-Rowan emphasis on persuasion:

In carrying out the mission assigned us by law and Presidential directive, USIA:

• Supports the foreign policy of the United States by direct communications with people of other nations.

• Builds understanding of the United States . . . among other people; and shares with them information, thought and experience that can contribute toward achieving mutual goals.

• Advises the U.S. goverment on public opinion abroad and its implications for the United States. . . .[6]

Five months later the Agency revised (for the first time in more than three years) its list of themes and subjects which the media

---

* In March, 1966, USIA's direct relationship with the President was further eroded when Johnson gave the State Department specific responsibility for "overall direction, coordination and supervision" of all U.S. activities abroad except military operations. A Senior Interdepartmental Group (SIG), headed by the Under Secretary of State, was created to oversee all operations with the help of lower-level Interdepartmental Regional Groups, chaired by the Assistant Secretaries of State for the various geographical regions. Marks was a member of SIG, and the area Assistant Directors of USIA were members of their respective Regional Groups. These did provide channels for USIA advice for a time, but they were mostly ignored after Under Secretary of State Ball resigned in the fall of 1966.

services were to give highest priority in their world-wide output. But the list was so long and so inclusive that its usefulness in setting priorities was questionable. In "building understanding of the U.S., its institutions, culture and ideas," the media services were told to stress America's "dynamic economy," its "pluralism in political and economic institutions," the "quality and availability" of its education, its vigorous attack on racial inequality, urban and social problems through Johnson's Great Society, its many achievements in science and technology, and the broad base of its cultural life.

In foreign affairs, the emphasis was put on U.S. efforts in Vietnam in "defense of self-determination," America's support of the UN and regional alliances, the "problem of indirect aggression and militant Communism," the search for workable arms control and disarmament, and U.S. trade and monetary policy, among others. Under the category of "U.S. efforts to help developing nations build the foundations of independent, modern states," the media services were instructed to stress the need for self-help, the threat of overpopulation, the importance of agriculture, the roles of private investment and U.S. governmental aid, the need for strong, democratic governments, and the dangers of Communist-led insurgency.[7]

The Word War over Vietnam

Vietnam, of course, was the prime example of Communist insurgency. Nearly a year before Marks's appointment, President Johnson decided that the national interest required an intensification of the U.S. effort there. On August 4, 1964, in response to North Vietnamese attacks on U.S. warships in the Tonkin Gulf, Johnson told the American people in a radio-television broadcast that "air action is now in execution against gunboats and certain supporting facilities of North Vietnam which have been used in these hostile operations. . . . [But] our response, for the present, will be limited and fitting. . . . We still seek no wider war."

The Voice of America lined up twenty-seven transmitters with a combined power of four million watts to carry Johnson's voice "live" to the Far East and Latin America, and the speech was repeated several times on each foreign-language service and disseminated through other Agency media. The President obtained from Congress a joint resolution reaffirming his powers to deal with the deteriorating Vietnamese situation, and USIA pointed to the measure's nearly unanimous vote as an indication of Johnson's solid backing in the country. (Three years later, however, the Agency as well as the President were embarrassed when some legislators who had supported the resolution charged that Johnson had interpreted it more liberally than they had intended.)

In early 1965 the war did widen. In the next of a series of major escalations, U.S. bombers began hitting strategic targets in North Vietnam and a massive influx of American troops took over the main burden of the ground fighting. For USIA, the widened war posed a series of challenges which were met with only limited success.

Both Kennedy and Johnson, and their Directors of USIA, while appreciating the importance of the psychological factors in the conflict, had never gotten around to doing much about them. Now, with the intensified war, the psychological tasks became more urgent.

Abroad, doubting allies and even more doubtful neutrals needed to be convinced that U.S. escalations of the war were justified and desirable. As the months passed and the war grew fiercer, this task became increasingly difficult. In 1965 a color documentary film on the war, *Night of the Dragon,* was sent to 110 countries in twenty-three languages. Pamphlets on Vietnam were published in Western Europe, and American officials fresh from service in Saigon lectured there. Similar activities were carried on in Latin America and the Middle and Far East.

These efforts did not, however, stem the increasing doubts. In April, 1965, USIA went all out in promoting a Presidential speech at Johns Hopkins University in which Johnson said the U.S. was willing to enter into "unconditional discussions" to end the war. An Agency survey of foreign reaction found that the speech was very favorably received—at first. Then, after further examination, many foreign commentators noted that the offer was not in fact unconditional, ruling out independent participation of the Vietcong, among other stipulations. Some foreigners (as well as some Americans) felt the U.S. position was deliberately misleading. When later it was revealed that Washington had delayed four months in replying to a September, 1964, suggestion by UN Secretary General U Thant—accepted by Ho Chi Minh—for secret talks between Washington and Hanoi, and then rejected his subsequent suggestion that the two nations' ambassadors meet in Rangoon, foreign skepticism mounted. Rebuttals and explanations proved unconvincing.

"The U.S. decision to help South Vietnam involves principles which were well established by 1950," an Agency Talking Paper asserted in early 1966. "They resulted from an appreciation of the lessons of the 1930s—Manchuria, Ethiopia, the Rhineland, Czechoslovakia—that aggression must either be met before it has gathered momentum or it will have to be checked later under more adverse conditions." Europeans, who felt they needed no lessons from the U.S. on the tragedy of the 1930s, did not believe the situations were comparable. And they resented American involvement in a faraway conflict that they feared might threaten their peaceful pursuit of affluence in a period of otherwise declining Cold War tensions.

As the war intensified so did the criticism, and as in this country not all of it was reasonable. In Brighton, England, a USIS Press Officer was barely rescued from a raving mob hurling rocks, paint, and eggs after he emerged from a university seminar on Vietnam. In Paris, President Johnson was burned in effigy. Five thousand marched in a Stockholm torchlight parade to condemn "the American war in Vietnam." Similar demonstrations took place in other cities around the world.

In Western Europe and Japan, television reporting of the war itself did great harm to the U.S. cause. It was the first war to be fought in front of TV cameras, and the harsh realities of battle disturbed millions abroad as well as at home. The Vietcong and North Vietnamese did not allow foreign TV correspondents to work with their combat forces (except in rare, carefully controlled instances), and what little television reportage they released to the world showed only their side of the story. But freedom to picture the U.S.–South Vietnamese situation was almost unlimited, and journalists made the most of their freedom. Some, mostly foreign, were delighted at the opportunity to show the United States in a bad light. Others were simply doing their job in depicting the grim details of modern warfare, but television made those details more graphic and more personal than in any previous war.

In mid-1966 West Germany's Vice Chancellor Erich Mende commented: "There is no question in my mind that the Vietnam war is unpopular largely because of television. People see the horrors and the misery of this war—burning villages, weeping mothers, maimed children. They see South Vietnamese troops manhandling Vietcong suspects, and they see the more sordid aspects of Saigon night life." Belgian statesman Paul-Henri Spaak was even more blunt: "The U.S. has completely lost the information war in Vietnam." Much of foreign TV reportage was a classic example of the medium being the message, and USIA was unable to counter it effectively.

Public opinion polls conducted in eleven countries in late 1967 showed overwhelming majorities in eight of them—including such diverse nations as West Germany, France, Finland, and Brazil— favored U.S. withdrawal from Vietnam. Even in Britain and Canada, two stout friends of America, more people thought the United States should begin to withdraw than thought it should step up its attacks. Only one of the nations polled, Australia, felt that the U.S. war effort should be intensified. It is doubtful that any USIA effort, no matter how large or skillful, could have materially changed the outcome.

But the most important psychological tasks were in Vietnam itself. The allegiance of the people needed to be won and held for the Saigon regime that had allied itself with the United States. This required, among other things, the creation of an effective propaganda machine within the South Vietnamese Government. Additionally, the Vietcong's will to fight and that of their North Vietnamese allies had to be undermined. And these tasks had to be done soon, before the war was irrevocably lost among the people before it was decided on the battlefield.

In April, 1965, after a Rowan visit to Saigon, President Johnson assigned responsibility for all U.S. psychological operations in Vietnam, both civilian and military, to the Director of USIA. He delegated policy direction to an "Interagency Psyops Working Group," chaired by Associate Director (later Deputy Director) Hewson Ryan. The group was composed of representatives of USIA, the State and Defense departments, AID, CIA, and the White House.

A Joint U.S. Public Affairs Office (JUSPAO) was established in Saigon, combining USIS with the Pentagon's psychological warriors and AID's communications media specialists. Put in charge of JUSPAO was USIA's talented and aggressive Public Affairs Officer in Saigon, forty-four-year-old Barry Zorthian. When JUSPAO came into being on July 1, 1965, it had 150 American and 400 Vietnamese employees, a high percentage from USIS. As the war continued to escalate in the months that followed, so did the size of JUSPAO. Its American staff rose to about 250, its yearly budget to $10 million.

Vietnam required an exceptional man to direct U.S. propaganda operations, and it had such a man in Zorthian. Born in Turkey of Armenian parents who fled to America to escape the 1921 massacres, Zorthian had been running hard ever since. After four years at Yale and a short stint as a reporter, young Zorthian joined the Marines and spent World War II in combat in the Pacific. He returned briefly to newspapering, then joined the Voice of America. In a few years, Zorthian rose to the number three job of Program Manager, where he helped, goaded, and competed with VOA chief Henry Loomis.

Recognizing Zorthian's exceptional ability and drive, Murrow persuaded him to join the Agency's Foreign Service. Skeptical at first, Zorthian went somewhat reluctantly to India as Deputy Public Affairs Officer and became an immediate success. One of Murrow's last decisions at the Agency was to send Zorthian to Saigon. When he arrived there in February, 1964, the propaganda situation appeared as gloomy as the military and political outlooks.

President Diem had been assassinated three months earlier; the Vietcong were becoming increasingly bold after repeated successes; American correspondents lacked confidence in what the embassy and USIS were telling them; and the military, AID, and USIS were squabbling over who should control propaganda operations.

What *Life* magazine described as his "burning conviction, energy and sheer physical courage" enabled Zorthian quickly to establish himself as the undisputed boss of U.S. propaganda even before Johnson made it official by creating JUSPAO. He won the respect of the cynical press corps by insisting on telling newsmen everything that possibly could be told. By 1967 *Life* could say that "Zorthian's word is one of the unsullied few in Saigon."[8] (He was not, however, above using a few PR tricks to make the war more palatable at home. As the commitment of U.S. troops grew larger, Zorthian urged military information officers to "find more Vietnamese heroes" so Americans would not think their young men were doing all the fighting.)

"Zorro," as he was soon nicknamed, won the confidence of successive U.S. ambassadors—Maxwell Taylor, Henry Cabot Lodge, Jr., and Ellsworth Bunker—and, equally important, of the U.S. military commander, General William Westmoreland. With good reason, Marks called him "one of the heroes of this war."

Żorthian pressed Washington to give him more and more resources. Johnson liked him, and the Agency responded by giving Vietnam unprecedented priority, especially after the creation of JUSPAO. In September, 1965, VOA increased its Vietnamese-language broadcasts (relayed to the North by a 50-kilowatt transmitter at Hue) to six and one-half hours daily, with a new segment designed to reach the North Vietnamese during their afternoon siesta hour. Talented officers from other areas were drafted to serve in Vietnam, and some were given intensive language training before being sent overseas (in contrast to fifteen years earlier when almost no U.S. propagandists were taught to speak Korean). Most, however, were rushed to Saigon with little preparation.

Knowledge of the Vietnamese language and culture was essential to the swarms of USIA officers who descended on the country, especially those who were assigned to the provinces, where few people spoke English and not many more knew French. A USIA-commissioned poll a few years earlier had shown that three-fourths of the Vietnamese considered Americans as the "foreigners most different from the Vietnamese," whereas 83 percent considered the Chinese to be the "foreigners most like us Vietnamese."[9] Knowledge of the language and people could not close that gap, but it could narrow it.

Most of the new staff went to JUSPAO's Saigon headquarters, where they taught and assisted their Vietnamese counterparts to produce leaflets, movies and TV shows, radio programs, and the other paraphernalia of propaganda. Radio programs also were produced in Saigon for broadcast by VOA. One, entitled *Uncommon People,* highlighted acts of valor by such people as village schoolteachers, health workers, heroic soldiers, and defectors from the Vietcong. Another, *Lesson from History,* recreated stories of Vietnamese heroes of the dim past who had fought "Chinese aggression."

A third of the new USIA staff went into direct psychological operations in support of massive "pacification" and "Revolutionary Development" programs, working in the relatively secure cities and the less safe hamlets and towns with their Vietnamese counterparts. Their goals were simple to define but intensely difficult to carry out:

- Win Vietnamese hearts and minds as well as "real estate"; en-

courage the people, especially in the disputed countryside, to side with
Saigon, even at the risk of Vietcong retaliation.

• Decrease sympathy for the Vietcong and Hanoi.

• Increase the participation of the Vietnamese people in U.S.-
supported efforts to achieve economic and social progress.

• Increase Vietnamese understanding and support for the United
States and U.S. policies and programs in Vietnam.

The enormity of the task was illustrated by JUSPAO's report to the
Agency on its first month of activity, July, 1965:

. . . the Vietnamese [are] becoming more concerned for their personal
safety and evidencing little or no interest in ideology and politics. In most
areas the attitudes of the people can be described as apathetic, showing
little or no support for either the GVN [Government of Vietnam] or the
Vietcong. . . .

The Vietcong's most significant action in the past month has been the
destruction of road and rail communications throughout much of the
highlands triggering a whirlwind of hoarding, rising prices, confusion on
the part of the people, and mounting resentment against the government
for not solving these economic problems.

Declining Vietnamese morale was primarily a problem of the
Vietnamese Information Service, but it was not up to the job.

JUSPAO Field Representatives continued to try to develop a more effective Vietnamese Information Service [VIS] . . . [but] where the government controls by day and the VC [Vietcong] by night, psychological activity has been difficult. VIS morale is low due to the absence of rural
security in many areas, lack of motivation and drive, meager salaries, and
the infrequent arrival of paychecks. . . . As usual the VIS cadre demonstrated their consistent tendency to talk down to the people instead of
with them . . . and to be entirely unwilling to share the hardships of the
target audience in order to put their ideas across.[10]

Zorthian was never very successful in prodding the Vietnamese
Ministry of Information into improving the performance of VIS.
For the most part, despite JUSPAO's infusion of ideas and equipment, it remained inept and apathetic. But the situation did improve
some.

What the Vietnamese Information Service could not or would not
do, JUSPAO did—in the name of VIS, or through joint U.S.-Viet-

namese "psyops committees" in each province. "Motivation training" courses were organized for the home-guard soldiers responsible for protecting most of South Vietnam's hundreds of villages; the purpose was to strengthen the ragged troops' understanding of why they were fighting and to tie them more closely to their remote and not always popular leaders in Saigon. JUSPAO provided teaching materials for AID-financed school buildings, which were quickly erected in villages as soon as the enemy was cleared out.

JUSPAO representatives goaded the "psyops committees" into increasing their activities. Citizens' committees were established to visit, write letters, and give gifts to troops. Provincial newspapers were published, portable exhibits circulated, and cultural teams organized to present propaganda skits and songs in recently pacified villages.

The use of drama troupes proved to be an especially effective device, and in late 1965 JUSPAO launched a nationally coordinated effort to reach all parts of the country under Saigon's control. The idea was not new; USIA had successfully operated similar projects in neighboring countries since 1955 and the Embassy in Saigon had begun a small effort in 1962. But JUSPAO found that while seventy troupes were touring the country under various auspices including that of the Vietnamese Ministry of Information, few were reaching the peasants.

JUSPAO helped train six-man *Van Tac Vu* (Cultural Drama Service) troupes and assisted in the production of their material. The entertainers—among them, attractive actresses unaccustomed to hardship—traveled in the black pajamas commonly worn by peasants, and lived with the villagers as they moved around the countryside, performing twenty or more shows per month. The troupes sang patriotic songs ("Vietnam, Vietnam" and "Our House"), amused and indoctrinated the peasantry with primitive dramas about villainous Vietcong and heroic South Vietnamese soldiers and officials, and off stage distributed medicines, seeds, food, and pamphlets, and helped at chores ranging from repairing damaged buildings to bathing infants.

"We try to make the rural people proud of their country and their government," explained one performer. "We tell why the Americans are with us. We show them what the Vietcong are trying to do, why they attack our villages and take our crops." Hanoi and the VC took note of the troupes, calling them "Black Pajama spies of American imperialism." More than once, performances were interrupted by grenades or gunfire. Two actors were killed in a midnight attack on their quarters in April, 1967. But the show went on.

"Revolutionary Development" propaganda directed at South Vietnamese emphasized good news: the Saigon Government's building of roads, bridges, and hospitals; protection of rice harvests being moved to market; victories in battle; and glowing promises for the day when the war would be won. In addition to the drama troupes and radio, the word was spread by provincial newspapers, hamlet bulletin boards, exhibits, movies, roving information teams, and—after early 1966 —by television.

Hundreds of TV sets were distributed to public reading rooms, community centers, and schools in towns and villages within a forty-mile radius of Saigon. Throngs gathered around them each night to hear Vietnamese officials speak and to watch propaganda movies. (U.S. Army telecasts to American troops on another channel were blacked out for that hour. "We don't want to put Premier Ky up against *Gunsmoke*," a USIS officer explained.)

Target: The Enemy

Much of JUSPAO's effort was aimed at enemy forces, urging them to defect to the South Vietnamese side or return peacefully to their families and villages. Cheap transistor radios, especially constructed to receive only U.S. and South Vietnamese stations, were sold to peasants and dropped into enemy territory in both North and South Vietnam. Toys, candy, and clothes were dropped in the North on Vietnamese holidays that traditionally had been occasions for showering gifts on children. Scores of similar ideas were volunteered by private citizens, although few were adopted.*

Working under Saigon's *Chieu Hoi* (Open Arms) program, Ameri-

---

* Among those considered and discarded were two from Congressman Craig Hosmer of California. He suggested dropping into North Vietnam thousands of ace-of-spades playing cards along with devices that would emit in succession three owl hoots. According to Hosmer, the ace of spades is considered a "deadly omen" to Vietnamese, while three hoots of an owl heard at night mean death is imminent in the immediate family.

can and Vietnamese psychological warriors tried every old trick and a number of new ones to induce enemy soldiers to stop fighting. By 1966, four to five million leaflets, many of them in the form of safe-conduct passes, were being dropped every week over Vietcong strongholds in the South and population centers in the North.

During *Tet,* the Lunar New Year holiday, in 1966 and again in 1967 and 1968, JUSPAO waged major campaigns, described as "the largest ever attempted in any war," to induce guerrillas on leave in their villages not to return to battle. Loudspeaker planes circled over every known guerrilla enclave, broadcasting recorded messages and scattering leaflets. VOA and the Vietnamese National Network shifted their program emphases to stress the desertion theme; a song, "*Tet* Without You," was broadcast hourly by every station.

The result of the *Tet* campaigns was a sharp increase in defections, and the effort was intensified between holidays. Its purpose was not only to spur desertions but also to encourage the surrender of arms, to impede Communist recruitment of guerrilla fighters, and to discourage local supply of food and information to the enemy.

In "Operation Rigor Mortis," the names of enemy dead were taken from papers found on their bodies and quickly broadcast to their home areas so that potential Vietcong recruits would know that these young men, contrary to VC promises, had been abandoned to die, far from their homes and ancestral burial grounds.

Low-flying loudspeaker planes awakened the enemy at night with somber Buddhist funeral music, followed by a recorded voice of a child pleading for his daddy to return home—or perhaps weird electronic cacophonies to frighten the superstitious who believed in forest demons. During one Mekong Delta battle, local girls were flown over Vietcong areas to warn the VC that they were "facing a unit that never loses." (This may not have frightened the enemy, but, according to one U.S. propagandist, "It turned the South Vietnamese troops into tigers!")

In the late summer of 1966, JUSPAO organized a massive "get-out-the-vote" campaign for Constituent Assembly elections. It helped bring out a high proportion of Vietnamese voters in the face of Vietcong harassment. A similar campaign was conducted during the 1967 presidential election.

In early September, 1966, two million copies of the first issue of a

JUSPAO-produced two-page tabloid newspaper, *Mien Nam Tu Do* (*Free South Vietnam*), were air-dropped over Communist areas of the South. Ten days later, just prior to the Assembly elections, five million copies of a special election edition were distributed. The newspaper carried "no polemical or tendentious writing," only "factual news reporting and features," JUSPAO explained. Later, USIA reported that its contents were devoted exclusively to "items supporting U.S. and Government of Vietnam objectives—the building of a viable government, revolutionary development, the *Chieu Hoi* defector program, understanding of the American presence, and news of victories over the Vietcong and North Vietnamese forces."[11]

A sequence of leaflets was aimed at North Vietnamese troops slated for battle in the South. In their training camps in the North, Ho Chi Minh's soldiers received air-dropped leaflets saying, "We know you are destined to come to South Vietnam to fight." Along the infiltration route they were told: "If you do come across, we'd like you to join us in our struggle against the Communists." Just before they crossed the border, the message read: "Here is a safe-conduct pass. It will pass you safely through our lines and save your life." And, at the end of the trip, they were given additional passes plus offers of money for arms brought with them, with prices ranging from 800 piasters (a little more than ten dollars at the official rate of exchange) for a pistol to 6,300 piasters for a heavy machine gun.

As U.S. air losses mounted, a modification of this device was tried. Leaflets were scattered over Communist-held areas North and South offering civilians five thousand dollars in gold for every shot-down pilot they brought to safety.

The effect of this war of words on the enemy was never easy to determine. When the battle was going well for the Vietcong and their North Vietnamese allies, the propaganda had little effect on most of them. But as defeat became more common, more of them listened seriously to offers of safety and food. Slowly the number of defectors rose from 450 a month in 1964 to a total of ten thousand in the last six months of 1966 and twenty thousand in the first half of 1967. A third of the defectors attributed their decisions to the *Chieu Hoi* effort.

Once a whole company surrendered with every member holding a safe-conduct pass. On another occasion, two men walked in with

only one pass between them and timidly asked if they could both surrender on it. To prevent defectors from changing their minds, each
was photographed with an American or South Vietnamese soldier
and told that copies of the photo would be dropped among his former
colleagues "to let them know of his right decision."

JUSPAO found that defections often started a chain reaction, and
every effort was made to encourage this. Each defector was inter-
rogated, fed, clothed, and given medical attention and some political
indoctrination. Sometimes, depending on his background—and current frame of mind—he was urged to make statements explaining why
he switched sides and describing his treatment. The statements were
printed in leaflets and scattered with the photographs, or recorded
and broadcast from airborne loudspeakers over the area from which
the defector came.

Meanwhile, back in Washington, high-level attention to the psychological side of the war varied with events. In February, 1966, Johnson, concerned by mounting criticism of the war and acutely
embarrassed by Senate hearings on the conflict sponsored by his
archcritic Fulbright, suddenly announced a "summit" meeting in
Honolulu with Premier Nguyen Cao Ky to discuss reconstruction and
social welfare in Vietnam, or what Johnson called "the other war."

Marks and Zorthian were among the 130 U.S. and Vietnamese
officials who attended the conference. Although Marks did not speak
up during the discussions, he had an opportunity at the end of the
meeting to remark briefly on the importance of the psychological warfare and "Revolutionary Development" efforts. Especially impressed
by the latter, Johnson told Zorthian: "Barry, every time I see a picture
of a battle in the papers, I want to see a picture of a pig," meaning he
hoped economic and social gains would receive as much attention
from the press as the violent aspects of the war.[12]

In another summit meeting in Manila ten months later, this one
involving the heads of a number of friendly Far Eastern governments,
USIA again played no substantive role. But the Agency was partly
responsible for arrangements for Johnson's visits to countries in the
area, and it provided extensive press coverage of the trip and kept
members of the U.S. delegation informed of world reaction. Similar
services were provided for a high-level meeting at Guam.

As the months passed without much progress toward military or psychological victory, Marks became increasingly concerned about Vietnam's cost to USIA—not only in dollars, but in its impact on Agency operations elsewhere. On the plus side were the Vietcong defections, a somewhat strengthened (although still wholly inadequate) Vietnamese Information Service, and some progress in rallying the people of South Vietnam behind the war. But these accomplishments had required the stripping of other USIS posts of men and money at the very time, ironically, that the war had markedly damaged America's reputation in the world.

Dozens of USIA's ablest officers, who normally would be sprinkled in key assignments in Washington and elsewhere, were tied up in Vietnam.* The Agency had always found it necessary, on occasion, to put second-rate men in jobs of first-rate importance, but not to the extent it was now doing it. And there was the future to consider, too. USIA needed its talent sensibly distributed around the world, working not only on today's problems but anticipating those of tomorrow.

Yet, despite the baring of the cupboard elsewhere, the Agency was never able to put enough staff into Vietnam to do the job there properly. Unlike some skeptical military men in World Wars I and II, General Westmoreland's officers for the most part appreciated the uses of propaganda and had confidence in JUSPAO. They were ready to follow USIA, both in noncombat psychological operations and combat psychological warfare. But they required trained advisers as well as policy guidance, and USIA could not fill the demand.

Pressed by Saigon for more men and money for JUSPAO, alarmed by the thinness in quality and quantity of Agency operations elsewhere, unwilling (and probably unable) to recruit vast new numbers of propagandists, and prompted by the U.S. Advisory Commission on Information, Marks began in late 1966 and early 1967 to slow the pace of USIA operations in Vietnam.

At the same time, Zorthian lost operational control over JUSPAO's field organization when it was merged, along with the field elements of other civilian agencies, into an Office of Civil Operations. Six

---

* One of the ablest was added to the White House staff in the fall of 1967 to help sell Congress and the American public on the Administration's Vietnam policy. Harold Kaplan, who had been Deputy PAO in Saigon in 1965-66, was recalled from a USIA assignment in Europe after only a few weeks there to assist the President's Press Secretary on Vietnam matters. He set up a small staff of researchers and speech writers.

months later, OCO was merged with noncombat military field activities into a Civil Operations and Revolutionary Support Office, which reduced much of Zorthian's policy influence.

"Zorro" understandably was unhappy with these developments, and he was weary and more than a little touchy after three years in Saigon. In a moment of pique he asked for a lesser job in the provinces, and Ambassador Lodge encouraged him to take it. But, as the weeks passed and he cooled down, Zorthian resolved to stay and see the war through to its end. Marks, however, decided that a change was desirable and began casting around for a successor.

The search went on all through 1967, while relations between Zorthian and Marks sank into sullen mutual suspicion. One candidate and then another escaped Marks's net, until he finally resolved the matter in early 1968 with this formula: Zorthian would become PAO in Tokyo, and the PAO there, Edward Nickel, would replace him in Saigon as head of JUSPAO. Handling of the foreign and American press would be split off from JUSPAO and put under Eugene Rosenfeld, an able ex-PAO.

But Zorthian was not so easily disposed of. Ambassador Bunker, with Zorthian whispering in his ear, wrote Marks that '68 was bound to be a sensitive and difficult year in Vietnam, what with the upcoming U.S. Presidential election and all, and he wanted to keep Zorthian in Saigon for at least another year to handle press relations. Rosenfeld could assist him and Nickel could become head of the JUSPAO propaganda operation. Marks had no choice but to acquiesce grudgingly, although he did plead with Bunker to keep Zorthian "out of Nickel's hair."

In the winter of 1968, as JUSPAO spokesmen were proclaiming a decline in enemy strength, the Vietcong launched massive surprise attacks in Saigon, Hue, and dozens of other cities. These attacks, which penetrated even the American Embassy compound, could not have been so successful had the populace firmly supported the Saigon regime and the U.S. presence. They underscored the hard lessons USIA learned in Vietnam:

• In war, especially civil war, conventional propaganda and psychological warfare are only effective when victories are won on the battlefield and morale-building political and economic reforms are achieved behind the lines.

>

- There is no U.S. Government agency truly qualified and staffed to conduct psychological operations in a war of this size. USIA comes closest, but to do its job properly requires men and money far in excess of what is available in "peacetime."
- Propaganda cannot make bad policy palatable.

Other Events, Other Problems

One consequence of the widened war in Vietnam was a blunting of the move toward U.S.-Soviet *détente,* cultural as well as political and economic, that had followed the Cuban missile crisis and the limited nuclear test ban treaty. The United States wanted to continue "building bridges" to Eastern Europe, but not at the price of unacceptable concessions on Vietnam. The Kremlin, for its part, was reluctant to exacerbate its dispute with Red China by appearing to be too cozy with Washington while the war raged in Southeast Asia.

Nonetheless, the war in Vietnam notwithstanding, the United States and the Soviet Union were able to reach agreement on a treaty barring the spread of nuclear weapons. And there was infrequent return in U.S. and Soviet propaganda to the heated exchanges of a decade earlier. Neither nation was very complimentary in talking about the other, but the emphasis usually was more on persuasion than on polemics—at least on the American side.

This change was dramatically illustrated in 1967 by the defections to the United States of Stalin's daughter, Svetlana Alliluyeva, and the Chargé d'Affaires of the Hungarian Legation in Washington. Mrs. Alliluyeva's defection was by all odds the most sensational (and, from a propaganda viewpoint, the most damaging) that had ever occurred, and the Hungarian was the highest-ranking Communist diplomat ever to defect. In the 1950s the Voice of America would have noisily exploited these events with repetitive features and commentary; in 1967 they received little more than straightforward news coverage.

In part, the restraint was due to Washington's desire to avoid unnecessarily annoying the leaders of the Soviet Union, whose cooperation would be required to make a suitable peace in Vietnam and push through a treaty barring the proliferation of nuclear powers. In part, however, it was also due to the greater sophistication of

USIA. The defections needed no embroidery; they spoke for themselves, and were more convincing (and devastating) without USIA pontificating.*

Reflecting this greater sophistication, USIA's Russian-language *Amerika* began to focus more on the substance rather than the surface of American life. The magazine's tenth-anniversary issue in September, 1966, which contained a lengthy message to the Soviet people from President Johnson, sold out in Moscow an hour after it went on sale.

"I think both sides must realize that neither is going to convert the other," Johnson wrote. "As great powers our two nations will undoubtedly have commitments that will conflict. But there is one commitment I hope we both share: the commitment to a warless world." Observing that "our people are more naturally friends than enemies," the President said he would "like to see us exchange goods and ideas and technology—all of the means to achieving common progress and prosperity."

Although *Pravda* responded with snorts of "hypocrisy" and the Kremlin obviously lacked enthusiasm for some aspects of the U.S.-Soviet cultural exchanges agreement which was renegotiated in 1966, exchanges did continue, in spite of Vietnam. In the autumn of 1966, "Hand Tools—USA," the eighth in the series of USIA exhibits in the U.S.S.R., toured Kharkov, Rostov, and Yerevan. "Industrial Design—USA" was shown in Moscow, Leningrad, and Kiev the following spring.

In May, 1967, for the first time, the United States participated in a Soviet Industrial Fair, INPRODMASH-67, which featured food processing, packaging, and distribution equipment.† USIA organized the exhibit, and other displays on highway construction machinery for 1967 showings in Hungary, Poland, and Bulgaria. The Communist nations put on similar exhibits in this country.

---

* The pain to the Kremlin caused by VOA reporting of Mrs. Alliluyeva's defection was well evidenced by the angry cries from Soviet media and Premier Kosygin's bitter attack on the lady when asked about her during his 1967 visit to the United States.

† INPRODMASH is a Russian acronym for "International Exhibition of Modern Mechanical and Automated Equipment, Packaging Equipment and Transportation Conveyances for the Food Industry," or so USIA solemnly explained.

Delegations of scientists, technicians, and bureaucrats traveled between Eastern Europe and the United States. The most important Soviet visitor to the United States was Premier Aleksei Kosygin, who led the U.S.S.R. delegation to the UN General Assembly in the aftermath of the brief June, 1967, war in the Middle East. While he was here, Kosygin met at the "summit" with President Johnson, the summit in this case being the little town of Glassboro, New Jersey, halfway between New York and Washington.

USIA was deeply involved in the U.S. effort to cope with the Arab-Israeli conflict. The crisis erupted in May when President Nasser of the United Arab Republic successfully demanded that the UN remove its buffer force separating Egyptian and Israeli troops and then closed the Strait of Tiran (at the entrance to the Gulf of Aqaba) to ships headed for Israel. Nasser made new military alliances with Iraq, Syria, and his old foe King Hussein of Jordan, Arab armies were mobilized, and Arab politicians and media began beating the drums for a "holy war" against the Jews. The Soviet Union, which had supplied Nasser with $2 billion worth of arms since the 1956 Suez war, spoke up strongly for its Arab allies.

In the wake of ineffectual UN and U.S. efforts to cool off the situation, war erupted on June 5 with lightning Israeli air strikes against the Arab air forces, most of which were caught on the ground and destroyed within a few hours. Desperately seeking a scapegoat for impending defeat, Nasser—with the connivance of King Hussein —falsely charged that U.S. aircraft had participated in the attack. A violent wave of anti-U.S. sentiment swept the Arab world.

Just prior to the outbreak of hostilities, the Voice of America's Arabic Service had gone from six to eleven hours a day of medium-wave broadcasting. Over and over again, VOA repeated denials of Nasser's charge. USIA urged State Department spokesmen to repeat daily Secretary Rusk's denial, and prompted the U.S. Mission to the UN to reiterate Ambassador Goldberg's offer of an impartial UN investigation. VOA and the Wireless File picked up domestic and foreign newspaper comment, especially from Turkey, Iran, and other Muslim countries, denouncing the "big lie." Movements of the Sixth Fleet, which Nasser had falsely accused of supporting Israeli military operations, were broadcast regularly in great detail.

The Agency did not answer each specific Arab allegation, because, as Assistant Director for the Near East Alan Carter explained, "I didn't want us to get into a lawyers' debate and I wanted us to sound cool and a little bit disdainful of such charges." Texts of U.S. statements, relayed abroad by the Wireless File, were delivered to heads of governments around the world.

All USIA employees and their families were evacuated from the U.A.R., Syria, and Iraq, and dependents were flown out of all other Arab countries except Saudi Arabia and Kuwait. U.S. embassies and libraries were stoned in several cities; in Alexandria the new USIS library was gutted by fire lit by an Egyptian mob. Throughout the area, regular USIS operations came to a halt, and it was months after the six-day war was over before many of them returned to normal.

Despite the Agency's best efforts, most of the hundred million Arabs could not accept the dismal and degrading fact that they had been thoroughly trounced by fewer than two million Israelis acting alone without outside help. So Nasser's lie continued to be believed by many. America's standing in the area sank to a new low.

While the war was in progress, Soviet attacks on the United States were muted (although Israel was subjected to violent denunciations). This was in sharp contrast to the earlier Suez war, when Moscow's propagandists had flayed the West and Soviet leaders had threatened missile attacks on London and Paris and promised hordes of "volunteers" for the Middle East. This time, although the Soviets had a larger stake in Arab victory, they were less willing to go to the brink.

In the weeks that followed, however, the virulence of Soviet criticism rose sharply. Moscow canceled the visit of sixty Soviet scholars to an international Orientalists Congress at the University of Michigan, blaming "a recent escalation of the United States war in Vietnam and Israel's aggression against Arab countries . . . supported by ruling circles in the United States." *Izvestia* described America as "the cruelest world gendarme, the rudest of the aggressors, the bloodiest of the stranglers of freedom."

As had happened before in times of acute crisis, the State Department depended heavily on USIA during the Middle East war, and coordination between the two agencies was close and effective. But when the war was over, the situation changed. As one high USIA official put it: "In times of calm, the State Department expects less from us than we are capable of doing. In time of crisis, they put an intolerable burden of expectation on our backs. Then, after the crunch, they revert to normal and tend to forget that they are still dealing with a psychological problem of considerable magnitude." USIA was not, for example, called in to advise on the foreign propaganda implications of the Glassboro meeting.

Glassboro, Honolulu, and Manila were not the only Johnson trips to the summit. The President met with Latin-American chiefs of government at Punta del Este, Uruguay, in April, 1967. Marks was a member of the U.S. delegation, and a large USIA team provided extensive coverage for the Agency's press, radio, and film outlets south of the border.

The meeting pointed up USIA's continuing problems in Latin America. President Kennedy's Alliance for Progress had bogged down, and it would have even if Kennedy had lived. But many in Latin America felt that Johnson had neglected the Alliance and Latin-American affairs generally, except for the unpopular U.S. intervention in the Dominican Republic. Long after his death, Kennedy's memory was kept alive through the use of his likeness on postage stamps and his name on hundreds of parks, schools, and housing projects. Despite USIA efforts, his popularity was not transferable to Johnson.

No mobs marched on USIS in Latin America, but the Agency was less successful than it had been in identifying the United States with the forces of progress and reform. In August, 1966, three days before the inauguration of a moderate president of Colombia, a bomb ripped through the USIS English-teaching center in Bogotá, killing an American instructor and three others, and injuring fifteen.

USIA's greatest problem with violence was how to explain the spreading and increasingly bloody racial upheaval in America, and particularly in its Northern cities. Riots in Harlem and Watts (Los Angeles) in the summers of 1964 and 1965 were followed by similar if less destructive outbreaks on both coasts and in the Midwest in 1966. Then, in the summer of 1967, came a frightening and unprecedented wave of shooting, burning, and looting in the overcrowded, slum-ridden Negro ghettos of Detroit, Newark, and more than a score of other Northern cities.

The failure of nonviolent techniques and the much-heralded civil rights and antipoverty legislation significantly to improve Negro housing, education, and employment opportunities resulted in the emergence of a new militant Negro leadership which scorned the traditional goal of gradual integration and called for "Black Power." This change was not overlooked abroad, nor was the House of Representatives' action in jeering down an Administration rat-control bill.

The new violence could not be explained away by USIA as a necessary if unfortunate by-product of progress in race relations, as had lesser outbreaks in the early 1960s. Continuing the Murrow-Rowan policy of candor, the Agency sought to put events into rational perspective. A USIA Talking Paper, trying in 1965 to explain why Watts had occurred, admitted the answer was "still not clear."

Many factors contributed to it—the midsummer heat, hostility towards police, a high rate of unemployment . . . lack of communications between Negroes and Whites, lack of exercise of leadership . . . the lag between recent, rapid political advancement and the slower rate of social and economic progress.[13]

Two years later these ills remained largely unremedied, and USIA was equally candid in admitting it. Roger Wilkins, head of the Justice Department's Community Relations Service, warned VOA audiences in June, 1967, that there was every likelihood of further Negro rioting because "the people are desperately unhappy."[14] When the Newark and Detroit riots exploded a month later, USIA audiences were prepared because they had been forewarned.

Foreign reaction was largely understanding and sympathetic. In a comment typical of many, *Spandauer Volksblatt* of Berlin expressed the belief that most American whites favored Negro integration and equal rights, and that only a country like America had the possibility of overcoming the sins of centuries in one generation.

In general, articulated foreign opinion took the view that any one-sided condemnation would be wrong because of the complexity of the problem. The situation was termed "paradoxical" and "ironic" because the Johnson Administration had done so much, if perhaps not enough, to improve the lot of Negro Americans. Negro extremism was viewed as an inevitable consequence of Negro impatience with the pace of progress.

The Agency advised its media services to report the riots "in some detail in order to maintain credibility," and instructed them to:

—Focus sharply on President Johnson's two-pronged response . . . : (1) measures aimed at a quick, final and permanent end to the violence and punishment of law breakers, and (2) "an attack . . . upon the conditions that breed despair and violence. . . ."

—Stress that only a tiny minority of the Negro population had taken part in the violence; that the great majority of Negroes, as well as whites, utterly deplore such tactics.

—Place the urban violence in socio-economic perspective. . . . Cities were not prepared to cope with the massive influxes, and overcrowding, inadequate housing and schooling, and unemployment followed. . . . All these complex problems are being tackled, but by their nature are solvable only over the long term.

Obviously, said the policy experts, "the story of quiet, steady progress of the Negro American cannot command comparable attention. But we must continue to plug away at that story." In this connection Roger Wilkins, himself a Negro, had told his VOA listeners that "there has never been another nation in the history of the world that has made the progress that we have made so far. . . . It is one of the most remarkable human stories in history." It was upon recognition of past progress and appreciation of present efforts and future plans that USIA pinned its hopes for understanding, even as the ghettos burned.

Progress and Controversy

A new vehicle for relating racial progress and other American developments to African audiences was launched in the autumn of 1965. *Topic* magazine, written and edited in Washington, is published monthly in English and French and mailed without charge to fifty thousand readers in sub-Saharan countries and to African students in European universities. Designed chiefly for educated Africans, its contents cover a broad spectrum of American life—social trends, the arts, sports, technology—with an emphasis on youth. Unlike most USIA magazines, *Topic* includes articles by and about Africans as well as Americans. A special issue on Negro American writers, painters, sculptors, architects, musicians, and actors was published in connection with the First World Festival of Negro Arts in Dakar in 1966.

USIA played a major role in the three-week festival, which brought together Negro artists and intellectuals from thirty-five countries including the United States. A high point of the conference was an evening of readings by American and African poets, among them the late Langston Hughes, at the USIS library. In the audience were the renowned Russian poets Yevtushenko and Dolmatovsky, whom the Kremlin—not having any Negro artists at its disposal—sent to Senegal anyway.

To attract more visitors to USIS libraries in Africa and elsewhere, Marks instituted permanent displays of American graphic arts in them, calling on U.S. printmakers, dealers, galleries, schools, and museums to contribute "the finest contemporary American prints."

These displays were well received, but another Marks move in connection with the libraries was not. In late 1965 he announced the virtual closing of the U.S. libraries in London and Paris, and there was much protest. An American professor facetiously suggested to a British poet that he "organize a mob and lead it in sacking and burning the American library in Grosvenor Square. . . . Only that way, paradoxically, could we preserve the Library." The British weekly *Spectator* mourned the loss of "possibly the single most important focus of goodwill towards the U.S. in Britain."

What happened was this: Congressional Appropriations Committees, still convinced that the Agency needed to do little in Western Europe where presumably America was best known and loved, demanded that USIA cut back its operations there. Marks, under Presidential instruction to get along with Congress, acquiesced to a greater extent than had Murrow or Rowan. The libraries in London and Paris were not closed, but most of their collections were disbanded.

In London a major portion of the library's collection was transferred to the University of London, with only reference works retained by USIS. Marks explained that this would "ultimately strengthen the University's planned Institute of American Studies." In Paris the bulk of the collection was moved to a USIS Student Center and to the private American Library of Paris. "We believe that these moves will increase the use of the American volumes rather than curtail the operation," Marks said.

There was, however, no stinting on money for the American exhibit in "Expo 67," the 1967 Montreal World's Fair. Many millions of dollars, obtained by special Congressional appropriation, were poured into the U.S. pavilion, which was designed and directed by USIA. The American exhibit was housed in a twenty-story-high spherical "geodesic dome" designed by Buckminster Fuller. It was the first exhibit planned solely by the Agency, without Commerce Department participation, and it was far livelier and more avant-garde than any previous U.S. exhibit. Some (reportedly including President Johnson) thought the exhibit too "far out," but the crowds loved it. Dollar for dollar, neither this nor any other highly expensive exhibit produces the results expected from other USIA expenditures, but in this instance at least there was no choice: the United States had to have a major exhibit at the fair, or grievously offend the sensitive Canadian government and people.

An important development in another medium was the production of a major film on President Johnson.* It was needed abroad, where opinions about Johnson were mixed at best. In terms of White House relations it was also a practical necessity, after the Agency had produced the feature-length film *Years of Lightning, Day of Drums* on President Kennedy. The new film, a twenty-eight-minute, wide-screen color documentary entitled *A President's Country,* sympathetically portrayed the countryside around the Pedernales River in Texas and the man who had emerged from that harsh terrain to lead his nation. Some Republicans in Congress grumbled, but there were no real protests; after all, USIA had made a number of films about Eisenhower when he was President.

There was a different reaction, however, when the U.S. Advisory Commission on Information recommended in 1967 that USIA be permitted to make its output available in this country, including such films as the one on Johnson. Frank Stanton, president of CBS and chairman of the Commission, explained:

It has to do with the people's right to know . . . what their government is telling the rest of the world about us. It has been USIA policy in the past, responsive to the sense of Congress, to deny this information to representatives of the United States news media and to the public at large,

---

* Equally important, but strictly in the negative sense, was the resignation in mid-1967 of George Stevens, Jr., the Murrow-appointed head of USIA's Motion Picture Service, to become director of the newly formed American Film Institute. As the ablest producer yet of Agency films, he would be, as Marks put it in announcing Stevens' departure, "sorely missed." Fortunately, he was succeeded by a young man of equal ability and energy, Bruce Herschensohn, who had produced the memorable *The Five Cities of June* and *Years of Lightning, Day of Drums* for USIA.

except on a selected basis. . . . It is our recommendation that "the walls can come down," and that while no efforts be made to *distribute* USIA materials in this country, they be made available for appropriate inspection on specific request by parties with a legitimate interest—their own or the public's.[15]

A number of legislators, and some newspapers that had often criticized the government for not telling enough about what it was doing, sharply disagreed. "I disapprove of the Federal Government . . . subsidizing this kind of propaganda to its own citizens," snapped Senator Fulbright. Senator Dirksen thought it would "set a very bad precedent." Senator Mundt, taking note of the film on Johnson, expressed fear that the party in control of the White House would use USIA material for its own political advantage.

The Washington *Post* objected that "if the ban [on domestic release of USIA material] is lowered, Government-produced matter ultimately will flood all the media [and] often be indistinguishable from material originating in other sources. It will compete with and diminish private media." The Los Angeles *Times* warned of "the admittedly remote but nonetheless real possibility that the Federal Government is laying a groundwork that other less scrupulous future leaders could use to build a propaganda machine."

Congress did not approve the Commision's recommendation. And perhaps it was right not to do so, but not for the reasons given. Former Director Carl Rowan commented:

As much as I sometimes wished, in my USIA days, that the Agency could get its light out from under Congress' bushel of inhibitions, I shudder at the Advisory Commission's proposal. . . . USIA's leaders would work twenty-five hour days just defending themselves. . . . Within hours after the first batch of USIA materials is distributed at home, the Agency will be besieged by an army of truck drivers, retired cowpokes and newspaper columnists, all offering free advice on how better to "sell democracy abroad." . . . A little reflection tells me that my USIA friends ought to realize when they're well off—and leave well enough alone.[16]

Other recommendations and conclusions of the Advisory Commission should have received more attention from the public—and from Congress and the President. Vietnam, racial disturbances, and controversy over the Warren Commission report on the Kennedy assassination had made the world "skeptical" of U.S. aims, the advisory group warned. USIA needed more attention and more money. Yet "neither the Legislature nor the Executive has yet approached this responsibility with the vigor it demands. Where the needs and challenges are greatest, where the task of making U.S. intentions clear is most difficult—it is in these areas that USIA has been most handicapped by Congressional reluctance."[17]

Congressional reluctance was not the only problem. The lack of Presidential enthusiasm for the Agency and its works had damaged USIA's influence within the government and its effectiveness abroad. Money was scarce, and—most important of all—no one seemed willing or able to fight for USIA and its vital functions as Murrow had. To appease Congress, which was demanding cuts in Federal spending before it would approve a tax increase, Johnson imposed upon the Agency a 10 percent reduction in the size of its Foreign Service and a freeze on recruitment, thus eliminating some able officers as well as some deadwood and shutting off the infusion of new talent (although the economy measures did not prevent USIA from giving a job to Warrie Lynn Smith, Lynda Bird Johnson Robb's best friend). Marks's managerial skills had enhanced the efficiency of the operation, but there was some doubt the Director would stay beyond three years in office and the Agency's staff dreaded still another change in leadership with all the problems that entailed. All this, combined with the malaise of spirit which by early 1968 had permeated the Johnson Administration generally, reduced Agency morale to a new low for the decade.

No help was an attack on USIA by the Republican Coordinating Committee, a group composed of national, Congressional, and state party leaders. The criticisms echoed those made by others in 1952 and 1960: America's "prestige" abroad had declined; the Agency was "chronically underfinanced" and its stance "timid—at times almost apologetic—in selling the American story abroad"; the Administration had ignored studies for improving the program. As in 1952 and 1960, there was some merit in the criticisms.

Once again, USIA faced a crisis of identity and purpose.

12 *The Strategy of Words*

Concepts of power have radically changed since World War II: today's H-bomb is to the device exploded over Hiroshima as that weapon was to the crude gunpowder invented by the ancient Chinese. But power alone cannot always prevail in relations among nations, as the British and French learned at Suez in the fifties and we Americans in Vietnam in the sixties. In a world where the benefits of education are being extended to the many instead of the few, the pen is increasingly mightier than the sword. Men are moved less by brute strength and more by ideas.

The population explosion threatens to engulf the world, and an explosion of new nations has doubled the number of sovereign powers in less than two decades. The "revolution of rising expectations" in the underdeveloped world, of which we became aware hardly more than a decade ago, has now spread from Latin America, Africa, and Asia to the grim ghettos of our own big cities, and we have not been very successful in satisfying it either abroad or at home.

In relations between the superpowers, the United States and the Soviet Union, the salves and solutions of past years—the Marshall Plan, NATO, SEATO, and CENTO, the Truman and Eisenhower Doctrines, "containment" and "massive retaliation"—are no longer entirely applicable. "International monolithic Communism" has fragmented into competing national Communisms, and Moscow has about as much influence with Bucharest as Washington does with Paris—and no influence at all with Peking.

We still compete intensely with the Soviet Union, but no longer on the brink of a nuclear war that both sides recognize would be mutually disastrous. Today's competition is more economic, scientific, political, and verbal than military. World leadership is determined by who can best deal with—and convince others it can best deal with—the problems of birth control, agricultural modernization, industrialization, urban congestion, education, and the development of viable political, economic, and social institutions. The nation that can solve its own problems and inspire others to do likewise is the nation that will lead the way into the twenty-first century.

This is not to say that Communism—Russian or Chinese—has become benign, or more democratic, or more desirable as a social or political system, or less competitive with democracy. But the nature of the game has changed (at least the game with the Soviet Union), the mood of the world has changed, and the need for skill and sophistication on our part has become greater.

All this has major implications for American propagandists. The U.S. Information Agency was born at the height of the Cold War. Most of today's senior officers were trained in Cold War combat. Consequently, much of the old vocabulary of the Cold War—"international Communism," "Communist conspiracy," "Iron Curtain," "free world"—continues to be employed, even when it is no longer applicable or persuasive. (I doubt whether much of it was ever very persuasive, except with the already persuaded.)

Too many of the world's peoples still believe the United States is concerned only with protecting its own skin against the Communist menace, rather than helping them build their own institutions in their own way. If confidence in American purposes is to be restored and maintained, our political leaders—and USIA—must forgo the turgid terminology of Cold War. Americans need to cultivate patience, tolerance, and the long view with the new nations, remembering as we view with distaste some of their men and methods that Europe viewed us the same way in our early years.

Perhaps most important of all, we Americans need to stop acting and talking as if we were omnipotent in the world—or at least stop showing frustration and anger when we do not have our way. We need to relinquish our cherished notion that we are God's chosen people, living in His land with His special blessing, and the conviction—as historian Henry Steele Commager has put it—that destiny has imposed "a special responsibility on the American people to spread the blessings of liberty, democracy and equality to other people of the earth." There is nothing wrong with wanting these blessings for others, of course, but we must point, not push, letting them find their way as we found ours.

This means emphasizing not the sins of others but the values we have found through trial and error to be best suited for ourselves. We should put less emphasis on our great wealth and power and more on the lofty dreams we hold in common with men everywhere. After Thomas Huxley visited America a century ago, he wrote: "I cannot say that I am in the slightest degree impressed by your bigness, or your material resources, as such. Size is not grandeur, and territory does not make a nation. The great issue . . . is what are you going to do with all these things?"

Giving the world our answer, even when we are agreed on what that answer should be, is no easy task. Thomas L. Hughes of the State Department points out that "the traditional singleness of our idealistic impact abroad is lost in a cacophony of competitive noises. . . . The insuperable exigencies of [Vietnam] wartime news coverage apparently require a relentless flood of releases on body counts, anti-personnel weapons, kill ratios, and cost-effectiveness curves which distort affirmative democratic discourse [and] take liberties with the nation's reputation. . . . The way we talk demeans us."[1]

Yet even when the message is heard above the cacophony, as indeed it is, those who hear do not always believe.

They look at us the way the poor people in the wretched valley gaze up at the laughing family that lives in the big white house on the hill. They know all about us. No matter that their impressions are formed in part by dreams and slander; they are firm. They expect the best and the worst from us, both miracles and destruction, and it is USIA's huge job to convince them that neither is totally forthcoming.[2]

Ed Murrow appreciated the difficulties, but he believed the job could be done. Asked to explain USIA's role, he told a small-town audience one night:

We will convey something of substance about this country and its people, this government and its aims, this land and its heritage. . . . And we shall try to so identify our aims and goals with theirs that all will realize that we truly seek not power but peace. We shall say to a world increasingly encumbered by the lust of want and a taste for haste that the way of the despot is not the sole design for satisfying desire.[3]

If it is to be successful in conveying something of substance during the coming decade, America's strategy of words needs sound policies that it can support without apology. But it also needs much more.

USIA must improve its recruitment efforts, especially among those who have already established reputations in communications and education, to assure a continuing supply of first-rate talent. Government salaries still are relatively low, but they are more competitive than formerly with private industry. The public's response to the Peace Corps revealed a high motivation among thousands of Americans for selfless public service; USIA must scramble to get its share of those who are both highly motivated and highly able.

At times, USIA sent its most available, i.e., least able, officers on recruiting trips around the country. Not surprisingly, they attracted some second-raters and discouraged some top-drawer talent. Since Murrow, the situation has improved. He required the Agency's ablest officers, no matter how busy, to be detached periodically to help with recruitment. Later, a senior officer was assigned the full-time task of searching out talent. Yet, given the Agency's world-wide responsibilities, its pool of truly able men and women should be larger.

In part, the weakness of some USIA officers may be blamed on their training, both before they come to the Agency and while in it. USIA boasts of its "professionalism," and certainly its people are far more professional than they were a decade or two ago. But this professionalism, which remains uneven, is based almost entirely on on-the-job trial and error.

Most universities, believing that "communications" and "public relations" are not academic subjects, have done little to prepare students for USIA careers of international, intercultural communication. Bits and pieces are taught, of course—foreign languages, diplomatic history, journalism, occasional courses in the theory of propaganda—but rarely are the pieces brought together in a meaningful whole. There are signs that this is beginning to change, if slowly; one of the most hopeful portents is the program being developed by the Edward R. Murrow Center of Public Diplomacy, a division of the Fletcher School of Law and Diplomacy.

If the failure of universities to respond to the need is deplorable, the failure of USIA to develop a professional training program worthy of the name is shocking. More than two decades have passed since the peacetime information program was launched, yet, although USIA has always had a "training division," the Agency's officers have had to learn nearly everything they need to know from more experienced colleagues on the job.

USIA requires a first-rate, greatly expanded training program for both new and mid-career employees. Propaganda history and strategy should be taught, as well as the techniques of intercultural communication, the uses of media and opinion research tools abroad, and the political and economic realities of the modern world. (Too many USIA officers are still economic illiterates.) The Agency's most promising young men should be required to take the time to learn at least one foreign language, no matter how urgently they are needed elsewhere.

Part of the blame for USIA's inadequate training program lies with Congress, which has not provided a pool of manpower sufficiently large to permit a significant fraction to be in training at all times. But every Director of the Agency has also been culpable, for more could have been done with existing resources. It is not that they haven't believed in the importance of training; all have. But they have been so concerned with immediate problems, with immediate vacancies to fill, that they have failed to build a program which could prepare at least a fair proportion of Agency officers to be more effective in the future. To his credit, Leonard Marks is taking some steps to make USIA training more pertinent and more meaningful.

Even apart from a formal training program, USIA officers should be encouraged to do more reading in propaganda, in American politics and culture, in current domestic and foreign problems, and in the history, politics, and culture of the countries to which they are assigned. There are some who do read widely. Most, however, including many of the ablest (who are also the busiest), do not. If this means allowing time on the job for reading and reflection, then time should be allowed. It is a wise use of the taxpayer's money.[4]

Another weakness USIA must overcome is the hardening of bureaucratic arteries that often occurs in any big organization. The maintenance of high motivation, creativity, independent thinking, and a climate encouraging innovation is essential to USIA's success. Every

Director of USIA should give it highest priority. Unfortunately, that has not always been the case.

International propaganda and cultural activities are significant elements of modern diplomacy. This makes USIA important to the State Department; it also makes State important to USIA. The Agency cannot be an isolated success. Much of what it does depends on the attitudes and commitments of State Department people in Washington and in the field. Yet relations between the two agencies have never been wholly satisfactory.

The State Department has many brilliant, dedicated, courageous men who have served their country well, but it is not the most creative branch of the Federal Government. Successive Presidents have complained about its unresponsiveness. Former ambassadors, educators, and journalists have criticized its administration. Even the department itself has in effect admitted (when it released without rebuttal a study of its personnel done by a team from Yale University) that it is dominated by a "social system" which encourages its career officers to avoid controversy and responsibility and penalizes those who "make waves."

To be effective, USIA needs a lively, creative, churning staff, unencumbered by the rigid regulations and inherent timidity of traditional diplomacy. That was one reason for taking the propaganda program out of the State Department in the first place. Yet USIA also must thoroughly integrate its activities with those of State, for propaganda in a vacuum is worse than no propaganda at all. This means more than merely accepting policy guidance; it means taking part in the decision-making process at every level. Today's separate Information Agency does not do that, but neither did it do so prior to 1953 when it was a much subordinated part of the State Department.

The experience of the last two decades indicates that the propaganda program is more likely to be vital and effective when it is independent of the administrative machinery of the State Department, yet integrated in day-to-day operations with the other tools of diplomacy. This requires a President and Secretary of State who understand the significance of psychological factors in foreign relations and appreciate the uses of propaganda. It requires that the rank and file of the State Department do likewise, and that USIA's people understand better the requirements of traditional diplomacy. It requires more interchange of personnel between State and USIA (as of this writing there are no ambassadors previously associated with USIA and only one State Department official in a top Agency job). And it requires creation of a USIA career Foreign Service Corps whose weakest members, as in State's Foreign Service, are subject to "selection out."

The need for good men has never been greater. There no longer are any "unimportant" countries, only countries of varying degrees of importance to the U.S. national interest and world peace. Vietnam, Cuba, the Congo, and the Dominican Republic have taught us that threats to peace can arise in the most unlikely places and in the most unexpected ways. USIA needs the skills and the manpower to deal with these threats. The Agency was unprepared for Vietnam, and it is unprepared should a similar conflict break out elsewhere.

Anticipating trouble and identifying the most effective means of dealing with it are, of course, prime functions of USIA research. Yet the Agency still knows woefully little about how its audiences are motivated, and which media are the most persuasive under varying circumstances. More attention and more resources need to be devoted to research.

USIA's own media services continue for the most part to operate in haphazard fashion, despite efforts to set priorities. They should concentrate their output on fewer, more important themes. Additionally, the quality of their output, although much improved in recent years, is still not as good as it could be. USIA has long been substantially hampered by a shortage of gifted writers and editors. Part of the problem is getting and keeping talented men and women, but there is more to it than that. Perhaps a government bureaucracy inherently discourages lively, thought-provoking writing; if so, Agency officials should devote more effort to recognizing and remedying the difficulty.

The most serious problems are with the "expensive" media: radio, motion pictures, and television. As previously noted, the Voice of America transmits mostly by shortwave, in order to stretch its signal over long distances. But most foreign radio listeners today, unlike ten or twenty years ago, either have receivers that only pick up medium-wave (broadcast band) transmissions or simply prefer medium-wave, which is the frequency used by their own broadcasters. Radio audiences are growing rapidly, but they will be lost to VOA unless it finds ways of doing more medium-wave broadcasting.

As for the visual media, the Agency has never had any clear idea as to whom it wants to reach through movies and television, what it wants to say to them, and what the best cinematographic devices are for doing it. As a result, USIA still too often makes pictures because they seem interesting to their producers, and too often uses them in the field because there are no alternatives other than dismantling the distribution mechanism—a course of action every Public Affairs Officer dreads, always hoping that the future will bring a larger number of films more useful to his purposes. The remedy is in more and better cooperation and communication between the Foreign Service propagandist and the motion picture specialist.

Television is, as we all know, an extraordinary medium, unlike all others. It is capable of creating its own events, of making its audiences feel they are a part of something actually going on—whether in fact it is going on, or is only a part of what is going on, or is just a figment of a producer's imagination.

As one perceptive observer has noted, "There is a vital margin of difference between saying 'Did you see the report in *The New York Times* of the massacres in the Congo?' and saying 'Did you see the massacres in the Congo on television last night?' The first remark implies only that one has seen a report (which may conflict with a report from another source). The second implies that one has seen the event itself. However carefully television is used, it cannot avoid this deception."[5] It is this phenomenon, more than any other, that makes television the most persuasive of the mass media.

After a slow start, television has grown rapidly abroad. Like an airline and a steel mill, TV has become an attribute of sovereignty that even the most backward and impoverished nations yearn for. Most of them now have it, or soon will. Audiences are large even where the people are poor, for group watching, in village squares and coffeehouses, permits the lowest peasant to watch the flickering images nightly.

For USIA, television is a great and growing opportunity, but it is one that the Agency has not taken adequate advantage of. Despite the enormous appetite of foreign TV stations for programs to flesh out their schedules, USIA provided almost nothing until recent years, and then only very little. The big problem, of course, is cost: the simplest shows are expensive to produce. What is needed is a decision by the Agency and Congress to spend the additional money required, $20 or $30 million annually, to make ample use of this medium.

That $20 or $30 million may turn out to be only the beginning. Today, communications satellites can beam "live" television programs from Washington to ground stations all over the earth for rebroadcast over local TV transmitters. Tomorrow, satellites will make direct international telecasting possible in the sense that we now have direct international broadcasting: from USIA's studios to the living rooms of its world-wide audiences, with no middlemen. It will be enormously expensive, not only to produce many programs in many languages every day, as VOA now does, but to finance the costly satellites.

When direct international telecasting becomes technologically possible, there is no question that the Soviets and others will do it. There is little question that, in the end, we will do it also, for as a means of communicating with others it will overshadow all other media. USIA needs to prepare for that day now, and to prepare Congress for additional annual expenditures of $100 million or more.

Money has always been a problem for America's foreign propaganda program. In its early years, its budgets went up and down like a yo-yo. More recently, USIA's budgets have stabilized, but there have been few periods when the operation was not starved for resources. Some years ago, Senator Jacob Javits of New York noted that "we expend $47 billion a year for defense without blinking an eyelash, and then put our propaganda apparatus through a wringer over a budget of $130 million. We have indeed lost our true perspective when we so subordinate the importance of ideas."[6] His words are equally true today. USIA's budget has gone up, but not as fast as military expenditures.

One reason for Congressional penuriousness is that our legislators have never really made up their minds as to what they want USIA to be and to do. They want it to "tell America's story to the world" and "fight Communism," but there is no consensus as to how the job should be done or what it entails in the way of resources. And the Congressional doubts are not surprising in light of the uncertainty over the Agency's role within the Executive Branch and in USIA itself.

President Kennedy's explicit 1963 Statement of Mission declared that the Agency's purpose is to further the achievement of U.S. foreign policy objectives by influencing attitudes abroad and by advising the

Executive Branch on the psychological factors of foreign relations. Although that directive still prevails officially, some in USIA ignore or misinterpret it, and there remain major pockets of ignorance or misunderstanding of the role of propaganda in the Departments of State and Defense—and in the White House.

This is not to say that miracles could be accomplished if the situation were otherwise. Just as negotiators cannot always reach agreements and economic aid cannot always prevent poverty, so propaganda cannot always persuade everyone to agree with us.

Some academicians and advertising men, while understanding the proper uses of propaganda, have tended to overrate its potential. They say that if only USIA's message were harder (or softer), more cultural (or more political), more subtle (or more obvious)—or if only we spent more money—then American propaganda could devastate its adversaries and we would all live happily ever after.

But it should be obvious that propaganda alone cannot stop Communist expansion or make it wither away in the countries where it now holds power. Nor can it be the key factor in ending a war in Vietnam or anywhere else, or in reuniting the Atlantic Alliance, or in halting the proliferation of nuclear weapons. Nonetheless, as Kennedy and Murrow demonstrated in their time, there is much it can do. And the need today is more, not less, urgent than in the early 1960s.

We need to use our communications skills to reduce tensions, not exacerbate them.

We need to restore confidence in American purpose in a world that has forgotten the past and is fearful of the future.

We need to win support for policies and goals which are imperfectly understood and increasingly suspected.

We need to reassure the world that we Americans have not lost faith in our traditional commitments to human dignity and democratic processes, either at home or abroad.

Ed Murrow's final words to his colleagues in USIA are as valid now as the day he spoke them. Even if Communism should disappear from the earth, he said, "we would still have the mission abroad of combating ignorance and fear, suspicion and prejudice. This struggle . . . will not be won in a single day or a single decade."

This effort requires a strong, vital foreign information program, backed by adequate financing and public support. Although Matthew said, "By thy words shalt thou be justified," words alone will not do the job. But it cannot be done without words, and spending words is cheaper than spending money and immeasurably less expensive than spending lives.

In the end, as in the beginning, is the word. The question is: what kind of word in what kind of world?

Bibliographic Notes

Chapter 1. We Become Propagandists

1. Walter Lippmann, "As Others See Us," syndicated column in the Washington *Post*, June 10, 1965.
2. Statement by Edward R. Murrow, Director of the U.S. Information Agency, before the Subcommittee on International Organizations and Movements of the Committee on Foreign Affairs, House of Representatives, Washington, D.C., March 28, 1963.
3. George Creel, *How We Advertised America* (New York: Harper & Brothers, 1920).
4. James R. Mock and Cedric Larson, *Words That Won the War* (Princeton: Princeton University Press, 1939), p. 61.
5. Edward L. Bernays, *Biography of an Idea: Memoirs of Public Relations Counsel Edward L. Bernays* (New York: Simon & Schuster, 1965), p. 177.
6. Creel, *op. cit.*, p. 402.
7. Mock and Larson, *op. cit.*, p. 332.
8. Creel, *op. cit.*, p. 408 and p. 402.
9. Bernays, *op. cit.*, p. 177.
10. Robert A. McClure, Foreword to Daniel Lerner's *Sykewar* (New York: George W. Stewart, Publisher, 1949), p. xvi.
11. Wallace Carroll, *Persuade or Perish* (Boston: Houghton Mifflin, 1948), p. 370.
12. *Ibid.*, p. 12.
13. Robert E. Sherwood, *Roosevelt and Hopkins* (New York: Harper & Brothers, 1948), p. 630.
14. Allen W. Dulles, *Germany's Underground* (New York: Macmillan, 1946), p. 133.
15. Leo Rosten, "The World of Leo Rosten: The Day I Bombed Berlin," *Look*, February 8, 1966.
16. Edward W. Barrett, *Truth Is Our Weapon* (New York: Funk & Wagnalls, 1953), pp. 13-14.

17. James P. Warburg, *Unwritten Treaty* (New York: Harcourt Brace, 1946).

18. Carroll, *op. cit.*, pp. 362-363.

19. Executive Order 9608, issued by President Truman, August 31, 1945.

20. Barrett, *op. cit.*, p. 54.

21. *Ibid.*, p. 75.

22. *Ibid.*, pp. 89-91.

23. Dean Acheson, "The American Image Will Take Care of Itself," *New York Times Magazine*, February 28, 1965.

Chapter 2. Villains and Heroes

1. *Hearings Before the Permanent Subcommittee on Investigations of the Committee on Government Operations, United States Senate, Eighty-Third Congress.*

2. Martin Merson, *The Private Diary of a Public Servant* (New York: Macmillan, 1955), p. 9.

3. *Ibid.*, p. 34.

4. *Ibid.*, pp. 68-69.

5. Richard H. Rovere, *Senator Joe McCarthy* (New York: Harcourt, Brace, 1959), p. 219.

6. Merson, *op. cit.*, p. 62.

7. *Ibid.*, p. 134.

8. Washington *Post*, July 22, 1953.

9. Merson, *op. cit.*, p. 148.

10. *Seventh Semiannual Report* of the United States Advisory Commission on Information, 1953.

11. Statement by the President, released to the press by the White House, October 28, 1953.

12. Letter to President Eisenhower by Theodore C. Streibert, Director of the U.S. Information Agency, October 27, 1953 (released to the press by the White House, October 28, 1953).

Chapter 3. Talking and Listening: The Propaganda "Dialogue"

1. Philip H. Coombs, *The Fourth Dimension of Foreign Policy* (New York: Harper & Row, 1964), pp. 122-123.

2. Charles Frankel, "The Era of Educational and Cultural Relations," Edward L. Bernays Foundation Lecture at the Edward R. Murrow Center of Public Diplomacy, the Fletcher School of Law and Diplomacy, Medford, Mass., April 26, 1966.

3. Coombs, *op. cit.*, pp. 124-125.

4. "A Cultural Officer Speaks . . . ," *USIA Correspondent*, August, 1966, p. 10.

5. Carl T. Rowan, "USIA's Polls and Why They Are Confidential," syndicated column in the Los Angeles *Times*, October 5, 1966.

6. Lloyd A. Free, "The Role of Public Opinion in International Relations," lecture at the Edward R. Murrow Center, the Fletcher School of Law and Diplomacy, Medford, Mass., November 1, 1965.

7. *Ibid.*

8. *Ibid.*

9. *Attitudes Toward American and South African Race Problems Among Lesser Educated Nigerians in Greater Lagos*, Research and Reference Service, U.S. Information Agency, June, 1964.

10. *Attitudes and Aspirations of African Students in France*, Research and Reference Service, U.S. Information Agency, April 18, 1963.

11. *Attitudes and Aspirations of African Students in West Germany*, Research and Reference Service, U.S. Information Agency, August, 1963.

Chapter 4. Hard Sell and Soft Sell

1. Dwight D. Eisenhower, "America's Place in the World," *The Reader's Digest*, October, 1965.

2. ———, *The White House Years: Waging Peace 1956-1961* (New York: Doubleday, 1965), p. 138.

3. Lloyd A. Free, "The Role of Public Opinion in International Relations," lecture at the Edward R. Murrow Center, the Fletcher School of Law and Diplomacy, Medford, Mass., November 1, 1965.

4. Andrew H. Berding, *Dulles on Diplomacy* (Princeton: D. Van Nostrand, 1965), p. 17.

5. Free, *op. cit.*

6. *General Conference Expectations and Confidence in Conference Participants*, Report No. 9, Research and Reference Service, U.S. Information Agency, July 11, 1955.

7. *Trends in Attitudes Toward the U.S. and the U.S.S.R. in the Wake of the Summit Conference*, Report No. 12, Research and Reference Service, U.S. Information Agency, September 16, 1955.

8. *Hungarian Refugees' Interpretations of Western Radio Broadcasts and Reactions to United States Non-Intervention (SR-6)*, Research and Reference Service, U.S. Information Agency, December 28, 1956.

9. *Eighth Review of Operations: January 1–June 30, 1957*, U.S. Information Agency, p. 5.

10. *Departments of State, Justice, the Judiciary, and Related Agencies Appropriations, 1958: Hearings Before the Subcommittee of the Committee on Appropriations, United States Senate, Eighty-Fifth Congress, First Session, on H.R. 6871* (Washington: United States Government Printing Office, 1957).

11. *New York Times*, May 11, 1957.

12. *Congressional Record*, May 15 and May 29, 1957.

13. Rowland Evans and Robert Novak, *Lyndon B. Johnson: The Ex-*

ercise of Power (New York: New American Library, 1966), p. 188.

14. Eisenhower, *The White House Years, op. cit.*, p. 138.

15. "USIA Basic Guidance Paper," issued to its staff by the U.S. Information Agency on October 22, 1957.

16. *Ninth Review of Operations: July 1–December 31, 1957*, U.S. Information Agency, p. 8.

17. *Public Reactions to Little Rock in Major World Capitals (SR-8)*, Research and Reference Service, U.S. Information Agency, October 29, 1957.

18. Berding, *op. cit.*, p. 96.

19. *Time*, October 28, 1957.

20. George V. Allen, Director of the U.S. Information Agency, in *Ninth Review of Operations, op. cit.*

21. *Thirteenth Report of the United States Advisory Commission on Information*, January, 1958, p. 9.

22. *The Impact of Sputnik on the Standing of the U.S. versus the U.S.S.R. (WE-52)*, Research and Reference Service, U.S. Information Agency, December, 1957.

23. *New York Times*, November 22, 1957.

24. Roscoe Drummond, "How U.S. Propaganda Errs," New York *Herald Tribune*, January 23, 1961.

25. Theodore C. Sorensen, *Kennedy* (New York: Harper & Row, 1965), pp. 203–204.

Chapter 5. American Propaganda Comes of Age

1. Roscoe Drummond in the New York *Herald Tribune*, January 23, 1961.

2. "Highlights of Recommendations by the President's Committee on Information Activities Abroad," and an exchange of letters between President Eisenhower and Mansfield D. Sprague, chairman of the committee, released to the press by the White House on January 11, 1961.

3. Statement by President Kennedy upon issuance of Executive Order 10920 abolishing the Operations Coordinating Board, released to the press by the White House on February 19, 1961.

4. "Report to the Honorable John F. Kennedy by the Task Force on United States Information Agency" (not released to the public), December 31, 1960; press statement summarizing the task force report, released by Senator Kennedy's Press Office on January 12, 1961.

5. Memorandum from Donald M. Wilson to Senator John F. Kennedy, "Preliminary Report on United States Information Agency" (not released to the public), December 13, 1960.

6. Remarks by Vice President Hubert H. Humphrey at the dedication of the Edward R. Murrow Center of Public Diplomacy, the Fletcher School of Law and Diplomacy, Medford, Mass., December 6, 1965.

7. Arthur M. Schlesinger, Jr., *A Thousand Days: John F. Kennedy in the White House* (Boston: Houghton Mifflin, 1965), pp. 611-612.

8. Mary McGrory, "A Startlingly Decent Man, He Symbolized Integrity," article in the Washington *Evening Star,* April 28, 1965.

9. Statement by Edward R. Murrow at a hearing of the Committee on Foreign Relations, United States Senate, regarding his nomination to be Director of USIA, March 14, 1961.

Chapter 6. The Murrow Years: Hot Words in the Cold War

1. Lloyd A. Free, "The Role of Public Opinion in International Relations," lecture at the Edward R. Murrow Center, the Fletcher School of Law and Diplomacy, Medford, Mass., November 1, 1965.

2. Statement by Edward R. Murrow, Director of USIA, before the Subcommittee on International Organizations and Movements of the Committee on Foreign Affairs, House of Representatives, March 28, 1963.

3. "Memorandum for the Heads of All Agency Elements and All USIS Field Posts" from Edward R. Murrow, Director of USIA, July 24, 1961.

4. Arthur M. Schlesinger, Jr., *A Thousand Days: John F. Kennedy in the White House* (Boston: Houghton Mifflin, 1965), p. 449.

5. Theodore C. Sorensen, *Kennedy* (New York: Harper & Row, 1965), p. 619.

6. *Ibid.*

7. USIA Potomac Cable No. 163, June 23, 1961.

8. USIA Potomac Cable No. 170, August 9, 1961.

9. Letter from President Kennedy to the Senate and House Minority Leaders on U.S. Information Activities Relating to Berlin, September 1, 1962.

10. Schlesinger, *op. cit.,* pp. 518-519.

11. *Eighteenth Report* of the U.S. Advisory Commission on Information, January, 1963, pp. 8-12.

Chapter 7. The Murrow Years: Successes and Failures

1. Address by Edward R. Murrow, Director of USIA, before the National Convention of the Federal Bar Association, Philadelphia, September 26, 1963.

2. "Attorney General Discusses Meredith Case on VOA," USIA Press Release No. 51, October 9, 1962.

3. Address by Donald M. Wilson, Deputy Director of USIA, before the Women's National Democratic Club, Washington, D.C., June 10, 1963.

4. Theodore C. Sorensen, *Kennedy* (New York: Harper & Row, 1965), p. 524.

5. Pierre Salinger, *With Kennedy* (New York: Doubleday, 1966), p. 134.

6. USIA Potomac Cable No. 181, September 29, 1961.

7. Arthur Schlesinger, Jr., "The U.S. Ignorance About Vietnam," San Francisco *Chronicle,* September 28, 1966 (Copyright 1966 by the *New York Times* and the *Chronicle*).

8. John Mecklin, *Mission in Torment* (New York: Doubleday, 1965).

9. Salinger, *op. cit.,* p. 324.

10. *USIA Correspondent,* September, 1963.

Chapter 8. The Murrow Years: Triumph and Tragedy

1. "USIA Commentary on TASS Statement," USIA Press Release No. 46, September 12, 1962.

2. Pierre Salinger, *With Kennedy* (New York: Doubleday, 1966), p. 264.

3. USIA Potomac Cable No. 245, October 22, 1962.

4. USIA Potomac Cable No. 246, October 24, 1962.

5. USIA Potomac Cable No. 247, October 28, 1962.

6. Theodore C. Sorensen, *Kennedy* (New York: Harper & Row, 1965), p. 726.

7. Larry L. King, "Lyndon Johnson as Literary Critic," *The New Republic,* November 12, 1966.

8. Address by Edward R. Murrow, Director of USIA, at the Fifty-Ninth Annual Convention of the Advertising Federation of America, Atlanta, Ga., June 19, 1963.

9. Address by Edward R. Murrow, Director of USIA, before the National Education Association, Detroit, Mich., July 1, 1963.

10. Remarks by Edward R. Murrow, Director of USIA, at the Seventh Annual USIA Honor Awards Ceremony, quoted in the *USIA Correspondent,* October, 1963.

11. Quoted by Jean White in "Luster Rubbed Off on USIA," an article in the Washington *Post,* March 15, 1964.

12. Arthur M. Schlesinger, Jr., *A Thousand Days: John F. Kennedy in the White House* (Boston: Houghton Mifflin, 1965), p. 612.

13. Edward R. Murrow, *In Search of Light: The Broadcasts of Edward R. Murrow 1938-1961,* edited by Edward Bliss, Jr. (New York: Alfred A. Knopf, 1967), p. 290.

Chapter 9. The Voice of America: Contribution and Controversy

1. Pierre Salinger, *With Kennedy* (New York: Doubleday, 1966), p. 213.

2. Remarks by Edward R. Murrow, Director of USIA, at the dedication of the Voice of America Relay Station at Greenville, N.C., February 8, 1963.

3. Edward W. Barrett, *Truth Is Our Weapon* (New York: Funk & Wagnalls, 1953), pp. 131-132.

4. Albert Bermel, "The Split Personality of USIA," *Harper's Magazine*, September, 1965.

5. Dwight D. Eisenhower, *The White House Years: Waging Peace 1956-1961* (New York: Doubleday, 1965), pp. 278-279.

6. "Directive to the Voice of America" (unsigned, but authorized by Director George V. Allen), U.S. Information Agency, November 1, 1960.

7. "Voice of America Policy," a directive from Edward R. Murrow, Director of USIA, December 4, 1962.

8. Memorandum from Edward R. Murrow, Director of USIA, to Henry Loomis, Director of the Voice of America, December 4, 1962.

9. Remarks by President John F. Kennedy at ceremonies marking the twentieth anniversary of the Voice of America, Washington, D.C., February 26, 1962.

10. Remarks by Henry Loomis on the occasion of his resignation as Director of the Voice of America, Washington, D.C., March 4, 1965.

11. Mary McGrory, " 'Voice' Chiefs Chafe at Curbs," Washington *Evening Star*, March 5, 1965.

12. " 'Voice' Policies Disturb Aides; Rowan Denies News Is Slanted," *New York Times*, June 5, 1965.

13. "America's Voice," editorial in the *New York Times*, June 11, 1965.

14. "His Master's Voice," story in *Newsweek* magazine, June 7, 1965.

15. Letter to the Editor by Carl T. Rowan, Director of USIA, in *Newsweek* magazine, June 28, 1965.

16. Bermel, *op. cit.*

17. Interview with Carl T. Rowan, Director of USIA, on the *Today* television program, National Broadcasting Company, June 4, 1965.

18. "Chancellor of the Voice," editorial in the Washington *Evening Star*, August 5, 1965.

19. "Aims of Voice Are Outlined by Chancellor," Associated Press news story published in the Washington *Evening Star*, July 29, 1965.

20. Remarks by John Chancellor, Director of the Voice of America, after taking the oath of office, September 1, 1965.

21. James B. Reston in the *New York Times*, September 2, 1966.

22. Warren Rogers, "America's Voice 'Swings a Little,' " *Look*, November 15, 1966.

23. David K. Willis, "Voice of America Chief Rebuts Propaganda Charge," *The Christian Science Monitor*, June 28, 1966.

24. Benjamin Welles, "Voice of America Sends Out 'New Sound,' " *New York Times*, November 8, 1966.

25. "Swinging Voice," *Time*, December 9, 1966.

26. *New York Times*, May 19, 1967.

27. Quoted in the *New York Times*, May 30, 1967.

28. Quoted in the *USIA Correspondent*, December, 1966.

Chapter 10. Carl Rowan: A Time of Transition

1. Address by Carl T. Rowan, Director-designate of USIA, at the Printing Week Convention, Minneapolis, Minn., February 21, 1964.
2. Interview with Rowan by Howard K. Smith on the ABC television program *Issues and Answers,* reported in the *USIA Correspondent,* February, 1964.
3. Address by Carl T. Rowan, Director of USIA, in Washington, D.C., May 6, 1964.
4. USIA Potomac Cable No. 287, March 11, 1965.
5. Address by Carl T. Rowan, Director of USIA, at the UCLA 1965 Foreign Journalism Awards Banquet, Los Angeles, Calif., May 14, 1965.
6. Interview with Rowan by Howard K. Smith, *op. cit.*
7. Remarks of Carl T. Rowan, Director of USIA, to the Washington staff of USIA, March 25, 1964.
8. Address by Carl T. Rowan, Director of USIA, at a Full Citizenship and World Affairs Conference of the International Union of Electrical, Radio and Machine Workers: AFL-CIO, Washington, D.C., March 30, 1965.
9. Address by Carl T. Rowan, Director of USIA, to the National Convention of the Military Chaplains Association, Chicago, Ill., May 20, 1964.
10. USIA Talking Paper No. 25, October 2, 1965.
11. Walter Lippmann in the Washington *Post,* June 10, 1965.
12. USIA Talking Paper No. 23, May 7, 1965.
13. Address by Carl T. Rowan, Director of USIA, at a United Nations Week Celebration, Los Angeles, Calif., October 22, 1964.
14. USIA Press Release No. 4, March 4, 1965.
15. Address by Carl T. Rowan, Director of USIA, at the University of Minnesota, Minneapolis, January 28, 1965.
16. Address by Carl T. Rowan, Director of USIA, at the annual dinner meeting of the Cleveland, Ohio, Bar Association and the Academy of Medicine, December 8, 1964.
17. Mary McGrory, "USIA Awaits Marks' Effect," Washington *Evening Star,* July 14, 1965.
18. Marquis Childs, "USIA's Affliction: Room at the Top," syndicated column in the Washington *Post,* July 30, 1965.
19. Richard Wilson, "Hard Season for the Johnson Image," syndicated column in the Washington *Evening Star,* July 14, 1965.

Chapter 11. Leonard Marks: A Time of War

1. Mary McGrory, "USIA Awaits Marks' Effect," Washington *Evening Star,* July 14, 1965.
2. "The USIA's New Chief," editorial in the *New York Times,* July 15, 1965.

3. Doris Fleeson, "Johnson Selects Boldly for USIA," syndicated column in the Washington *Evening Star*, August 5, 1965.

4. *USIA Correspondent*, September, 1965.

5. Douglas Kiker, "Report on Washington," *Atlantic Monthly*, January, 1967.

6. *USIA Correspondent*, April, 1967.

7. Memorandum from Hewson A. Ryan, Deputy Director (Policy and Research) of the U.S. Information Agency, to the heads of all Agency elements, August 14, 1967.

8. Maynard Parker, "Close-Up: The Mark of Zorthian," *Life*, May 12, 1967.

9. *Some South Vietnamese Views and Opinions about the United States and Other Nations*, Research and Reference Service, U.S. Information Agency, March 26, 1963.

10. JUSPAO-Saigon Field Message No. 23 to USIA-Washington, August 25, 1965.

11. *USIA Correspondent*, November, 1966.

12. *Time*, February 18, 1966.

13. USIA Talking Paper No. 24, August 31, 1965.

14. "Voice of America Audience Told More Negro Riots Are Likely," *New York Times*, June 25, 1967.

15. Press release, U.S. Advisory Commission on Information, March 8, 1967.

16. Carl T. Rowan, "Leave It Alone, Fellows . . . ," syndicated column in the Los Angeles *Times*, April 14, 1967.

17. *Twenty-Second Report to the Congress*, U.S. Advisory Commission on Information, Washington, D.C., March 8, 1967.

Chapter 12. The Strategy of Words

1. Speech by Thomas L. Hughes, Director of Intelligence and Research, Department of State, at the eighth annual convention of the International Studies Association of Columbia University and New York University, New York City, April 14, 1967.

2. Douglas Kiker, "Report on Washington," *Atlantic Monthly*, January, 1967.

3. Remarks by Edward R. Murrow, Director of USIA, at the twenty-third annual Distinguished Service Award banquet of the Kinston, N.C., Junior Chamber of Commerce, February 11, 1963.

4. A selective bibliography, for those in USIA or laymen interested in American propaganda, follows these notes.

5. Henry Fairlie, "Can You Believe Your Eyes?," *Horizon*, Spring, 1967.

6. "Needed: A Crash Program for USIA," speech by Senator Jacob K. Javits of New York, Kingston, N.Y., September 27, 1961.

Selective Bibliography

(Books cited in the bibliographic notes have been omitted.)

Books and Miscellaneous Material

American Assembly, Columbia University. *Cultural Affairs and Foreign Relations* (Englewood Cliffs, N. J.: Prentice-Hall, 1963. 184 pp.)

Berding, Andrew H. *Foreign Affairs and You!* (New York: Doubleday, 1962. 264 pp.)

Browne, Donald Roger. *The History and Programming Policies of RIAS: Radio in the American Sector (of Berlin).* (University Microfilms, 1963. 365 pp. University of Michigan, Ph.D. thesis, 1961. "An authorized reprint produced by microfilm-xerography.")

Cleveland, Harlan, Gerard J. Mangone, and John Clarke Adams. *The Overseas Americans* (New York: Mc-Graw-Hill, 1960. 316 pp.)

Committee on Foreign Affairs. *Personnel for the New Diplomacy* (Carnegie Endowment for International Peace, 1962. 161 pp.)

DeVos, Ton Pieter. *A Field Study in the Effectiveness of the United States Information Service in the Netherlands* (University Microfilms, 1963. 247 pp. University of Oklahoma, Ph.D. thesis, 1962. "An authorized reprint produced by microfilm-xerography.")

Dizard, Wilson P. *The Strategy of Truth: The Story of the U.S. Information Service* (Washington, D.C.: Public Affairs Press, 1961. 213 pp.)

Dyer, Murray. *The Weapon on the Wall* (Baltimore: Johns Hopkins Press, 1959. 269 pp.)

Goodfriend, Arthur. *The Twisted Image* (New York: St. Martin's Press, 1963. 264 pp.)

Goralski, Robert S. "Radio Broadcasting in Asia and the Voice of America." In *Studies on Asia,* vol. 1. (Lincoln: University of Nebraska Press, 1960, pp. 88-97.)

325

Gordon, George N., Irving Falk, and William Hodapp. *The Idea Invaders* (New York: Hastings House, 1963. 256 pp.)

Holt, Robert T., and Robert M. van de Velde. *Strategic Psychological Operations and American Foreign Policy* (Chicago: University of Chicago Press, 1960. 243 pp.)

Joyce, Walter. *The Propaganda Gap* (New York: Harper & Row, 1963. 144 pp.)

Martin, Leslie J. *International Propaganda: Its Legal and Diplomatic Control* (Minneapolis: University of Minnesota Press, 1958. 284 pp.)

Massoud, Mahmoud Ahmed. *The United States Information Program in the Middle East and South Asia* (University Microfilms, 1963. 282 pp. American University, M.A. thesis, 1963. "An authorized reprint produced by microfilm-xerography.")

Meyerhoff, Arthur E. *The Strategy of Persuasion: The Use of Advertising Skills in Fighting the Cold War* (New York: Coward-McCann, 1965. 191 pp.)

Posner, Ben. *Major Budgetary and Programming Problems of the United States Information Agency in its Operations of Overseas Missions* [n.p.]. (264L. American University Ph.D. thesis, 1962.)

Stephens, Oren. *Facts to a Candid World; America's Overseas Information Program* (Stanford: Stanford University Press, 1955. 140 pp.)

Swing, Raymond. *"Good Evening!" A Professional Memoir* (New York: Harcourt, Brace & World, 1964. 311 pp.)

Thomson, Charles A. H., and Walter H. C. Laves. *Cultural Relations and U.S. Foreign Policy* (Bloomington: Indiana University Press, 1963. 227 pp.)

Thomson, Charles A. H. *Overseas Information Service of the United States Government* (Washington, D.C.: Brookings Institution, 1948. 397 pp.)

Whitaker, Urban George, ed. *Propaganda and International Relations* (San Francisco: Chandler Publishing Co., 1962. 264 pp.)

Basic Laws and Regulations

United States Information and Educational Exchange Act of 1948, as amended (P.L. 402, 80th Congress, approved January 27, 1948; 22 U.S.C. 1431 *et seq.*), known as the Smith-Mundt Act.

Mutual Education and Cultural Exchange Act of 1961 (P.L. 87-256, approved September 21, 1961), known as the Fulbright-Hays Act.

Reorganization Plan No. 8 of 1953 (18 F.R. 4542), which established the U.S. Information Agency as a separate organization of the Executive Branch; issued by President Eisenhower on June 1, 1953, and effective July 31, 1953.

Index